Nature, Society and Environmental Crisis

A selection of previous *Sociological Review* Monographs

Actor Network Theory and After*
eds John Law and John Hassard
Whose Europe? The Turn Towards Democracy*
eds Dennis Smith and Sue Wright
Renewing Class Analysis*
eds Rosemary Cromptom, Fiona Devine, Mike Savage and John Scott
Reading Bourdieu on Society and Culture*
ed. Bridget Fowler
The Consumption of Mass*
eds Nick Lee and Rolland Munro
The Age of Anxiety: Conspiracy Theory and the Human Sciences*
eds Jane Parish and Martin Parker
Utopia and Organization*
ed. Martin Parker
Emotions and Sociology*
ed. Jack Barbalet
Masculinity and Men's Lifestyle Magazines*
ed. Bethan Benwell
Nature Performed: Environment, Culture and Performance*
eds Bronislaw Szerszynski, Wallace Heim and Claire Waterton
After Habermas: New Perspectives on the Public Sphere*
eds Nick Crossley and John Michael Roberts
Feminism After Bourdieu*
eds Lisa Adkins and Beverley Skeggs
Contemporary Organization Theory*
eds Campbell Jones and Rolland Munro
A New Sociology of Work*
eds Lynne Pettinger, Jane Parry, Rebecca Taylor and Miriam Glucksmann
Against Automobility*
eds Steffen Böhm, Campbell Jones, Cris Land and Matthew Paterson
Sports Mega-Events: Social Scientific Analyses of a Global Phenomenon*
eds John Horne and Wolfram Manzenreiter
Embodying Sociology: Retrospect, Progress and Prospects*
ed. Chris Shilling
Market Devices*
eds Michel Callon, Yuval Millo and Fabian Muniesa
Remembering Elites
eds Mike Savage and Karel Williams
Un/knowing Bodies
eds Joanna Latimer and Michael Schillmeier
Space Travel and Culture: From Apollo to Space Tourism
eds Martin Parker and David Bell

*Available from John Wiley & Sons, Distribution Centre, 1 Oldlands Way, Bognor Regis, West Sussex, PO22 9SA, UK

Most earlier monographs are still available from: Caroline Baggaley, The Sociological Review, Keele University, Keele, Staffs ST5 5BG, UK; e-mail srb01@keele.ac.uk

The Sociological Review Monographs

Since 1958, *The Sociological Review* has established a tradition of publishing one or two Monographs a year on issues of general sociological interest. The Monograph is an edited book length collection of research papers which is published and distributed in association with Blackwell Publishing Ltd. Our latest Monographs have been *Market Devices* (edited by Michel Callon, Yuval Millo and Fabian Muniesa), *Remembering Elites* (edited by Mike Savage and Karel Williams), *After Habermas: New Perspectives on the Public Sphere* (edited by Nick Crossley and John Michael Roberts), *Feminism After Bourdieu* (edited by Lisa Adkins and Beverley Skeggs), *Contemporary Organization Theory* (edited by Campbell Jones and Rolland Munro), *A New Sociology of Work* (edited by Lynne Pettinger, Jane Parry, Rebecca Taylor and Miriam Glucksmann), *Against Automobility* (edited by Steffen Böhm, Campbell Jones, Chris Land and Matthew Paterson), *Sports Mega-Events: Social Scientific Analyses of a Global Phenomenon* (edited by John Horne and Wolfram Manzenreiter) and *Embodying Sociology: Retrospect, Progress and Prospects* (edited by Chris Shilling). Other Monographs have been published on consumption; museums; culture and computing; death; gender and bureaucracy; sport and many other areas. We are keen to receive innovative collections of work in sociology and related disciplines with a particular emphasis on exploring empirical materials and theoretical frameworks which are currently under-developed. If you wish to discuss ideas for a Monograph then please contact the Monographs Editor, Chris Shilling, School of Social Policy, Sociology and Social Research, Cornwallis North East, University of Kent, Canterbury, Kent CT2 7NF C.Shilling@kent.ac.uk

Nature, Society and Environmental Crisis

Edited by Bob Carter and Nickie Charles

Wiley-Blackwell/The Sociological Review

BLACKWELL PUBLISHING
350 Main Street, Malden, MA 02148–5020, USA
9600 Garsington Road, Oxford OX4 2DQ, UK
550 Swanston Street, Carlton, Victoria 3053, Australia

First published 2010 by Blackwell Publishing Ltd

Library of Congress Cataloging-in-Publication Data

Nature, society and environmental crisis / edited by Bob Carter and Nickie Charles.
    p.   cm.
    Includes bibliogrpahical references and index.
    ISBN 978-1-4051-9333-7 (pbk. : alk. paper)
1. Nature–Social aspects.   2. Social ecology.   3. Sociology–Environmental
aspects.   I. Carter, Bob, 1948–   II. Charles, Nickie.
    HM856.N38 2010
    304.2–dc22

                                                                        2009052273

A catalogue record for this title is available from the British Library

Set in 10/12 Times NR MT

by Toppan Best-set Premedia Limited

Printed and bound in the United Kingdom

by Page Brothers, Norwich

For further information on Blackwell Publishing, visit our website:
http://www.blackwellpublishing.com

Contents

Society, nature and sociology 1
Bob Carter and Nickie Charles

Part One: Changing Conceptions of the Natural and the Social 21

Race, sex and the 'earthly paradise': Wallace versus Darwin on human evolution and prospects 23
Ted Benton

Alienation, the cosmos and the self 47
Peter Dickens

Normality and pathology in a biomedical age 66
Nikolas Rose

Sociology and climate change 84
John Urry

Part Two: Social Worlds, Natural Worlds: Sociological Research 101

The dangerous limits of dangerous limits: climate change and the precautionary principle 103
Chris Shaw

A stranger silence still: the need for feminist social research on climate change 124
Sherilyn MacGregor

Broadcasting green: grassroots environmentalism on Muslim women's radio 141
Daniel Nilsson DeHanas

Part Three: Sociological Futures   157

The 'value-action gap' in public attitudes towards sustainable energy:
the case of hydrogen energy   159
Rob Flynn, Paul Bellaby and Miriam Ricci

Technologies in place: symbolic interpretations of renewable energy   181
Carly McLachlan

'Doing food differently': reconnecting biological and social
relationships through care for food   200
Elizabeth Dowler, Moya Kneafsey, Rosie Cox and Lewis Holloway

Unnatural times? The social imaginary and the future of nature   222
Kate Soper

Notes on contributors   236

Index   240

Acknowledgments

Many of the chapters in the present volume were first presented at the 2008 BSA Annual Conference 'Social Worlds, Natural Worlds' held at the University of Warwick. We jointly organised this conference with Hazel Rice, Christina Hughes and Gurminder Bhambra, our colleagues in the Department of Sociology at Warwick, and with the organisational assistance and expertise of the BSA, particularly Liz Jackson, the BSA conference organiser. We wish to thank all of them for the considerable amount of work they put into the conference and to thank the BSA for allowing us to use the design from the conference poster for the cover of the book. Our colleagues within the Sociology department also contributed in different ways to the conference's success. Responsibility for this volume, although the inspiration for it came from the conference, remains with us.

Society, nature and sociology

Bob Carter and Nickie Charles

The social sciences have been faced with a series of challenges to their relevance since the beginning of the 21st century. In particular, the growing urgency of environmental crises and the remarkable increase in knowledge of genomics have raised questions about sociology's ability to analyse the contemporary world and, especially, its ability to understand the relationship between the natural world and human societies. The argument of this volume is that sociology has a significant contribution to make to this understanding and that it is imperative that sociologists become involved in what are often seen as purely scientific and technical discussions. In this opening chapter we contribute to this engagement by considering the question of how sociology understands the natural and the social and why many sociologists are re-thinking this relationship. We argue that this rethinking is due, on the one hand, to political and theoretical developments within and without sociology and, on the other hand, to the challenge of climate change and recent scientific interventions in, and transformations of, 'nature'. First, however, we discuss the relationship between nature and society that underpinned the development of sociology as a discipline.

The natural and the social in sociology

Debates about the relation between the natural and the social have been central to the development of sociology in the USA and Europe. There are various reasons for this, but two in particular are significant for the present chapter: the manner in which the efforts of classical sociologists[1] to demarcate a realm of the social entailed a contrast with a realm of the natural; and the profound intertwining of social thought and the natural sciences in 19th and early 20th century thinking, especially in various forms of social Darwinism.

Early efforts to establish a coherent object of study for social science pressed in a dualist direction, seeking to establish the social as a discrete entity separate from the natural and requiring its own methods of empirical enquiry, whilst simultaneously stressing its commonalities with the established project of natural science. This tension is captured in the very term 'social science' and in the epistemological claim that the social world can be known in ways similar to the natural world. This claim in turn rests upon ontological presumptions about reality and about the ways in which social and natural reality may be said to be distinct.

Nature as an object of study distinct from the social world is the product of a relatively recent world view, developing from the mid 18th century onwards, one broadly associated with the rise of industrial capitalism, and the establishment of a system of nation-states globally interconnected through colonialism and imperialism (Hobsbawm, 1992; Bayly, 2004). The powerful emphasis placed on technological development, especially military technology, sharply accelerated the global emergence of scientific thought. During this process,

> the meaning and social significance of concepts such as science, reason, and empirical verification were greatly modified, often blending with preexisting ideas in still vigorous indigenous systems of thought. These modern concepts often came to carry unintended new meanings for people, whether within or outside Europe and North America. (Bayly, 2004: 307)

From the very outset of industrial capitalism, which was always a global process, as Bayly (2004) has forcefully argued, ideas about science and ideas about the social were inextricably commingled. Nevertheless, the notion that they could somehow be separated, and that one could be used to assess, correct and improve the other, became a key feature of certain forms of modernist thought. This was especially so where natural scientific ideas could be used to explain social inequalities or handily account for elite privileges and political projects (Malik, 1996).

Eugenics and other ideas about race, for example, were important features of much 19th century thought, especially, but not exclusively, in Europe and the USA. As several writers have pointed out (Pichot, 2009; Bayly, 2004; Kevles, 1985), ideologies of race war and racial fitness could be applied as a set of practices in rapidly growing cities because they appealed to a diverse range of cross-class interests: ruling elites who saw in them a ready justification for imperial expansion, the middle classes for whom they expressed their conviction in their own social superiority, and the (mainly white) industrial working classes, the glow of whose own immiseration dimmed when set into the larger space of national pride and xenophobia.

The strength of such ideas was also a product of their scientific status, of the widespread belief that social, racial and gender hierarchies were grounded in a natural order whose workings had been revealed by the application of scientific thought to the natural world. The rise of industrial capitalism relentlessly drove the extensive application of technologies to production; in so doing it encouraged the view, familiar to contemporary environmentalists, that the planet is a 'garden' made for the delights of humankind, capable of limitlessly sustaining human production and consumption. From this perspective, common in 19th and early 20th century Western thought, the interdependence between the social and the natural was entirely one way: nature was passive, there to be taken, a provider of resources (the gendered nature of this way of thinking seems obvious now). This is an illustration of what Pichot (2009) has termed the 'scientization of the natural', the subordination of nature to human purposes with its anthropocentric privileging of human needs and wants and an unshakable commitment to the beneficent effects of technological applications and fixes.

There was, however, another contradictory moment contained in the rise of industrial capitalism. This is the other arm of Pichot's depiction, namely the 'naturalization of the social'. One form of this has already been alluded to, namely the efforts of eugenics and racism to ground social hierarchies as natural orders, thereby removing their political content and rendering them impervious to reform. Another form, again familiar to contemporary environmentalists, is to use nature normatively, as a basis for a critique of the artefactual and the unnatural, of the urban and the industrial. This Romantic revolt has a long pedigree in European thought (Berlin, 1990) and appeals to an authentic, often originary, idea of human nature rediscoverable only on the basis of an unconstrained, purer mode of living purged of the shallow distractions of polite culture and the superfluous needs of consumerism. Nature was a powerful source, for the German Romantics in particular, of the unkempt, the wild and the disordered; from the poems of Wordsworth to the paintings of David Friedrich Caspar, Nature was seen as a source of spiritual renewal in an age of desiccating materialism and rationalist order.

Sociology, newly emerging towards the end of the 19th and the beginning of the 20th century, was not altogether immune to these influences: Durkheim's fond glances towards the medieval guilds as a possible model for the new forms of organic solidarity are an example. Unsurprisingly, perhaps, the only one of the founding triumvirate of classical sociology whose work has had a lasting impact on the debates about the social and the natural, particularly in its environmentalist and political forms, is Marx. At the core of Marx's social theory is the concept of practice, the embodied capacity of human beings to transform themselves and their world through labour. Human emancipation, for Marx, is realizable only, and precisely, because human labour changes our relation to nature; this, in turn, alters the possibilities for human fulfilment. Marx's scorn of Utopian socialists, for example, was founded on his view that without the development of productive forces – that is, a changed relationship to nature – the abolition of want and poverty was not practically possible and so, neither, was human emancipation.

As Benton (1993) has argued, Marx's position is not without tension. Marx's view, particularly in his earlier work such as the *Economic and Philosophic Manuscripts of 1844*, seems to encourage an instrumental or anthropocentric approach to the natural world: it is something to be subordinated to, and used for, the purposes of human fulfilment. 'Nature, it seems,' notes Benton, 'is an acceptable partner for humanity only in so far as it has been divested of all that constitutes its otherness, in so far, in other words, as it has become, itself, human' (Benton, 1993: 31). As we have already suggested, this position is a common one in Western social theory and has frequently justified rapacious and exploitative policies by governments towards natural resources. Elsewhere, though, Marx takes a different perspective. In later work, especially that following the publication of Darwin's *Origin of Species* in 1859, he took a more consistently materialist approach, regarding nature as 'a complex causal order, independent of human activity, forever setting the condition and limits within which human beings, as natural beings, may shape and direct their activities' (Benton, 1993: 31). There is a strong insistence here on the ineluctable necessity of a different sort of relationship between the social and the natural worlds, one that gives a proper place to the specificity and distinctiveness of the human species without undermining the recognition that, as part of nature, human beings are critically dependent on the natural environment as a condition of survival.

Indeed, as Burkett (1999) has persuasively argued, Marx places great emphasis on the *natural* basis of labour productivity: the human capacity to work (labour power) is itself a natural property of being human. Moreover, an inherent component of human labour is its appropriation of materials produced spontaneously by nature, without human assistance. Marx's materialist emphasis on the natural basis of labour productivity means that use value necessarily contains a natural element and therefore the productivity of labour must be conceptualized in terms of definite natural conditions (Burkett, 1999: 33). Marx's materialism from this perspective rests on an ontological distinction between social relations and nature, a distinction that allows for an examination of their interplay and the development of a materialist environmental politics:

> [Marx's] vision of a more concordant co-evolution of society and nature depends on the distinction between human production conditions, as formed by non-exploitative social relations, and nature as such. (Burkett, 1999: 31)

This dualist account, we would suggest, is central to Marx's great achievement, namely the development of a political analysis of the relation between the natural and the social.

Thus far we have argued, along with many others, that sociology as a discipline was founded on an ontological distinction between society and nature; sociology and the social sciences were concerned with uncovering the laws governing the workings of society, while the natural sciences dealt with those underpinning the natural world. The picture is, of course, more complicated than this and biology – particularly eugenics and theories of evolution – remained influential well into the 20th century (see Osborne and Rose, 2008; Goldman, 2007; Fuller, 2007; Carter, 2007). Nikolas Rose (this volume) reminds us of the close connections between sociology and biology at that time and of the links between British sociologists and the Eugenics Society. Also influential were human ecological approaches such as those of Patrick Geddes and Lewis Mumford whose 'regional approach to social development' sought to 'link natural and social knowledges into a coherent whole' (Jamison, 2001: 80; Studholme, 2007). The influence of biological thinking – and especially eugenics – on sociological theorizing partly explains the attempts of sociologists, feminists and anti-racists to demarcate 'the social' and culture as something distinct from 'the natural' that could be studied and explained without recourse to biology. The distinction between society and nature was used as a basis for differentiating sociology and the social sciences from the natural sciences and became increasingly important in the light of attempts to naturalize and scientize all social inequalities and differences. Indeed, it is one of the dualisms which characterizes Western philosophical thought and enables society, culture and the individual to be defined in relation to each other and in opposition to their 'other' – nature (Strathern, 1992).

Challenging 'society' and 'nature'

The social movements that emerged in the 1950s and 1960s challenged these dualisms and developed a critique of what has been termed 'big' science and the 'scientific-technological state' (Jamison, 2001: 66); in the process they produced new knowledges, redefined reality, and translated 'scientific ideas into social and political beliefs' (Eyerman and Jamison, 1991: 92; Touraine, 1985). According to Jamison, the 'new movements of feminism and environmentalism articulated an alternative approach to science and technology' and 'involved a rejection of modern science's exploitative attitude to nature' (Jamison, 2001: 68). They also developed an extensive critique of dualistic conceptualizations of society and nature and the way in which social and political thinkers have used 'nature' as a justification for social inequalities; in other words they challenged 'established thought in the social sciences' (Benton, 1991: 2).

The civil rights movement and challenges to eugenics

Prior to the emergence of second wave feminism and environmentalism, however, a key challenge to an uncritical belief in a beneficent science and its ability to explain the social world came with the emergence of the Civil Rights movement in the USA. Eugenics had played a central role in the maintenance of social hierarchies of race in the USA (as well as in Europe, and through colonialism, much of the rest of the world: see, for example, Balibar and Wallerstein, 1991; Bayly, 2004; Dikotter, 1992). Tucker (1994) has pointed to the 'enormous influence' exerted by 'the racist wing of the eugenics movement'; one of its leading figures, Charles Davenport, was publicly praised by President Roosevelt on the publication of Davenport's magnum opus *The Passing of the Great Race* (Tucker, 1994: 92). From the late 1950s, the Civil Rights movement began to challenge eugenics and the biological explanations it advanced for racism and discrimination. In doing so, the movement drew on anthropological and sociological research to demonstrate that social differences were environmental and cultural. (There are obvious parallels here with the women's movement and feminism, where a similar rejection of biological reductionist accounts of sex inequalities and discrimination was taking shape; see, for example, Charles, 1993). This strategy was undeniably effective, and may even have been a necessary stage in the development of an anti-racist politics in the USA, but significantly it left unchallenged the concept of race as biologically based, thereby failing to critique the role of science in politics. It is not possible, we would contend, to use the notion of race without implicating some notion of biological determinism and mobilizing a muddled ontology of the natural and the social, one that was unable to challenge the conviction that 'science' can provide solutions to a wide range of social anxieties, including those arising from the prospect of ecological catastrophe. The civil rights movement, nevertheless, mounted a significant challenge to conventional understandings of the natural and the social, something that was taken further by the environmental movement.

The environmental movement

The emergence of the most recent wave of the environmental movement is often linked to the publication of Rachel Carson's *Silent Spring* in 1962, which exposed the potentially disastrous consequences of exploitative scientific practices for the environment and popularized the idea of 'systems ecology' (Jamison, 2001: 69), and to the 1970 Earth Summit (Hannigan, 2006; Castells, 2009). These different starting points reflect the fact that the environmental movement emerged earlier in the USA than in Britain and Europe. Be that as it may, there are three elements of the movement which are significant for our discussion: its relationship with science, its critique of dominant conceptualizations of 'nature' and its transformative impact on ways of seeing, particularly on ways of seeing the relationship between human societies and the natural world.

The environmental movement has had, from its inception, a contradictory relationship with science. This is apparent in the fact that the environmental dangers posed by science and technology were initially popularized by a scientist and a woman, Rachel Carson. So, while the environmental movement has developed a profound critique of 'big' science and its technological applications, it is dependent upon scientists to alert it to environmental threats and, in turn, scientists are dependent on the environmental movement to popularize their ideas (Castells, 2009). Moreover scientists and scientific knowledges can be found on both sides of the environmental debate (Beck, 1992; Mol and Spaargaren, 1993: 442). The movement also developed a critique of dominant conceptions of nature by building on and transforming conservationist and preservationist views (Jamison, 2001). Such views predated the environmental movement and argued, in different ways, for a modification of the exploitative relation between human society and the natural world; they tended, however, to be based on an anthropocentric and masculinist view of the relationship between humans and the environment (Kheel, 2008). The environmentalists of the 1960s and 1970s built on these views but challenged their anthropocentrism, arguing that humans had no pre-eminent place in the ecological systems of which they were part. Finally, the environmental movement both challenged the dominant view of nature as something to be exploited and facilitated the diffusion of the idea of ecological crisis (Hannigan, 2006: 45); in other words it reframed and redefined the relationship between society and nature as one of crisis rather than stability. It also paved the way for the wider diffusion of ideas about human ecology and their application to the understanding of social and political problems (Jamison, 2001) and, in the 1980s, for the emergence of environmental sociology (Hannigan, 2006). It therefore contributed to new ways of seeing and understanding the world which particularly affected conceptualizations of nature and its relation to society. In Castells' words, it changed 'the way we think about our collective relationship to nature' (Castells, 2009: 6).

The feminist movement and ecofeminist thought

While the environmental movement emphasized the connectedness of society and nature, and embraced an ecological world-view that saw humankind as only one part of nature, feminism took a different view. Feminists developed a critique of the supposed 'naturalness' of women's subordination, taking issue with the gendered subtexts of the founding 'fathers' of sociology and with the ways in which women's alleged closer relationship with nature was constructed within social and political thought and used as legitimation for their subordinate social and political status. Furthermore, they developed social and, especially, cultural explanations of gender, separating it from a consideration of biological sex (see Oakley, 1972; de Beauvoir, 1972). These explanations attempted to get away from the biological reductionism which had characterized understandings of women's subordinate social position (Sayers, 1982) and, in the process, denied any place to 'nature' or 'biology' in their explanatory frameworks.

Feminists also developed a critique of Western knowledge and of the dichotomies underpinning Western philosophical thought, both of which were important to the development of ecofeminism. They argued that, far from being objective and impartial, Western knowledge was the product of a partial, masculinist world-view. It was predicated on the viewpoint of white, middle-class Western men who were able to abstract themselves from the social and material world and produce knowledge which was claimed to be objective and universal but which was actually subjective and partial (see Charles, 1996 for a summary of these arguments). Science was characterized as a 'masculinist project' (Mellor, 1997: 118) and the rise of scientific rationality was linked to the release of 'the full destructive potential of Western patriarchal culture' (Mellor, 1997: 116). Prior to the emergence of rational science, it was argued, nature had been conceptualized as 'a living being and nurturing mother' albeit one that could be 'wild, uncontrolled, and evil' (Kheel, 2008: 212). With the development of capitalism and modern industry, an image of nature as a machine emerged and this, so Carolyn Merchant argues, encouraged the exploitative relation to nature that characterizes both science and capitalist production (Merchant, 1980). Thus feminists critique the claim that knowledge is 'disembodied, impersonal and transcendent' and argue that 'the detachment of the scientific model...has led to the technologies of life or death such as nuclear physics and molecular biology' (Mellor, 1997: 118). Furthermore, it was argued, Western knowledge is opposed to embodied ways of knowing. Ecofeminists view nature and the natural world as embracing humanity rather than as something which is separate and separable from it; in this they concur with views advanced within the wider environmental movement.

Ecofeminists also argue that the dualisms of Western philosophical thought are underpinned by a 'logic of domination' which legitimates the abuse of nature, women and other oppressed groups. This logic of domination elevates the masculine over the feminine associating it with reason, the mind, autonomy and culture. The feminine, by contrast, is associated with emotion, the body and the material world, including nature. This conceptual system 'underlies the abuse of nature, women, and other marginalized humans in the Western world' (Kheel, 2008: 210). Contrary to some critics (eg Meyer, 1999), ecofeminists do not necessarily argue that a transformation in dualistic modes of thought is sufficient to eliminate an exploitative relation to 'nature'; on the contrary, oppressive and masculinist modes of thought are linked to material practices, and capitalist production in particular is identified as the cause of environmental degradation (Merchant, 1999).

These dualisms associating women with nature and men with culture were assumed to be universal, thereby providing an explanation for women's 'universal' oppression. This assumption, however, came under attack from within social anthropology. Anthropologists recognized that cultures other than their own had different world views and cosmologies and did not necessarily distinguish nature from culture or associate women with nature (see for eg Descola, 1996; Howell, 1996). These cosmologies, according to Descola, could be classified as totemic, animic and naturalism. A totemic classificatory system makes 'use of empirically observable discontinuities between natural species to organize, conceptually, a segmentary order delimiting social units'; an animic classificatory system 'endows natural beings with human dispositions and social attributes' (Descola, 1996: 87) while naturalism is 'the belief that nature does exist, that certain things owe their existence and development to a principle extraneous both to chance and to the effects of human will' (Descola, 1996: 88). Naturalism 'creates a specific ontological domain, a place of order and necessity where nothing happens without a reason or a cause' (Descola, 1996: 88). And, as Descola points out, this is the Western view of nature and, in his view, is no more 'true' than totemism or animism; all are culturally relative. Ethnographic evidence of this sort demonstrated that there was no universal understanding of nature as a realm separate from human society. This meant, firstly that not all societies viewed women as closer to nature than men and nature as separable from and subordinate to culture; second that the evidence of women's universal subordination was questionable; and thirdly that the way different societies understood their relation to their environment did not necessarily involve relations of hierarchy and power. This opened the way to cultural relativism and a stepping back from advancing universal explanations of allegedly universal phenomena. These issues are addressed by Peter Dickens (this volume) who links dualistic modes of thought and cosmologies both to the ways in which societies are organized and to the structure of the psyche.

The civil rights, environmental and feminist movements have clearly challenged dominant conceptions of society and nature by pointing to their fundamental interconnections and by demonstrating their cultural relativity and their association with gendered and racialised hierarchies. They have, in different ways, questioned the values and assumptions associated with modernity, the valuing of progress, growth and risk-taking for example, analysing them not only as capitalist but also as masculinist and racist. In this sense they have been engaged in a cultural politics which challenges the way we think about the world and the practices in which we engage. These reconceptualizations were to have significant repercussions for sociology as a discipline and, arguably, constitute a continuing challenge to its very existence (eg Law, 2008; Jamison, 2001).

'Nature' in crisis: 'society' under threat

The other challenges to sociological thinking came, on the one hand, from threats to the continued existence of human society such as that posed by nuclear weapons and the release of radiation from Chernobyl (1986) and, on the other hand, from the development of technologies of the body in particular and biotechnology more generally. These developments have led some sociologists (notably Beck) to suggest that modernity is being replaced by what he terms 'risk society'. Risk society has been brought about by the emergence of risks which are unbounded, potentially catastrophic and global. It signals a shift from a society marked by distribution-based conflicts to one marked by 'the production, definition and distribution of risks' (Mol and Spaargaren, 1993: 440). Along with others, Beck takes the emergence of 'new' social movements in the 1960s and 1970s as indicating a transition to a new type of society. In his view, science and technology have contributed to the emergence of these risks and are 'no longer capable of providing the security that is sought by the population to reduce their own anxieties and fears'; as a result, they have been 'demystified' (Mol and Spaargaren, 1993: 443). The idea of risk society contrasts with the suggestion that a third phase of modernity, ecological modernity, is emerging which involves a transformation of industrial production such that it becomes 'an ecologically rational organization of production and consumption' (Mol and Spaargaren, 1993: 437) taking 'into account the maintenance of the existing sustenance base' (Hannigan, 2006: 25).

Developments in technologies of the body, such as reproductive technology, have also changed understandings of what is 'natural'. Marilyn Strathern argues that the debates about reproductive technology, specifically surrogate motherhood during the 1980s, were about 'the intrusion of technology into biological process' and 'interference with natural relations'; she suggests that Nature itself was under threat (Strathern, 1992: 41). In her words, 'Artificial processes are seen to substitute for natural ones, and thus present themselves as "interfering with nature"... What is interfered with is the very idea of a natural fact. Or, to

9

put it another way, of the difference between natural and cultural ones' (Strathern, 1992: 43). This coming together of 'nature' and 'culture' in reproductive technology is also a characteristic of genetic technology and Strathern's arguments are echoed by Nikolas Rose (this volume). Beck argues in a similar way that nature no longer exists outside society or, indeed, society outside nature, because it has been so changed by human intervention (Beck, 1992: 80; see also Jamison, 2001). Industrial processes and the environmental degradation that they cause have resulted in nature becoming 'a historical product' (Beck, 1992: 80). Moreover, the 'destruction of nature…becomes an integral part of the social, political and economic dynamic' (Beck, 1992: 80). This he calls the societalization of nature, which, through the creation of 'global social, economic and medical threats to people', gives rise to newly emergent social, political and economic conflicts. Environmental problems thereby become social problems with attendant 'risks' for the future of democracy.

The question of whether nature any longer has an independent existence has therefore emerged both from environmental degradation associated with capitalist industrial production and from developments in biotechnology. There no longer appears to be a natural realm which is independent of human activity. These developments – scientific, technological and industrial – mesh with ideas about cultural relativism and cosmologies which have no concept of 'nature' that is separate from something called 'society' or 'culture', and provide support for the argument that 'nature' is socially constructed. Such positions, however, ignore the compelling argument that aspects of nature may be modified but nature is not created by human activity. As Ted Benton puts it:

> [E]vidence of the potentially catastrophic implications of ecological degradation on a global scale might serve to remind us of the role of non-human nature, as well as human embodiment itself, in providing the bedrock conditions of possibility for any sort of human activity at all. (Benton, 2009: 226)

New social movements, together with scientific and technological developments which create threats to the survival of both nature and society, have challenged sociology to incorporate 'nature' into theories of social reality, to recognize that human beings are part of a social and natural environment and that the natural environment, far from being infinitely exploitable, sets limits on what humankind is able to do. New social movements are also associated with the emergence of a new type of society, one which supersedes the modern epoch and the understandings of nature in which sociological notions of society and individual are grounded (Strathern, 1992). This has given rise to two different approaches to society and nature. The first retains a notion of nature which is connected to but conceptually distinguishable from society, while the second argues that it is no longer possible to make this conceptual distinction (or that it is one 'choice' amongst many). In what follows we look first at approaches that retain a notion of 'nature' and then at those which supersede it in one way or another.

Reconceptualizing nature and society

Nature as real

The concern with the body and sexuality reasserts the materiality of bodies and their social and cultural effects. There has also been a move to reconceptualize sex and gender, with some arguing that sex as well as gender is socially constructed (Delphy, 1996) and others suggesting that our biology is influential in the way we experience gender. Similarly, some variants of ecological or environmental sociology insist that nature is not only 'real' with real effects on human societies but that sociology needs to take it into account in order fully to understand human societies. This insistence that 'nature' is an important dimension of human existence and that it ought to be encompassed within a properly sociological imagination poses a challenge to sociology as a discipline. This is because it would require not only that sociology consider the social, economic and political consequences of environmental degradation, as argued by Beck, but that it take into account the action of biological materiality on social processes. Ted Benton has discussed this at length in various works and he, in common with Peter Dickens, argues that it is possible to do this without resorting to biological reductionism, something that sociologists, with reason, have been at pains to avoid. His contribution to this volume illustrates this contention through an exploration of naturalistic explanations of human evolution. The importance of his chapter is that he shows how, in explaining human evolution, Darwin investigated not only the influence of 'nature' but also that of 'society' on human development, showing that their effects were different. This supports arguments for the retention of an idea of nature with different laws of causality from those operating at the social level.

Such a view of nature can also be found in both Marx and contemporary forms of ecological Marxism. Marx's work, despite its ambiguities, provides the basis for environmentalist arguments that recognize the influence of political ideas and structures on the character of the relationship between the natural and the social. It thereby avoids reducing the natural to the social, since for Marx the natural world possesses its own properties and powers, independent of human activity yet whose effects are mediated through the forms of that activity; and it avoids reducing the social to the natural, since the social world has emergent properties of its own that are themselves the product of the exercise of distinctively human properties and powers of language and reflexivity.

Marx's analysis contains a powerful critical theory of environmental crisis, one which identifies 'capital's hunger for materials and energy' as '*quantitatively* anti-ecological' (Burkett, 1999: 112). There are two sources of environmental crisis for Marx according to this interpretation. The first is a crisis of capital accumulation, where the technological advances and rising productivity associated with the expansion and reproduction of capital accumulation generate an increase in the quantity of natural forces and objects that capital must appropriate as materials and as instruments of production; more and more of the earth's resources must be turned into *saleable* objects of exchange value. Those resources that cannot be produced and sold at a profit, that are not socially valued within capitalist social relations, such as fertile land or an unpolluted environment, are simply neglected. The crisis of capital accumulation generates imbalances between capital's material requirements (fossil-based fuels, for instance) and the natural conditions of raw materials production (global warming creates droughts which in turn significantly impair crop growth).

The second form of crisis Marx points to is in the quality of human social development, particularly the increasing material and energy circulation produced by capitalism's industrial division of town and country. Urban spaces and industrial production generate vast amounts of human and industrial waste matter which has to be disposed of or re-circulated. This is another example of a use value that cannot be converted readily into exchange value.

Ecological Marxism argues that capitalist production is exploitative, not only of the working class but also of nature. Nature, or the environment, is both a source of raw materials and a depository for waste; the metaphors of 'tap' and 'sink' (O'Connor, 1998) or 'mine' and 'dumping ground' (Sachs, 1999: 26) have been used to describe this relationship. O'Connor has suggested, building on Marx's analysis, that this constitutes a second contradiction of capitalism, one in which humanity is on a collision course with the natural world (O'Connor, 1998: xii). Capitalism, because it is a self-expanding system of economic growth (O'Connor, 1998: 10), is unable to operate in an environmentally sustainable manner and is the root of the current environmental crisis. Ecological Marxism, for O'Connor, recognizes the 'irreducible autonomy of nature, as enabling and constraining human projects' (O'Connor, 1998: 4) and that the 'rhythms and cycles' of nature 'are governed by a different logic than the rhythms and cycles of capital' (O'Connor, 1998: 10). Ecological Marxism argues further that the struggle over the conditions of production should be understood as including struggles over nature; over the conditions which enable the reproduction of the conditions of production to continue. This struggle is engaged in by new social movements and aims to protect the 'viability of the social and natural environment *as means of life and life itself*' (O'Connor, 1998: 12). Thus nature is conceptualized as constituting a fundamental part of the conditions of production, conditions that capitalist production itself is destroying.

'After nature'

An alternative approach argues that 'nature' no longer has an autonomous existence, if it ever did, and that we are 'after nature' (Strathern, 1992). This is not necessarily because the material, biological world no longer exists but because the idea of nature no longer provides the grounding in relation to which human beings construct societies and culture: nature is no longer conceptualized as an 'autonomous domain' (Strathern, 1992: 194). Furthermore this transformation in the way in which 'nature' functions conceptually has partly been brought about by the effect of biotechnology; relationships which were previ-ously thought to be 'natural', such as that between mother and child, can now be seen 'either as socially constructed or as a natural state of affairs (socially) assisted'. This means that choice is exercised about 'what to consider natural' (Strathern, 1992: 196). This destabilization of context is what, in Strathern's view, explains the perception of ecological crisis.

> If nature has not disappeared, then, its grounding function has. It no longer provides a model or analogy for the very idea of context. With the destabilising of relation, context and grounding, it is no surprise that the present crisis (epoch) appears an ecological one. (Strathern, 1992: 195)

Strathern argues that 'the End of Nature is really After Nature: a point of apprehension, in this case of the constructional roles that particular concept has played in our perceptions' (Strathern, 1992: 191). We have moved beyond the modern epoch which was characterized by a distinction and connection between society and nature, each being defined in relation to the other and, although sharing similarities, also differing.

> Culture and nature may be connected together as domains that run in analogous fashion insofar as each operates in a similar way according to laws of its own; at the same time, each is also connected to a whole other range of phenomena which dif-ferentiate them – the activities of human beings, for instance, by contrast with the physical properties of the universe. (Strathern, 1992: 73)

For Strathern, we are now 'after nature'; there is no longer a grounding notion of nature in relation to which we are able to understand society, culture and the individual. Others, such as Haraway (2003) with her notion of nature-culture, and Swyngedouw (1999) with the idea of socio-nature, take this further, refusing any distinction, conceptual or otherwise, between society and nature. Neither society nor nature exist independently of the practices and perfor-mances which create the realities of which they are part and which bring them into being (Law, 2009); there is therefore no essential difference or boundary between them. This shift in thinking about society and nature is marked by a move from asking why things happen to charting the 'how' of social processes in minute detail, a move from causal explanation to phenomenological descrip-tion; indeed phenomenology and ethnomethodology came under attack in the 1970s for having no concept of society so it should not be a surprise that their resurgence is associated with a denial of the conceptual distinction between society and nature (Worsley, 1974).

Some of these differences are represented in this volume. Thus Ted Benton, Peter Dickens and Kate Soper argue for recognition of an external reality, the different layers of which are governed by different types of causality, while Nikolas Rose takes the view that nature can no longer be seen as a realm sepa-rate from society. He argues this in relation to biotechnology, specifically genet-ics, and approaches the issue through an exploration of the normal and the pathological. For him this raises ethical questions about what sorts of human beings we would like to become, questions also touched upon by Kate Soper in the final chapter of the volume.

Challenging the discipline

Some variants of environmental sociology, such as the new ecological paradigm which was advanced in the late 1970s, argue that sociology has to change in order to be able to 'make it environmental in its preconceptions'; thus rather than 'avoiding' the concept of nature, sociology should incorporate it (Foster, 2002: 56). Arguably such incorporation is only possible by a transformation of sociology and of its object of study – the social. Indeed there are many who argue that for environmental issues to be taken seriously there has to be a reconfiguration of the disciplines such that disciplinary boundaries are broken down and society and nature can be conceptualized as different parts of a single whole (Jamison, 2001; Descola and Palsson, 1996). Such reconceptualizations serve to displace concepts such as 'society' thereby 'fundamentally altering the sociological tradition' and have developed *inter alia* from the sociology of networks and flows (Mol and Spaargaren, 2005: 96). Material flows 'become the unit of analysis' and this, it has been argued, represents a radicalization of the new ecological paradigm advanced in the 1970s. Furthermore, environmental flows are made 'inherently social' and are not 'necessarily or exclusively material. They also can be for the most part social, or a combination or hybrid: a social-material flow' (Mol and Spaargaren, 2005: 99).

Mobility is another key concept that is elaborated in Urry's chapter (this volume) and explored empirically in the chapter by Flynn *et al*. Thus the 'mobility of environmental ideas, information, and interpretation frameworks flowing between networks and nodes around the globe can – according to the sociology of flows – be interpreted in much the same way as material flows' (Mol and Spaargaren, 2005: 99). Urry's 'sociology of flows' is influenced by actor-network theory and 'argues for a merge of the natural and the social into hybrids, putting "material worlds" or hybrids at the center of analysis' (Mol and Spaargaren, 2005: 99). Thus the sociology of flows does not distinguish between nature and society or the material and the social.

Mol and Spaargaren note that the merging of society and nature has serious consequences for sociology as a discipline. For Urry the division between society and nature is outdated, as is the division between the natural and social sciences, and what is now needed is 'complexity sciences' in order to understand contemporary developments. This model is clearly derived from complexity and chaos theory, as is talk of flows, fluids, fractals, autopoiesis and so on, all concepts which are mobilized by Urry and borrowed from models developed within the natural sciences. The call for an integration of social and natural sciences has been on the agenda since the 1970s and the emergence of the environmental movement; indeed it is said to be one of the consequences of this movement (Jamison, 2001) and is supported by several of our contributors.

The final development to mention here concerns the conflict between constructionism and realism that erupted into the 'science wars' in the 1990s (Law, 2008). At its most extreme this was a conflict over whether reality exists – a perennial philosophical problem which arguably is not the proper concern of sociology (Turnbull and Antalffy, 2009) – and raised the question of the extent to which 'nature' was constructed by scientific practice or existed externally to it. This has been a problem for those feminists wishing to hang on to 'reality' while recognizing that knowledges are situated and embodied. Donna Haraway puts this cogently when she says that she wants to have 'an account of radical historical contingency for all knowledge claims... *and* a no-nonsense commitment to a faithful account of the "real" world' (Haraway, 1991: 187 our emphasis).

Within sociology there are many who take a similar view, arguing for a social constructionist position without taking the view that reality has no independent existence. Social constructionists, according to Hannigan, do not claim that 'environmental risks do not exist or that natural reality plays no identifiable role in producing knowledge about these risks' (Hannigan, 2006: 29). On the contrary, they are interested in the different ways in which environmental problems are understood and how, through the pressures brought to bear by social movements, NGOs, the media and government, to name but a few, and the different discursive framing of environmental problems that are associated with different social actors, policies and practices emerge which may themselves have material consequences. Such processes are investigated by Chris Shaw (this volume) who combines a social constructionist with a critical realist approach to explore how the idea of a dangerous limit has been constructed and its potential consequences for efforts to halt global warming. His chapter is important because it shows that scientific uncertainties have been made into certainties in the process of developing policy. He calls for a recognition both of uncertainty and that science cannot provide all the answers; instead the development of climate change policies has to be subjected to a democratic process, which will embody a more positive precautionary principle and which will not be dominated by science and technology. In this he agrees with many of the contributors that the problem of climate change is something that cannot be solved through a reliance on science and technology alone.

Sociology and environmental politics

Sociology and the social sciences more generally have a critical part to play in understanding how the ecological crisis has come about, investigating its hugely unequal impact on human societies and contributing towards the development of social and political programmes that will avert or ameliorate the crisis. Although science and technology clearly have a critical part to play, it is unlikely that there will be a technological fix to solve the crisis. John Urry, in his chapter, issues a passionate plea for sociology to engage with the debates about climate change, in this sense agreeing with the sentiments expressed by Chris Shaw that it is not sufficient to leave the question of climate change to the scientists. Other sociologists have taken up Urry's challenge. As we have already seen, Beck's concept of risk society is a contribution to understanding the profoundly undemocratic future that may be a consequence of ecological crisis. More recently Giddens has intervened in the debate by providing a prescription for tackling climate change based on sociological analysis of the problem and the possible ways in which global warming might be addressed. His approach has much in common with the ideas of ecological modernity, that modernity is now entering a phase where ecological concerns will be central to industrial production, although he also argues that an ensuring state that monitors what is happening and enables agreed goals to be achieved is essential. He therefore recognizes that capitalist enterprises left to their own devices will not necessarily deliver on climate change (Giddens, 2009). He argues that environmental justice is important, recognizing that those who are living in poverty will suffer disproportionately from climate change; what he fails to acknowledge, as MacGregor points out in her chapter, is that the majority of the poor are women and it is therefore women and children who will be affected disproportionately. Climate change is, in this sense, profoundly gendered, something that is not recognized by most environmental sociologists.

Sherilyn MacGregor adopts a feminist social constructionist approach to illustrate a gendered analysis of climate change. For her gender is important to the way in which climate change is understood, in how it is experienced in daily life, and in institutional and individual responses to climate change (see also Mellor, 1997). MacGregor's chapter shows that environmental degradation and climate change are not gender neutral; this raises the important question of environmental justice and how it is to be achieved if a concept of gender is missing from analyses of climate change. The chapter by Daniel De Hanas provides an example of women's activism in relation to the environment and illustrates one of the points made by MacGregor, that women's activism often takes place within the constraints of gender divisions of labour. He situates his research in the context of discussions about the relationship of religions to environmental issues, arguing that Islam has more potential for environmental protection than does Christianity. He illustrates this through an exploration of a women's programme on Muslim Community Radio, showing that the broadcasts sacralize environmentalism, promote the idea that Islam is modern, and challenge accepted gender divisions of labour.

The three chapters that follow focus on alternative sources of energy and food production. Rob Flynn, Paul Bellaby and Miriam Ricci explore people's attitudes to hydrogen, an alternative source of energy, investigating the gap that exists between values and action on environmental issues. They ask why it is that, even though people are now aware of the risks of global warming, they do not seem to have made appropriate changes in their behaviour, and provide evidence to show that people are 'locked in' to behaviours that rely on the use of non-renewable energy. They also show that women are often 'greener' than men in their environmental attitudes.

While Flynn *et al.* explore views on hydrogen technology amongst those who are not directly affected by its generation, Carly McLachlan's focus is on local reaction to renewable energy generation. She explores the reaction of 'stakeholders' and the public more generally to two specific developments, linking them to the different symbolic meanings of place and technology. She shows that ideas about the relationship between technology, nature and place are critical in people's responses to the siting of alternative technology. Environmental arguments can be mobilized both in favour of, and against, such technologies, not only in terms of where they are sited, but also in terms of their desirability and the contribution they are likely to make to alleviating global warming.

Perhaps a more fundamental way of countering climate change is to develop ways of producing which do not rely on practices that are exploitative and destructive of the environment. Such practices are explored by Liz Dowler, Moya Kneafsey, Rosie Cox and Lewis Holloway in their chapter on food production where they investigate those involved in 'alternative' or 'sustainable' food networks. They argue that ideas of reconnection and an 'ethic of care' are fundamental to these networks and that behaviour, in terms of values and practices, can and does change, given the right social context.

This sort of change in values and practices, which has been characterized as post-material (Inglehart, 1990), is also advocated by Kate Soper. Along with many of the contributors, she argues that it is not sufficient to seek alternative sources of energy so that we can continue with our existing lifestyle; more radical changes are needed. As an early environmental campaigner put it:

> the accent must be far more on *reducing* the amount of travel than on looking for the technological 'fix'. The crucial changes must be *social* rather than technological. We shall have to live closer to our work and shop locally, buying locally grown food and locally made goods, consisting far more of local materials.... In short, the key to alternative transport lies in the alternative to transport. (Rivers, 1976: 227 cited in Jamison, 2001)

Soper poses the question of whether we can any longer distinguish between that which is artificially contrived and that which is naturally given – a question that is answered by Nikolas Rose in the negative but which others answer in the affirmative. Soper argues that, despite all the ways in which humans intervene in natural processes, nature continues to exist independently of human activity in the sense that 'all our interventions... are dependent on the workings of physical law and process, and have their outcomes determined by them'. And she points out that her position, along with that of critical realists like Ted Benton and Peter Dickens, relies on a '"realist" or theoretical concept of nature rather than 'other more phenomenological or metaphysical concepts'. Soper's argument about an alternative hedonism and care for the environment resonates with the arguments of Dowler *et al.* about a new ethic of care that they identify among alternative producers and consumers of food.

The contributors to this volume present a powerful argument for sociological intervention in debates about climate change, particularly in understanding the socio-economic and cultural processes which have given rise to it and how they might be changed so as to avoid ecological catastrophe. And in order for sociologists to intervene effectively, sociology needs to engage across disciplinary boundaries. This means moving away from an insistence that sociology is only able to deal with the social or cultural, defined in contradistinction to the natural, and engaging with 'nature', however it is defined. The chapters in this book provide different illustrations of how this is happening and how sociology is beginning to address one of the most urgent problems facing humankind.

Note

1 We are aware that there is disagreement about whether or not Marx, Weber and Durkheim can be considered, *strictu sensu*, sociologists (see for example Osborne and Rose, 2008). Sociologists or not, however, they have been of fundamental importance for the development of sociology as a discipline and it is for this reason that we consider their understandings of the relation between society and nature to be relevant to our discussion.

References

American Sociological Association (2002), *Official Statement on Race*, http://www2.asanet.org/media/asa_race_statement.pdf

Balibar, E. and Wallerstein, L., (1991), *Race, Nation, Class: Ambiguous Identities*, London: Verso.

Bayly, C. A., (2004), *The Birth of the Modern World 1780–1914*, Oxford: Blackwell.

Beck, U., (1992), *Risk Society: Towards a New Modernity*, Los Angeles: Sage Publications.

Benton, T., (1991), 'Biology and Social Science: Why the Return of the Repressed should be given a Cautious Welcome' in *Sociology*, 25 (1): 1–29.

Benton, T., (1993), *Natural Relations: Ecology, Animal Rights and Social Justice*, London: Routledge.

Benton, T., (2009), 'Conclusion: Philosophy, Materialism, and Nature – Comments and Reflections' in S. Moog and R. Stones (eds), *Nature, Social Relations and Human Needs: Essays in Honour of Ted Benton*, Basingstoke: Palgrave Macmillan, pp. 208–243.

Berlin, I., (1990), *The Crooked Timber of Humanity*, London: John Murray.

Burkett, P., (1999), *Marx and Nature: A Red and Green Perspective*, London: Macmillan.

Callon, M., (1986), 'Some elements of a sociology of translation: domestication of the scallops and the fishermen of St Brieue bay' in J. Law (ed.), *Power. Action and Belief: A New Sociology of Knowledge?* London: Routledge and Kegan Paul, pp. 196–233.

Carter, B., (2007), 'Genes, genomes and genealogies: The return of scientific racism?' *Ethnic and Racial Studies*, 30 (4): 546–556.

Castells, M., (2009), *Communication Power*, Oxford: Oxford University Press.

Charles, N., (1993), *Gender Divisions and Social Change*, Hemel Hempstead: Harvester Wheatsheaf.

Charles, N., (1996), 'Feminist practices: identity, difference, power' in N. Charles and F. Hughes-Freeland (eds), *Practising Feminism: Identity, Difference, Power*, London and New York: Routledge: 1–37.

de Beauvoir, S., (1972), *The Second Sex*, Harmondsworth: Penguin.

Delphy, C., (1996), 'Rethinking sex and gender', in D. Leonard and L. Adkins (eds), *Sex in Question: French Materialist Feminism*, London: Taylor and Francis: 30–41.

Descola, P. and Palsson, G., (1996), 'Introduction' in P. Descola and G. Palsson (eds), *Nature and Society: Anthropological Perspectives*, London and New York: Routledge: 1–21.

Descola, P., (1996), 'Constructing natures: symbolic ecology and social practice' in P. Descola and G. Palsson (eds), *Nature and Society: Anthropological Perspectives*, London and New York: Routledge: 82–102.

Dikotter, F., (1992), *The Discourse of Race in Modern China*, London: Hurst.

Everyman, R. and Jamison, A., (1991), *Social Movement: A Cognitive Approach*, Cambridge: Polity Press.

Foster, J., (2002), 'Environmental Sociology and the Environmental Revolution' in *Organization and Environment*, 15 (1): 55–58.

Fuller, S., (2007), 'A path better not to have been taken' in *Sociological Review*, 55 (4): 807–815.

Giddens, A., (2009), *The Politics of Climate Change*, Cambridge: Polity Press.

Goldman, L., (2007), 'Foundations of British Sociology 1880–1930: contexts and biographies' in *Sociological Review*, 55 (4): 431–440.

Hajer, M. and Fischer, F., (1999), 'Beyond Global Discourse: The Rediscovery of Culture in Environmental Politics' in F. Fischer and M. Hajer (eds), *Living with Nature: Environmental Politics and Cultural Discourse*, Oxford: Oxford University Press.

Hannigan, J., (2006), *Environmental Sociology* (2nd edn), London and New York: Routledge.

Haraway, D. J., (1991), *Simians, Cyborgs, and Women: The Reinvention of Nature*, London: Free Association Books.

Haraway, D. J., (2003), *The Companion Species Manifesto: Dogs, People and Significant Otherness*, Chicago: Prickly Paradigm Press.

Hobsbawm, E., (1992), *Nations and Nationalism Since 1780*, Cambridge: Cambridge University Press.

Howell, S., (1996), 'Nature in culture or culture in nature? Chewong ideas of 'humans' and other species' in P. Descola and G. Palsson (eds), *Nature and Society: Anthropological Perspectives*, London and New York: Routledge: 127–144.

Inglehart, R., (1990), *Culture Shift in Advanced Society*, Princeton, NJ: Princeton University Press.

Jamison, A., (2001), *The Making of Green Knowledge: Environmental Politics and Cultural Transformation*, Cambridge, Cambridge University Press.

Kevles, D. J., (1985), *In the Name of Eugenics: Genetics and the Uses of Human Heredity*, New York: Alfred A. Knopf.

Kheel, M., (2008), *Nature Ethics: An Ecofeminist Perspective*, Lanham: Rowan and Littlefield Publishers.

Law, J., (2008), 'On sociology and STS' in *The Sociological Review*, 56 (4): 623–649.

Law, J., (2009), 'Practising Nature and Culture: An Essay for Ted Benton' in S. Moog and R. Stones (eds), *Nature, Social Relations and Human Needs: Essays in Honour of Ted Benton*, Basingstoke: Palgrave Macmillan: 65–79.

Malik, K., (1996), *The Meaning of Race: Race, History and Culture in Western Society*, London: Macmillan.

Mellor, M., (1997), *Feminism and Ecology*, Cambridge: Polity Press.

Merchant, C., (1980), *The Death of Nature: Women, Ecology, and the Scientific Revolution*, New York: Harper and Row.

Merchant, C., (1999), 'Partnership Ethics and Cultural Discourse: Women and the Earth Summit' in F. Fischer and M. Hajer (eds), *Living with Nature: Environmental Politics and Cultural Discourse*, Oxford: Oxford University Press: 204–223.

Meyer, J. M., (1999), 'Interpreting nature and politics in the history of Western thought: The environmentalist challenge' in *Environmental Politics*, 8 (2): 1–23.

Mol, A. P. J. and Spaargaren, G., (1993), 'Environment, Modernity and the Risk-Society: The Apocalyptic Horizon of Environmental Reform' in *International Sociology*, 8 (4): 431–459.

Mol, A. P. J. and Spaargaren, G., (2005), 'From Additions and Withdrawals to Environmental Fows' in *Organization and Environment*, 18 (1): 91–107.

Oakley, A., (1972), *Sex, Gender and Society*, Temple Smith: London.

O'Connor, J., (1998), *Natural Causes: Essays in Ecological Marxism*, New York, London: Guilford Press.

Omi, M. and Winant, H., (1994), *Racial Formation in the United States: From the 1960s to the 1990*, New York: Routledge.

Osborne, T. and Rose, N., (2008), 'Populating sociology: Carr-Saunders and the problem of population' in *The Sociological Review*, 56 (4): 535–551.

Pichot, A., (2009), *The Pure Society: From Darwin to Hitler*, London: Verso.

Rich, P., (1984), 'The long Victorian sunset: anthropology, eugenics and race in Britain, c1900–48' in *Patterns of Prejudice*, 18 (3): 3–17.

Rivers, P., (1976), 'There's no transport like no transport' in G. Boyle and P. Harper (eds), *Radical Technology*, London: Wildwood House.

Sachs, W., (1999), 'Sustainable development and the crisis of nature: on the political anatomy of an oxymoron' in F. Fischer and M. A. Hajer (eds), *Living with Nature: Environmental Politics as Cultural Discourse*, Oxford: Oxford University Press: 23–41.

Sayers, J., (1982), *Biological Politics*, London: Tavistock.

Strathern, M., (1980), 'No Nature, No Culture: The Hagen Case' in C. MacCormack and M. Strathern (eds), *Nature, Culture and Gender*, Cambridge: Cambridge University Press, pp. 174–222.

Strathern, M., (1992), *After Nature: English Kinship in the Late Twentieth Century*, Cambridge: Cambridge University Press.

Studholme, M., (2007), 'Patrick Geddes: founder of environmental sociology' in *Sociological Review*, 55 (3): 441–459.

Swyngedouw, E., (1999), 'Modernity and Hybridity: Nature, Regenracionismo, and the Production of the Spanish Waterscape, 1890–1930' in *Annals of the Association of American Geographers*, 89 (3): 443–465.

Touraine, A., (1985), 'An introduction to social movements' in *Social Research*, 4: 749–787.

Tucker, W. H., (1994), *The Science and Politics of Racial Research*, Urbana and Chicago: University of Illinois Press.

Turnbull, N. and Antalffy, N., (2009), 'Bourdieu's distintion between philosophical and sociological approaches to Science Studies' in *The Sociological Review*, 57 (4): 547–566.

Worsley, P., (1974), 'The state of theory and the status of theory' in *Sociology*, 8: 1–17.

Part One
Changing Conceptions of the Natural and the Social

Race, sex and the 'earthly paradise': Wallace versus Darwin on human evolution and prospects

Ted Benton

There is grandeur in this view of life, with its several powers, having been originally breathed into a few forms or into one; and that, whilst this planet has gone cycling on according to the fixed law of gravity, from so simple a beginning endless forms most beautiful and most wonderful have been, and are being, evolved (Darwin, *Origin of Species*)

In their provocative confrontation with renascent religiosity, militant atheists Richard Dawkins and Daniel Dennett rely heavily on the intellectual resources of a certain reading of Darwinism for their intellectual ammunition (Dawkins, 2006; Dennett, 2006). Paradoxically, an earlier version of 'Darwinism applied to the human case' would have had much in common with the homophobia, sexism and racial ideology of some versions of contemporary religious radicalism (see, for example, Caplan, 1978). By contrast, the new Darwinian secularists are keen to emphasise their elevated view of human nature – our capacity for empathy, altruism, the moral ordering of our lives, and egalitarian sentiments. In fact, however, the impoverished conceptual resources on offer from this version of neo-Darwinism give precious little rational support for such an optimistic view. Would a rigorous Darwinian be required, in the end, to fall back on the bleak vision of nature red in tooth and claw, and of humans as destined for an unending and ruthless 'struggle for existence'? Might one not, in the face of such a conclusion, be tempted into the more comforting arms of a moderate religiosity – even perhaps, of belief in 'intelligent design'? Or – as for many sociologists – might one rather altogether avoid serious engagement with the implications of our standing as evolved primates?

In many respects the tensions and dilemmas of this contemporary clash of world-views mirrors a much earlier dispute: one between co-inventor of the concept of evolution by natural selection, Alfred Russel Wallace, and his far more celebrated fellow philosopher-naturalist, Charles Darwin, and his supporters – most notably Thomas Huxley. Arguably, however, a study of their exchanges offers a much more fruitful direction for secular thinking about human nature and prospects than can be gleaned from the mutual incomprehensions of our current spectacle. What follows is an overview and analysis of some key differences of view that arose between these figures from the mid-1860s onwards – with the emphasis on human distinctiveness, racial and gender divisions, and the future prospects of human kind.

Darwin and Wallace before the 'Origin'

The great 19th century explorer, collector, radical political activist and naturalist-philosopher, Alfred Russel Wallace achieved much-deserved eminence in his own day. However, since that time he has remained in relative obscurity despite the efforts of numerous historians and biographers (for examples, McKinney, 1969; Fichman, 2004; Raby, 2001; Smith & Beccaloni, 2008). The 'official' celebrations of Darwin's achievement that abound in his bicentenary year represent Darwin as a solitary genius – a reluctant revolutionary. Some accounts make no mention at all of Wallace, while others introduce him as the stimulus to Darwin's publication of his ideas, so as to preserve his 'priority'. But this stimulus was the simple fact that Wallace had quite independently arrived at an essentially similar account of the 'origin of species' to Darwin's own, and in all innocence sent his paper, setting out the hypothesis, to Darwin for comment. Odd, then, that we should now give all the credit for the new view of living nature and our place in it to Darwin alone.

Wallace was much less well connected than Darwin, from early on in his life a firm religious sceptic and Owenite socialist. He did not suffer as Darwin did from deep anxiety about the metaphysical implications of evolutionary naturalism – and he did not have to fear loss of the approbation of respectable society as Darwin did – he never had it in the first place. There were similarities, however, in the routes that took both men to the problem of speciation and its solution. Both were from their early days close observers and deep lovers of the natural world. Both were endowed with great intellectual curiosity and, to be inferred from their correspondence and notebooks, both animated by the question of human origins and nature. In December 1857 Darwin wrote to Wallace: 'You ask whether I shall discuss "man". I think I shall avoid the whole subject, as so surrounded with prejudices; though I fully admit it is the highest and most interesting problem for the naturalist.' (Darwin, 1887 Vol. II: 109). Both men were prompted by their intellectual quest (and in Wallace's case, by the need to earn a living) to take long and hazardous overseas excursions: Darwin's voyage of the Beagle, and Wallace's ill-fated adventures in the Amazon (1848–52) and subsequent eight years of travel and exploration in the 'Malay Archipelago' (mostly on the islands of what we now know as Indonesia). Both men were confronted by the immense diversity of living species, the patterns of their distribution and the myriad forms of adaptation to their varied conditions of life. Again, for both, their experiences and the interpretations they put on them were strongly shaped by their prior intellectual influences: significantly theological in Darwin's case, and political-philosophical in Wallace's. Both, however, had read earlier advocates of evolution and the transmutation of species and shared a great admiration for the geological work of Lyell – with its exposition of the diversity of the living forms of the past, its suggestion of the antiquity of the earth and its key methodological principle: 'uniformitarianism'.

Both men, too, encountered humans of different civilizations, races and cultures – and were perhaps most deeply impressed by their encounters with indigenous 'savage' peoples, living, as Wallace put it, in a 'state of nature'. As an old man, reflecting on his experience of the Amazon forests, Wallace listed 'three great features which especially impressed me'. The first was 'the virgin forest, everywhere grand, often beautiful and even sublime'. The second was 'the wonderful variety and exquisite beauty of the butterflies and birds'. The third...

> ...and most unexpected sensation of surprise and delight was my first meeting and living with man in a state of nature with absolute uncontaminated savages.... In every detail they were as original and self-sustaining as are the wild animals of the forests, absolutely independent of civilization, and who could and did live their lives in their own way, as they had done for countless generations before America was discovered....The true denizen of the Amazonian forests, like the forest itself, is unique and not to be forgotten. (Wallace, 1905 Vol. I: 288).

Though Wallace was never again quite so awed by his encounters with other cultures, he did write home, while in Borneo: 'The more I see of uncivilized people, the better I think of human nature on the whole, and the essential differences between civilized and savage man seem to disappear' (Wallace, 1905 Vol. I: 342–3). This was of a piece with Wallace's egalitarian political philosophy, but also reflected his deep aversion to the inequalities, exploitation and materialism of his own 'civilization': the moral elevation of 'savage' society was an effective foil to Wallace's life-long progressive commitment to change in his own.

Darwin was much less fortunate in his encounters with 'savage' society. Having enjoyed the company of three captive and 'part-civilized' Fuegians on the Beagle voyage, he was horrified by the 'degraded' state of existence of their fellows, and by the speed with which his released former companions reverted to their former ways. Nevertheless, Darwin was a liberal and progressive figure for his day on questions of cultural and racial difference. He (like Wallace) did not hesitate to distinguish 'barbarous' or 'savage' societies from 'civilized' ones, and (unlike Wallace) seemed unequivocal about the superiority of the latter. However, as is well-known, he was a firm opponent of the 'great crime' of slavery, and decried what we would now call racism: 'If, indeed, such men are separated from him by great differences in appearance or habits, experience unfortunately shows us how long it is, before we look at them as our fellow creatures' (Darwin, 1874: 122–3).

For both Darwin and Wallace, observation of the behaviour, emotional expressions and social lives of non-human animals figured centrally in their evolutionary thinking, and, through that, in their re-positioning of humans in relation to the rest of the natural world. Interestingly, encounters with one of the 'anthropomorphous apes', the orangutan, were seminal for both. For

Darwin, the opportunity was provided by the captive orang, 'Jenny', in London Zoo, in 1838 (see, for example, Darwin's 'M' notebook, pp. 85, 129, 138–40, in Grüber, 1974: 281–93).

In Wallace's case, the encounter was somewhat more extensive, dramatic, and poignant. Wallace embarked on his second great journey in 1854. His 'Species Notebook', written in the course of his travels from 1855 to 1856, reveals him, as a 'philosophic naturalist', concerned not just with empirical recording and collecting of species, but with linking his observations to wide questions of methodology, morals, religion and metaphysics. He follows Lyell in his commitment to a view of nature as ordered and law-governed; but he is sharply critical of Lyell's inconsistency in seeking to explain all the historical transformations of the earth according to the 'ordinary' operation of natural laws, but resisting this in the case of the emergence of new species. This insistence on the special creation of each species is, for Wallace, not only methodologically unsound, but inconsistent with the evidence of variation and distribution. So Wallace is already disposed to the view that new species are formed from ancestral populations by some (unknown) natural mechanism. Further, there is some evidence that his choice of the geographical area for his adventures was at least partly motivated by the prospect of encountering the orang, and also that his interest in this species was connected with his growing conviction that humans were themselves descended from ape-like ancestors.

In his accounts of the various racial groups of the Amazon and the 'Malay Archipelago' Wallace provides dispassionate accounts of their physical features, modes of dress, material culture and so on, almost in the style of his accounts of the diversity of animal species, and in his celebrated contribution to the biogeography of the latter region, he includes the human races and their distribution as simply part of the story (for examples, Wallace, 1865, 1962 [1869]). This 'naturalistic' approach to anthropology would be consistent with his uniformitarian beliefs and commitment to species-transformation, with humans as just another species, having evolved from ancestor-populations by whatever mechanism might explain the origins of the other species.

However, the apparent coherence of this framework of thought is disrupted at several points. First, Wallace's view of evolutionary change formed just one aspect of a more general notion of inherent progress in the history of the human and natural worlds. He sometimes speaks of 'progressive development' as though it were a synonym for species-transformation, and accordingly expresses no qualms in speaking of species as forming an ascending hierarchy from 'lower' to 'higher'. He also uses this way of speaking in referring to the different peoples of the Amazon and 'Malay Archipelago'. At the same time, his political egalitarianism disposes him to see no 'essential' differences between savage and civilized, and his evident belief in the educability of 'savages' seems to rule out any notion of a fixed hierarchy of racial differences within the human. His estimation of the high moral character of some indigenous cultures, and rejection of the 'vices' of his own European civilization rule out any simple narrative of human cultural 'progress' from savagery to civilization. Still more difficult for the coherence of his views at this stage is the implication that the 'gap' between humans and the rest of the animal kingdom cannot be filled (a strategy some-times adopted by Darwin) with intermediate grades of 'primitive' human races. The uniformitarian doctrine that change occurs continuously by small steps seems to be called into question by the absence of intermediates between the 'anthropomorphous' apes and the 'full nobility' of 'man'.

This site of inner tension in Wallace's outlook is crucially manifest in his treat-ment of the orang. In his 'Species Notebook 5' Wallace notes March 19th 1855 as a 'white letter day': his first sighting of the 'Orang utan or "Mias" of the Dyaks in its native forest' (Wallace, 2002). His excitement notwithstanding, Wallace's main concern is to recruit local native help in tracking and shooting as many of these great beasts as possible, so they can be measured, skinned and packaged as specimens to be sent back to England. His accounts of the mias-hunts suggest a quite ruthless disregard for the suffering of his quarry but, at the same time, a recognition of the various emotional states of fury and surprise expressed by his victims. Set in absolute contradiction to all this are the moving accounts Wallace gave at the time (including a playful one sent to his family back home) of his attempt to rescue and rear a baby 'mias' whose mother he had shot and killed. The powerful paternal feelings this relationship evoked are unmistakable – and he even begins his letter home by referring to the mother mias as a 'wild woman of the woods' who he has killed. He is constantly struck by the resemblance of the mias's behaviour to that of a human baby, and concludes his letter with this expression of his grief at the death of the infant: 'From this short account you will see that my baby is no common baby, and I can safely say, what so many have said before with less truth, "there never was such a baby as my baby", and I'm sure nobody ever had such a dear little duck of a darling of a little brown hairy baby before' (Wallace, 1905 Vol. I: 345; see also Benton, 1997).

So, by the mid-1850s Wallace is committed to the transformation of species and to uniformitarianism, but is full of unresolved contradictions in his under-standing of the relationships between the different human races, the origins of humans from some ape-like ancestor and, especially, the moral and metaphysi-cal status of one of our closest non-human relatives: a being to be killed, mea-sured, and collected as just another 'specimen', or to be nurtured, loved and mourned, as a fellow being?

However, the key scientific question posed by the transformation of species continued to engage Wallace's thinking: what was the mechanism? Wallace's article 'On the Habits of the Orang-Utan of Borneo' (Wallace, 1856) illustrates how far Wallace was, at that time, from his breakthrough on this question. He notes that the male orang is equipped with massive and powerful canines, yet is a benign frugivore, is rarely attacked, and, even when it is, defends itself with its powerful arms (notwithstanding the image of a mias goring a Dyak used in Wallace, 1962!). So, why is it equipped with organs that appear to be of no use to it? Wallace insists that this is an inappropriate question – many animals and plants are adorned with colours and extraordinary structures that can be of no use to them: 'We conceive it to be a most erroneous, a most contracted view of the organic world, to believe that every part of an animal or of a plant exists solely for some material and physical use to the individual, to believe that all the beauty, all the infinite combinations and changes of form and structure should have the sole purpose and end of enabling each animal to support its existence.' In part, this insistence on non-adaptive traits can be understood as of a piece with Wallace's critique of the creationist doctrine that the perfect adaptation of species to their conditions of life is evidence of their creation by a supreme being. On the contrary, Wallace is arguing, organisms have many characteristics that are quite unconnected with 'adaptation'. Darwin's response to the same set of creationist doctrines was to search for a natural mechanism that might explain the *appearance* of design. Wallace, however, rejected the premise of the creationist argument: such functional thinking reduced to empty tautology, and, as here, was also contradicted by the presence of non-adaptive traits in many species. But the context reveals another, metaphysical, motivation in Wallace's anti-utilitarianism. He concludes his broadside against it with: '...as if one of the noblest and most refining parts of man's nature, the love of beauty for its own sake, would not be perceptible also in the works of a supreme creator.' Wallace, at this time, was opposed, on methodological grounds, to attempts to explain *specific* events or processes as acts of divine creation, but he did not rule out the possibility that some essentially unknowable creative agency might have been at work in designing the world as a whole, with its fundamental laws and patterns – including, perhaps, its sublime beauty, and the human potential to recognize and love it.

Wallace, natural selection, and human evolution

But Wallace was soon to arrive at a solution to his key problem of the mechanism of species-change, and this would set in train a radical transformation of his own world-view. While enduring a bout of fever, on the island of Gilolo, and recalling his earlier reading of Malthus's *Principles of Population*, Wallace hit on what Darwin was to recognize as the 'identical' hypothesis to his own: an explanation of the origin of new species as the outcome of a 'struggle for existence' in which only the 'fittest' or best-adapted survive, and succeed in passing on their advantageous attributes to their offspring. As is well-known, Wallace sent a paper (Wallace, 1858) explaining these ideas to Darwin, who immediately saw a threat to his own priority. Wallace's paper and a sketch of Darwin's own version were hastily read at a meeting of the Linnaean Society in 1858, and Darwin was provoked into completing a more extensive manuscript that was published the following year as *The Origin of Species*. While still in the Far East, Wallace read the *Origin* over and again, extolled its great virtues, and immediately declared himself an advocate of what he now, with extraordinary generosity of spirit, acknowledged as 'Darwinism'.

Perhaps the most significant shift in Wallace's outlook induced by his discovery/ conversion to the explanatory power of the idea of 'natural selection'

(Wallace, less influenced than Darwin by the analogy with domestication, preferred the phrase 'struggle for existence') was abandonment of his opposition to utilitarianism. In his 1858 paper he does, in fact, allude to the persistence of 'relatively unimportant' traits such as colours, crests and the like across relatively distantly related forms. This suggests that at that time he did not conclude that the exigencies of the struggle for existence would modify every organic trait – only those that had some significance in either advantaging or hindering an organism in its attempts to feed itself, defend itself against predators and so on. However, his repeated accounts of the severity of the struggle for existence, and the utmost exertions it called for, tell against this: 'There is no muscle of its body that is not called into daily and hourly activity; there is no sense or faculty that is not strengthened by continual exercise' (Wallace, 1867a: 38). It is as if Wallace is simply hanging on to his former insistence on useless traits, albeit, now as mere 'unimportant' features, rather than as evidences of the non-utilitarian beauty of natural forms.

However, even these last vestiges disappear when he later expounds the core of Darwin's view of natural selection: '... none of the definite facts of organic nature, no special organ, no characteristic form or marking, no peculiarities of instinct or of habit, no relations between species or between groups of species – can exist, but which must now be or once have been *useful* to the individuals or the races which possess them.' (Wallace, 1867a: 47). From 1859 Wallace becomes an eloquent defender of the Darwinian thesis, and goes on to demonstrate the explanatory power of the idea of natural selection in a wide range of empirical applications (Wallace, 1864a; 1867a, b, c; 1868). In subsequent editions of the *Origin*, and, as we shall see, in later works, Darwin came to accept some of the arguments of his critics, and to acknowledge an evolutionary role for some other mechanisms, operating as modifications of, or alongside, natural selection. By contrast, Wallace remained uncompromisingly faithful to natural selection until his attempt to test it to the limit in explaining human evolution brought him to yet another critical turning point.

The 'test' in question took the form of a celebrated paper entitled 'The Origin of Human Races and the Antiquity of Man Deduced from the Theory of Natural Selection' (Wallace, 1864b). Uncharacteristically the original paper was presented to a meeting of the Anthropological Society of London, a racist breakaway from the Ethnological Society (see Raby, 2001: 176; Fichman, 2004: 154). The core of Wallace's highly original treatment of this topic is a contrast between the intensity of the pressure of natural selection on the bodily structures of 'solitary' species, with the limitations imposed on this pressure once a being evolves who is 'social and sympathetic' and has the mental faculties required for invention. As these capacities emerge in a population – ancestral humans – natural selection no longer acts to change their bodily character, but increasingly works on their social and mental faculties, intensifying and augmenting them. The introduction of a division of labour, sympathy as a motive for mutual assistance, self-restraint, the ability to make tools and weapons, control the use of fire, make clothes, domesticate other animals and grow crops would all deliver advantages in the struggle for life, and so be favoured by natural selection.

Unfortunately, Wallace was unclear (as was Darwin, later) about precisely how natural selection would have acted in enhancing the sociability and intellectual powers of ancestral humans. Would it have done so directly, by increasing the survival and reproductive success of the more inventive and socially disposed individuals, or indirectly, by way of the competitive success of groups, or 'tribes' that were the better endowed with such individuals? Long after the deaths of Darwin and Wallace, this came to be seen as a rather important distinction, but both of them tended to work with the latter hypothesis. In Wallace's case: 'Tribes in which such mental and moral qualities were predominant, would therefore have an advantage in the struggle for existence over other tribes in which they were less developed, would live and maintain their numbers, while the others would decrease and finally succumb' (Wallace, 1864b: clxii).

Of course, when Wallace writes of the enhancement of mental and moral faculties, rather than bodily structures, he is referring indirectly to the brain and central nervous system as the organic basis of these capacities (in so far as they are inherited): 'His brain alone would have increased in size and complexity and his cranium have undergone corresponding changes of form.' (Wallace, 1864b: clxvii). Wallace imagines a homogeneous population of a 'barely social' ancestor of modern humans acquiring the physical distinguishing features of the races – skin colour, 'the scanty or abundant hair, straight or oblique eyes', etc as they adapted to different regions of the earth. As selection ceased to bear significantly on bodily form but increasingly tended to augment the mental and moral faculties, these racial differences would have become fixed, and the bodily appearance of the human species as a whole would remain little different from the ancestral, ape-like species.

In support of his theory, Wallace claims that it 'neither requires us to depreciate the intellectual chasm which separates man from the apes, nor refuses full recognition of the striking resemblances to them which exist in other parts of its structure' (Wallace, 1864b: clxix). But the argument takes Wallace still further. As the social, moral and intellectual capacities of humans are augmented by the action of natural selection, their exercise in the shape of practical inventions cumulatively takes humans out of the power of natural selection altogether, and, indeed, partially reverses this relationship. As human inventions gradually give them power to control or direct the forces of nature for their own benefit, humans themselves come to usurp the power of natural selection: 'Man has not only escaped "natural selection" himself, but he actually is able to take away some of that power from nature which, before his appearance, she universally exercised.' (Wallace, 1864b: clxviii).

This gradually acquired enlargement of human moral and mental faculties, together with the consequent ability of 'man' to 'direct and govern nature to his own benefit', leads Wallace to foresee a future utopian human existence of full social harmony, justice and material well-being:

We can anticipate the time when the earth will produce only cultivated plants and domestic animals; when man's selection shall have supplanted "natural selection"; and when the ocean will be the only domain in which that power can be exerted, which for countless cycles of ages ruled supreme over all the earth…the world is again inhabited by a single homogeneous race, no individual of which will be inferior to the noblest specimens of existing humanity. Each one will then work out his own happiness in relation to that of his fellows; perfect freedom of action will be maintained, since the well balanced moral faculties will never permit any one to transgress on the equal freedom of others; restrictive laws will not be wanted, for each man will be guided by the best of laws; a thorough appreciation of the rights, and a perfect sympathy for the feelings, of all about him; compulsory government will have died away as unnecessary (for every man will know how to govern himself), and will be replaced by voluntary associations for all beneficial public purposes; the passions and animal propensities will be restrained within those limits which most conduce to happiness; and mankind will have at last discovered that it was only required of them to develop the capacities of their higher nature, in order to convert this earth, which had so long been the theatre of their unbridled passions, and the scene of unimaginable misery, into as bright a paradise as ever haunted the dreams of seer or poet. (Wallace, 1864b: clxvii–clxx)

Seemingly, Wallace has at last achieved a fully coherent marriage of his version of evolutionary theory with his socio-political values. The rigorous application of the idea of natural selection to the questions of human origins and the relationships between the human races yields a view of human progress towards a utopian future embodying the humanist and socialist values Wallace had long-espoused.

However, Wallace's new synthesis is deeply problematic in (at least) three important respects. The first, and perhaps most troubling, of these is the means by which the future 'bright paradise' is to be realized. The 'great law' of the 'preservation of favoured races in the struggle for life' leads to the 'inevitable extinction of all those low and mentally undeveloped populations with which Europeans come into contact'. The Europeans are superior morally, mentally and physically, and 'the same powers and capacities which have made him rise in a few centuries from the condition of the wandering savage…enable him when in contact with savage man, to conquer in the struggle for existence, and to increase at his expense…'. Suddenly lost are Wallace's admiration for the moral character of indigenous cultures, as well as his long-standing hostility to the moral degradation, materialism and injustice of his own European civilization. Instead, the 'races' of man are arranged in a hierarchy of moral and mental development, progress coming only from the extinction of the 'lower' races and the victory of a racially homogeneous superior European form. Wallace's new view of the struggle between the races is not only at odds with his own experiences and enduring beliefs but also has an internal contradiction. The mental and moral attributes of the denizens of Wallace's utopia are imbued with sympathy for the feelings of all about them, fully acknowledge the freedom and rights of others, and have a voluntary command of their passions. These are hardly virtues that one would expect to conduce to victory in a racial struggle for existence – nor are they the sort of virtues one would expect to be nurtured and enhanced by such a struggle.

The second uncomfortable feature of Wallace's new view is its abandonment of the radical re-positioning of humans in nature that was a key element in the Darwinian revolution. The outcome of the action of natural selection in perfecting human mental and moral character is a being who is in important respects set over and above the rest of that nature from which it came. The great gulf that separates even the 'lowest savages' from the apes has come about as a result of thousands, possibly millions, of years, of action of natural selection on the mental and moral faculties of our ancestors. This gives us a 'new argument for placing man apart, as not only the head and culminating point of the grand series of organic nature, but as in some degree a new and distinct order of being'. And, as we have seen, this superiority of humans over nature also consists in their usurpation of the power of natural selection itself through advances in cultivation and domestication. The extraordinary hubris of this thesis was, interestingly, questioned by some in Wallace's audience (Wallace, 1864b: clxxii, Messrs. Bollaert and Bendyshe). It takes us directly to the third problematic feature of Wallace's 'new synthesis'.

For Wallace to contemplate with apparent equanimity the prospect of a 'time when the earth will produce only cultivated plants and domesticated animals' is hard to grasp. His accounts – especially his personal notebooks – of his travels in the Amazon and in the Far East abound with expressions of wonder and excitement at the beauty of the animals and plants he encounters – indeed the brilliant colours and patterns of the birds of paradise and papilionid butterflies were among the most favoured topics for his scientific writings. As we saw, in Wallace's paper of 1856 on the habits of the orang, the beauty of natural forms prompted one of Wallace's early references to the possibility of a higher creative power. And, in late old age, he still recalled 'the wonderful variety and exquisite beauty of the birds and butterflies,' as well as the sublime grandeur of the Amazonian forest.

Perhaps the abandonment of some of his most deeply felt and persistent moral and aesthetic values in this paper should be seen as a mark of Wallace's exceptional intellectual rigour – and the power of his commitment at that time to the explanatory value of the idea of natural selection. But Wallace must have been uncomfortable with these implications of his attempt to press the idea of natural selection to its limit in the human case. In any event, he soon severed his connection with the Anthropological Society and returned, in the latter years of the 1860s, to less contentious attempts to resolve a number of hitherto puzzling questions of natural history.

Wallace the heretic

However, this was to be only a brief lull. In 1869 Wallace released the first of what Fichman (2004: 157) refers to as his 'bombshells'. This was contained in the concluding remarks of review of new editions of two works by Lyell (Wallace, 1869). Following laudatory comments on Lyell's achievements and his (rather late) conversion to the idea of natural selection, Wallace announces his own conversion to the view that natural selection is insufficient to explain the 'higher mental and moral faculties' of humans. Not only this, but the formative power complementary to natural selection must be some form of purposive guidance connected to an 'overruling intelligence'. The following year, Wallace published, as the concluding essay in his *Contributions* (1870), a more fully developed version of his new position on human evolution and prospects.

Wallace's argument has four distinct elements: first, that humans have a range of capacities and related physical features that could not have been acquired by natural selection unaided. Second, that the human potential of these attributes is fully realized only under conditions of advanced civilization. Third, that in view of this, the originally acquired capacities can only be understood as preparations for their later exercise in a more advanced state of human progress. Fourth, that the only satisfactory explanation for such anticipated development must be the intervention in human evolution of some superior intelligence that has guided it for some higher purpose.

Wallace, of course, remained committed to the view that humans are descended from some ape-like ancestor, and that natural selection played its part in that development. His new position is solely that some attributes cannot be accounted for in terms of natural selection alone. The most fully developed argument Wallace gives for this is based on comparison of the cranial capacities of contemporary human races, and such fossil evidence as was then available. His conclusion is that contemporary 'savages', early humans and 'civilized' humans differ very little from one another in cranial capacity. Given standard materialist assumptions about the relationship between the size and complexity of the brain and mental abilities, Wallace concludes that the mental and moral capacities of savages, early humans and 'civilized' humans must also differ very little from each other – but very greatly from their nearest relatives among the anthropoid apes.

However, Wallace claims that natural selection could have endowed human ancestors with barely more mental capacity than that of the apes with which they competed – any more would have been surplus to what would have been required in the 'struggle for existence'. Moreover, if we consider the lives of contemporary 'savages', the demands made on their mental abilities are very few: 'What is there in the life of the savage, but the satisfying of the cravings of appetite in the simplest and easiest way? What thoughts, ideas, or actions are there, that raise him many grades above the elephant or the ape?' (Wallace, 1870: 342). This must have been still more true of 'the men whose sole weapons were rudely chipped flints'. So, from their origins, humans were endowed with a mental capacity far greater than the actual wants of their mode of life, and far greater than they either could or did exercise. Comparing the 'savage' either with the 'brutes', or with the more highly developed human cultures, Wallace says, 'we are alike driven to the conclusion that in his large and well-developed brain he possesses an organ quite disproportionate to his actual requirements – an organ that seems prepared in advance, only to be fully utilized as he progresses in civilization.' (Wallace, 1870: 343). Savages, claims Wallace, for all the high development of their brains, have no words for abstract ideas, have no foresight beyond the simplest necessities, and do not reason far beyond what is available to their senses. As to the savage's moral and aesthetic sensibilities, he 'has none of those wide sympathies with all nature, those conceptions of the infinite, of the good, of the sublime and beautiful, which are so largely developed in civilized man.' (Wallace, 1870: 340). Their mental endowment, unusable by them in their condition of 'savagery', cannot, therefore, have been acquired by natural selection, and, as a form of anticipatory development, can only be understood as the work of some purposive agency.

Supplementary arguments used by Wallace include the loss of most of our body-hair, linked with the adoption of the upright posture and enhanced physical beauty. Wallace fails to see how our original coat of hair could have been so disadvantageous to our ancestors as to have been lost – and not restored as they migrated to cooler climates. He is also struck (understandably enough) by the marvellous delicacy and flexibility of the human hand. How, he asks, could the crude material cultures of stone-age man and contemporary savages have necessitated such perfection? Again, Wallace contemplates the immense complexity of the mental operations and physical changes involved in human speech – and the beauty of voice involved in music – and argues they could never have been of use to the lowest savages, and so could not have been evolved by natural selection. Finally, the development of a moral sense – conscience and the sense of right and wrong over and above mere utilitarian calculation – could not have been an outcome of natural selection acting unaided.

From 1865 Wallace had been introduced to spiritualism, and had made a systematic study of the evidence and claims made by spiritualist mediums and their advocates (Wallace, 1866). Initially he sought to bring spiritualist phenomena within the scope of empirical science, and appears to have become a convert himself only gradually. Even then, he continued to insist that the study of these occult phenomena was a proper topic for scientific research. It seems that Wallace's conversion to spiritualism coincided with the emergence of his scepticism about the role of natural selection in human evolution. It certainly provided him with a mode of making intelligible the apparent teleology of the acquisition of human attributes and potentials long before they could be actualized in a fully civilized society. However, it could also be that the unwelcome implications of his 1864 attempt to press the idea of natural selection to its limit in accounting for human evolution was also at work in his retreat from that earlier position (and even, possibly, in his conversion to spiritualism itself).

Whatever Wallace's motives, it is worth noting how far this new position has taken him from his former views (this interpretation is controversial – see Smith, 2004, Benton and Smith in Smith & Beccaloni, 2008). The doctrine of 'uniformitarianism' has been abandoned in the shape of the immense gap that now opens up between humans and their nearest relatives, and in the retreat into the advocacy of a 'special intervention' – distinct from the 'ordinary course of nature' – in explaining the evolution of a single species. Humans, despite their lowly antecedents, are set apart from the rest of nature – the product, in their 'higher' natures, of disembodied spiritual guides – and shaped for some future fulfilment in the after-life. 'Progress' to full human realization is no longer to culminate in the earthly paradise of the 1864 essay but has been displaced to the world of the spirit-life. Even the new doctrine of the 'disproportionately' mentally endowed savage, while avoiding hard-edged racism, and giving room for enlightened 'education' of the savage mind, still involves a bizarre caricature of the lives of indigenous people. Wallace from his own experience certainly knew differently.

Aware of the 'bombshell' his new departure from Darwinian orthodoxy would detonate, Wallace wrote to Darwin that a few years previously he would himself have regarded his current views as 'equally wild and uncalled-for'. Darwin was suitably distressed by Wallace's apparent recantation: 'As you expected, I differ grievously from you, and I am very sorry for it' (Darwin, F., 1887: 116).

Darwin's reply: *The Descent of Man*

It seems likely that, for a second time, Wallace's challenge provoked Darwin into print (Wallace, 1905 II: 7–8). Having long feared the controversy that an explicit treatment of human evolution would cause, Darwin had, with his usual caution, held back. As his early exchange of letters with Wallace made clear, Darwin had long been interested in the bearing of his evolutionary ideas on the question of human origins. His notebooks on 'Mind, Matter and Materialism' (Grüber, 1974), written in 1838 and 1839, carry recurrent thoughts and evidence-gathering relevant to this great question. Famously, however, Darwin in presenting his evolutionary hypothesis in *The Origin* concluded by merely noting that by it 'Light will be thrown on the origin of man and his history'.

But Darwin was not in control of the life taken on by his ideas once he had committed them to print. The wider intellectual and lay public was less inter-ested in the lives of barnacles – or even finches and giant tortoises – than in the dramatic implications of the evolutionary hypothesis for the elevated status of human kind and its relation to god the creator. Even without Wallace's chal-lenge, Darwin would have had to address the question eventually. This he did with a vengeance in his great work *The Descent of Man and Selection in Relation to Sex* (1874 [1871]).

In large measure, this book can be read as a response to Wallace's departure from evolutionary naturalism, and, interestingly, it draws heavily and approv-ingly from Wallace's 1864 essay – though Darwin modifies and supplements the argument of that work in important ways. First, Darwin sets out the grounds for concluding that humans did descend from some ape-like ancestor. This was, of course, not at issue between Wallace and Darwin, but Darwin ends his first chapter with a tilt at human-centred arrogance that Wallace might not have fully endorsed: 'It is only our natural prejudice, and that arrogance that made our forefathers declare that they were descended from demi-gods, which leads us to demur to this conclusion' (Darwin, 1874 [1871]: 25).

Darwin next sets out on the explanatory task that certainly did divide himself and his closest allies from Wallace: the causal mechanisms, or processes by which this descent took place. As always, Darwin provides a wealth of empirical evidence to back up each stage in his argument, but the bare bones are that the human species is highly variable – both within and between sub-populations. Reproductive rates were probably very high in our ancestral populations, but they must also have suffered periodically from famine and other 'checks' to the increase of population. Consequently, 'they must, therefore, occasionally have been exposed to a struggle for existence, and consequently to the rigid law of natural selection, (Darwin, 1874 [1871]: 48). Here Darwin cites Wallace's 1864 'celebrated' paper with approval, noting that the reader would be surprised by the latter's current position. Against Wallace's current view, Darwin argues that the tools and weapons made by 'primitive' man involved great skill and dexterity, and would, indeed, have required the perfection of the hand. In the context of a change from an arboreal mode of life to bipedalism and greater hand/ foot differentiation, increased flexibility of the hand for different uses would have conferred a selective advantage. The survival of the anthropomorphous apes, at an intermediate stage towards bipedalism, is evidence that development short of full perfection of the hand still confers advantages, and so indicates that a gradual evolution to bipedalism and perfect development of the hand would have been possible. Bipedalism would also allow changes in the shape of the head, with a reduction in the size of the teeth and jaws, and a corresponding increase in cranial capacity. A related line of development might have led from the 'signal cries' or musical cadences of apes to articulate language through 'adaptation by the inherited effects of use'. On the loss of body-hair, Darwin considers possible explanations in terms of natural selection, but proposes an alternative explanation in terms of sexual selection: the preservation and augmentation of characters that are attractive to the opposite sex, as distinct from those that confer an advantage in the general 'struggle for life'. This idea was a continuing source of controversy between Wallace and Darwin – and, of course, among evolutionary biologists more generally (see Cronin, 1991).

So far, then, Darwin has rebutted Wallace's claims that a number of distinctive human traits would not have been useful to our progenitors, and has made out a strong case for the plausibility of their having been acquired by degrees through the operation of natural selection 'either directly or indirectly'. However, as we shall see, Darwin has made some interesting concessions on the way.

Where Wallace's challenge really comes into its own is in the explanation of the sources of the mental, emotional, moral and social dimensions of human nature – man's 'higher' faculties. Darwin attributes 'man's' current dominance to three characteristics: his highly developed intellectual faculties (most especially the capacity for articulate language), his social habit, and his corporeal structure. Darwin's case for the gradual evolution of distinctively human mental traits relies on extensive evidence to the effect that humans do not differ fundamentally from other animals, especially the primates, in their senses, the small number of instincts (self-preservation, sexual love, maternal love etc) they retain, their emotional repertoire (happiness, terror, suspicion, humour, jealousy and so on), and in their capacity to reason, imagine, dream and so on. Against those who would place an 'insuperable barrier' between humans and other animals he comments that, in the development of human infants and children, the adult mental faculties are acquired by degrees, so there is no reason to suppose this might not have happened in the evolution of the species. In the specific case of language he suggests that human language might have emerged from musical calls of apes like the gibbons of today by sexual selection, and then been developed, along with the vocal organs themselves, by a combination of inheritance by repeated use and development of the brain. The tendency to use language Darwin takes to be a human instinct, but the acquisition of a specific language is learned – as is the case with widespread songbirds which have local dialects. Even the human aesthetic sense – one of Wallace's key examples – can be understood as not different in kind from that shown by other species. Both humans and other animals are attracted to regular and symmetrical forms. In the case of the courtship displays of male birds to the female, it is 'impossible to doubt that she admires the beauty of her male partner'. Darwin even seems to suggest that perceptions of beauty are objective, commenting that women like to adorn themselves with the brightly coloured plumes of birds. However, he does claim that 'high tastes' depend on complex associations and are acquired culturally – and not enjoyed by 'barbarians or uneducated persons'.

Next, Darwin devotes a whole chapter to the most challenging question – the origin of human moral sense. He supposes that human progenitors were already social animals. As such they would – like other social species – have some social instincts, probably derived by extension from parental and filial love. The social instincts include sympathy for others and a disposition to come to their aid, desire for the approval of others, pleasure in their company, and misery in their absence. Darwin argues that in the human case these social instincts are less specific than in other species, and occur as rather generalized 'impulses', e.g. to help one another, without any definite instinctual 'guide' as to how to do so. Here, Darwin is probably best understood as committed to the idea of what Mary Midgley (1979) has called 'open instincts' in the human case: general motivational dispositions that may be shaped and given definite form by learning and reasoning, rather than rigid behavioural repertoires.

Now, moral sense, Darwin argues, would necessarily emerge in a species with social instincts and which also approached humans in the development of its general intellectual faculties. Like other social animals we have, as well as our social instincts, others that dispose us to act in self-interested ways – the instincts for self-preservation, hunger, sexual desire, vengeance, and others. These instincts tend to give rise to more intense, but short-term and readily satisfied desires, compared with the more enduring but often less intense social instincts. An intelligent being, however, would be able to compare past and future acts, and would be able to approve or disapprove of them, feeling misery at the thought of an enduring social instinct being over-ridden by a short-term and self-interested impulse. In this way a moral sense would emerge and be developed by the desire of the social being to be approved of by his/ her social group. Remorse and repentance would follow from breaching a 'rule held sacred by the tribe'. Eventually the ability is acquired to rule one's conduct by asserting the priority of the social over the self-preservative instincts. This is what Darwin calls 'self-command'. Thus far, Darwin considers the evolution of the capacity for the 'social virtues' is necessary for the continuity of social life itself – both for 'rude' and civilized humans.

But Darwin still thinks this is a low stage in the development of the moral sense. In uncivilized societies, what is condemned and punished as a crime when committed against another member of the tribe may be acceptable – and even celebrated – when practised against a member of a different group. Against advocates of the high moral standing of 'savages', Darwin notes that uncivilized societies (also civilized ones until quite recently) practise slavery, even treating the women of the community as slaves, and have no sympathy in their treatment of animals. So, the further development of morality arises from the joining together of tribes into nations, and the associated use of reason to extend the social and sympathetic instincts to include all members of the nation, and ultimately to 'men' of all nations and races. Finally, this extension of sympathy should be enlarged in scope to include all sentient beings:

> Sympathy beyond the confines of man, that is, humanity to the lower animals, seems to be one of the latest moral acquisitions...This virtue, one of the noblest with which man is endowed, seems to arise incidentally from our sympathies becoming more tender and more widely diffused, until they are extended to all sentient beings. As soon as this virtue is honoured and practised by some few men, it spreads through instruction and example to the young, and eventually becomes incorporated in public opinion.' (Darwin, 1874 [1871]: 123)

In broad outlines, then, Darwin's argument can be read as a development and elaboration of Wallace's 1864 paper, with the emphasis on the evolutionary importance of the combination of sociality and intellectual development, together with a systematic rebuttal of the arguments used by Wallace from the late 1860s onwards to justify his retreat from his earlier view. However, Darwin manages to avoid several of the unwelcome implications drawn by the Wallace of 1864 from his rigorous attempt to apply the idea of natural selection to the understanding of human evolution. So, we can see from the above quotation that Darwin is far from envisioning, let alone commending, a future in which humans so dominate nature that only cultivated plants and domesticated animals remain. In fact, Darwin's moral vision is remarkably close to what we might now recognize as a deep green, or ecocentric, ethic. This moral vision dates back to at least the late 1830s in Darwin's thought, as expressed in this astonishing passage from an early notebook:

> Animals – whom we have made our slaves we do not like to consider our equals. Do not slave-holders wish to make the black man other kind?...the soul by consent of all is superadded, animals not got it, not look forward if we choose to let conjecture run wild then animals our fellow brethren in pain, disease, death, & suffering & famine; our slaves in the most laborious work, our companion in our amusements. They may partake, from our origin in one common ancestor we may all be netted together. (Darwin, 1987 [1837]: 228–9. Notebook B 231–2)

The parallel between the racial ideology that justifies slavery and the dichotomy between humans and other animals that legitimates our unjust treatment of them is very striking – and of a piece with the most radical thinking of our own time.

The second unwelcome implication of Wallace's 1864 essay was the harsh vision of struggle between 'higher' and 'lower' races of humans, with progress coming from the elimination of the latter. As we saw, Wallace later retreated from this bleak perspective, acknowledging the high mental *capacity* of our progenitors and modern 'savages' – but only at the cost of extreme denigration of their actual intellectual and cultural *achievements*. Neither position squares with Wallace's well-known and frequently uttered high praise for both the culture and the moral standing of indigenous society. The conclusions to which Wallace felt himself driven by the logic of his successive positions in evolutionary theory continued to be at odds with his long-standing political and moral values, and the testimony of his own direct experience.

In Darwin's treatment of race there is no such inner tension. Despite his occasional self-admonition, Darwin continues to write of 'higher' and 'lower' in relation to both non-human species and the human races. He also, like Wallace, devotes considerable attention to questions of the origins and extinction of the human races. In Darwin's treatment of the latter topic, however, there is much less emphasis on racial extinction as a result of the 'struggle for existence' with 'higher' races and cultures. He rather discusses a series of particular examples, stressing the complexity of the causes, and the limits to our knowledge. Moreover, cutting across the hierarchical language, Darwin lays great emphasis on the unity of human kind, and the relative superficiality and insignificance of racial differences. In criticizing the view that human races should be seen as different species, he notes such differences as skin-colour and some other structural variations, but considers them insignificant in relation to the 'multitude' of points of resemblance. As to mental traits, he continues:

> The American aborigines, negroes and Europeans are as different from each other in mind as any three races that can be named; yet I was incessantly struck, whilst living with the Fuegians on board the "Beagle", with the many little traits of character,

showing how similar their minds were to ours; and so it was with a full-blooded negro with whom I happened once to be intimate. He who will read Mr. Tylor's and Sir J. Lubbock's interesting works can hardly fail to be deeply impressed with the close similarity between the men of all races in tastes, dispositions and habits.' (Darwin, 1874 [1871]: 178)

As to the origins of racial differences, Darwin considers that there may be some element of adaptation to different conditions of life experienced by human populations in different geographical regions, but for most of the differences some other agency must have been responsible. This agency is sexual selection. In fact, Darwin's subsequent discussion attributes rather more than racial differences to this agency: differences in mental and physical attributes between men and women, as well as several important distinctive features of the human species in general are derived by this means. Darwin distinguishes the general struggle for existence from what he calls the sexual struggle – that is, the competition between members of each sex to mate with and secure offspring with members of the other. Sexual struggle in this sense is general throughout the animal kingdom, and has two aspects: direct struggle between rivals of the same sex (usually males, as the more 'eager' of the two sexes) for access to 'passive' females, and competition among members of the same sex (again, usually males) to excite or 'charm' members of the opposite sex into choosing them as mates. Sexual struggle is analogous to the general struggle for existence in that success in the struggle for reproductive opportunities will lead to differential proportions of offspring on the part of the more attractive or powerful suitors. Sexual selection, like natural selection, will thus, over numerous generations, bring about and augment organic change. In some cases sexual selection preserves and develops traits that are inherited by both sexes and in others by only one sex, according to laws of inheritance which, Darwin concedes, are both complex and largely unknown.

The great advantage, for Darwin's argument, of this distinct selective agency is that it can be used to explain the persistence and intensification of traits that are either useless in the general struggle for life, or even a definite disadvantage, and so could not have been acquired by natural selection. So, for example, Darwin refers directly to Wallace's *Contributions* on the disadvantages of the loss of body-hair in humans (Darwin, 1874 [1871]: 600). He agrees with Wallace, too, on the non-utility of music: 'As neither the enjoyment nor the capacity of producing musical notes are faculties of the least use to man in reference to his daily habits of life, they must be ranked amongst the most mysterious with which he is endowed' (Darwin, 1874 [1871]: 570). But the mystery is resolved by the idea of sexual selection, as Darwin supposes that beauty of voice would have been among the ways in which the progenitors of humans attracted one another – and, further, he speculates that this may have been a significant agency in the evolution of human language. In all human cultures, opposite sexes attract one another according to conventions of physical beauty or adornment, though there are very wide differences between cultures in the 'standards of beauty' recognized. Darwin speculates that many generations of sexual selection may have given rise to the differences between the races in skin-colour, facial features and so on.

Darwin vs. Wallace; naturalism vs. humanism

So, for Darwin, there is no difficulty in supposing not just that humans descended by a process of gradual evolution by natural causes from some ape-like ancestor, but also that *all* of their attributes – including sociability, high intellectual ability, moral sense, language, music and the love of beauty for its own sake – could have been so derived. In philosophical terms, Darwin's view of human evolution and nature is a comprehensively naturalistic one. In presenting this account, Darwin draws on and develops themes from Wallace's 1864 essay, while resisting Wallace's later retreat into what might now be called 'human exceptionalism'. It seems likely that Wallace's conversion to spiritualism had some role in his abandonment of his earlier naturalistic view but, as we saw, there were other respects in which the implications he drew from that position must have been uncomfortable for him. To sustain both his spiritualism and his enduring progressive role in public life, as a socialist, advocate of land nation-alization and the rights of women, he seems to have felt he needed to break from his former naturalistic view of human evolution.

On closer inspection, however, Darwin and Wallace have more in common than this contrast suggests. Neither man was entirely consistent in his views of racial and gender differences, but both were, in the context of their time, at the progressive end of the available spectrum of positions. Both recognized human distinctiveness, favoured gender equality, and were critical of racial oppression. In one respect, Darwin seems to have gone further than Wallace, in envisaging a time when human morality would include all sentient beings, not just the human community.

But even in their apparently very different views on human evolution, there is more agreement than might initially appear. Wallace's key case against com-prehensive naturalism is that humans early on acquired attributes that could have been of no use to them in the struggle for life, and so could not have been acquired by natural selection. Darwin's response is a complex and many-sided one. In the case of some attributes, such as sociability, Darwin argues (as Wallace had in his 1864 essay) that this would certainly have conferred selective advantages, as would the adoption of upright posture and the perfec-tion of the human hand for many different tasks. But for many other attributes, Darwin, too, thinks that natural selection could not have been the sole agent of transformation. He is quite explicit in the *Descent* that he had attributed too much to the action of natural selection in the earlier editions of the *Origin*, and that this was due to the continuing influence of the argument from design. This had led to his 'tacit assumption that every detail of structure, excepting rudiments, was of some special, though unrecognised, service.' He continues: '...I did not formerly consider sufficiently the existence of structures, which,

41

as far as we can at present judge, are neither beneficial nor injurious' (Darwin, 1874 [1871]: 61).

So, Darwin, too, concedes that the agency of natural selection alone is not sufficient to account for the origin of many of the distinctive human traits – as well as gender and racial differences. But Darwin's response is to complement natural selection with a series of other hypothetical mechanisms. Among the most significant of these are the inheritance of characters after generations of habit ('use-inheritance'), correlations of growth (traits acquired as a result of some other modification by unknown laws of inheritance), social, or 'group' selection and sexual selection. Use-inheritance was to be later discredited by the greater understanding of genetic inheritance, but Darwin's ingenious uses of the ideas of social and sexual selection retain their interest.

The significance of social life for human evolution was recognized by Wallace in his 1864 essay but is given a more central place in Darwin's *Descent*. Especially significant is his account of the emergence of the moral sense as a consequence of the combination of social instincts with increased intellectual ability in the human lineage. This saves Darwin from the necessity to explain such troubling traits as conscience and virtue in terms of the direct action of natural selection; instead they can be seen as the further consequence of other aspects of human nature which were so explicable. Other distinctively human traits, such as love of beauty and musicality, which Darwin concedes could not be wholly explained in terms of natural selection, *could* be understood in terms of *sexual* selection.

Both Wallace's 1864 essay, and Darwin's *Descent* attribute the development of human social instincts and emotions primarily to group selection – that is, to the selective advantage given to sub-populations by relatively large numbers of socially-orientated individuals. So, 'tribes' with more sympathetic individuals willing to help one another or defend the group against attack will succeed in competition with other tribes, and so produce relatively more offspring. Current orthodoxy in evolutionary biology tends to discount group selection as likely to have played a large evolutionary role except under rare circumstances; but the issue remains both complex and controversial (see, for a useful introduction, Sterelny, 2001, chapter 5). However, neither Darwin nor Wallace was entirely clear in his thinking about the evolutionary mechanisms associated with sociality. Occasionally Darwin, in particular, seems to recognize an alternative possibility. This is that society itself acts as a selective agency:

> With those animals which were benefited by living in close association, the individuals which took the greatest pleasure in society would best escape various dangers; whilst those that cared least for their comrades, and lived solitary, would perish in greater numbers' (Darwin, 1874 [1871]: 105).

Development of this notion of social life as a causal order in its own right, with determinate consequences for the survival and reproductive chances of individuals, is consistent with what is now known about genetic inheritance and is an important resource for a comprehensively naturalistic understanding of human nature which, however, resists the reductionism of much contemporary socio-biology and 'evolutionary psychology' (see Barkow *et al.*, 1992; Pinker, 1997; Benton, 1999; Rose & Rose, 2000).

As we have seen, Darwin's case for a comprehensive naturalism depends not just on the evolutionary importance of human sociality but also on the idea of sexual selection. Interestingly, Wallace expressed some reservations about this idea even in his earlier phase. That males might have acquired greater aggressive tendencies, physical strength and 'weapons' such as large canine teeth as a result of their conflict over access to females is something that Wallace accepted. However, he increasingly resisted the other dimension of sexual selection – the exercise of 'choice', mainly by females, on the basis of aesthetic judgment of the quality of the male's ornamentation or courtship performance. His reservation in this respect became still clearer as he abandoned naturalism in favour of his spiritualist-teleological view of the direction of human evolution. Love of beauty is so elevated an achievement of human civilization, how could it have been a shaping influence on human progenitors – let alone 'lower' animals – even insects? Darwin concedes that this is remarkable:

> . . . yet I fully admit that it is astonishing that the females of many birds and some mammals should be endowed with sufficient taste to appreciate ornaments, which we have reason to attribute to sexual selection; and this is even more astonishing in the case of reptiles, fish, and insects. But we really know little about the minds of the lower animals. (Darwin, 1874: 616)

But, he continues, anyone who finds this difficult to accept should reflect that 'the nerve-cells of the brain in the highest as well as in the lowest members of the Vertebrate series, are derived from those of the common progenitor of that great Kingdom'. The mental faculties of widely differing groups of animals may thus have developed in very similar ways.

Less 'fundamentalist' than Wallace ('Hence it is that some of my critics declare that I am more Darwinian than Darwin, and in this, I admit, they are not far wrong.' (Wallace, 1905 Vol. II: 22)), Darwin was able to consider the possibility of a naturalistic account of human distinctiveness that did not rely exclusively on a single evolutionary mechanism. His more pluralist but still naturalistic approach to understanding human distinctiveness is of particular interest for social scientists but has, surprisingly, been rather neglected – even by sociologists who have adopted an evolutionary approach. Central to Darwin's argument is his recognition that our evolutionary ancestors were themselves social beings, and his drawing out of that an account of the ways our emotional, moral and cognitive powers and dispositions can be seen as outcomes of social life as itself a selective agency. This is in sharp contrast to the reductionism of much of our contemporary neo-Darwinism. Secondly, Darwin draws on a notion, 'sexual selection' – first developed to explain marked sexual dimorphism in such taxa as birds of paradise and the peacock – as a significant agency in human evolution. By contrast with Wallace, his emphasis on the importance of this mechanism was associated with a much greater sense of the similarity of the mental lives of humans and animals than Wallace could countenance.

Darwin's scientific and philosophical synthesis has a great deal to offer for our own times. His way of combining full acknowledgement of human distinctiveness and capacity for moral progress with his powerful sense of our kinship and ecological interconnectedness with the other species with whom we share the planet, and the sense of ethical responsibility he draws from that, could hardly be more apposite. But Wallace, too, has something indispensable to add. Despite his tendency to see humans as set above the rest of nature, he never lost sight of the necessity of a proper relationship to nature as central to human well-being – and continued to campaign against the sufferings wreaked upon the working population by industrial capitalism's environmental destructiveness:

> Yet it is among those nations that claim to be the most civilised.... that we find...the greatest recklessness, in continually rendering impure this all-important necessity of life, to such a degree that the health of the larger portion of their populations is injured and their vitality lowered, by conditions which compel them to breathe more or less foul and impure air for the greater part of their lives. The huge and ever-increasing cities, the vast manufacturing towns belching forth smoke and poisonous gases, with the crowded dwellings, where millions are forced to live under the most terrible insanitary conditions, are the witness to this criminal apathy...(Wallace, 1903, cited in Knapp, 2008)

Wallace's commitment to what might now be called environmental justice, and Darwin's philosophical legacy of a non-reductive naturalism about human origins and nature are both crucially important resources for the kind of radical new thinking demanded by our current ecological and economic impasse (for further development of this line of argument, see Benton, 1993 and Moog & Stones (eds), 2009).

References

Barkow, J., Cosmides, L. and Tooby, J., (1992), *The Adapted Min*. Oxford: Oxford University Press.

Benton, T., (1993), *Natural Relations: Ecology, Animal Rights and Social Justice*, London: Verso.

Benton, T., (1997), Where to draw the line? Alfred Russel Wallace in Borneo, *Studies in Travel Writing*, 1:96–119.

Benton, T., (1999), Evolutionary psychology and social science: a new paradigm or just the same old reductionism? *Advances in Human Ecology*, 8:65–98.

Benton, T., (2008), Wallace's dilemmas: the laws of nature and the human spirit', In C. H. Smith and G. Beccaloni (eds), (2008), *Natural Selection and Beyond: The Intellectual Legacy of Alfred Russel Wallace*, Oxford: Oxford University Press.

Caplan, A. L., (ed.), (1978), *The Sociobiology Debate*, New York: Harper Row.

Cronin, H., (1991), *The Ant and the Peacock*, Cambridge: Cambridge University Press.

Darwin, C., (1859), *On The Origin of Species by Means of Natural Selection*, London: John Murray.

Darwin, C., (1874), [1871], *The Descent of Man and Selection in Relation to Sex*, London: John Murray.

Darwin, C., (1987), [1837], *Charles Darwin's Notebooks 1836–1846* P. H. Barrett, P. J. Gautrey, S. Herbert, D. Kohn and S. Smith (eds), London & Cambridge: British Museum (Natural History)/ Cambridge University.

Darwin, F., (ed), (1887), *The Life and Letters of Charles Darwin* (2nd edn., in 3 volumes), London: John Murray.

Dawkins, R., (2006), *The God Delusion*, London: Transworld.

Dennett, D., (2006), *Breaking the Spell: Religion as a Natural Phenomenon*, London: Allen Lane.

Fichman, M., (2004), *An Elusive Victorian: The Evolution of Alfred Russel Wallace*, Chicago & London: University of Chicago Press.

Grüber, H. E., (1974), *Darwin on Man*, London: Wildwood.

Knapp, S., (2008), Wallace, conservation and sustainable development, In C. H. Smith and G. Beccaloni (eds), 2008 *Natural Selection and Beyond: The Intellectual Legacy of Alfred Russel Wallace*. Oxford: Oxford University Press.

McKinney, H. L., (1972), *Wallace and Natural Selection*. New Haven and London: Yale University.

Midgley, M., (1979), *Beast and Man: the Roots of Human Nature*, Brighton: Harvester.

Moog, S. and Stones, R., (eds), (2009), *Nature, Social Relations and Human Needs: Essays in Honour of Ted Benton*, Basingstoke & New York: Palgrave Macmillan.

Pinker, S., (1997), *How the Mind Works*, Harmondsworth: Allen Lane.

Raby, P., (2001), *Alfred Russel Wallace: A Life*, London: Chatto & Windus.

Rose, S. and Rose, H., (eds), (2000), *Alas, Poor Darwin: Arguments against Evolutionary Psychology*, London: Jonathan Cape and New York: Harmony.

Smith, C. H., (2004), Alfred Russel Wallace on man: a famous 'change of mind' – or not? *History and Philosophy of the Life Sciences*, 26(2):257–70.

Smith, C. H., (2008), Wallace, spiritualism and beyond: 'change' or 'no change', in Smith and Beccaloni (2008).

Smith, C. H. and Beccaloni, G., (eds), (2008), *Natural Selection and Beyond: The Intellectual Legacy of Alfred Russel Wallace*, Oxford: Oxford University.

Sterelny, K., (2001), *Dawkins vs. Gould: Survival of the Fittest*, London: Icon.

Wallace, A. R., (1856), On the habits of the Orang Utan of Borneo, *Annals and Magazine of Natural History*, July:26–32.

Wallace, A. R., (1858), On the tendency of varieties to depart indefinitely from the original type, *Journal of the Proceedings of the Linnaean Society*, Vol. 3:53–62. (reprinted without alteration in Wallace, 1870).

Wallace, A. R., (1864a), 'On the phenomena of variation and geographical distribution, as illustrated by the Papilionidae of the Malayan region' in *Transactions of the Linnaean Society*, Vol. XXV.

Wallace, A. R., (1864b), The origin of human races and the antiquity of man deduced from the theory of 'natural selection', *Journal of the Anthropological Society of London*, 2:clviii–clxxxvii. (reprinted, but with a new title and significant alterations, in Wallace, 1870).

Wallace, A. R., (1865), The varieties of man in the Malay Archipelago, *Transactions of the Ethnological Society of London*, Vol. 3:196–215.

Wallace, A. R., (1866), *The Scientific Aspect of the Supernatural*. http://www.wku.edu/~smithch/wallace/S118A.htm

Wallace, A. R., (1867a), Mimicry, and other protective resemblances among animals, *Westminster Review*, July:1–43. Republished in Wallace, A. R., (1870), *Contributions to the Theory of Natural Selection*, London: Macmillan.

Wallace, A. R., (1867b), Creation by law, *Quarterly Journal of Science*, October:471–488. Republished in Wallace, A. R., (1870), *Contributions to the Theory of Natural Selection*, London: Macmillan.

Wallace, A. R., (1867c), The philosophy of birds' nests, *Intellectual Observer*, July:413–420. Republished in Wallace, A. R., (1870), *Contributions to the Theory of Natural Selection*, London: Macmillan.

Wallace, A. R., (1868), A theory of birds' nests, *Journal of Travel and Natural History*, 2:73–89. Republished in Wallace, A. R., (1870), *Contributions to the Theory of Natural Selection*, London: Macmillan.

Wallace, A. R., (1869), 'Sir Charles Lyell on Geological Climates and the Origin of Species', *Quarterly Review*, April:359–394.

Wallace, A. R., (1870), *Contributions to the Theory of Natural Selection*, London: Macmillan.

Wallace, A. R., (1903), *Man's Place in the Universe*, London: Chapman & Hall.

Wallace, A. R., (1905), *My Life: A Record of Events and Opinions* (in two volumes), London: Chapman & Hall.

Wallace, A. R., (2002), *Alfred Russel Wallace's Malay Journals*, transcribed by M. B. Pearson (unpublished manuscript. I am obliged to George Beccaloni for bringing this to my attention).

Alienation, the cosmos and the self

Peter Dickens

Abstract

This paper is concerned with the alienation between the self and the cosmos. On the one hand, the binaries involved in this process (including the division between society and nature and between mental and manual labour) have been widely described and commented on. Social scientists and activists alike have shown that dichotomies of this kind are used by social elites to legitimate control over nature and over 'inferior' human beings. These insights are all vital but this paper attempts to combine them with elements of psychoanalysis. Binary ways of thought also appeal to elements (especially infantile elements) of the human psyche that divide parts of society and nature into 'good' and 'bad'. These binaries are the product of psychic defence mechanisms operating under uncertain, challenging or difficult- to-understand circumstances. They result in a narcissistic rather than an anaclytic relation to the cosmos, one in which a divided cosmos is mirroring a divided self rather than (as in archaic societies) a self which develops in close relation to 'others' on which it depends. The paper concludes by arguing that a highly general, 'universal', knowledge of the cosmos and external nature is unstable and eminently challengeable.

Why a dualistic cosmos?

A particular form of cosmology has remained dominant, at least since the Ancient Greek era. Typically, the most distant parts are deemed to be Heavenly, pure, subject to regular movement and most easily understandable via mathematics (often of an advanced nature) and abstract reasoning. Those parts nearer Earth and on Earth itself, on the other hand, are seen as having precisely opposite qualities. They are impure, profane, Godless and chaotic. Why is this dualistic picture so dominant? This paper attempts to answer this question. First it addresses some of the more objective features of society given prominence by conventional sociology. Secondly, psychoanalysis is explored, the suggestion being that a dualistic cosmos can in part be understood as a product of a dichotomized human psyche.

On dualisms and dichotomies

Dualisms, in which some aspect of society and nature are split into two contrasting elements, can be useful heuristic devices for understanding the complexity of the world. As Levi-Strauss (1966) famously argued, dualisms are a feature of both 'savage' and 'domesticated' thinking. Binary oppositions such as death versus creation or 'raw' versus 'cooked' are used to make symbols, which help create order in a complex world (1966: 8).

On the other hand, binary language is frequently imbued with meaning and is often used by the socially powerful as creating high value to some features of society and low value to others. The left-hand column of Figure 1 shows some of the concepts often construed as 'bad', 'inferior' or of low value. On the right-hand side are concepts often construed as 'good', 'superior' or 'positive' and of higher value. Such binaries are used to exercise power; the domination of nature by society, for example, or the superiority of mental over manual work and of men over women. Discourse of this kind is also used to legitimate imperialism, colonialism and the exploitation of non-human species.

Merchant (1982) has traced the images of nature that have prevailed from the early mediaeval period up to the beginnings of the industrial revolution in Britain. She also shows how these dualisms are subject to change. In line with the dualisms outlined in Figure 1, external nature has been consistently envisaged in terms of a living organism; specifically a female. And 'female' is frequently linked to, or equated with, a number of other qualities and entities such as 'earth' and 'emotional'.

But this 'female nature' has been transformed over time. At the start of the mediaeval period it was widely projected as a kindly nurturing woman whereas towards the end of the 17th century the female was being widely construed as more 'primitive', 'wild' and even threatening. And, in line with the development of early capitalism and the growing industrialisation of the countryside, a female nature construed as temperamental was an object or body needing control by (male) scientific knowledge and rationality. Similarly, John Locke (1632–1704) and Thomas Hobbes (1588–1697) expressed, albeit in rather different forms, a view of external nature as something wild. Again it needed taming and using in an instrumental way by property-owning individuals to serve human ends (See Benton, 2007 for discussion).

The number of binaries or dualisms such as those in Figure 1 could be multiplied indefinitely. Furthermore, different concepts within the 'good' and 'bad' columns are often linked. These dichotomies and their connection to social power are now a familiar feature of the contemporary social sciences, with feminist scholars and activists to the fore in exposing these binaries as a way of exposing how power is exercised (Ortner, 1974; Plumwood, 1993; 2002, Warren, 1994, 1996, 1997, 2000; Mellor, 2009). Women are identified with the natural world while 'consciousness is seen as resting with the male knower' (Mellor, 2007).

'Bad'/Low Value	'Good'/High Value
Nature	Culture
Death	Life
Ecosystems	Exploitable resources
Subsistence	Market value
Female	Male
Emotional	Rational
Manual	Mental
Feelings/wisdom	Skills/Tradeable knowledge
Object	Subject
Primitive	Civilized
Earth	Heaven

Figure 1: *Binaries in Western Thought (adapted from Plumwood 1993, Mellor 2009).*

Dualisms and cosmology: social and economic explanations

Important social relations and social processes underlie these alternative visions (Lerner, 1991). These were first outlined by Marx (1976) and have since been elaborated by, amongst others, Sohn-Rethel (1975, 1978), Thomson (1961), Lukacs (1968) and Postone (1996). One obvious suggestion is that cosmic elites (priests, philosophers, scientists and others) have promoted abstraction by arguing that the further realms of the cosmos are zones of God, purity and mathematics. Conveniently these same cosmic elites deem themselves (and are widely deemed by others) as closer to God and purity. Their mastery of abstract ideas, including their mathematical knowledge locates them in the superior, if still earthly, realms.

But explaining forms of cosmology with reference to the division between mental and manual labour is only part, if an important part, of why abstract ideas achieve importance. The rise of abstract thinking such as that used to understand the outer realms of the cosmos is also rooted in the workings of society, specifically the money economy beloved by neoclassical economics (Mirowski, 1989). This is the sphere in which commodities are bought and sold. A premium is placed on abstraction because abstraction has steadily been made integral to virtually everyone's social life as they buy commodities for money.

Using money as a means of valuing and comparing things is an abstract yet increasingly pervasive practice.

Money, in the form of capital, is also an abstraction with seemingly magical powers. The simple process of investment shows, or appears to show, that money mysteriously creates yet more money (Sohn-Rethel, 1975, 1978). Money has, in Marx's words 'the occult ability to add value to itself. It brings forth living offspring, or at least lays golden eggs' (Marx, 1976: 255). This mysterious process of investment itself creating profits helps to sustain the myth that profits are somehow made independent of the sphere of production, the sphere in which labour-power is appropriated.

Exchanging money for commodities and magically expanding value in this process has led to a widespread 'abstraction mentality', one attributing special significance to abstraction in general, including the abstraction of mathematics and numbers. This general mentality lies behind the highly abstract forms of cosmology that have prevailed throughout the last 2000 years of human history. These cosmologies usually have precarious or even non-existent bases in observed or experienced reality, a gap mirroring the separation of investment and market exchange from production. Market exchange has of course greatly multiplied and extended as capitalism has developed, particularly with the recent extension of privatization, commodification and levels of consumption by the middle classes. Note that the market economy was virtually absent in the 'primitive' or 'archaic' societies where this kind of abstract mysticism was also absent. The people in these societies lived by hunting, fishing and the rearing of domestic animals. There was little by way of market exchange.

The growth of market economies, particularly as they have developed under capitalism, signalled the start of the kind of dualism with which we are now very familiar. As outlined above, the cosmos has been consistently associated with the rise of a mystical abstraction based in the money economy. This abstraction has been extended to include magical notions of a God-filled, pure, cosmos; one admired and revered by lay people despite (or precisely because of) the fact that they have a minimal understanding of the heavens described by cosmologists and other cosmic elites such as quantum physicists.

Alienation and the public universe

Some indication of the alienation from the cosmos stemming from abstraction can be gained by looking at responses to a recent survey by Mass Observation of lay people's responses to contemporary cosmologies. (Details of the survey are given at the end of this paper, in Appendix 1). The long-standing association between God, Heaven and the outer reaches of the Universe is well exemplified by one teaching assistant when she writes that:

> it would be wonderful to glide through space, visit other galaxies, look at our world from another perspective. As a Christian, I believe I will one day, from Heaven (C2677).

The overwhelming impact of contemporary scientific theories of the cosmos such as the Big Bang/Big Crunch model is the creation of powerlessness.

> The thing that fascinates me most about outer space is the idea that the universe is constantly expanding. It's difficult to visualize this. This constant expansion means there are infinite possibilities in space: other life forms, doppelgangers; and we are just specks. It puts all petty worries and anxieties of everyday life into perspective (F3137).

> The only effect that these mind-blowing figures have on me is to make us feel no more important than a grain of sand (B2605).

> I don't need, or want to be reminded of, how little I/we actually matter (M3132).

Cosmologies based on observation have competed with those based on the assertion of ideal forms. But they have achieved rather little success (Lindberg, 2007). A contemporary example of a materialist alternative is the work of Hannes Alfven who argued that the cosmos is constituted by a plasma 'criss-crossed by vast electrical currents and powerful magnetic fields, ordered by the cosmic counterpoint of electromagnetism and gravity' (Alfven cited in Woods and Grant, 1995: 201). Such plasma can be replicated in a laboratory and they are central to fluorescent lighting. In the 1970s the Pioneer and Voyager space-craft appear to have confirmed an alternative theory of this kind by detecting the presence of electrical currents and magnetic fields filled with plasma filaments.

This is just one example of a materialist cosmological tradition, one which has potentially challenged idealist theories such as those advanced by Plato, Aristotle and subsequent better-known cosmologies. Another example of an alternative is that which emerged in the early Ionian trading cities. Here a relatively democratic social order was created based on traders, craftsmen and freeholding peasants. Myths about the cosmos purveyed by priests claiming divine powers were resisted in this distinctive social context. The abstract reasoning usually associated with Ancient Greek philosophy (what Sohn-Rethel (1975) called 'the Greek miracle') did not extend to this region of the country. High value was instead placed on knowledge based on observation and practical experience (Lerner, 1991). But such approaches were not to prevail or become widespread. Idealism, linked to market exchange and the domination of intellectual over manual labour, has had by far the greatest influence on cosmology.

Dualisms, the Cosmos and the self: a Kleinian perspective

The above accounts of cosmology-formation are certainly useful, particularly in terms of their stress on the objective features of society that generate particular ways of thinking. But there is a third approach, one focussing on subjectivity and the ways the psyche tends to split the outside world into contrasting elements. This emphasis on the subjective level needs combining with the more objective understandings outlined above. Such combination would help over-come yet another pervasive dichotomy, that between subjective and objective. It would also help explain how dichotomous ways of understanding promoted by elites and by the exchange-process have come to acquire hegemonic signifi-cance for large numbers of people.

Melanie Klein's work on the self helps us develop this line of argument. Like Freud, Klein recognized the independent causal powers of the human psyche, a power built into humans' bodily constitution. She closely examined the devel-oping ego of the infant, how it protects itself and how it can disintegrate in response to anxiety and the threat of death. She participated in minute detail in children's play, exploring in particular the psychic meaning children give to toys. This form of psychoanalysis (one often lasting over a protracted length of time) allowed her to immerse herself in children's anxieties and to tease out conflicts within the young, developing, psyche. Furthermore, and against more conventional forms of scientific activity, her work allowed intuition and accu-mulated experience to form a central part of her theory-making. Immersion in the child's activities and perceptions also allowed Klein to argue that psychic life is by no means a story of unproblematic 'progress' from infancy to adult-hood (Mitchell, 1986). Conflicts between co-existing inner drives are a common feature of psychic life, as are ambivalent feelings towards the outside world.

In the process of birth and in the very earliest stages of life the infant is subject to a number of experiences such as light, noise, cold and feeding. The infant feels a particularly close association with the mother, she being what Klein calls 'the whole of the external world.' (Klein cited by Sibley, 1995: 6). The mother, particularly the mother's breast, is the source of both positivity and negativity, of 'good' and 'bad'.

The infant's sense of self-hood starts to be developed by two closely inter-linked processes: introjection and projection. The process of 'introjection' is that in which the infant's self absorbs what it experiences of the external object. Both 'bad' and 'good' parts of the child's environment (again particularly the mother's body) are identified with and incorporated back into the self. Projec-tion entails an aspect of the self, that is sensed as unbearable, being projected on, or attributed to, somebody or something else. But a 'good' part of the self is also projected back on to an object, an infant also identifying itself in this way with an external object. The outcome, in Klein's terms, is the 'paranoid-schizoid position', this being characterized by ambivalence in relation to the environment. Life and death instincts war within an infant, the first seeking the love of the mother and the life-giving breast, the second attacking the mother and the breast as a threatening 'bad'. This violent 'death instinct' is a means of attacking a perceived source of pain and frustration, these being the result of the mother's inevitable failings. At the same time the infant, by attacking the fantasized 'bad' element of the mother, is also preserving the 'good' mother and, as a result, protecting her from the infant's aggressive impulses.

These processes of splitting, projection and introjection are envisaged by Klein as subconsciously generated by the infant psyche as a means of coping with her or his inner world and the perceived threat to persecute, suffocate and even annihilate the self. They are phantasies used as means of making sense of the world and dealing with such anxieties about survival.

However, human development, according to Klein, normally consists of the ego gradually coming to recognize that both 'good' and 'bad' parts of people and the environment can co-exist. 'The depressive position' is one in which the infant comes to recognize the wholeness of the external object and the coexistence of 'good' and 'bad' in the same person or entity. But the subject now feels guilty for the damage originally caused to the mother by treating her (the person on whose life the infant depended) as a 'bad' object. The depressive condition is therefore one of guilt, sadness and mourning for the lost object, but one which recognizes external reality existing in a more complex and realistic way (Klein, 1998). So while some troubling aspects of the self may be left behind in the paranoid-schizoid position, new internal troubles arise concerning the lost 'pure' object and its perceived ruination (Phillips and Stonebridge, 1998). At one level the psyche has been made more integral but at another it is left disturbed and vulnerable. The psyche, as it develops into adulthood, must learn to live with the sadness and mourning associated with its lost childhood. Similarly, development entails a recognition that there will never be a perfect, trouble-free, 'finished' end-state for the psyche. A very important feature of Klein's work is that ambivalences and contradictions within the human psyche persist and there can easily be reversals in later life towards a split, infantile, form of psyche (Mitchell, 1986).

The adult social world actually receives relatively little attention in Klein's account. On the other hand, those who have developed and used her work have made such extensions (Rustin, 1999; Segal, 2004; Sibley, 1995). They show in different ways how, if a psyche does not learn to develop a more complex understanding as they progress from the paranoid-depressive position, individuals are likely to have an alienated and unhappy relationship with themselves and their environment.

Instances of splitting are shown by these authors to be adult versions of the neonate's defence mechanisms. They are latent infantilizing processes being realized under social conditions generating fear and anxiety. The developing human being is not allowed to mature into a 'depressive' state, one in which it comes to terms with the complexities of the adult world.

Splitting the Cosmos, splitting internal nature: an historical account

Early childhood's dualising propensities remain latent in adults and are also realized and articulated by, amongst others, the 'cosmic elites' outlined earlier, those claiming special knowledge of the cosmos (Dickens and Ormrod, 2007a,b). On the one hand, these elites' own psyches are therefore reflected in their models of the cosmos. On the other hand, people's dichotomizing tendencies stemming from earliest infancy can recognize themselves reflected *in* the cosmos.

Yet the ways in which such splits are constructed has varied tremendously across different societies in various historical epochs. And these differences have immense social and political significance. It is often remarked that in 'primitive', pre-modern, societies there was no discontinuity between humans, nature and the cosmos. The dichotomy 'society' and 'nature' was largely unknown in these societies (Ingold, 2000). Furthermore, the cosmos itself was envisaged as 'alive' with the same spirit or soul that animated human beings and their surroundings. There was not, as is the case in contemporary societies, a radical distinction between the self on the one hand and the cosmos on the other. The self in primitive or archaic societies is made through interacting *with* its environment, this including other selves as well as organic and inorganic nature (Ingold, 2000; Tarnas, 2006).

However, a binary splitting process is nevertheless a consistent feature of these societies. Durkheim's famous study of Aboriginal tribes notes the horizontal stratification of the tribe into opposing binary phratries (1995). Not only were different clans of humans divided according to these phratries, but all non-human nature and celestial bodies were assigned to one phratry or another. Examples were the Sun to one and the Moon to an 'other'. A divide therefore ran through the whole of the primitive cosmos (Figure 2) (See also Parsons, 1966; Levi-Strauss, 1968; Ingold, 2000).

There are two noteworthy features of dichotomizing by archaic or 'primitive' societies. First, they were primarily a means of classifying parts of the cosmos and, as Levi-Strauss showed, developing myths about its origin and creation of matter. Dichotomies were not used in an evaluative way, defining one part of the dichotomy as 'bad' another as 'good' and using these divisions to legitimate the exercise of power. Second, as Durkheim noted, the divide between phratries and their different parts of the cosmos was not only of a dichotomous nature but was of a 'horizontal' character (See Figure 2).

Taking these features together, dichotomies were not used to distinguish a 'high' (non-human) part of nature from a 'low' part of which humans are part.

Figure 2: *The horizontal division of the universe in 'primitive' societies.*

Durkheim described how 'others' in these societies are indeed defined in terms of opposites, but these are opposites at the same level. Thus, as shown in Figure 2, the Sun and planets might be associated with one phratry while the Moon and the stars might be associated with another. Similarly, a black cockatoo, war and land might be a means of characterizing one phratry, while a white cockatoo, peace and water might be used for another.

Durkheim's account is therefore clearly compatible with Kleinian and object relations theory, these supposedly 'primitive' people developing social selves in relation to others on whom they depend; the latter including animals and inanimate objects as well as other people (Ingold, 2000). 'Primitive' or archaic selves therefore define themselves in relation to outside 'others', a process of 'anaclysis' in which the self develops to recognize and comfortably coexist with entities, some of which may well be *un*like the self (Freud, 1977). In Kleinian terms, a form of self develops which is not infantilised by a continuing psychic split.

The division of labour within these archaic societies was almost non-existent. The position of elders is important to note. They were, and in the few remaining societies of this kind still are, engaged in interpreting the relationships between an 'alive' cosmos and the phratry. This contrasts significantly with later elites distinguishing between a supposedly 'superior' cosmos and supposedly 'inferior' human beings on earth.

The dominant picture is drastically changed during the long era between primitive and fully modern societies. The most influential of the Ancient Greek philosophers, most notably Aristotle and Plato, advanced the idea of an hierarchically ordered universe composed of 'crystalline spheres'. The outer sphere was the realm of God, the *primum mobile*. Next came the stars, the planets, the moon and then the Earth, Aristotle posited a 'sublunary realm' between the moon, the Earth. Differences between celestial bodies therefore now took on a hierarchical order of superior and inferior elements. Such cosmic ordering of course mirrored and extended the Earthly social order. Likewise, some humans (including priests) were 'above' others and were furthermore deemed nearer to the higher realms of the cosmos than the great mass of the people. As Figure 3 shows, a hierarchical order ran through the entire universe.

Figure 3: *The Greek hierarchical universe.*

Some Ancient Greek philosophers nevertheless resisted the idea of a pure heavenly zone contrasted with a chaotic and changing earthly realm (Dickens and Ormrod, 2007a,b). Anaxagoras (c.500–428 BC) argued, for example, that the heavens were actually made of much the same stuff and the same processes that could be seen and experienced on earth. It was another materialist view, one again based on observation rather than imposing detached abstract ideas on to the cosmos. Epicurus (341–270 BC) argued that gods may well occupy the cosmos but humans should not be over-concerned with them since the gods are not attempting to control or influence human affairs (Inwood and Gerson, 1994).

Models of the cosmos based on abstract reason nevertheless prevailed, albeit in modified forms, up to and including the West European Middle Ages. An Aristotelian view underlay, for example, the hierarchical Great Chain of Being notion made prevalent in Europe during this era. It was again a vertically-split cosmos, one in which the Gods and angels inhabited the most stratospheric levels while kings and high-ranking earthlings were seen as at least partly inhabiting the 'higher' realms of the universe. Socially subordinate people, animals and inanimate nature were deemed to be at the 'lower' end of the spectrum, that most distant from the superlunary realm. It was another picture, despite the fact that it made the social order seem natural and God-given, in which the concept of a split cosmos and its inhabitants would have resonated with the psyches of many 'lay' human beings (Dickens and Ormrod, 2007a).

The dichotomy between the self and the cosmos took a rather different form with the 15th century Renaissance picture of the cosmos and the position of 'man' within it. Now 'he' was considered a miniature version of the cosmos as a whole, the human head being equivalent to the superlunary realm and the body being equated with the earthly, 'natural', sphere (Tarnas, 2006; Dickens and Ormrod, 2007b). The 'split' between 'mind' and 'body' now became envisaged, at least by dominant social strata, as built into the cosmos itself. Significantly, these developments took place at the same time as the emergence of early capitalism in Northern Italy and the opening of trade routes and early imposition of private property relations around the globe.

The self was re-construed, again by dominant social orders, in a form familiar to our own era. This individual is free, independent, able to travel over the whole world. Most important of all, he (and it was almost always 'he') was able to own and control this world. As Tarnas writes:

> a new form of human being announces itself: dynamic, creative, multidimensional, protean, unfinished, self-defining and self-creating, infinitely aspiring, set apart from the whole, overseeing the rest of the world with unique sovereignty, centrally poised in the last moments of the old cosmology to bring forth and enter into the new (Tarnas, 2006: 4).

A binary order re-emerged in Enlightenment thinking as materialists asserted that the universe was 'mere matter in motion' (Tarnas, 2006) and an object to be exploited in the human interest. In some senses this reversed the religious and metaphysical assertion that the universe was the dwelling place of god(s), powerful *subjects* controlling human affairs. Increasingly emptied of its gods, the cosmos was now made an *object* for the exercise of human power (Dickens & Ormrod, 2007a). The pre-modern horizontal binary that cleft the whole of the universe in two was replaced by a vertical split which divided humans (the privileged subjects and masters of reason) from a supposedly cold and mechanical universe from which they are expelled (Figure 4).

Abstraction, as outlined earlier, has an economic basis in the exchange of goods for money. And this process has increasingly governed society's relations with the cosmos and with the whole of external nature. From the late 17th century onwards there has developed a radical distinction between a supposedly all-knowing (and again mainly male) subject and the object of the universe. The result is what Weber called 'disenchantment' of humanity from the cosmos. A black or a white cockatoo now offers little or no emotional connection with the cosmos. At best they are objects to be observed. What really matters now is cash value, a white cockatoo perhaps being worth more than a black one in the animal trade. Space and time alike are now increasingly construed as homogenous entities, this again directly reflecting the steady commodification of land and labour under early capitalism. Variations in landscape, hours of the day, seasons and body-clocks are, as far as possible, homogenized by universal money-values. These attempts to abstract from, or over-ride, the fact that space and time remain lived-in realities nevertheless leave contradictions, a point to which this chapter returns (Lefebvre, 1991; Harvey, 1996).

Addressing the Kleinian starting-point of this chapter, the 'good' or 'positive' is now equated with Enlightenment science and rationality. These are envisaged as expelling the 'bad' in the form of dark superstition and mysticism, with the eventual prospect of everything being understood via a rational science. Note that although Figure 4 appears to suggest there are no divisions between human beings, this is not because all humans *are* equal. It merely represents the Enlightenment ideal that humans are born equal and 'free', a myth which continues to disguise structural inequalities.

Figure 4: *The Enlightenment dualism.*

Given a Kleinian starting-point, the constant dualisation of the cosmos throughout human history since the era of the archaic civilizations has had profound infantilizing implications, appealing to and activating the dualisms relied on by infants to establish their place in the world. Again, Freud's original distinction between anaclytic and narcissistic object choice is useful. If people in archaic societies developed an anaclytic view of the cosmos (one in which the cosmos is conceived as different yet depended on by the self), people in subsequent societies have tended towards a narcissistic object choice, one in which the split form of the cosmos simply mirrors the split form of the self. The narcissistic vision has been maintained partly because such dualism reflects the psyches of cosmic elites themselves. But, as suggested earlier, the narcissistic vision also mirrors the psyches of the socially-subordinated. Social domination is hegemonic if it is made to penetrate the psyches, albeit the infantile and ill-developed psyches, of whole human societies in this way. Yet, as discussed shortly, such hegemony is incomplete and unstable.

Dichotomous cosmologies from Newton to Hawking

Galileo's telescopes showed the moon to be rough, uneven, and not unlike the earth. Sun spots indicated that the far cosmos was far from immutable. It might be assumed that such developments were the death-knell for ancient binaries between 'good' and 'bad' parts of the universe. But contemporary cosmology shows that this has by no means happened. Dichotomies of this kind have not disappeared. In fact they have made a dramatic reappearance in modern cosmology. This has profound implications for modern self-identity.

Klein's ideas offer insights into Newton and his science of the cosmos. He is sometimes seen as the ultimate embodiment of Renaissance 'universal man'. But as a practising alchemist *and* a physicist who also worked out the principles of modern physics, he was personally at the centre of the division between 'reason' on the one hand and 'irrationality' on the other. Indeed both such world-views interacted with one another, Newton's Laws of Motion being a direct result of his struggling with alchemy. The latter asserted that the Earth was a form of animate entity, drawing in and expelling something equivalent to 'breath' across an 'aether', thereby creating attractions and repulsions between different types of material.

Newton realized that entities repelled and attracted one another but, on the basis of his own experiments, he also realized that such attractions and repulsions between entities took place without the medium of aether. There had to be another explanation of 'action at a distance' and this realization was eventually to be the basis of the famous laws of gravity and motion that bear Newton's name (White, 1998). Meanwhile, as these immense intellectual struggles took place within this one person they appear to have had, possibly in combination with a latent (in that era 'bad') homosexuality, a deleterious effect on his own mental health (Manuel, 1968). His interest in alchemy was largely repressed, this also being a 'bad' which could certainly threaten his eminent standing as the proponent of 'good' science (White, 1998).

Contemporary cosmology contains many similar dichotomising tendencies. Perhaps today's most famous theory is the Big Bang/Big Crunch theory of the universe, the idea being that the universe was created from a singular point of infinite density, eventually collapsing back in on itself. Such a theory may well have connections with developments in the social world. Woods and Grant (1995) suggest, for example, that a collapsing universe was a common feature of the Classical Greek, and mediaeval eras. The cosmos was predicted to collapse in all of these periods when in reality it was society that was collapsing. 'What was imminent was not the end of the world, but the collapse of slavery and freedom' (Woods and Grant, 1995: 199). The early Christians, suffering from persecution by the Romans, appear to have been the first to develop the first version of 'Big Crunch' thinking.

The argument that dominant models of the cosmos are reflections of social change and social struggle has much to support it. Furthermore, these models systematically inhibit any sense of human agency. The cosmic order as represented by Aristotle and the Great Chain of Being, for example, all mirrored a social order which was supposedly fixed. Similarly, The Big Bang/Big Crunch model implies a preordained long-term doom, one over which people have little or no control (Lerner, 1991). But dominant forms of the cosmos also have consistently appealed to a tendency of the human psyche to conceive the world in binary, oppositional, terms.

Stephen Hawking's model of the universe, which is predicated on Big Bang thinking, also contains elements of 'good' and 'bad' (Rose, 1993). But whereas Newton repressed the 'negative' aspect of his psyche in his model of the universe, Hawking's model of the 1990s contains both 'positive' *and* 'negative' elements. The former again implies 'scientific' and the latter 'mysterious' and 'bad' or 'negative' in the sense of not understood by science.

The vision of the cosmos stemming from Einstein and postulated by Hawking and others posited black holes which are so dense and so massive that the gravitational force they generate prevents even light from escaping from them. Everything else near a black hole simply disappears into these 'black' holes. The laws of quantum physics have supposedly been over-ridden and unravelled by these intense gravitational fields. Such abstract speculations about black holes are used by contemporary physics to explain the highly concentrated and violent outbursts of energy occurring at the centre of galaxies (Lerner, 1991). There is more than a hint of danger associated with these mysterious black holes apparently not obeying the chief tenets of science. Hawking (2005: 81) shows a future space traveller being swallowed up forever into a black hole, a fate reproduced in science fiction movies such as Star Trek and Star Wars (Connor, 2008). Hawking's model is another picture of the cosmos which can be illuminated by Klein's theories, the cosmos now being widely envisaged as two opposing (positive and negative) elements combined and interacting with each other.

Yet note that in 2004 Hawking announced that 'black holes' were not so threatening or devastating after all. The information or the traveller contained within them does not totally disappear. It is transformed and returned in a different form. As Hawking explained, 'if you jump into a black hole your mass energy will be returned to our Universe but in a mangled form, which contains information about what you were like, but in an unrecognizable form' (Hawking cited by Hogan, 2004). So the 'bad' parts of the universe are now comparatively 'good' or 'positive'. The laws of physics had not been over-ridden, even if they return humans that are unrecognizable as such.

But even this is not the end of the story since other 'bad' parts of the cosmos have since been apparently discovered. Positive and negative qualities projected by cosmologists on to the cosmos have taken an interesting new form in recent years with what are known as 'Dark Matter' and 'Dark Energy'. Dark Matter constitutes 23 per cent of the universe (Clark, 2008). Yet it is invisible and there is no scientific understanding whatsoever of this key substance. Yet, since Dark Matter holds galaxies and cluster of galaxies together, an understanding of this all-encompassing substance is necessary to shore up the Big Bang model. As Woods and Grant put it:

> If the universe was created 15 billion years ago, as the model predicts, there has simply not been enough time for the matter we observe to have congealed into galaxies like the Milky Way, without the help of invisible 'dark matter' (1995: 190).

Dark Energy constitutes 73 per cent of the universe and it too is largely a mystery. It is generally believed to increase the expansion of the universe at an accelerating rate. Nevertheless some cosmologists now argue that it may in due course go into reverse and act like more conventional gravity. Rather than cause cosmic expansion it may bring galaxies rushing towards each other and lead them to collide. It therefore may or may not generate the end of the universe. As one contemporary commentator puts it 'cosmologists are still very much in the dark about dark energy' (Ananthaswamy, 2008: 34).

Dark Matter and Dark Energy therefore join Newton's alchemical 'aether' and Hawking's 'black holes' as massive, almost completely non-understood, but nevertheless needed to shore up the models of the cosmos asserted by contemporary cosmology. These parts of the cosmos are being consciously fantasized, or subconsciously phantasized, as 'bad' or 'unscientific'. As such they again activate humans' most primitive psychic defence mechanisms, including those of the cosmologists themselves. Significant too is the abiding interest amongst cosmologists with what happens when scientifically understood matter and Dark Matter are fused. The belief is that energy is released but also that matter is destroyed, cancelling each other out and producing a nothingness. Perhaps this model can be interpreted as the sheer impossibility of reuniting the fractured universe. A permanently split psyche is projected on to a permanently split cosmos, with the latter in turn only confirming the splintered nature of the psyche.

These highly speculative models of the cosmos can therefore be envisaged as influential cosmologists projecting their own split psychic qualities on to the cosmos. On the one hand they are projecting elements of themselves ('good' and 'bad') on to the cosmos but with these same cosmic elements in turn being read back on to, or introjected by, the self. Meanwhile all this speculation has a decreasing reference to actual observation of the universe (Norris, 2000; Frankel, 2003).

Perhaps the most basic social dichotomy of all is that between mental and manual labour, with the first being ranked amongst 'the good' and the second amongst 'the bad' or 'inferior' (See Figure 1). There are many social and political ways in which this type of division has been made and reinforced over the millennia since Aristotle's and Plato's day. But 'mental labourers' often express this dichotomy in 'superior' mathematicized forms. But, again, such elites are not simply imposing alienating visions of a 'good' and/or 'bad' cosmos on subordinate earthlings. They are creating and re-creating such models while the psyches of the population as a whole are also prone to seek and endorse such models as defence mechanisms and as means of making sense of their anxieties and childhood experiences.

It might seem that lay people are alienated from their universe simply because they cannot understand the highly abstruse mathematical language being deployed. Yet this is too simple. They are also definitely intrigued by and drawn into such notions as Big Bang and 'black holes'. The fact that Hawking's *Brief History of Time* (1988) has sold over 9 million copies since its publication in 1988 is part-testament to this ambivalence. But so too is the fact that very few people indeed have actually understood the book they have bought.

Ambivalence towards modern cosmology comes through in responses to the Mass Observation survey. Co-existing scientific and mysterious elements of the cosmos seem to make sense to many of the Mass Observation correspondents. This despite the fact that, as the correspondents are the first to admit, their grasp of quantum physics and mechanics is at best tenuous. Correspondents typically describe Stephen Hawking's theories as 'fascinating', despite the fact that they hardly understood them. The fact that lay people do not understand modern cosmology as represented by Hawking is seen as a product of their inadequate intellectual capacities. The result is profoundly disabling and alienating.

I can't get my head round most of the theories like the Big Bang. If the universe started like that, what existed before it? And where is it expanding into? And what lies beyond it? For me it is impossible to conceptualize these issues. But I accept that there must be many things in existence beyond my knowledge or comprehension (C2256).

The black holes take some getting your head around but at the same time hints at the enormity of understanding you need just to try and put some of it in context (H1703).

The scientific theories are difficult to understand, even with the help of Richard Dawkins books (sic). String theory, black holes, worms in time. It is definitely worth trying though (W632).

The psyche and unstable hegemony

Incorporating a Kleinian understanding of the psyche, one admitting both 'good' and 'bad' elements of the infant and adult psyche, suggests that hegemonic power has a strong psychoanalytic element. This fact also offers some insight into the puzzle a number of theorists refer to when they point to the limitations of the supposedly 'universal' understandings offered by mental labourers. Supposedly 'universal' understandings actually consistently fail to describe the cosmos and external nature adequately. Such failures give rise to what Lukacs (1968) calls 'the antinomies of the bourgeoisie', the fact that apparently universal laws actually do *not* explain the circumstances and particularities which people experience. Universalism is, as Lukacs puts it, 'incapable of fulfilment', promising a total understanding of society and of the cosmos which in practice cannot be delivered. This ultimate failure of universals means that dominant classes eventually 'lose the possibility of gaining intellectual control of society as a whole and with that [lose their] own qualifications for leadership' (1968: 121).

But, as outlined earlier, one way in which attempts are made to gain or restore intellectual control is through cosmic elites also classifying some realms of the natural world as '*non*-science' or '*non*-rational'. In Kleinian terms these are again the 'bad' and 'valueless' qualities which have still not been understood but which will in due course be cracked by further scientific endeavour. 'Bad' and 'good' are therefore means by which the contradictions of 'antinomies of the bourgeoisie' are partially and provisionally papered over. But constant covering still cannot conceal the fact that universalism constantly remains uncertain, unstable and always challengeable.

Conclusion: the division of labour, the Cosmos and developing the depressive position

Marrying psychoanalytic and sociological approaches to the cosmos and to external nature suggests that what in the end is positive or negative, 'bad' or 'good', is not 'people', 'the cosmos' or parts of the cosmos. What is 'bad' is alienation from nature, which started with the abstractions of the more influential of Ancient Greek philosophers and continued with the rise of a distinct class of intellectual labourers under capitalism. The split is between what Lerner (1991) calls 'those who learn and those who work'. The more powerful labourers (the distinguished cosmologists discussed above being good examples) not only use and develop their mental capacities but are often handsomely rewarded for doing so. Furthermore, it is in their interests consistently to overestimate the potential of science to offer an eventually complete and perfect understanding of the cosmos. Meanwhile the mental capacities of the least powerful are neglected and their rewards are much more minimal.

As Marx and his followers suggest, these processes cannot be simply ascribed to the machinations of intellectual labourers, each protecting and promoting their particular part of the division of labour. The move towards increasing abstraction was greatly facilitated and enabled by the lived abstraction stemming from the abstraction of market exchange, a process again escalating with the penetration of the capitalist exchange into many spheres of social life, especially from the 17th century onwards. This chapter has attempted to show that the dichotomization between 'good' and 'bad', 'scientific' and 'mysterious' strikes deep into the human psyche. Such divisions are means by which human beings see themselves *in* the cosmos, even if such a recognition appeals to some of the most infantile of psychic mechanisms. On the other hand, dominant social orders using these distinctions cannot necessarily rely on these distinctions as a means of holding on to their authority.

Alternatives to universalism necessitate developing much more sophisticated, multi-layered understandings of the cosmos and of society. These would undermine the 'good' and bad' projected by dominant social orders and appealing to the infantile self. Recognition of such greater complexity can best be achieved through critical realist ontology, one recognizing the causal mechanisms working at different levels of abstraction. Different disciplines (physics, biology, sociology, psychology and so on) offer insights into the causal mechanisms operating in the cosmos. Critical realism offers an ontology which helps combine these mechanisms into a coherent and structured whole (Bhaskar, 1989; Sayer, 1992; Dickens, 2004).

An ontology of this kind would simultaneously be a means by which Klein's more mature 'depressive position' could start to be realized. A depressive position entails recognizing an uncomfortable fact. Important as Enlightenment scientific ideals remain, there never will be a time at which it has progressed to such an extent that it offers a complete and perfect knowledge of the cosmos and humanity's place within it. There will always be some aspect that is 'unknown'. But, as Klein's work suggests, anaclysis entails recognizing that an incomplete understanding of the 'other' is a necessary and emancipatory part of human development. An anaclytic, rather than narcissistic, relation with a largely unknown cosmos should not be a cause of terror or wild, unsupported, speculation. Rather, it should be a spur to gaining still better understandings based on observation and experience.

Acknowledgements

This chapter is a modified version of Dickens, P. (2008) 'Split Cosmos, Split Psyche, Split Society' published in *Flows and Networks of Environmental Sociology. Essays in honour of Professor Timo Järvikoski on his 60th birthday,* edited by Timo P. Karjalainen, Pentti Luoma, Kalle Reinikainen, Thule Institute, University of Oulu, Finland. Many thanks to James Ormrod, to members of the SASS Social Science Forum, University of Brighton and to members of the

International Association for Critical Realism for comments on this and the earlier version of this paper. The material from the Mass Observation Archive is reproduced with permission of Curtis Brown Group Ltd, London on behalf of the Trustees of the Mass Observation Archive © The Trustees of the Mass Observation Archive

References

Ananthaswamy, A., (2008), 'From big bang to big bounce', *New Scientist*, 200, 2686: 32–5.
Benton, T., (2007), 'Humans and Nature: From Locke and Rousseau to Darwin and Wallace' in J. Pretty, A. Ball, T. Benton, J. Guivant, D. Lee, D. Orr, M. Pfeffer and H. Ward (eds), *The Sage Handbook of Environment and Society*. London, Sage.
Bhaskar, R., (1989), *The Possibility of Naturalism*, Hemel Hempstead: Harvester Wheatsheaf, 1989.
Clark, S., (2008), 'Cosmic enlightenment', *New Scientist*, 8 March: 28–31.
Connor, S., (2008), 'The Man Who Got to the Bottom of Black Holes', *Independent*, 16th April.
Dickens, P., (2004), *Society and Nature. Changing Our Environment, Changing Ourselves*, Cambridge: Polity.
Dickens, P. and Ormrod, J., (2007a), *Cosmic Society. Towards a Sociology of the Universe*, London: Routledge.
Dickens, P. and Ormrod, J., (2007b), 'Outer Space and Internal Nature: towards a sociology of the universe', *Sociology*, 41 (4): 609–626.
Durkheim, E., (1995), *The Elementary Forms of Religious Life*, New York: Free Press. (First published 1912).
Frankel, H., (2003), *Out of This World. An Examination of Modern Physics and Cosmology*, Cardiff: Cardiff Academic Press.
Freud, S., (1977), 'Three Essays on the Theory of Sexuality' in *On Sexuality*, Pelican Freud Library, Vol.7, Harmondsworth: Penguin. (First published 1905)
Harvey, D., (1996), *Justice, Nature and the Geography of Difference*, Oxford: Blackwell.
Hawking, S., (1988), *A Brief History of Time*, London: Bantam.
Hawking, S., (2005), *A Briefer History of Time*, London: Bantam.
Hogan, J., (2004), 'Hawking concedes black hole bet', *New Scientist* 21.7., http://www.newscientist.com/article/dn6193-hawking-concedes-black-hole-bet.html
Ingold, T., (2000), *The Perception of the Environment. Essays in livelihood, dwelling and skill*, London: Routledge.
Inwood, B., and Gerson, L., (eds), (1994), *The Epicurus Reader*, Indianapolis: Hackett.
Klein, M., (1998), *Love, Guilt and Reparation*, London: Vintage.
Lefebvre, H., (1991), *The Production of Space*, Blackwell: Oxford.
Lerner, E., (1991), *The Big Bang Never Happened*, New York: Vintage.
Levi-Strauss, C., (1966), *The Savage Mind*, London: Weidenfeld and Nicholson.
Levi-Strauss, C., (1968), *Structural Anthropology*, Vol.2, London: Allen Lane.
Lindberg, D., (2007), *The Beginnings of Western Science*, Chicago University Press.
Lukacs, G., (1968), *History and Class Consciousness*, London: Merlin.
Manuel, F., (1968), *A Portrait of Isaac Newton*, New York: Da Capo.
Marx, K., (1975), *Early Writings*, Harmondsworth: Penguin.
Marx, K., (1976), *Capital*, Harmondsworth: Penguin.
Mellor, M., (2007), 'Ecofeminism: Linking Gender and Ecology' in J. Pretty, A. Ball, T. Benton, J. Guivant, D. Lee, D. Orr, M. Pfeffer and H. Ward (eds), *The Sage Handbook of Environment and Society*. London, Sage.
Mellor, J., (2009), 'Ecofeminist economics and the politics of money' in Salleh, A. (ed.), *Eco-Sufficiency and Global Justice*, London: Zed Books.

Merchant, C., (1982), *The Death of Nature*, London: Wildwood House.

Mirowski, P., (1989), *More Heat than Light*, Cambridge University Press.

Mitchell, J., (ed), (1986), *The Selected Melanie Klein*, New York: Free Press.

Norris, C., (2000), *Quantum Theory and the Flight from Realism. Philosophical Responses to Quantum Mechanics*, London: Routledge.

Ortner, S., (1974), 'Is Female to Male as Nature is to Culture?' in M. Rosaldo and L. Lamphere (eds), *Woman, Culture and Society*, Stanford, CA: Stanford University Press.

Parsons, T., (1966), *Societies: evolutionary and comparative perspectives*, Englewood Cliffs, NJ: Prentice-Hall.

Phillips, J. and Stonebridge, L., (1998), Introduction, *Reading Melanie Klein*, London: Routledge.

Plumwood, V., (1993), *Feminism and the Mastery of Nature*, London: Routledge.

Plumwood, V., (2002), *Environmental Culture: the Ecological Crisis of Reason*, London: Routledge.

Postone, M., (1996), *Time, Labour and Social Domination*, Cambridge University Press.

Rose, J., (1993), 'Negativity in the Work of Melanie Klein' in *Why War? Psychoanalysis, Politics, and the Return to Melanie Klein*, Oxford: Blackwell.

Rustin, M., (1999), *The Good Society and the Inner World*, London: Verso.

Sayer, A., (1992), *Method in Social Science. A Realist Approach*, 2nd edn., London: Routledge.

Segal, J., (2004), *Melanie Klein*, 2nd edn., London: Sage.

Sibley, D., (1995), *Geographies of Exclusion*, London, Routledge.

Sohn-Rethel, A., (1975), 'Science as Alienated Consciousness', *Radical Science*, 2, 3: 65–101.

Sohn-Rethel, A., (1978), *Intellectual and Manual Labour: a critique of epistemology*, Atlantic Highlands, N.J: Humanities Press.

Tarnas, R., (2006), *Cosmos and Psyche. Intimations of a New World View*, London: Viking.

Thomson, G., (1961), *The First Philosophers. Studies in Ancient Greek Society*, London: Lawrence and Wishart.

Warren, K., (ed.), (1994), *Ecological Feminism*, London: Routledge.

Warren, K., (ed.), (1996), *Ecological Feminist Philosophies*, Bloomington: Indiana University Press.

Warren, K., (ed.), (1997), *Ecofeminism*, Bloomington: Indiana University Press.

Warren, K., (2000), *Ecofeminist Philosophy*, Lanham, Rowman and Littlefield.

White, M., (1998), *Isaac Newton. The Last Sorcerer*, London: Fourth Estate.

Woods, A. and Grant, T., (1995), *Reason and Revolt*, London: Welred.

Appendix 1

The Mass Observation Archive Directive, Summer 2005

The Directive referred to was called 'The Universe and Outer Space'. A range of questions was asked including, for example, queries over possible life in the universe, placing weapons in space and whether Government space programmes are a good use of money. The questions relevant to this chapter were:

– Science: can it give us all the answers to understanding the universe?
– Scientific theories of the universe; are there any that you find particularly interesting?

A full account of the survey is given in Dickens and Ormrod (2007a), Appendix B. Further information on the Mass Observation Archive can be found on their website: www.massobs.org.uk

Normality and pathology in a biomedical age[1]

Nikolas Rose

In conclusion, we hold that human biology and medicine are, and always have been, necessary parts of an 'anthropology'. But we also hold that there is no anthropology that does not presuppose a morality, such that the concept of the 'normal', when considered within the human order, always remains a normative concept of properly philosophical scope. (Georges Canguilhem, *The Normal and the Pathological*, [1951] p. 133, 1978)[2]

Are you normal? We all know the layers of meaning and judgement conflated within a question like this: the normal as average, typical, physically and mentally healthy, statistically close to the mean in a population. Hence those associations summoned by its antithesis, pathological: unhealthy, deviant, dangerous. These terms interweave different modes of judgement, statistical, social, medical, moral, ethical. Perhaps most sociologists would accept that the idea of the norm has its place in relation to the body – the vital norms of temperature, of blood pressure, of heartbeat and the like, perhaps of anatomy and physiology more generally. But they – we – tend to look with suspicion when this apparent natural sense of normativity is displaced from the realm that today we call biological (or perhaps biomedical) to that which we term social. Hence they would probably agree with that great historian of the life sciences, Georges Canguilhem, when he differentiated vital norms from social norms. In his doctoral thesis, written in 1943, Canguilhem argued that biological thought derived its ideas of the normativity of the organism from the dynamic normativity of life itself: 'It is life itself, and not medical judgment which makes the biological normal a concept of medical value and not a concept of statistical reality' (Canguilhem, 1978: 73). In his 'new reflections on the normal and the pathological' written between 1963 and 1966, inflected by the radical spirit of those times, he distinguished such vital norms from social norms. Social norms – the norms of docility, legality, productivity, punctuality, civility and the like – were not a reflection of the normativity of a vital order and its struggle against death, but of the normativity of socio-political authorities and their attempts to maintain order and pursue their objectives of control.

Of course, this distinction between the organic norms of the body and the artificial norms of society was not accepted by the first sociologists. Sociological styles of thought have long been intertwined with those of biology – indeed, biology and sociology were born close together. The Oxford English Dictionary tells us that the term 'biology' for the sciences of life emerged and stabilized in the period from 1820 to 1840; it gives 1844 for the first use of the term sociology for a new science of social ethics. Metaphors drawn from the biology of the time have played a large part in each generation's analysis of social phenomena. For functionalist sociologists it seemed that social norms had the same relation to the healthy functioning of society that vital norms had to the healthy functioning of the human organism: in the former case as in the latter, departure from those norms was evidence of a kind of pathology. Few would accept this today, in the wake of decades of criticisms of functionalism, the rise of the sociology of deviance, cultural relativism and the criticisms of the nature-culture binary. But what, then, of the normal and the pathological, and of the vital and the social? This is the theme I would like to discuss in this paper.

The personalized genome

I don't know how many of you have recently visited the website of deCODEme.[3] Those of you who have will have discovered that, 'For only $985, we scan over one million variants in your genome' and that you can 'Calculate genetic risk for 18 diseases based on the current literature; find out where your ancestors came from and compare your genome with others; get regular updates on future discoveries and a growing list of diseases and traits'. You may be surprised to be told, however, that 'deCODEme is not a clinical service to be used as the basis for making medical decisions. While the Genome Scan includes genetic variants that have been linked in our own and others' research to risk of certain diseases, we believe that individuals interested in utilizing such information for making healthcare decisions should do so in the context of clinical diagnostic tests.' And also that 'the deCODEme Genetic Scan does not include genetic variants that have been shown to cause purely genetic diseases or indicate a near certainty of developing any diseases'. But there is another way to turn all this 'getting to know your genome' into health-relevant information, apparently, because deCODEme offers to sell genetic tests ordered with the authorization of a physician at a discount to subscribers, and these may be reimbursable by healthcare providers.[4]

So a new business model is taking shape. And whatever this warning may say, for legal reasons no doubt to do with US FDA guidance on the marketing of genetic tests,[5] the information on risk will have consequences for individuals who receive it. And deCODEme is not alone. You could try '23andme' where 'genetics just got personal'.[6] Or you could go to 'Navigenics' for after all it is 'my genes, my health, my life'.[7] Or, if you are suspicious of commercial motives, visit the site of George Church's Personal Genome Project at Harvard,[8] or can consult this blog of one of the participants, Misha Angrist, aka, GenomeBoy.[9] In Harvard's personal genome project, as with the commercial sites, you participate in a new 'gift relation' – in the very same moment that you deposit your own 'personal genome' and health data into the genome bank to discover your own risks, you contribute your own data to the population on which future risk estimates are based. As these projects gather data from across the world, on a person by person basis, and in doing so collect larger and larger databases to provide the statistical power to discover genetic markers of small effect associated with disease risk, perhaps a new form of global genomic citizenship – individualized and consumerized – is in the making.

From tainted germ plasm to genome wide association studies

However durable this business model proves, it is clear that something has happened to genetics, to its style of thought, its forms of evidence, its technologies for generating truths, and their implications. Sociologists have long been among the most fervent believers in genetic exceptionalism – that is to say the belief that there is something exceptionally powerful in genetic information. Almost all British sociologists of the first half of the 20th century had close links with the Eugenics Society – although some of them, notably Titmuss, wanted to shift the emphasis away from genetic improvement and towards environmental and social measures to improve the quality of the population – the approach that would become known as 'social medicine' (Oakley, 1991). Sociology in this period was transfixed with problems of fertility, with differential fertility between social classes, and its consequences for population size and quality, and the Eugenics Society was one of the progenitors of academic sociology in Britain as well as of demography (Osborne and Rose, 2008).

But when it comes to the social implications of genetic knowledge the contemporary sociological imagination is shaped by hindsight. From the stories of the Jukes and the Kallikaks, with their images of tainted germ plasm coursing down the generations, to the murderous eugenics of the Nazi state and the pastoral eugenics of the Nordic welfare societies, genetics has been associated in the sociological imagination with fatalism, reductionism, individualization of social problems, and a range of profoundly negative policies for the management of the quality of the population through reproductive control – what contemporary Norwegians call a 'sorting society' which divides people in terms of an idea of individual worth fixed at birth in a given genetic complement. Such a genetic imaginary is regularly reinforced by the absurd simplifications of social Darwinists, for whom 'the gene' is a black box and selection is accorded a social teleology. Not to mention the occasional outburst by those like James Watson who should know better – you can check out his own personal genome, sequenced in two months in 2007 by 454 Life Sciences – Measuring Life One Genome at a Time – for less than $1M, and available on the web for all to see, only lightly edited.[10]

Perhaps this perception of genetics as intrinsically linked to a kind of biological determinism was justified in the early years of the Human Genome Project with the regular narratives proclaiming that this was a search for the code of codes, the book of life, and the belief that the genome contained the 'digital instructions' for making human beings – the so-called genetic programme approach (Kay, 2000). Many suggested that the number of distinct genes, now thought of as coding sequences consisting of strings of nucleotide bases – the Gs, Cs, As and Ts of the three letter code for amino acids that make up proteins, as in the familiar GATTACA, on the 23 human chromosomes was between 100,000 and 300,000 (Gilbert, 1993). Estimates of the number of different proteins in the human body vary, but many put this at about 100,000. So it did not seem impossible that there was, indeed, one gene for each protein, together with some additional sequences concerned with the regulation of gene transcription and expression, modelled on the classic studies by Jacob and Monod in the 1960s (Jacob and Monod, 1961).

On this basis, one could conceive of a clear genomic distinction between normal and pathological. Most individuals would have 'normal' genomes with a common sequence coding for the proteins necessary to produce healthy functioning except when disrupted by pathogens from outside. Those destined to sicken would have 'mutations' in one or a few genes which would either predispose them, or even determine them, to ill health. This was, indeed, the promise of genomic medicine. Leroy Hood, writing in 1992 under the title 'Biology and Medicine in the Twenty First Century', in the book he co-edited, *The Code of Codes*, believed that, 'Once the 100,000 human genes have been identified' it would transform our ways of dealing with human diseases:

> The genome project in the twenty-first century will have a profound impact on medicine, both for diagnosis and therapy . . . Perhaps the most important area of DNA diagnostics will be the identification of genes that predispose individuals to disease. However, many such diseases – cardiovascular, neurological, autoimmune – are polygenic; they are the result of the action of two or more genes. Human genetic mapping will permit the identification of specific predisposing genes and DNA diagnostics will facilitate their analysis in many different individuals... Perhaps in twenty years [he was writing in 1992] it will be possible to take DNA from newborns and analyze fifty or more genes for the allelic forms that can predispose the infant to many common diseases...For each defective gene there will be therapeutic regimens that will circumvent the limitations of the defective gene. Thus medicine will move from a reactive mode...to a preventive mode. Preventive medicine should enable most individuals to live a normal, healthy, and intellectually alert life without disease. (Hood, 1993: 155–157).

But this quote illustrates that genomics in the closing decades of the 20th century, even when it had a rather simple 'one gene-one protein' model, was not bound up with fatalism, but with hope. As Carlos Novas and I have argued, even in relation to the most apparently fatal of the single gene disorders, Huntington's Disease, diagnosis led not to passivity but to activism – campaigning organizations, websites and web-lists for mutual advice and support, fund raising and tissue donation to find the genetic basis of the disorder and the funding of research to develop therapies (Novas and Rose, 2000; Rose and Novas, 2005). And, more generally, we suggested that we were seeing the rise of what we termed active biological citizenship – a new active consumer-like turn in the strategies of even quite old support groups for those with particular illnesses or disabilities, together with new groups formed around specific diseases, especially genetic diseases; new relations between these groups and medical researchers in which sufferers and carers campaigned for research funding, donated money, tissues and time, and sought to direct research towards cures. Also new relations between patients and medical expertise, and indeed new 'active' modes of governing the self, involving self-education in the nature of a disorder, and self-management; a characteristic combination of autonomization and responsibilization that one might term 'biomedical prudence'. Many of these contemporary examples have been well studied. Paul Rabinow's work on Association Française contre les Myopathies (AFM) led him to propose the idea of 'biosociality' as a play on the then popular ideas of socio-biology (Rabinow, 1999). Carlos Novas's work on Huntington's Disease and PXE international led him to suggest that a 'political economy of hope' characterized this new field (Novas, 2006). The work of Deborah Heath, Rayna Rapp and Karen-Sue Taussig on Epidermolysis Bullosa suggested that we were seeing the emergence of new active forms of 'genetic citizenship, (Heath *et al.*, 2004). And, of course, these new active modes of self-management, part of what I have elsewhere termed 'ethopolitics', led to their own forms of judgment and indeed of exclusion brilliantly captured in the paper by Vololona Rabeharisoa and Michel Callon entitled 'Gino's lesson on humanity' (Callon and Rabeharisoa, 2004).

This situation was to mutate again when, in 2001, after much diplomatic negotiation, the draft sequences from both public and private sequencing programmes were simultaneously published. Each showed not 100,000 genes, but as few as 30 to 40,000 coding sequences (Lander *et al.*, 2001; Venter *et al.*, 2001). As Craig Venter asserted at the time, the basic premise of the genetic programme approach – one gene for one protein – could no longer be sustained: the reductionist approach had to be abandoned in favor of models of complexity: 'networks that exist at various levels and at different connectivities, and at different states of sensitivity to perturbation' (Venter *et al.*, 2001: 1347). When the Human Genome Sequencing Consortium published their final sequence in *Nature* in 2004 (Collins *et al.*, 2004) we had decisively left what Evelyn Fox Keller termed 'the century of the gene' (Keller, 2000) and we also seemed to have moved decisively beyond the 'genetic programme' approach (Neumann-Held and Rehmann-Sutter, 2006). There were simply 'not enough genes' for the sequence to be regarded as a 'code of codes' or the digital instructions for making a human being. We were in a much more complicated world, where alternate reading frames could read the same sequence of bases in different ways, where proteins were assembled from sequences spread across many chromosomes. We were in the world of alternative splicing, where parts of one sequence would be connected up with parts of another sequence, in a world where the same sequence could produce different proteins at different stages of development, in a world where, far from the DNA regulating the development of the cell, it appeared that in crucial respects it was the cell, and the humble

RNA previously merely assigned to the role of messenger, that seemed to be in charge of development.

And, if this was not bad enough news for those who had placed such hopes in the future of genetic medicine, the bottom seemed to be falling out of that particular market. By the start of 2007, billions of pounds and dollars had been spent in attempts to 'translate' the results of the Human Genome Project into clinically relevant measures that would improve the health of patients, yet there was little to be shown in the way of new therapeutic options available for the common complex diseases that ail most of us in the developed world, let alone in relation to the burden of disease in developing countries. While companies specializing in biomedical genomics saw their stock market values rise sharply with the initial developments in sequencing the human genome, the downturn began in 2002. Commercial companies whose business plan was predicated on the discovery of the genetic bases for such common disorders saw their share values drop sharply over the opening years of the 21st century. And by 2005 *Nature Biotechnology* commented that 'roughly ¾ of the companies that listed during the 1999/2000 biotech bubble are still not making money'; and even in 2006 Genentech and Amgen finished the year down in share value by around 12 per cent. Leroy Hood's hope of finding a few significant alleles of large effect, which would allow clinically meaningful genetic tests for susceptibility to conditions such as diabetes, heart disease, or the dementias had proved largely fruitless, and no effective genetically informed therapies for common disorders were even on the horizon. Where then for genomic medicine?

Personalized genomics

The flurry of publications from Genome Wide Association Studies in Autumn 2007 can be seen as one response to this crisis in genetic medicine (for one influential piece, see Wellcome Trust Case Control Consortium, 2007). Economies of scale have come to the rescue and enabled the emergence of a new way of thinking, a new wave of hope, and a new business model. The industrialization of the process of sequencing large numbers of SNPs has led to an exponential drop in the prices of sequencing each location – so that it is feasible for researchers with large sample sizes to sequence up to 500,000 SNPs in each subject for less than $1000. SNP level information from HapMaps has enabled this many SNP markers to be identified and localized. And case control studies, comparing large numbers of individuals with a disease diagnosis with normal controls, have enabled the generation of data showing differences between cases and controls at multiple sites. A new way of thinking – disease susceptibility as the result of interactions between many, maybe two or three hundred, SNPs of small effect, has been made possible. Hypothesis free, it is claimed – no need to opt for candidate genes, no need to begin from functional hypotheses – statistical associations will generate risk assessments with clinically useful consequences.

Not that this approach has been without scientific criticism – for poorly defined phenotypes, poor study designs, and, perhaps most important, for failing to emphasize the low utility of the associations found for assessing the risks of developing complex diseases (effect sizes of the new loci found are modest or small) (Higgins *et al.*, 2007; Manolio and Collins, 2007; Pearson and Manolio, 2008). Nonetheless, a new way of thinking is taking shape. For most common complex disorders, the genetic basis, if that is indeed the right word, lies in the highly complex interactions of many 'genes of small effect' each of which may, in combinations with others, increase or decrease risk by a small percentage. Perhaps one cannot even call these SNP level variations *'genes'* of small effect, as many of the signals picked up in these studies actually identify significant differences between cases and controls in regions that were once termed 'junk' – that is to say, that do not contain the triplets that code for amino acids at all.

This way of thinking has been central to the new buoyancy of the market in genomics. Consider the words of Steven Burrill, whose group acts as biotechnology consultants to the industry:[11]

> The transition to a more personalized medicine world is creating the need for molecular diagnostics, biomarkers, genotyping assays, etc. and so companies specializing in these areas have received positive investor attention…Sequenom, for example, a provider of fine mapping genotyping, methylation and gene expression analysis solutions, saw its share price rocket and closed the year up 588 per cent.

This, to return to our starting point, is the kind of research that animates Navigenics, 23andme, and deCODEme. Indeed deCODEme is an attempt, by those who carried out one of the first population wide studies of the association between genomic information, medical records and genealogy in Iceland, to develop a new business model. The one on which they had placed their bets – that one could use this method to develop tests for common complex disorders and ultimately therapeutics that targeted their genetic basis – had generated few if any medically useful findings. Hence the new target audience is less pharma companies and medics than it is you – your own personal genome. You are to be empowered, to discover your own levels of genomic risk, to become an active participant in genomic research, and to have to make your own kind of sense of the new spectrum of risk data with which you are provided – it is 'your genes, your health, your life' and hence in your power to use genetic information to assemble a pathway to optimal health. And, in the moment when you accept the obligations of this new offer of genomic freedom, you enrol your own genome in the database that will eventually, or so the companies hope, provide the statistical power necessary for more and more pronouncements of more and more sites associated with small variations in population risk for particular disorders. Indeed, according to *Nature* in February 2008, over the five and a half months since October 2007, the number of diseases for which genetic tests were available to patients had grown by 8.4 per cent, to 1,236 (Editorial, 2008).

But what has become of the notion of normality – the healthy, the average, the absence of pathology? At the genomic level, the answer may seem surprising – none of us – none of you – are 'normal'. We are all at risk, of higher risk for some conditions, of lower risk for other conditions, but all of us harbour, in those three billion base pairs that make up our 23 chromosomes, multiple minor variations that are potentially knowable, and which appear (although I would like to stress that word) to render our future risks of everything, from Alzheimer's disease to obesity, knowable and calculable. We are all asymptomatically, presymptomatically ill – and perhaps all suitable cases for treatment. Now of course this is not itself a radical shift. On the one hand it just extends what we already know about the emerging landscape of risk susceptibility, presymptomatic and asymptomatic diseases etc. Most of you – at least those of a certain age – will be personally familiar with procedures for the allocation of individuals to risk groups, on a genealogical basis, in terms of a family history of illness or pathology, and/or on a factorial basis, in terms of combinations of factors statistically linked to a condition. Men presenting to their doctors with high blood pressure are risk profiled in terms of age, weight, family history, smoking and so forth, are allocated to a risk group using a scale based on epidemiological and clinical research and, if at high risk, may be advised to make changes to behavior, diet or lifestyle, or preemptively placed on a drug regime intended to reduce the risk of the occurrence of such disorders. Pregnant women are risk profiled by their doctor or midwife, and if allocated to a high-risk group for miscarriage, premature birth or associated difficulties are subject to enhanced surveillance by midwives and gynaecologists (Weir, 1996). And so on.

Many of us working in these areas have drawn attention to the apparently illimitable expansion of this territory of risk under pressures from several directions. Preventive medicine, of course, prioritizes identification and intervention, both at the collective and at the individual level, prior to the emergence of frank disease. The growing precautionary principle, coupled with foresight and horizon scanning exercises, predicts the future burden of current health trends and demands early interventions into conditions such as obesity not previously encompassed within the territory of treatment; pharmaceutical companies seek products that will treat chronic conditions, as these make more sense in a business model, and what could be more profitable than medications used for a lifetime to treat a pre-disease – high lipid levels, for example – that is to say, to treat parameters that are not themselves diseases but are thought to increase the likelihood of future disease. And patients themselves, enjoined to be prudent about their own health, to manage their bodies in the name of health, willingly or unwillingly are coming to ally themselves with such presymptomatic measures in the name of health.

As I have said, none of this is without precedent. In some recent papers the fine historian Charles Rosenberg has pointed out two important senses in which nothing much new is happening (Rosenberg, 2003; 2006). First, there have always been disputes about the boundaries of disease, or perhaps better, the boundaries of the territory of medicine and the legitimate activities of medics –

from back pain to pregnancy, the characterization of disease has been disputed. Second, what Rosenberg terms 'technocreep' has a long history: diagnostic tools elicit signs that are taken as evidence of pathologies that were previously invisible – generating what Rosenberg terms 'protodiseases' (Rosenberg, 2003). What changes, then, when we move to the molecular scale, the scale of molecular genomics? The prediction was that gene sequencing would identify the genomic bases of diseases at birth, if not before, with all sorts of consequences. Sequences were identified that coded for the defects causing rare and often fatal diseases – such as the famous or infamous 'Jewish Genetic diseases' such as Tay-Sachs, Canavan Disease and Fanconi Anemia – known to be more common among Ashkenazi Jews. These became the subject of a controversial genetic register, run by communities themselves, that tested young people for their carrier status before they entered into marriage and advised them whether or not it was genetically appropriate for them to marry and procreate. But attempts to discover diagnostically meaningful genetic information for common complex disorders were largely unsuccessful – even the much publicized 'breast cancer genes' BRCA1 and BRCA2 account for only a small proportion of the heritability of breast cancer, let alone for the bulk of the condition that is not known to be linked to family history. And so, although with a few exceptions again for simple and rare conditions, attempts to develop genetically targeted treatments or clinical interventions were similarly unsuccessful. But nonetheless, the idea that genetics held the key to future risk, to susceptibility, was hard to dislodge – as witness the number of people seeking to have those tests when they first became available on the web.

Of course, as I have suggested, the new ventures in gene sequencing also hold out that idea that your genome carries variations that may affect your future disease susceptibility – that tiny SNP level variations in sequences increase or decrease susceptibility to all the ills that flesh is heir to. And Craig Venter, one of the few individuals who has had his whole 'diploid' genome sequenced, peppers his recent autobiography *A Life Decoded* with inserts letting the reader know that he does or does not carry the specific variant that would increase his risk of developing a particular disorder (Venter, 2007). But this simply makes the point: there is NO normal genome. At the genomic level, no-one is 'normal', at least in the sense that this term acquired from the 19th to the 20th century, overlaying a statistical average, a judgment of desirability, and an idea of health and illness. The developments in the genomics of disease that I have outlined suggest a different way of thinking, one that is perhaps difficult to comprehend – that of pathology without normality. I want to propose that, in the area of disorders of body and mind at least, we are moving from dividing practices based on the binary of normality and abnormality to practices based on the idea that all individuals vary, and that most, if not all, carry molecular variations that can in particular circumstances lead to disorders of body or mind but which, once known, are potentially correctible. In the human genome, 'the normal is rare.'[12] Or rather, there is no normal human genome; variation *is* the norm. In this new configuration, what is required is not a binary judgment of normality and pathology, but a constant modulation of the relations between biology and forms of life, in the light of genomic knowledge.

Is my brain normal?

Let me turn from genes to brains. Is my brain normal? Of course, the validity of psychiatric diagnosis of abnormality or mental disorder has long been contested and not just by sociologists – although sociologists will remember the famous paper by David Rosenhan, 'On being sane in insane places' which concludes that sanity is hard to diagnose (Rosenhan, 1973). But you might be forgiven for thinking, given all the popular hype about brain scanning, that we now had technologically sophisticated ways of seeing at least if your brain was normal, if not your mind. Images of brains of people with Alzheimer's and other disorders that appear to have a firm neurological aetiology often seem to confirm this. However things are not so simple. Take the case of Alzheimer's. Many clinicians consider that imaging of persons thought to be showing symptoms of Alzheimer's can be helpful in ruling out other causes of dementia such as tumours, if it is carried out when the behavioural and cognitive signs of disorder are quite marked. However, imaging the brains of those persons with mild symptoms, which might indicate that they are at an early stage in developing the disorder, is not helpful diagnostically. Perhaps, then, we might focus for a moment on brain imaging.

The work of anthropologists who have done field work among the brain mappers has shown us that such images are not simple representations of the living brain, but are highly mediated inscriptions of changes in blood flow, measured not in 'your brain' itself – since they have little idea of the size of the scanned brain or its actual configurations until post-mortem – but in terms of pixels in a three-dimensional space which is mapped on to a 'standard' brain space, and coloured according to certain conventions (Beaulieu, 2000; Dumit, 2003). A lot, then, is 'black boxed' in that image, and brain mappers themselves view with some concern the proliferation of these images as if they were simple photographs or X-Rays, and their utilization in popular and professional discourses. Nonetheless, the images have undoubted power. Scans of the brains of children from Romanian orphanages, for example, have been deployed to give us hard proof at last of the importance of early mother-child interaction – it is written in the brain (Nelson *et al.*, 2007). Defence lawyers have used scans of the brains of those accused of impulsive or violent conduct to indicate that their brain was maladaptive and so their responsibility for the act was mitigated: while this has largely been unsuccessful in the courtroom it is the focus of much ongoing research (I discuss this in Chapter 8 of Rose 2006b). And so on. Now I do not want to cast doubt on the importance of scanning technology, the great advances in resolution, and its potential role in diagnosis of some conditions. But we should pause for a moment to consider the relation between the state of your brain – the wet, meaty stuff – and your mental capacities.

Again, we can refer to Alzheimer's – and I am drawing extensively on the excellent work of Margaret Lock on this issue (Lock, 2007; 2008). Now Alzheimer's is one of the rather rare psychiatric conditions that appears to have a clear neurological bias: the neurofibrillary tangles and amyloid plaques that Alois Alzheimer identified in the first decade of the 20th century, using novel staining techniques, in tissue obtained from the brains of a number of patients who died with the condition that Emile Kraepelin would later name after him. This is not the place to go into the tangled history of this condition and the rival claims for its discovery.[13] The point for our purposes is what it might reveal about the relation between pathology in the brain and pathology of conduct. And to put it simply, the answer is this: there is *no* simple relation between the numbers of plaques and tangles in a person's brain and the symptoms of dementia.

Brain state, that is to say, is not correlated with mind state – if I can use that old fashioned term for a second – in any simple way. First, such plaques and tangles are found in several other conditions, not in senile dementia or Alzheimer's alone. Second, and more importantly, one cannot predict brain state – the quantum of plaques and tangles present at autopsy – from the degree of cognitive decline of the person when alive. Although in the 1960s and 1970s many researchers, research institutions, patient support groups and others coalesced around the hypothesis of the cerebral basis of the disorder – and hence agreed on the direction for research into aetiology, prevention, treatment, perhaps even cure – doubts have continually resurfaced about the coherence of the diagnostic category of Alzheimer's, about the role of the best known 'risk factor' – carrying one or two copies of the allele APOE4 (which I won't discuss here). More important for our purposes, there were continual doubts about the relation between the brain state and the mental state. The much-quoted Nun's study makes the point most clearly. Almost 700 Catholic sisters from The School Sisters of Notre Dame in the US participated, agreeing to have neuropsychiatric assessments regularly from age 75, and to donate their brains for autopsy after death. Despite the fact that pictures posted by the researchers on their website seem to show clear gross anatomical differences between the brain of a normal centenarian and an 'Alzheimer Brain',[14] as the autopsy evidence accumulated, it seemed that a proportion of the nuns who performed rather well on the test battery actually had extensive plaques and tangles in their brains, while some of those who had few anatomical changes in their brains performed badly on the tests and exhibited the behavioural signs of dementia. What, then, predicted cognitive performance or decline, if not the state of the brain? It appeared that this was 'cognitive reserve'; for each of the nuns had written an account, at admission, of their reasons for wanting to join the order and these had been preserved. When they were analysed, there was a negative correlation between the elaboration and complexity of the account and the level of cognitive decline shown by the neuropsychiatric tests.[15]

So is Alzheimer's linked to plaques and tangles in the brain? Probably. If one could visualize those plaques and tangles in the living person, would that predict their cognitive capacities? No. Indeed many of those living perfectly normal lives unto death would, on autopsy, show brain abnormalities. Despite all the research, and the very important basic science that has been done, the relation between brain anatomy and cognitive capacity remains mysterious. While research continues to focus on Alzheimer's as a 'brain disorder', the multitude of environmental, social and cultural supports for the disorder – its ecological niche, to use Ian Hacking's nice term, remain relatively unstudied. As Margaret Lock has put it 'dementia will not be better accounted for without consideration of the embodied, minded, self having a unique life history embedded in singular social and environmental contexts.'[16]

So what is a normal brain? Brains are not, of course, routinely scanned for early signs of dementia. Nonetheless, one does see the spread of a new diagnosis, not based on brain scanning, called Mild Cognitive Impairment. MCI is a diagnosis made by clinical judgement, usually requiring memory loss and perhaps unexpected decline in other cognitive functions. There is controversy over the status of this diagnosis and of its utility (See the papers collected in Macher 2004). Some claim that the diagnosis can be made with relative certainty, others say that the phenotype is too blurry to be of much clinical or predictive use. Estimates of prevalence in those aged over 65 range from 5.2 per cent to 16.8 per cent (Golomb *et al.*, 2004: 354). Some claim MCI is an early stage of Alzheimer's and will progress to the full disease, others dispute this inevitable progression. Some claim that recent advances in brain imaging enable the visualization of plaques and tangles at an early stage, and hence allow prediction of who among those who meet the behavioural criteria of MCI will progress to Alzheimer's, although the evidence from the Nun Study and elsewhere suggests we should be wary. Some say that the diagnosis enables early treatment, which will slow progression; others doubt that such treatment is available. There is much to be said, here, given the blurry character of Alzheimer's itself, of the apparent capacity of a diagnosis of MCI to shift an individual on to a social and experiential pathway to Alzheimer's. Nonetheless, since the naming of this phenomena in 1988 re-organized a complex and competing field of categories and definitions, citations have increased exponentially – according to the Institute for Scientific Information's Web of Science, there was one article on this topic in 1990, 158 in 2000, and 943 in 2007. But here I can only focus on one issue that relates to my opening question – what is it to be normal?

Of course, there are many reasons for this renewed interest in this condition on the borders of normality: as Golomb *et al.* put it 'this explosion of interest reflects a shift in dementia research away from established disease and toward early diagnosis' (Golomb *et al.*, 2004: 353) linked to the hope of early therapeutic intervention – for who could argue with the view expressed in the introduction to the edition of *Dialogues in Clinical Neurosceince* in which their article appears; 'Earlier is almost always better' (Lebowitz, 2004: 350). The logic of preventive medicine is to aim for early diagnosis – surely it is better to know early and intervene early in disorders such as Alzheimer's. Hence the increasing use of diagnostics in the clinic to identify patients with MCI, and perhaps to treat them with the one drug that is currently suggested to delay the development of Alzheimer's – donepezil, marketed as Aricept – 'Does spending time with your loved one mean everything to you? If your loved one has Alzheimer's, Aricept may help.... Aricept may help your loved one be more like themselves longer.'[17] In the face of the fear of such a devastating condition, and with such a possibility, who could resist this hope?

Now MCI and Alzheimer's are linked together by organizations such as the European Brain Council under the heading of 'brain disorders' – a category that, for them, includes Anxiety disorders, Addictive disorders, Affective disorders, Psychotic disorders, Multiple Sclerosis, Dementia, Parkinson's disease, Migraine and other headaches, Stroke, Epilepsy, Brain trauma and Brain tumour. Their 2004 study on 'The Cost of Brain Disorders' estimated that across 28 European countries (the EU plus Iceland, Norway and Switzerland) with a total population of 466 million, 127 million people or 27 per cent are affected by at least one brain disease and that the total cost of brain disorders amounted to 386 billion Euro, of which the largest cost component was indirect costs totalling 179 billion Euro (47 per cent), with a direct healthcare cost of 135 billion Euro (35 per cent) and a direct non-medical cost of 72 billion Euro (18 per cent).[18] Such figures act as powerful mobilizers of public health agencies, repeating the arguments made by the World Health Organization, epidemiological estimates made in the United States of the prevalence of psychiatric disorders among the general population – not just those in touch with psychiatric services – and those made in Europe by such organizations as the European College of Neuropsychopharmacology (Kessler *et al.*, 2005; Wittchen and Jacobi, 2005; Wittchen *et al.*, 2005; World Health Organization, 2004).

Of course, these numbers don't merely represent – they create realities – they create a world of mental states, of mental normality and abnormality, that is made intelligible, practicable, governable through numbers. We could say a lot about the specific ways in which these numbers were generated, assembled, framed and rendered public, notably about the ways in which diagnostic manuals are transformed into checklists, which invite members of the general population to transform their feelings of malaise into symptoms that then appear as indicators of the presence of undiagnosed disorder. But these numbers, however 'constructed', have consequences and index something about our forms of life. Such numbers mark out what is salient and to who; as in the case of psychiatric diagnoses, they group us into categories and divide us between categories, transform moral and political judgments into impersonal and technical data upon which they confer the moral authority of objectivity. Numbers legitimate, and make demands, and here we can especially see what Anthony Hopwood termed 'the power of the single figure' (Hopwood, 1987). Numbers render a space governable yet contestable – indeed these very numbers open a contest between those who proclaim the challenge of the rising 'burden of mental illness' and those who proclaim the challenge of the 'medicalization of normality' – as in the recent book by Horwitz and Wakefield on the extension of the diagnostic category of depression – entitled *The Loss of Sadness* (Horwitz and Wakefield, 2007).

Nonetheless, these numbers seem to show us the birth of what I have termed elsewhere 'disorders without borders' (Rose, 2006a). And we can find other indicators than these. Take, for example, rising rates of the use of psychiatric drugs – data that I have discussed extensively elsewhere (Rose, 2003; 2004). You will probably not be surprised by the data on the use of stimulant drugs for the treatment of 'Attention Deficit Hyperactivity Disorder' in children; rates of diagnosis in different areas range from around 2 per cent of schoolchildren to around 17 per cent in some states in the USA. And you probably won't be surprised, given all the public debate, at the figures, even in Europe, for the rising use of the selective serotonin reuptake inhibitors – drugs initially marketed for depression, but whose remit has widened to anxiety disorders such as Social Anxiety Disorder and Panic Disorders. But you may be surprised at the rising rates of diagnosis of young children in the United States with bipolar affective disorder. And of course the list could go on.

Sociologists are not short of explanations. Today they seldom cite social causes for the rise of mental ill health diagnoses, as was the case for an older sociological psychiatry. On the contrary, they favour constructionist accounts in terms of medical imperialism, medicalization of social problems, energetic proselytising by parents and support groups, the egregious power of the drug companies with their disease awareness campaigns, the suborning of psychiatric and clinical judgement and so forth. I don't want to evaluate these different accounts here – my purpose is rather different. What I have tried to gesture towards, with these selected data, is the strange fact that in the most wealthy sector of our globe, in the century when more human beings are living longer than ever before, we seem beset by a virtual epidemic of disorders – not just of mind or psyche, but of brain. Madness, we were once told by sociologists, was a residual category, to be deployed when all other accounts of deviant conduct failed (Scheff, 1966). But no longer; it appears that a lifetime without mental disorder, at least in this expanded definition, and now mapped onto the brain, would be somewhat abnormal or, to put it another way, mental abnormality has practically become normalized, simultaneously a condition to be treated and a mode of existence to be expected.

Think back, for a moment, to the message that accompanies these medications – because it's a message to you. It is a certain image of a form of life to which you should aspire, and which the drug will aid you to achieve – you can get your life back, you can become yourself again – you too can say 'I feel like myself again, I feel like me'. Actually, if you Google 'feel like myself again' you will find this phrase repeated over and over, not just in psychiatric drug testimonials, but in websites for drugs to promote female libido, dietary supplements, breast augmentation testimonials, menopause treatments, plastic surgery and much more. Normality has to be worked at, or at least this version of normality as an ideal of autonomous self-fulfilment of the self. In fact most of the quotes come from women, so perhaps this is a specific gendered normality, although the images in the pharmaceutical advertisements are of both sexes and all races and ethnic groups. Here as elsewhere we see the rise of the obligation to manage one's self as a kind of enterprise of itself – a continuous work of modulation of the self in relation to an ideal. The critics are wrong in saying what is promised here is a shallow, illusory happiness in a pill (President's Council on Bioethics (US) and Kass, 2003). The work on the self that is enjoined is multiple: diet, exercise, self-reflection and self monitoring, goal setting and evaluation, not to be displaced by, but to be supported with, the use of medication. And you can see here, I hope, why some of the recent 'neuroethical' discussion of enhancement technologies rather misses the point. For what is involved here cannot be divided according to the binary logic of treatment versus enhancement; it is a constant work of modulation of the self in relation to desired forms of life.

Social norms and vital norms today

Where does all this leave us, in relation to the normal and the pathological, the social and the vital today? I am not sure that I have an answer, or rather I am quite sure that I do not! I have suggested that recent developments in medical genomics lead us into a world where there is no norm, no single standard or reference 'normal' genome, but rather a world of multiple molecular variations of small effect shaping for each individual a specific profile of risks in relation to which prudent life choices are to be made, in the name of the newly empowered autonomy of – and obligations of – the contemporary genomic biological citizen. And I have suggested that, in the new world of molecular neuroscience and psychopharmaceuticals, a perception has taken shape of the burden of mental disorder, as brain disorder, which makes abnormality into a new kind of norm and requires a continual work of the self on the self in order to manage that immanent possibility by the will, by lifestyle, by drugs, in order to achieve an ideal form of life – which is the life of the autonomous self.

I am, however, certain of one thing. The distinction made by Georges Canguilhem, with which I began, is difficult to maintain; the distinction between the vital norms of the body and the disciplinary norms of society. On the one hand, those vital norms, of height, weight, longevity, fertility, obesity etc. are much more historically and socially variable than this formulation suggests. On the other hand, today the norms of the body itself have been opened to re-engineering at the molecular level in the name of a certain kind of freedom. It would be facile to try to judge these changes with a reference to some naturalness that we modern human beings have now lost. We humans have never been natural. So the question that confronts us is perhaps an ethical one. Perhaps we need to ask, not just the question of historical ontology – what kind of human beings have we become – but a question of ethics as *Lebensführung*: 'what kind of creatures do we think we *should* become'?

Notes

1 This paper was written for a keynote lecture entitled The Normal and The Pathological: Managing Bodies and Minds in the Age of Molecular Biomedicine, to be given at the Annual Conference of the British Sociological Association, in March 2008. In the event, it could not be delivered. In revising it for this publication, I have kept to the style of a spoken, speculative talk, rather than a formal paper, and it should be read in that light.

2 Canguilhem originally published an article title 'Le Normal et Le Pathologique' in 1951, and a version of this was included in the original French edition of *La Connaissance de la View*, published in 1965, I have quoted this passage from the translation of this text under the title *Knowledge of Life.*

3 http://www.decodeme.com/ – since the time this paper was written, the costs have reduced and the numbers of risk conditions have increased – both considerably. Further, in November 2009, deCODE, the parent company, ran into severe financial difficulties, but is still Frading.

4 http://www.decodeme.com/ accessed 17 February 2008. Note that the text on the website has been revised several times since that date.

5 http://www.fda.gov/cdrh/oivd/guidance/1549.pdf accessed 18 February 2008.

6 https://www.23andme.com/ accessed 18 February 2008.

7 http://www.navigenics.com/corp/Main/ accessed 18 February 2008.

8 http://www.personalgenomes.org/ accessed 18 February 2008.

9 http://genomeboy.com/ accessed 18 February 2008.

10 http://www.454.com/ accessed 18 February 2008 – the sequencing of James Watson was announced in their press release dated May 31, 2007.

11 http://www.burrillandco.com/pdfs/q4_12_2006.pdf accessed 18 February 2008.

12 In his 1997 book, Pharmacogenetics, Wendell W. Weber quotes from Somerset Maugham's account of his experiences as a young medical student.... 'I have always worked from the living model. I remember that once in the dissecting room when I was going over my "part" with the demonstrator, he asked me what some nerve was and I did not know. He told me; whereupon I remonstrated, for it was in the wrong place. Nevertheless he insisted that it was the nerve I had been looking in vain for. I complained of the abnormality and he, smiling, said that in anatomy it was the normal that was uncommon. I was annoyed at the time, but the remark sank into my mind and since then it has become forced upon me that it was true of man as well as anatomy. The normal is what you find but rarely. The normal is the ideal. It is a picture that one fabricates of the average characteristics of men, and to find them all in a single man is hardly to be expected.' Maugham's observation – that the normal is rare – is at the heart of the challenge and promise of pharmacogenomics' (Wendell W. Weber (1997) Pharmacogenetics, Oxford: Oxford University Press, quoted in Norton, 2001: 180). Thanks to Oonagh Corrigan for this quote.

13 There is actually some disagreement about priority here but this is not pertinent to this paper.

14 http://www.mc.uky.edu/nunnet/ accessed 14 February 2008

15 For a list of publications from the Nun Study, see http://www.healthstudies.umn.edu/nunstudy/scientific.jsp accessed 14 February 2008.

16 Quoted from p. 23 of the MS of 'Seduced by Plaques and Tangles' given by Margaret Lock at the Workshop of the European Neuroscience and Society Network "Our Brains, Our Selves?" held in Harvard in May 2008, for details of the event see www.neurosocieties.eu/pdf/Harvard_2008_Programme.pdf

17 http://www.aricept.com/index.aspx, accessed 14 February 2008.

18 http://www.europeanbraincouncil.org/projects/CDBE.htm accessed 14 February 2008.

References

Beaulieu, A., (2000), 'The space inside the skull: digital representations, brain mapping and cognitive neuroscience in the decade of the brain', PhD. Dissertation, University of Amsterdam.

Callon, M. and Rabeharisoa, V., (2004), 'Gino's lesson on humanity: genetics, mutual entanglement and the sociologist's role', *Economy and society* 33(1): 1–27.

Canguilhem, G., [1951] (1978), *On the normal and the pathological*, Dordrecht: Reidel.

Canguilhem, G., (2009), *Knowledge and Life*, New York: Fordham University Press.

Collins, F. S., Lander, E. S., Rogers, J. and Waterston, R. H., (2004), 'Finishing the euchromatic sequence of the human genome', *Nature* 431(7011): 931–945.

Dumit, J., (2003), *Picturing Personhood: Brain Scans and Biomedical Identity*, Princeton NJ: Princeton University Press.

Editorial, N., (2008), 'Genetics benefits at risk', *Nature* 451(7180): 745–746.

Gilbert, W., (1993), 'A Vision of the Grail', in D. J. Kevles and L. Hood (eds), *The Code of Codes: Scientific and Social Issues in the Human Genome Project*, Cambridge, MA: Harvard University Press.

Golomb, J., Kluger, A. and Ferris, S. H., (2004), 'Mild cognitive impairment: historical development and summary of research', *Dialogues in Clinical Neurosceince: Mild Cognitive Impairment* 6(4): 351–367.

Heath, D., Rapp, R. and Taussig, K. S., (2004), 'Genetic Citizenship', in D. Nugent and J. Vincent (eds), *Companion to the Anthropology of Politics*, Oxford: Blackwell.

Higgins, J. P. T., Little, J., Ioannidis, J. P. A., Bray, M. S., Manolio, T. A., Smeeth, L., Sterne, J. A., Anagnostelis, B., Butterworth, A. S., Danesh, J., Dezateux, C., Gallacher, J. E., Gwinn, M., Lewis, S. J., Minelli, C., Pharoah, P. D., Salanti, G., Sanderson, S., Smith, L. A., Taioli, E., Thompson, J. R., Thompson, S. G., Walker, N., Zimmern, R. L. and Khoury, M. J., (2007), 'Turning the pump handle: Evolving methods for integrating the evidence on gene-disease association', *American Journal of Epidemiology* 166: 863–866.

Hood, L., (1993), 'Biology and Medicine in the Twenty First Century', in D. J. Kevles and L. Hood (eds), *The Code of Codes: Scientific and Social Issues in the Human Genome Project*, Cambridge, MA: Harvard University Press.

Hopwood, A. G., (1987), 'The Archaeology of Accounting Systems', *Accounting Organizations and Society* 12(3): 207–234.

Horwitz, A. V. and Wakefield, J. C., (2007), *The Loss of Sadness*, Oxford: Oxford University Press.

Jacob, F. and Monod, J., (1961), 'Genetic Regulatory Mechanisms in the Synthesis of Proteins', *Journal of Molecular Biology* 3: 318–356.

Kay, L. E., (2000), *Who wrote the book of life?: a history of the genetic code*, Stanford, CA: Stanford University Press.

Keller, E. F., (2000), *The century of the gene*, Cambridge, Mass.: Harvard University Press.

Kessler, R. C., Berglund, P., Demler, O., Jin, R. and Walters, E. E., (2005), 'Lifetime prevalence and age-of-onset distributions of DSM-IV disorders in the national comorbidity survey replication', *Archives Of General Psychiatry* 62(6): 593–602.

Lander, E. S. *et al.*, (2001), 'Initial sequencing and analysis of the human genome', *Nature* 409(6822): 860–921.

Lebowitz, B. D., (ed.), (2004), *Mild Cognitive Impairment*, Vol. 6: 4.

Lock, M., (2007), 'Alzheimer's Disease: A Tangled Concept', in S. McKinnon and S. Silverman (eds), *Complexities: Beyond Nature and Nurture*, New York: Routledge.

Lock, M., (2008), 'Seduced By Plaques and Tangles', Unpublished Paper presented at 'Our Brains, Our Selves?' Workshop, Harvard, May 2008.

Macher, J.-P., (ed.), (2004), *Mild Cognitive Impairment*, Vol. 6: 4.

Manolio, T. A. and Collins, F. S., (2007), 'Genes, environment, health, and disease: Facing up to complexity', *Human Heredity* 63(2): 63–66.

Nelson, C. A., III, Zeanah, C. H., Fox, N. A., Marshall, P. J., Smyke, A. T. and Guthrie, D., (2007), 'Cognitive Recovery in Socially Deprived Young Children: The Bucharest Early Intervention Project', *Science* 318(5858): 1937–1940.

Neumann-Held, E. M. and Rehmann-Sutter, C., (2006), *Genes in development: re-reading the molecular paradigm*: Durham, NC: Duke University Press.

Norton, R. M., (2001), 'Clinical pharmacogenomics: applications in pharmaceutical R&D', *Drug Discovery Today* 6(4): 180–185.

Novas, C., (2006), 'The Political Economy of Hope: Patients' Organizations, Science and Biovalue', *Biosocieties* 1(3): 289–305.

Novas, C. and Rose, N., (2000), 'Genetic risk and the birth of the somatic individual', *Economy and Society* 29(4): 485–513.

Oakley, A., (1991), 'Eugenics, Social Medicine and the Career of Richard Titmuss in Britain 1935–50', *The British Journal of Sociology* 24(2): 165–194.

Osborne, T. and Rose, N., (2008), 'Populating sociology: Carr-Saunders and the problem of population', *The Sociological Review* 56(4): 552–578.

Pearson, T. A. and Manolio, T. A., (2008), 'How to interpret a genome-wide association study', *Jama – Journal of the American Medical Association* 299(11): 1335–1344.

President's Council on Bioethics (U.S.) and Kass, L., (2003), *Beyond therapy : biotechnology and the pursuit of happiness*, 1st Edition, New York: Regan Books.

Rabinow, P., (1999), *French DNA: trouble in purgatory*, Chicago IL: University of Chicago Press.

Rose, N., (2003), 'Neurochemical selves', *Society* 41(1): 46–59.

Rose, N., (2004), 'Becoming neurochemical selves', in N. Stehr (ed.), *Biotechnology, Commerce And Civil Society*, New York: Transaction Press.

Rose, N., (2006a), 'Disorders Without Borders? The Expanding Scope of Psychiatric Practice', *BioSocieties* 1(4): 465–484.

Rose, N., (2006b), *The Politics of Life Itself: Biomedicine, Power and Subjectivity in the Twenty First Century*, Princeton, NJ: Princeton University Press.

Rose, N. and Novas, C., (2005), 'Biological Citizenship', in A. Ong and S. Collier (eds), *Global Assemblages: Technology, Politics and Ethics as Anthropological Problems*, Malden, MA: Blackwell Publishing.

Rosenberg, C., (2003), 'What is disease? In memory of Owsei Temkin', *Bulletin of the History of Medicine* 77: 491–505.

Rosenberg, C., (2006), 'Contested boundaries – psychiatry, disease, and diagnosis', *Perspectives In Biology And Medicine* 49(3): 407–424.

Rosenhan, D. L., (1973), 'On being sane in insane places', *Science* 179: 250–258.

Scheff, T. J., (1966), *Being mentally ill: a sociological theory*, London: Weidenfeld & Nicolson.

Venter, J. C., (2007), *A Life Decoded: My Genome, My Life*, New York: Viking.

Venter, J. C. *et al.*, (2001), 'The sequence of the human genome', *Science* 291(5507): 1304–1351.

Weir, L., (1996), 'Recent developments in the government of pregnancy', *Economy and society* 25(3): 372–392.

Wellcome Trust Case Control Consortium, (2007), 'Genome-wide association study of 14,000 cases of seven common diseases and 3,000 shared controls', *Nature* 447(7145): 661-U7.

Wittchen, H. U. and Jacobi, F., (2005), 'Size and burden of mental disorders in Europe – a critical review and appraisal of 27 studies', *European Neuropsychopharmacology* 15(4): 357–376.

Wittchen, H. U., Jönsson, B. and Olesen, J., (2005), 'Towards a better understanding of the size and burden and cost of brain disorders in Europe', *European Neuropsychopharmacology* 15(4): 355–356.

World Health Organization, (2004), 'Prevention of Mental Disorders. Effective Interventions and Policy Options, Summary Report', Geneva: World Health Organization.

Sociology and climate change

John Urry

Capitalism and contradiction

This chapter examines some major changes relating to the contemporary condi-tions of life upon earth. It deals especially with emergent contradictions that stem from shifts within capitalism over the course of the last century or so. These shifts involve moving from low carbon to high carbon economies/socie-ties, from societies of discipline to societies of control, and more recently from specialized and differentiated zones of consumption to mobile, de-differentiated consumptions of excess. Sociological analysis, I argue, is thus central to examin-ing high carbon societies and climate change.

Marx and Engels wrote of how modern bourgeois society: 'is like the sor-cerer, who is no longer able to control the powers of the nether world whom he has called up by his spells' (Marx and Engels, 1888 [1848]: 58). The sorcerer of contemporary capitalism has generated major emergent contradictions. This paper discusses how capitalism through global climate change is bringing: 'dis-order into the whole of bourgeois society, endanger[ing] the existence of bour-geois property' (Marx and Engels, 1888: 59). In the 21st century capitalism is not able to control those powers that it called up by its mesmeric spells that were set in motion during the unprecedented high carbon 20th century. As Leahy writes: 'capitalism could come to a sticky end... without the supposedly essential ingredient of a revolutionary proletariat. Capitalism as a growth economy is impossible to reconcile with a finite environment' (Leahy, 2008: 481); I am not suggesting that any other modern economic system has a 'better' environmental record.

Economic and social sciences generally presume that systems are naturally in equilibrium and negative feedback mechanisms will restore equilibrium if movement occurs away from such a stable point. This notion of naturally rees-tablishing equilibria can be found in general equilibrium models in economics and in sociological models of structure and agency. However, notions of emer-gent contradiction problematize equilibrium models (Beinhocker, 2006: chs 2, 3). In this chapter, I presume that no distinction should be made between states of equilibrium and states of growth. All systems are dynamic, processual and generate emergent effects and systemic contradictions, especially through positive feedback mechanisms (Beinhocker, 2006: 66–7). In particular the high carbon economy/society of the last century is the emergent contradiction with positive feedbacks that 20th century capitalism unleashed. It was the genie that got let out of the bottle and cannot be 'easily' put back again into that 'bottle'. Capitalism is no longer able to control the exceptional powers which it generated especially through new forms of excessive consumption and which are, it seems, changing climates and eliminating some of the conditions of human life and of its predictable improvement as experienced by a fair proportion of the world's population for much of the last century.

Climate change and peak oil

These arguments about non-equilibrium and contradictions relate to the most significant issue facing contemporary human societies, namely global climate change. Notions of complex systems, feedbacks and nonlinearities are central to the emerging sciences of climate change (Rial *et al.*, 2004; Lovelock, 2006; Pearce, 2007). Rial and his climate change collaborators summarize how the earth's climate system is: 'highly nonlinear: inputs and outputs are not proportional, change is often episodic and abrupt, rather than slow and gradual, and multiple equilibria are the norm' (Rial *et al.*, 2004: 11). We will see how these features are central to the analysis of climate change.

Global temperatures have risen over the past century by at least 0.74°C and this appears to be the consequence in part of higher levels of greenhouse gases in the earth's atmosphere. Greenhouse gases trap the sun's rays. As a result of this 'greenhouse' effect the earth warms. Such greenhouse gas levels and world temperatures will increase significantly over the next few decades. Such warming will change patterns of temperatures, rainfall, crops, animals and life worldwide. Climate change, which may well be rapid and abrupt, constitutes the major threat to human life and patterns of economic and social organization. Even the Pentagon has announced that climate change will result in a global catastrophe costing millions of lives in wars and natural disasters. Its threat to global stability is, they estimate, far greater than that of terrorism (see Abbott, Rogers and Sloboda, 2007).

The scientific evidence for climate change is less uncertain than when the first Intergovernmental Panel on Climate Change (IPCC) Report appeared in 1990. The organized actions of many scientists around the globe have come to transform public debate; and this 'power of science' is probably unique in the case of mobilizing actions and events around the perceived and looming crisis of global climate change, according to Stehr (2001). And the climate change orthodoxy has now largely marginalized the 'climate change deniers'; with 2005 marking the year when the climate change debate tipped according to Lever-Tracy (2008: 448–50). Social science research has revealed the complex and 'interested' funding that has supported much of the research that denies the thesis of climate change (McCright and Dunlap, 2000). However, none of this is to suggest that there is anything but immense uncertainty with regard to the sciences of climate change and especially of the models that are deployed to predict rates of greenhouse gases or of temperature increases.

Nevertheless, by the time of the 2007 Report the IPCC was able to declare that the warming of the world's climate is now 'unequivocal' (IPPC, 2007). This is based upon extensive observations of increases in global average air and ocean temperatures, of widespread melting of snow and ice and of rising global average sea levels. The Report further shows that carbon dioxide is the most important of the human-produced or anthropogenic greenhouse gases. Its concentration levels exceed by far the natural range identified over the past 650,000 years. Its high and rising levels must thus stem from 'non-natural' causes. Moreover, there is very high confidence amongst the thousands of IPCC scientists that global warming is at least in part the effect of human activities which have resulted in dramatically raised levels of carbon emissions. And there are many elements of global warming: increase in arctic temperatures, reduced size of icebergs, melting of icecaps and glaciers, reduced permafrost, changes in rainfall, reduced bio-diversity, new wind patterns, droughts, heat waves, tropical cyclones and other extreme weather events (for recent popular science accounts, see Lovelock, 2006; Kolbert, 2007; Linden, 2007; Lynas, 2007; Pearce, 2007; Monbiot, 2006).

Moreover, the IPCC Reports are based on reaching a complex scientific and political consensus and as a consequence do not factor in all the potential and more uncertain feedback effects. World temperatures will increase significantly over the next few decades and these increases will almost certainly trigger *further* temperature rises as the earth's environmental systems are unable to absorb the original increases. Monbiot states that climate change begets climate change (Monbiot, 2007). Notions of complex systems, feedbacks and nonlinearities are central to the multiple processes involved in changing climates (Rial *et al.*, 2004; Lovelock, 2006; Pearce, 2007). The most dramatic of these positive feedbacks would involve the whole or partial melting of Greenland's ice cap, which would change sea and land temperatures worldwide, including the possible turning off or modification of the Gulf Stream. Another potentially significant feedback involves how climate change has led to the first recorded melting of the Siberian permafrost with the potential subsequent release of billions of tons of methane (http://www.guardian.co.uk/environment/2005/aug/11/science.climatechange1). Thus various diverse yet interconnected changes within the earth's environmental systems could create a vicious circle of accumulative disruption occurring, as Pearce expresses it, 'with speed and violence' (Pearce, 2007). Overall Lovelock argues that 'there is no large negative feedback that would countervail temperature rise' (Lovelock, 2006: 35).

Moreover, the study of ice cores shows that in previous glacial and interglacial periods abrupt and rapid changes occurred in the earth's temperature. Earth, according to Pearce, does not engage in gradual change (Pearce, 2007: 21). Rapid changes have been the norm, not the exception. Moreover, temperatures at the time of the last Ice Age were only 5°C colder than they are now.

And in the Arctic increases in temperature have been really marked, with feed-backs creating local warming of 3–5°C over just the past thirty years.

With 'business as usual' and no significant reductions in high carbon systems, the stock of greenhouse gases could treble by the end of the century. The Stern Review states that there is a 50 per cent risk of more than a 5°C increase in temperatures by 2100 and this would transform the world's physical and human geography through a 5–20 per cent reduction in world consumption levels (Stern, 2007: 3). Even a temperature increase worldwide of 3°C is completely beyond any recent experience and would transform human and animal life as it has been known (see the various scenarios in Lynas, 2007).

Thus the overall consequences of such unique changes are global and, if they are not significantly reduced, will very substantially reduce the standard of living, the capabilities of life around the world, and the overall population, as catastrophic impacts begin, starting off in the 'poor' south (see Roberts and Parks, 2007). The World Health Organization calculated as early as 2000 that over 150,000 deaths are caused each year by climate change, such changes being global, cross-generational and highly unequal around the world. The planet will endure but many forms of human habitation will not. Climate change is more-over increasingly intersecting with a global energy crisis since oil (and gas) supplies around the world are simultaneously starting to run down.

Today's global economy is deeply dependent upon, and embedded into, abundant cheap oil. Most industrial, agricultural, commercial, domestic, and consumer systems are built around the plentiful supply of 'black gold' (and gas; see Darley, 2004, on *High Noon for Natural Gas*). Peak oil production occurred in the USA as far back as 1971 and oil production worldwide has probably peaked because of the failure to discover new fields at the same rate during most of the 20th century (Heinberg, 2005; Rifkin, 2002: ch. 2; but see Jackson, 2006). Energy is increasingly expensive and there will be frequent shortages especially with the world's population continuing to increase in size, in its profligate con-sumption of oil and in its urbanization. There is not enough oil and this will generate significant economic downturns, more resource wars and probably lower population levels. Rifkin claims that the oil age is: 'winding down as fast as it revved up' (Rifkin, 2002: 174). The delivery of fresh water also depends upon fossil fuels while severe water shortages face one third of the world's population (Laszlo, 2006: 28–9).

Rifkin goes on to argue: 'Like Rome, the industrial nations have now created a vast and complex technological and institutional infrastructure to sequester and harness energy' (Rifkin, 2002: 62). This infrastructure was a 20th century phenomenon with especially the US as *the* disproportionately high energy pro-ducing and consuming society. Its economy and society were based upon the combination of automobility *and* electricity. While it possesses 5 per cent of the world's population it consumes a quarter of the world's energy and produces almost a quarter of global carbon emissions (Nye, 1999: 6). Kunstler considers the systems effects of the peaking:

At peak and just beyond, there is massive potential for system failures of all kinds, social, economic, and political. Peak is quite literally a tipping point. Beyond peak, things unravel and the center does not hold. Beyond peak, all bets are off about civilization's future (Kunstler, 2006: 65).

Leggett describes the 'Empire of Oil' as being 'without doubt the most powerful interest group on the planet', much more powerful than most nation-states (Leggett, 2005: 12, 15). Hence 'The Great Addiction' [to oil] remained with oil becoming vital to virtually everything that is done on the planet. And these vested interests have misrepresented the size of their reserves, suggesting that the peaking of global oil is much further away in time. Moreover, American and European foreign policies are significantly driven by global oil interests. In the USA the desire to increase access to oil sources from outside the USA, since its decline in oil production commenced from around 1970, is the context for its attempted subjugation of Middle Eastern oil interests in the name of the 'freedom' of citizens to drive and to heat/air-condition their homes.

Adding to increasing temperatures and reduced oil is the growth in the world's population by about 900 million people per decade, the largest absolute increase in human history (Gallopin, Raskin and Swart, 1997). By the end of the 20th century the world population passed 6 billion and is expected to reach 9.1 billion by 2050 if the effects of global heating, the peaking of oil, wars or global epidemics do not intervene. And according to estimates, the world went urban on May 23rd 2007, this being 'transition day' when the world's urban population exceeded the rural for the first time (http://news.ncsu.edu/releases/2007/may/104.html. accessed 28.05.08).

The following are some of the dramatic consequences of these interdependent developments (see Dennis and Urry, 2008, for further detail): increases in the number and scale of 'failed states' (and failed 'city states' such as New Orleans in late 2005); rising sea levels involving the flooding of roads, railways, transit systems, and airport runways in coastal areas especially through surges brought on by more intense storms; growing insecurities in the supply of clean water, since it is calculated that a temperature increase of 2.1 degrees would expose up to a staggering figure of 3 billion people to water shortages; increasingly significant problems of food security, large protest marches and flooding, desertification and generally rising grain costs. These consequences are far worse in the poor south since there is here a shocking 'climate of injustice' (Roberts and Parks, 2007).

High mobility systems

How then did the genie of climate change get let out of the bottle? It is a problem of the 20th century, when powerful high carbon path dependent systems were set in place, locked in through various economic and social institutions. And as the century unfolded those lock-ins meant that the world was left a high and growing carbon legacy. Electricity, the steel-and-petroleum car, and suburban living and associated consumption are three of those locked-in legacies. The 20th century is reaping its revenge upon the 21st century and massively limiting the choices and opportunities available within the new century. And to slow down, let alone reverse, increasing carbon emissions and temperatures requires the reorganization of social life, nothing more and nothing less. The nature of 'social life' is central to the causes, the consequences and the possible 'mitigations' involved in global heating. Yet nowhere in the major analyses of climate change are there good sociological analyses of how to bring about transformed low carbon human activities that could get locked-in and move most societies into a different path-dependent pattern (see Lever-Tacey, 2008; Urry, 2008, on sociology's neglect of such issues).

Indeed, most analyses of climate change are written by scientists either for other scientists or for governments. They are uninformed by social science although Rial and his co-authors do emphasize the need for researchers to build bridges across artificial disciplinary boundaries (Rial *et al.*, 2004: 33). This neglect of social science is true even of the very significant Stern Review which, written by an economist, does not develop analysis of how human practices are organized over time and space and how they might be significantly transformed. Changing human activities is mostly seen as a matter of modifying economic incentives for individuals through varying tax rates (Stern, 2007: Part IV).

Around the world, though, there are various organizations and states that are making it clear that there is a limited window of opportunity within which climate change could be slowed down. James Hansen, Bush's main climate change adviser, is very clear: 'We are on the precipice of climate change tipping points beyond which there is no redemption' (quoted in Pearce, 2007: xxiv). After that window of opportunity the various 'human activities' that are generating increased carbon emissions will make further warming of the planet inevitable *and* probably catastrophic. This is what Lovelock terms the revenge of Gaia that produces 'global heating' (Lovelock, 2006). Climate change is thus the outcome of enormously powerful systems that are rather like a 'juggernaut' careering at full pace to the edge of the cliff (see Giddens, 1990). And slowing down the juggernaut even slightly requires the engendering of equally if not more powerful systems than those which are currently powering it towards this fast approaching abyss. In this paper I specifically focus upon high carbon mobility systems (see Urry, 2008, on the specific implications for car systems).

While in 1800 people in the US travelled 50 metres a day, they now travel 50 kilometres a day (Buchanan, 2002: 121). Today world citizens move 23 billion kilometres; by 2050 it is predicted this will increase fourfold to 106 billion (Schafer and Victor, 2000: 171). Carbon use within transport accounts for 14 per cent of total greenhouse emissions and is the second fastest growing source of such emissions. What has happened are the development of social practices which presuppose huge increases in the speed of travel (by humans) and in the distances covered (by both goods and humans).

Forms of life we might say are now 'mobilized'. The growth of new kinds of long distance leisure, the establishment of globally significant themed environments, the growing significance of car and lorry transport within China and India, the rapid growth of cheap air travel, and the increased 'miles' flown and travelled by the world's 90,000 ships by manufactured goods, foodstuffs and friends all index such mobilized forms of life (see Larsen, Urry and Axhausen, 2006, on 'friendship' miles).

Central to global heating has been the reconfiguring of economy and society around 'mobilities'. There is an emergent 'mobility complex', a new system of economy, society and resources that has been spreading around the globe (see Urry, 2007, for more detail). Large scale mobilities are not new but what is new is the development of this 'mobility complex'. This involves a number of interdependent components that in their totality remake consumption, pleasure, work, friendship and family life. These components are:

- the contemporary scale of movement around the world
- the diversity of mobility systems now in play
- the especial significance of the self-expanding automobility system and its risks
- the elaborate interconnections of physical movement and communications
- the development of mobility domains that by-pass national societies
- the significance of movement to contemporary governmentality
- the development of places of excess that mostly have to be travelled to
- the development of a language of mobility, the capacity to compare and to contrast places from around the world
- an increased importance of multiple mobilities for people's social and emotional lives

Bauman argues that as a consequence of this complex: 'Mobility climbs to the rank of the uppermost among the coveted values – and the freedom to move, perpetually a scarce and unequally distributed commodity, fast becomes the main stratifying factor of our late-modern or postmodern times' (Bauman, 1998: 2). In particular consumption in the 'rich north' towards the end of the 20th century *escapes* from specific sites, as populations are mobile, moving in, across and beyond 'territories'. And as people move around and develop personalized life projects through being freed from certain structures, so they extend and elaborate their consumption patterns *and* their social networks. Many are less determined by site-specific structures, of class, family, age, career and especially neighbourhoods, as Giddens (1994) and Beck (1999) both argue. The site-specific disciplining of consumption becomes less marked. At least for the rich third of the world, partners, family and friends are a matter of choice, increasingly spreading themselves around the world. There is a 'supermarket' of friends and acquaintances, and they depend upon an extensive array of interdependent systems of movement in order to connect with this distributed array of networks by meeting up from time to time within distinct places (Larsen, Urry and Axhausen, 2006).

Paralleling this is the way that touring the world is how the world is increasingly performed, with many people being connoisseurs and collectors of places.

This connoisseurship and hence the further amplification of mobility applies to very many places, such as good beaches, clubs, views, walks, mountains, unique history, surf, music scene, historic remains, sources of good jobs, food, landmark buildings, gay scene, party atmosphere, universities and so on.

Contemporary capitalism presupposes and generates some increasingly expressive bodies or habituses relatively detached from propinquitous family and neighbourhoods. They are emotional, pleasure-seeking and novelty-acquiring. Such bodies are on the move, able to buy and indulge new experiences located in new places and with new people. This develops the 'experience economy' (Pine and Gilmore, 1999). So, as people escape the disciplinary confines of family and local community based on slow modes of travel, they then encounter a huge array of companies that comprise the experience economy. Capitalist societies involve new forms of pleasure, with many elements or aspects of the body being commodified (for those that can afford it). Expressive capitalism develops into a mobile and mobilizing capitalism with transformed, and on occasions, overindulged bodily habituses while, at the same time, many other people are employed in 'servicing' such habituses, often also on the move (see Lash and Urry, 1994, for early formulations of this mutual dependence). There are many ways in which the body is commodified in and through it moving about and being moved about, through what might be described in the late 20th century as 'binge mobility'.

Excess capitalism

What we might say then is that late 20th century capitalism generated 'excess capitalism' and this significantly contributes to the high carbon consumption of the 'rich north' at the end of the 20th century and at the beginning of the 21st.

This shift in consumption processes can be examined by reference to the changing places of leisure. The early development of seaside resorts in northern Europe provided original places of pleasure (see Walton, 2007, on 'riding on rainbows' at Blackpool). These places of working-class mass pleasure were premised upon a number of strong and marked contrasts, between work and leisure, home and away, workspace and leisure space, and ordinary time and holiday time. Pleasure derived from these contrasts, to be away for a week from domestic and industrial routines and places. Such places of leisure and pleasure provided a chance to 'let your hair down' for a week in a site of carnival before returning to normal (Shields, 1991). And that pleasure was highly regulated through the co-presence of one's family and to some degree one's neighbourhood, who also travelled at the same time to the very same place. Leisure, we might say, was neighbourhood-based even where the neighbourhood is temporarily on the move.

This, I want to suggest, was 'disciplined' pleasure with conspicuous consumption specific to individuals. Discipline came to be realized within specific *sites of confinement* such as the family, local community, school, prison, asylum, factory, clinic and so on (Foucault, 1976, 1991; Goffman, 1968; Lacy, 2005). Individuals moved from one such site to another, each possessing its own laws, procedures and mode of regulation. Surveillance was based upon fairly direct co-presence within that specific locus of power. The panopticon was 'local' and more or less directly visual. Power was internalized, face-to-face and localized within that site. And consumption was specific and regulated through each site, including the family and the 'neighbourhood'. It was based upon slow modes of travel (except for the occasional annual break to Blackpool and other places of temporary pleasure). These disciplinary societies with their high levels of spatial and functional differentiation reached their peak in mid-20th century Europe and North America.

But over the 20th century another system of power emerges, what Deleuze terms *societies of control*. Here power is fluid, de-centred and less site specific (Deleuze, 1995). The sites of disciplinary confinement become less physically marked. Critiques of the effects of 'institutionalization' lead to the closure of former places of confinement. Treatment and correction increasingly take place within the 'community' but a community involving fast modes of travel and not neighbourhood based. Surveillance is less face-to-face. Many sets of social relations are not spatially internalized within specific sites. Gender relations are less confined to the family, work is both globalized and in part carried out in the home, schooling partly occurs within the media and so on. States increasingly involves complex control systems of recording, measuring and assessing populations that are intermittently on the move, beginning with the system of the passport (Torpey, 2000) and now involving a 'digital order' able to track and trace *individuals* as they move about searching new places of excess.

And this undermining of neighbourhoods was given a hugely enhanced emphasis with the development of 'neo-liberalism' as the predominant form of economic and social restructuring over the past twenty to thirty years. This globalizing doctrine spread out from its birthplace in the Economics Department at the University of Chicago through the extraordinary influence of the 'Chicago boys' (Harvey, 2005a, 2005b; Klein, 2007). By 1999 Chicago School alumni included 25 Government Ministers and more than a dozen central bank presidents (Klein, 2007: 166).

Neo-liberalism asserts the power and importance of private entrepreneurship, private property rights, the freeing of markets and the freeing of trade. It involves deregulating such private activities and companies, the privatization of previously 'state' or 'collective' services, the undermining of the collective powers of workers and providing the conditions for the private sector to find ever-new sources of profitable activity. Neo-liberalism seeks to minimize the role of the state, both because it is presumed that states will always be inferior to markets in 'guessing' what is necessary to do and because states are thought to be easily corruptible by private interest groups. It is presumed that the market is 'natural' and will move to equilibrium if only unnatural forces or elements do not get in the way, especially through countless 'gambles' being freely made on alternative futures (Sheller, 2008a: 108).

States, however, are often crucial to eliminating these 'unnatural' forces, to destroying many pre-existing sets of rules, regulations and forms of life that are seen as slowing down economic growth and constraining the private sector. And sometimes that destruction is exercised through violence and attacks upon democratic procedures, as with Augusto Pinochet's first neo-liberal experiment in Chile in 1973. Neo-liberalism elevates market exchanges over and above all other sets of connections between people. It believes that the 'market' is the source of value and virtue. Any deficiencies in the market are the result of imperfections of that market.

And on many occasions the freedom of the market is brought about by the state that is used to wipe the slate clean and to impose sweeping free-market solutions. These have been found from 1973 onwards across most of the world. The state is central to what Klein terms the rise of 'disaster capitalism' (Klein, 2007). Harvey describes neo-liberal processes as involving 'accumulation by dispossession' (2005b: ch. 4). Peasants are thrown off their land, collective property rights are made private, indigenous rights are stolen and turned into private opportunities, rents are extracted from patents, general knowledge is turned into intellectual 'property', there is biopiracy, the state forces itself to hive off its own collective activities, trade unions are smashed and financial instruments and flows redistribute income and rights away from productive activities.

This neo-liberalism has become the dominant global orthodoxy. It is articulated and acted upon within most corporations, many universities, most state bodies and especially international organizations such as the World Trade Organization, World Bank and the International Monetary Fund. Harvey summarizes how neo-liberalism is: 'incorporated into the common-sense way many of us interpret, live in, and understand the world' (Harvey, 2005a: 3).

And one output of neo-liberalism over the past two to three decades has been to generate capitalist places of consumption excess. These often involve 'dispossessions', of workers' rights, of peasant land-holdings, of the state's role in leisure, of neighbourhood organizations, and of customary rights. Each such place or zone of excess is characterized by a sub-set of the following characteristics: travel to distinct zones is often made possible by large infrastructural projects; there are gates controlling entry and exit; they are highly commercialized with many simulated environments; there is only pleasure, no guilt; norms of behaviour are unregulated by family or neighbourhood; there are liminal modes of consumption; bodies are subject to commodification; there is digital control; these sites are increasingly globally known for their consumption and pleasure excess; and they are sites of potential mass addiction. Davis and Monk refer to these places of consumption excess as 'evil paradises' citing many examples around the world (Davis and Monk, 2007).

Giddens analyses such development as the outcome of increased 'freedom' (Giddens, 2007). People are forced from site-specific forms of surveillance to more varied forms of activity, often distant from neighbourhood and being the product of movement. And part of that is the freedom to become 'addicted', to be emotionally and/or physically dependent upon excessive consumption of certain products and services of global capitalism, legal, illegal or semi-legal. Places of excess that get travelled to are places of potentially significant addiction. Giddens suggests that compulsive behaviour is common in modern society because it is:

> linked to lifestyle choice. We are freer now than 40 years ago to decide how to live our lives. Greater autonomy means the chance of more freedom. The other side of that freedom, however, is the risk of addiction. The rise of eating disorders coincided with the advent of supermarket development in the 1960s. Food became available without regard to season and in great variety, even to those with few resources (http:// www.guardian.co.uk/comment/story/0,,2191886,00.html; accessed 22.11.07).

Mobilities, we thus might say, are all about choice, of food, products, places, services, friends, family, gambling and addictions.

Dubai is the current iconic place of such excess, as it has moved from being a major producer of oil to the major site of excess consumption including the oil to get people there and to fuel the sites of consumption excess (see the YouTube video on *Do Buy*). It is said to be the world's largest building site with dozens of megaprojects including the palm islands, the 'island world', the world's only 7 star hotel, a domed ski resort, the world's tallest building (Burj Dubai) and carnivorous dinosaurs (Davis and Monk, 2007). This is a place of monumental excess where the goal is to be number 1 in the world. If Dubai is to be the luxury-consumer paradise of the Middle East and South Asia: 'it must ceaselessly strive for visual and environmental excess' (Davis and Monk, 2007: 52). And it achieves this through architectural gigantism and perfectibility with simulacra more perfect than the original. Dubai might be described as a vast gated community of excess with state and private enterprises being virtually indistinguishable (Davis and Monk, 2007: 61). This is a place of vice, of over-consumption, prostitution, drink and gambling where guilt in a nominally Islamic country is confined to the idea of not consuming to the 'limit'. This is all made possible by migrant contract labourers from Pakistan and India who are bound to a single employer and subject to totalitarian control. Indeed labour relations in such places are excessively exploitative although this is carried to the extreme in Dubai where almost all labour is imported and passports are removed from migrants on entry (Davis and Monk, 2007: 64–6). This is truly accumulation through dispossession, as Harvey would say (Harvey, 2005b).

There are many other examples of such neo-liberal exemplars of excess (see Gottdiener, 2000; Davis and Monk, 2007; Cronin and Hetherington, 2008). Sheller describes such processes within the Caribbean, one of the original places of paradise. Here the 'all-inclusive resort' carves out spaces for liminal consumption largely cut off from the surrounding territory and from local people, apart from those providing 'excess services'. Gated and often fortified they secure temporary consumption of excess away from the prying eyes of both locals and those back at home. Indeed on occasions whole islands are gated and provide secure sites for consumption. Crucial also to much Caribbean tourism are huge cruise ships, which are floating gated communities again organized around consuming to excess. The largest cruise ship in the history of the world has recently been launched by Royal Caribbean Cruise Lines. It includes 1815 guest staterooms, the first-ever surf park at sea, cantilevered whirlpools extending 12 feet beyond the sides of the ship, a waterpark complete with interactive sculpture fountains, geysers and a waterfall, a rock-climbing wall and the Royal Promenade with various shops and cafés, all located in the middle of the ocean (www.royalcaribbean.com. accessed 29.5.08; Sheller, 2008b).

More generally, Sheller argues that such developments are paradigmatic of recent trends, effects of neo-liberal developments of migration and return visits, resort development and new forms of select tourism and the splintering of public infrastructures. She particularly investigates one planned development involving 'starchitect' Zaha Hadid on the island Dellis Cay in the Caribbean. This is aimed, we might say, at the 'private jet-set', those who accumulate houses and servants as others accumulate cars. Sheller summarizes how: 'entire Caribbean islands are being curated into exclusive resorts for the super-rich, and removed from the control and governance of local communities and...their governments' (Sheller, 2008b). She also describes how 21st century Atlantic City is a temple of gambling, greed and a neo-liberal 'casino capitalism' (Sheller, 2008a). And these dreamworlds especially for the celebrity super-rich provide models, through multiple media, that enflame the desires for similar kinds of experience from much of the rest of the world's population. As Davis and Monk argue:

> On a planet where more than 2 billion people subsist on two dollars or less a day, these dreamworlds enflame desires – for infinite consumption, total social exclusion and physical security, and architectural monumentality – that are clearly incompatible with the ecological and moral survival of humanity (Davis and Monk, 2007: xv).

So far, excess has been used in this analysis to capture a series of shifts: from low carbon to high carbon economies/societies; from societies of discipline to societies of control, and from specialized and differentiated zones of consumption to mobile, de-differentiated consumptions of excessive, wasteful consumption.

Two theoretical notions can develop the argument here. First, Veblen famously analysed various aspects of wasteful consumption (Veblen, 1912: 85, 96). The possession of wealth is shown by the waste of time, effort and goods. In order to be conspicuous it must be wasteful. He applies this notion to the consumption practices of individuals. But what has happened in the neo-liberal phase of capitalism has been to transform whole cities, regions or islands economies/ societies into centres of 'wasteful' production and consumption (Macau, Dubai or Las Vegas). Much of capitalist production in the neo-liberal era takes place without regard to need or public good. So the scale and impact of 'waste' production has moved upwards, especially with much of this economy of waste focusing upon gambles on the future, whether on the casino table or global commodities or junk bonds or mortgages. It is also we might say a kind of casual production and consumption as places come and go, being produced and then used up (as Sheller, 2008a, shows in the case of Atlantic City). And one consequence of such waste is to generate climate change, which is, according to Stern: 'the greatest and widest-ranging market failure' (Stern, 2006: i).

But second, these excesses can be understood in relationship to Bataille's notion of the 'excess energy' that cannot be deployed for a system's growth but which nevertheless has to be used up (Bataille, 1991: 20). This he refers to as the 'accursed share', the surplus energy that a system must expend through luxury goods and wasteful consumption. It is from the viewpoint of general economy functionally necessary (Sheller, 2008a: 110). But from the overall relationship with its environment it is waste and excess that is generated. In the neo-liberal period, these systems of excess production and consumption have become dominant as societies of discipline morph into societies of control, and specialized and differentiated zones of consumption morph into mobile, de-differentiated consumptions of excess. As Sheller writes: 'Atlantic City is not alone in spawning a virulent form of casino capitalism and real-estate speculation; it is just one example of a wider global trend in economies of excess, spectacle, and speculation' (Sheller, 2008a: 123).

Futures

Thus economies and societies of such an accursed share, of excess, have moved 'the world' in seemingly inexorable fashion towards more extensive carbon consumption and into possibly irreversible climate change. The adaptive and evolving relationships between enormously powerful systems, especially those of a de-regulated economy and excessive forms of consumption are careering at full pace to the edge of the abyss.

So if global heating continues to escalate through positive feedback loops then one scenario for the middle of this century is what I term 'regional warlordism' (derived from the UK Government's Foresight Programme scenario building 2006; Urry, 2007: ch. 13). This involves the substantial breakdown of many mobility, energy and communication connections currently straddling the world. There would be a plummeting standard of living, a relocalization of mobility patterns, an increasing emphasis upon local warlords controlling recycled forms of mobility and weaponry, and relatively weak imperial or national forms of governance. There would be increasing separation between different regions, or 'tribes'. The first places to be washed away would be paradise beaches, islands and other coastal settlements of excess (see Amelung, Nicholls and Viner, 2007, on the implications of global climate change for tourism flows). September 2005 New Orleans shows what this scenario would be like for a major city in the rich but unequal 'north' (see Hannam, Sheller and Urry, 2006; Giddens, 2007: 156–7). Systems of repair would dissolve with localized recycling of bikes, cars, trucks, computer and phone systems. Only the super-rich would travel far and they would do so in the air within armed helicopters or light aircraft, with very occasional tourist-type space trips to escape the hell on earth with space as the new place of excess (see http://www.economist.com/display-story.cfm?story_id=3500237 accessed 19.12.06; see Cwerner, 2006). Those who could find security in gated and armed encampments would do so, with the neo-liberal privatizing of collective functions and the further gating of zones of excess pleasure.

Elsewhere I suggest two other future scenarios, local sustainability and a digital panopticon (Dennis and Urry, 2008). The likely outcomes are increasingly constrained by adaptive and co-evolving systems and emergent contradictions that the world has inherited from the 20th century. And in a recent study Diamond notes how environmental problems have in the past produced the 'collapse' of societies (Diamond, 2005). And he suggests that human-caused climate change, the build-up of toxic chemicals in the environment and energy shortages will produce abrupt, potentially catastrophic effects in the 21st century. Increased urbanization, growing resource depletion, population expansion, and accelerated climate change constrain the possibilities of reengineering future mobilities and energy uses so as to avoid such 'societal collapse'. But it may already be too late because of those high carbon societies of the 20th century and their enduring path dependent impacts. Leahy maintains, after reviewing potential energy sources available in the 21st century, that there: 'is no way forward without a drastic reduction in consumption and production. As far as energy is concerned, the reduction has to be maintained indefinitely.' (Leahy, 2008: 480).

20th century capitalism generated the most striking of contradictions. Its pervasive, mobile and promiscuous commodification involved utterly unprecedented levels of energy production and consumption, a high carbon society whose dark legacy we are beginning to reap. This contradiction could result in a widespread reversal of many of the systems that constitute capitalism as it turns into its own gravedigger. As Davis and Monk apocalyptically argue: 'the indoor ski slopes of Dubai and private bison herds of Ted Turner represent the ruse of reason by which the neoliberal order both acknowledges and dismisses the fact that the current trajectory of human existence is unsustainable' (Davis and Monk, 2007: xvi). Excess pleasure would seem to be breeding an exceptional excess of disaster; this is another illustration of Al Gore's 'Inconvenient Truth'. In the 21st century capitalism is not able to control those powers that it called up by its spells set in motion during the unprecedented high carbon 20th century, which reached its peak of global wastefulness within the neo-liberal period.

Specifically with regard to mobilities, there will not be an end to movement. But there may be much less movement chosen for connoisseurship and to establish co-presence, and much more to escape heat, flooding, drought and extreme weather events. Climate change will, it seems, generate tens of millions of 'environmental refugees' sweeping around the world and scratching to get inside one or other set of gates before they get shut for good. The sorcerer has indeed conjured up some spectacular spells for 21st century magicians to deal with. And sociology needs to be in those debates and analyses and not, as at present, playing a minor fiddle to the physical sciences and even to economics. Life on the planet needs us even if we have been very slow in knocking on the door.

References

Abbott, C., Rogers, P. and Sloboda, J., (2007), *Beyond Terror. The truth about the real threats to our world*, London: Rider.
Amelung, B., Nicholls, S. and Viner, D., (2007), 'Implications of global climate change for tourism flows and seasonality', *Journal of Travel Research*, 45: 285–96.
Bataille, G., (1991), *The Accursed Share, Volume 1*, New York: Zone.
Bauman, Z., (1998), *Globalization: The Human Consequences*, Cambridge: Polity Press.
Beck, U., (1999), *Individualization*, London: Sage.
Beinhocker, E., (2006), *The Origin of Wealth*, London: Random House.
Buchanan, M., (2002), *Nexus: Small Worlds and the Groundbreaking Science of Networks*, London: W.W. Norton.
Cronin, A. and Hetherington, K., (eds), (2008), *Consuming the Entrepreneurial City*, London: Routledge.
Cwerner, A., (2006), 'Vertical flight and urban mobilities: the promise and reality of helicopter travel', *Mobilities*, 1: 191–216.
Darley, J., (2004), *High Noon for Natural Gas*, Vermont: Chelsea Green.
Davis, M., (2007), 'Sand, Fear, and Money in Dubai', in M. Davis and D. Monk (eds), *Evil Paradises. Dreamworlds of Neoliberalism*, New York: The New Press.
Davis, M. and Monk, D., (eds), (2007), *Evil Paradises. Dreamworlds of Neoliberalism*, New York: The New Press.
Deleuze, G., (1995), 'Postscript on control societies', in G. Deleuze (ed), *Negotiations, 1972–1990*, New York: Columbia University Press.
Dennis, K. and Urry, J., (2008), *After the Car*, Cambridge: Polity.
Diamond, J., (2005), *Collapse: how societies choose to fail or survive*, London: Allen Lane.
Foresight, (2006), *Intelligent Information Futures. Project Overview*, London: Dept for Trade and Industry.
Foucault, M., (1976), *The Birth of the Clinic*, London: Tavistock.
Foucault, M., (1991), 'Governmentality', in G. Burchell, C. Gordon and P. Miller (eds), *The Foucault Effect. Studies in Governmentality*, London: Harvester Wheatsheaf.
Gallopin, G., Raskin, P. and Swart, R., (1997), *Branch Points: Global Scenarios and Human Choice*, Stockholm: Stockholm Environment Institute – Global Scenario Group, pp. 1–47.
Giddens, A., (1990), *The Consequences of Modernity*, Cambridge: Polity.
Giddens, A., (1994), 'Living in a Post-Traditional Society', in B. Beck, A. Giddens and S. Lash (eds), *Reflexive Modernization: politics, tradition and aesthetics in the modern social order*, Cambridge: Polity.
Giddens, A., (2007), *Europe in the Global Era*, Cambridge: Polity.
Goffman, E., (1968), *Asylums*, London: Penguin.
Gottdiener, M., (ed.), (2000), *New Forms of Consumption*, Maryland: Bowman and Littlefield.
Hannam, K., Sheller, M. and Urry, J., (2006), 'Editorial: Mobilities, Immobilities and Moorings', *Mobilities*, 1: 1–22.
Harvey, D., (2005a), *A Brief History of Neo-Liberalism*, Oxford: Oxford University Press.
Harvey, D., (2005b), *The New Imperialism*, Oxford: Oxford University Press.
Heinberg, R., (2005), *The Party's Over: Oil, War and the Fate of Industrial Society*, New York: Clearview Books.
IPCC, (2007), http://www.ipcc.ch/ (accessed 2.6.08).

Jackson, P., (2006), *Why the Peak Oil Theory Falls Down: Myths, Legends, and the Future of Oil Resources, http://www.cera.com/aspx/cda/public1/news/pressReleases/pressReleaseDetails. aspx?CID=8444* (accessed 21.11.06)

Klein, N., (2007), *The Shock Doctrine*, London: Penguin Allen Lane.

Kolbert, E., (2007), *Field Notes from a Catastrophe. A Frontline Report on Climate Change*, London: Bloomsbury.

Kunstler, J. H., (2006), *The Long Emergency: Surviving the Converging Catastrophes of the 21st Century*, London: Atlantic Books.

Lacy, M., (2005), *Security and Climate Change*, London: Routledge.

Larsen, J., Urry, J. and Axhausen, K., (2006), *Mobilities, Networks, Geographies*, Aldershot: Ashgate

Lash, S. and Urry, J., (1994), *Economies of Signs and Space*, London: Sage.

Laszlo, E., (2006), *The Chaos Point*, London: Piatkus Books.

Leahy, T., (2008), 'Discussion of "Global warming and Sociology"', *Current Sociology*, 56: 475–84.

Leggett, J., (2005), *Half Gone. Oil, Gas, Hot Air and Global Energy Crisis*, London: Portobello Books.

Lever-Tracy, C., (2008), 'Global warming and sociology', *Current Sociology*, 56: 445–66.

Linden, E., (2007), *Winds of Change. Climate, Weather and the Destruction of Civilizations*, New York: Simon and Schuster.

Lovelock, J., (2006), *The Revenge of Gaia*, London: Allen Lane.

Lynas, M., (2007), *Six Degrees. Our Future on a Hotter Planet*, London: Fourth Estate.

Marx, K. and Engels, F., [1848], (1888), *The Manifesto of the Communist Party*, Moscow: Foreign Languages.

McCright, A. and Dunlap, R., (2000), 'Challenging global warming as a social problem: an analysis of the conservative movement's counter-claims', *Social Problems*, 49: 499–522.

Monbiot, G., (2006), *Heat. How to stop the planet burning*, London: Allen Lane.

Nye, D., (1999), *Consuming Power*, Cambridge, Mass: MIT Press.

Paskal, C., (2007), 'How climate change is pushing the boundaries of security and foreign policy', Chatham House, http://www.chathamhouse.org.uk/files/9250_bp0607climatecp.pdf (accessed 04/03/08).

Pearce, F., (2007), *With Speed and Violence. Why Scientists fear Tipping Points in Climate Change*, Boston: Beacon Press.

Pfeiffer, D., (2006), *Eating Fossil Fuels*, Gabriola Island, BC: New Society Publishers.

Pine, B. J. and Gilmore, J., (1999), *The Experience Economy*, Barvard Business School Press.

Polanyi, K., (1954), *The Great Transformation*, Boston: Beacon Press.

Rial, J., Pielke, R., Beniston, M., Claussen, M., Canadell, J. and Cox, P., (2004), 'Nonlinearities, feedbacks and critical thresholds within the Earth's climate system', *Climatic Change*, 65: 11–38.

Rifkin, J., (2002), *The Hydrogen Economy*, New York: Penguin Putnam.

Roberts, J. T. and Parks, B., (2007), *A Climate of Injustice*, Cambridge, Mass: MIT Press.

Schafer, A. and Victor, D., (2000), 'The future mobility of the world population', *Transportation Research A*, 34: 171–205.

Sheller, M., (2008a), 'Always turned on', in Cronin, A. and K. Hetherington (eds), *Consuming the Entrepreneurial City*, London: Routledge.

Sheller, M., (2008b), 'The new Caribbean complexity: mobility systems and the re-scaling of development', *Singapore Journal of Tropical Geography*, 14: 373–84.

Shields, R., (1991), *Places on the Margin*, London: Routledge.

Stehr, N., (2001), 'Economy and ecology in an era of knowledge-based economies', *Current Sociology*, 49: 67–90.

Stern, N., (2006), *Stern Review. The Economics of Climate Change.* (http://www.hm-treasury.gov. uk/independent_reviews/stern_review_economics_climate_change/sternreview_index.cfm accessed 6.11.06).

Stern, N., (2007), *The Economics of Climate Change. The Stern Review*, Cambridge: Cambridge University Press.

Torpey, J., (2000), *The Invention of the Passport*, Cambridge: Cambridge University Press.

Urry, J., (2007), *Mobilities*, Cambridge: Polity.

Urry, J., (2008), 'Climate change, travel and complex futures', *British Journal of Sociology*, 59: 261–79.

Veblen, T., (1912), *The Theory of the Leisure Class*. New York: The Macmillan Company.

Walton, J., (2007), *Riding on Rainbows*. St Alban's: Skelter.

Part Two
Social Worlds, Natural Worlds:
Sociological Research

The dangerous limits of dangerous limits: climate change and the precautionary principle

Chris Shaw

The European Union (EU) is commonly described as a world leader in the building of international environmental agreements (Jordan, 2008; Schlosberg and Rinfret, 2008; Gerhardsa and Lengfeldb, 2008). It was the driving force behind the Kyoto Protocol: this is the only existing international climate change treaty to include legally binding targets for reductions in emissions of carbon dioxide and requires developed countries to cut carbon dioxide emissions by an average of 5 per cent by 2012. It is, however, unlikely that EU member states will achieve these targets (Anderson and Bows, 2008). Despite this failure, the EU has already unilaterally committed itself to further reductions in emissions of carbon dioxide, with targets of 20% cuts by 2020, and 60% by 2050, in order to avoid warming the earth by more than two degrees centigrade over the pre-industrial average (Europa, 2009). However, a new discourse is emerging which claims that two degrees is in excess of anything that might be considered safe, and that we are already living with dangerous climate change (Anderson and Bows, 2008; Harvey, 2007a, 2007b; Hansen *et al.*, 2008; Schneider, 2008).

Identifying if, or when, climate change becomes dangerous is made difficult by the absence of any consensus on what counts as 'dangerous' climate change (Oppenheimer and Petsonk, 2005; Hulme, 2007). This difficulty stems in large part from the fact that attitudes to risk and concepts of danger are socially and culturally embedded (Douglas and Wildalvsky, 1982). In addition, vulnerability to changes in the climate is not distributed evenly across all the world's ecosystems and human communities. The variable nature of the way climate change is understood and experienced places a question mark over the idea that there can be one dangerous limit for the whole earth. Examination of these issues has been neglected by the mainstream media and NGOs, which have, alongside the state and elements of the corporate sector, been central to reproducing the discourse of a two degree dangerous limit. This acceptance of an overly simplistic account of dangerous climate change has been attributed to a strong and ongoing desire to discuss risk in a way 'that circumvents or at least limits the complications inherent in drawing on the social science perspective or incorporating value judgments' (Oppenheimer, 2005: 1401). This aversion to ethics and values in favour of a purely quantitative framing of climate change is deliberate, in that quantitative targets are 'first order questions used to divert attention away from questions about the political and social order' (Elliot, 1998, cited in Smith, 2007: 202).

In order to avoid second order questions, mainstream media, NGO, corporate and policy discourses invoke climate science as the source of the idea that two degrees is a dangerous limit. However, the climate science community has been very insistent that it is not the role of science to define the amount of climate change that should be considered dangerous (for example Oppenheimer, 2005; Pachauri, 2007; Moss, 1995; Adger *et al.*, 2003; Marburger, 2007). Where the scientists have felt moved to comment on the dangerous limit it is often to suggest that two degrees is more warming than could be considered safe (Hansen *et al.*, 2007).

The dangerous limit target dominates the climate policy agenda (Anderson and Bows, 2008: 3863). Given the gravity of the impacts forecast to result from climate change, defining a dangerous limit would seem to be a prime case for the application of the precautionary principle. The precautionary principle was characterized in the 1998 Wingspread Statement as follows: 'When an activity raises threats of harm to human health or the environment, precautionary measures should be taken even if some cause and effect relationships are not fully established scientifically'. The statement listed four central components of the principle: (1) taking preventative action in the face of uncertainty, (2) shifting burdens onto proponents of potentially harmful activities, (3) exploring a wide range of alternatives to possibly harmful actions, and (4) increasing public participation in decision making (Tickner, 2003: xiii–xiv). Whilst EU environmental policy continues to be of great interest to social scientists (Jordan, 2008) there has been no significant examination of the extent to which the EU emissions target is an expression of the precautionary principle. In what follows I discuss the way in which the precautionary principle has informed policy development and how the two degrees of warming idea has become an acceptable limit. Climate change policy has not to date benefited from the application of the precautionary principle and scientific evidence indicating that humanity is already committed to exceeding dangerous levels of climate change means that it is now too late for precaution. First, however, I discuss the need to combine social constructivist and critical realist approaches and describe the data that I draw on.

Social construction and critical realism

Bray and Shackley define climate change as a 'quasi-reality', in so far as it is a phenomenon defined by expert knowledge and surrounded by uncertainty, and claim a social-constructivist methodology as the best approach to understanding such a problem (Bray and Shackley, 2004: 2). The need for a social-constructivist methodology is underscored by the socially and culturally embedded nature of concerns about climate change risks, and the way these varying perspectives are mediated through discourse.

Latour, concerned about the paralysing effect of relativism, was moved to ask 'Why does it burn my tongue to say that global warming is a fact whether you like it or not?' (Latour, 2004: 227). My adoption of a social-constructivist epistemology does not seek to deny the objective and physical existence of anthropogenic climate change but is instead specific to the construction of the two degree dangerous limit. In this sense, my approach draws on aspects of critical realism, which allows us to accept that we are dealing with a real event, a warming of the earth's atmosphere induced at least in part by human activity, whilst recognizing that the meanings we give to this phenomenon may be constructed through language (Willig, 1998).

I also draw on elements of green critical theory. Critical theory claims that modernity, in its privileging of instrumental reason, has corrupted the ideals of the Enlightenment. The dominance of instrumental reason is believed to work against the flourishing of human potential and the achievement of liberty. Green critical theory, such as that espoused by Bookchin in his philosophy of Social Ecology (1987), sees a connection between a human spirit deformed by hierarchical society and an ongoing corruption and degradation of the natural environment. Though critiques of instrumental reason, ecological manifestos and concern about the impact of industrial technology on society are well established, the fast moving pace of the climate debate gives scope for new tensions to be brought to these old thoughts. EU climate change policy and the precautionary principle both seek to serve the goal of ecological modernization, a paradigm which favours industrial efficiency and technological development in order to ensure economic development and environmental quality (Schlosberg and Rinfret, 2008: 254). However, after 17 years of trying to meet the UNFCCC's (United Nations Framework Convention on Climate Change) requirement to avoid dangerous climate change (see p. 110), observations show that atmospheric concentrations of carbon dioxide are rising at over twice the rate of increase during the 1990s (Black, 2006). There is, therefore, no empirical evidence base for the belief that dangerous climate change can be avoided within the paradigm of ecological modernization and its attendant invocation of the precautionary principle. We have therefore either to maintain our faith in a technology as yet unseen to provide the means of our salvation or search for alternative perspectives to guide a meaningful policy response. In my view it is green critical theory which provides the perspective required.

Eckersley (2006) suggests that there have been two waves of critical theory, with the second wave, including green theory, being a response to criticisms levelled at the first wave; this is most closely associated with the Frankfurt School. Following on from this initial body of work, a second wave of green political theory of the mid-1990s and beyond has been less preoccupied with critical philosophical reflection on humanity's posture toward the non-human world and more concerned to explore the conditions that might improve the 'reflexive learning capacity' of citizens, societies, and states in a world of mounting yet unevenly distributed ecological risks (Eckersley, 2006: 248). This post-modern turn in green political theory, concerned with a retreat from meta-narratives about how the world should be, and instead contenting itself with local, context specific narratives about how the world is experienced, is a long way from the totalizing vision seen to be the defining feature of critical social science. A totalizing vision requires us to stand apart from the prevailing order of the world, so that we can ask how that order came about. By standing apart we cease to take the institutions and social and power relations for granted and instead call them into question (Smith, 2007: 199). I argue for the continued necessity of the totalizing vision to be found in critical theory, on the basis that the truncated and partial narratives of the last thirty years have accompanied an acceleration in the destruction of the natural environment.

Recent analyses of green diplomacy and the building of international environmental regimes have contributed to our understanding of the ways in which the mainstream green agenda has been shaped by economic and geo-political norms. Green diplomacy has been described as a means by which the global North has been able to extend its control over distant and subordinate places (Stipple and Paterson, 2007: 162). Others have sought to argue that all imposed harms (such as might result from allowing the climate to warm dangerously) are a form of expropriation of the powerless by the powerful (Ravetz, 2006: 282). As one scientist I spoke to ironically noted

> I do often point out I use two degrees centigrade and I haven't come up with the definition. It is one certain people in the UK and EU have come up with and broadly we acknowledge it, and most of us are aware that this is going to kill people elsewhere in the world but they are a long way away, they're poor and they're generally black and we don't care. (UK climate scientist, September 2008)

One of the dominant criticisms of critical theory has centred on its anti-science agenda (Wellmer, 1983). The research presented in this chapter, however, indicates that it is not the science itself but the way it has been interpreted, by non-scientists, that is the problem. The two degree dangerous limit has become an orthodoxy as the result of non-scientists (corporations, NGOs, the mass media and policy makers) using science as a cover for value choices. The two degree limit to dangerous warming is an expression of values. By assuming the danger lies in the future, when two degrees of warming have taken place, the need for radical and immediate changes in the current social order is replaced by the belief that danger can be averted through go-slow policy prescriptions and the ecological modernization of existing technologies.

In order to explain the reproduction of the two degree limit over the last thirty years, I rely primarily on discursive data. They take the form of 28 semi-structured interviews from the climate science and NGO communities generated through convenience and snowball sampling techniques. In addition, email exchanges and recordings of presentations at demonstrations (such as the Climate Camp at Heathrow in July 2007) and conferences (for example Exeter University Dangerous Rates of Change Conference, September 2008) are drawn on. Interviews have also been conducted with organizations that straddle the policy and business communities (for example the Carbon Trust, a UK government funded body charged with helping UK businesses meet emission reduction targets) and I have used commentary from the mass media.

The precautionary principle

The precautionary principle is a concept used to guide policy-making in the face of what Ravetz has defined as 'high uncertainty/high stakes' environmental problems (Ravetz, 2006: 276). These urgent, complex problems require policy decisions to be made in advance of any certainty about potential harm. Consequently these decisions must rely as much on subjective judgment as objective scientific evidence (Roberts, 2004: 12). Theoretically the precautionary principle demands that these subjective judgements should err on the side of caution. In practice, there are no hard and fast rules for the application of the precautionary principle, and its implementation is subject to a number of different factors over and above judgements about harm to humans and the natural environment. For example, how does one justify potentially costly measures in the absence of scientific evidence about the potential harm a substance or process may cause? (Roberts, 2004: 99; European Environment Agency, 2002: 12). Consideration also needs to be given to the harm that may arise from application of the precautionary principle, as for example has occurred around discussions over the banning of DDT and the claimed subsequent increase in cases of malaria.

The precautionary principle has been embedded within a range of different environmental interventions, including those relating to acid rain and protection of the ozone layer and fisheries depletion (for detailed examinations of these interventions see European Environment Agency, 2002; Tickner, 2003). There are a large number of treaties which have sought to formalize the idea of precaution in environmental policy including the 1987 Montreal Protocol on Substances that Deplete the Ozone Layer, the 1992 Rio Declaration (including the UNFCCC), the 1992 Maastricht Treaty, the Wingspread Statement on the Precautionary Principle from 1998, the European Commission's Communication on the Precautionary Principle and the Council of Ministers Nice Decision both from 2000 and the 2001 Stockholm Convention on Persistent Organic Pollutants.

It is the EU, however, with its incorporation of the precautionary principle as a legal norm, which is seen to be unique in the primacy it affords to considerations of health and environmental protection in its policy making (Christoforou, 2003: 241). The European Court of Justice judgement on BSE provides evidence of how much importance the EU places on precaution:

> where there is uncertainty as to the existence or extent of risks to human health the institutions may take protective measures without having to wait until the reality and seriousness of those risks become fully apparent. (BSE [1998], at paragraph 63, cited in Christoforou, 2003: 243)

In addition, Article 174(2) of the EC treaty as modified by the Maastricht treaty in 1992 states that the community policy on the environment should aim at a high level of protection (Christoforou, 2003: 242).

Despite these lofty ideals, however, the precautionary principle has been criticized for being nothing more than a disguised cost-benefit analysis. Funtowicz and Ravetz have addressed the inadequacy of cost-benefit analyses of environmental problems in their paper 'The worth of a songbird' (Funtowicz and Ravetz, 1994). This critique was also extended to the cost-benefit analysis of climate change (Baer, 2007). Both these critiques attack the cost-benefit analysis of environmental problems as always favouring the *status quo*, continuing the demand for scientific certainty and being more concerned with protecting vested interests and political expediency than the environment (Quijano, 2003: 21). Under these constraints, policy will continue to rely on standard scientific risk assessments, which attempt to justify 'living with danger' rather than pay the costs of prevention (Raino, 2008: 663). Criticism from this perspective points to the Dutch experience for evidence of the claim that the precautionary principle is merely symbolic. The Dutch have been key drivers in pushing forward the EU climate change policy and the precautionary principle has been prevalent from the beginning in Dutch documents dealing with climate change, yet annual Dutch carbon-dioxide emissions rose from 210.3 million tonnes in 1990 to 216.9 million tonnes in 2000 (Pettenger, 2007: 61). Supporters of the belief that the precautionary principle is just another name for a cost–benefit analysis point to the EU Commission statement on the precautionary principle from 2000, which states that application of the precautionary principle should not aim at zero risk, that the costs and benefits should also be taken into account, and any application of the principle should be provisional pending additional scientific research (European Commission 2000, cited Christoforou, 2003: 247).

Application of the precautionary principle is further hindered by the lack of any shared understanding of what exactly is meant by the precautionary principle, and an agreed methodology for its application (Kaiser, 2003: 39). Without such definitions there are a multitude of get-out clauses preventing consistent use of the precautionary principle.

The construction of a dangerous limit

The first appearance in print of the two-degree limit seems to be in a 1967 paper whose authors write of 'a convincing calculation that a doubling of CO_2 would raise temperatures by roughly 2 degrees centigrade' (Manabe and Weatherald, cited in Weart, 2003: 203). Oppenheimer & Petsonk identify a 1979 paper by the economist W.D. Nordhaus as the first attempt to describe two degrees of warming as a dangerous limit (Oppenheimer and Petsonk, 2005).[1] Oppenheimer and Petsonk's citation of the Nordhaus paper focuses on his argument that two degrees centigrade of warming is the limit of warming which has occurred naturally over the last 10,000 years. Humanity has survived these previous levels of warming and so two degrees can reasonably be claimed as a desirable limit to human forcing of the climate (Nordhaus cited in Oppenheimer and Petsonk, 2005: 197). This idea of two degrees as a natural limit in climate variation is central to the construction of the two-degree limit and is reiterated in a highly influential set of reports from the German Advisory Council on Global Change (WBGU, 1995, 1997, 2003), which I return to below.

The 1967 and 1979 papers reach their conclusions about a two degree limit on the basis of climate sensitivity calculations. Whilst the topic of climate sensitivity is important to climate science and much of the climate change commentary in the social sciences, I can only briefly outline the main features of the concept here.

A question of central concern to a technical construction of climate change is 'How much warming will arise from x increases in atmospheric concentrations of carbon dioxide?' This relationship is known as climate sensitivity. Attempts to calculate climate sensitivity have focussed on modelling what happens when atmospheric concentrations of carbon dioxide are doubled. In fact, so ubiquitous has the assumption of a doubling of carbon dioxide been in these calculations that the term 'climate sensitivity' does not refer to calculations of warming from a range of different increases in carbon dioxide, but refers only to the consequences of a doubling of carbon dioxide. A climate scientist who has written extensively on the climate sensitivity story explained to me the standardization of the climate sensitivity calculations as a structurally imposed constraint. Climate sensitivity was being calculated by a large body of scientists over a large span of space and time, requiring standardization of the models so that comparisons could be made between the results being generated. This process was beyond the computational power of any one computer, hence the need for this co-ordination. And why a doubling of carbon dioxide? Firstly because one needs the parameters used for the modelling to be sufficiently different from current conditions for the results to have any statistical significance. And secondly:

> doubling looked like it was a plausible likelihood. It was going to happen anyway given the trend of increasing emissions that was going on. It wasn't going to be that long, that unimaginably far in to the future. It counts as an interesting extension of existing modelling so...in that sense it was plausible. It's going to happen sometime, whether it's 50 years or 100 years doesn't really matter. (Climate scientist and academic researcher, June 2008)

Looking at the early work on climate sensitivity and warming, it would appear that a certain inevitability about a doubling of carbon dioxide and two degrees of warming has been entrenched in the research from the very beginning. Van der Sluijs and others, in a history of the climate sensitivity concept, concluded the 'sensitivity to doubling' concept was a hypothetical research entity which has become reified in scientific assessment. In addition they claimed that their research revealed that the concept of climate sensitivity is much more complex and indeterminate than acknowledged by the climate science community and that climate scientists are hostile to a re-examination of assumptions which might reflect badly on their community (Van der Sluijs *et al.*, 1998: 312–313). The aversion to any reappraisal of the assumptions of the climate sensitivity model has been matched by the absence, until very recently, of any re-examination of the assumptions about the safety of two degrees of warming.

Weart (2003), Oppenheimer and Petsonk (2005), Boehmer-Christiansen (1994), Newell (2000), Pearce (2007), and Walker and King (2008) have all provided an extensive history of the development of the climate change debate since the middle of the twentieth century. For reasons of space I content myself here with an overview of some key papers that appeared after the UNFCCC came into force in 1992. The two-degree target developed out of the UNFCCC, which requires signatories to take steps to avoid dangerous climate change (UNFCCC, 1992 Article 2). The UNFCCC did not quantify what amount of climate change should be considered dangerous, leaving it to the signatories to reach agreement on such a definition.

As shown in Table 1 (below), the period from 1994 to the present day saw the idea of a two degrees dangerous limit become increasingly central to discourses about the climate change risk. This table lists only a sample from a very extensive range of papers and conferences which featured discussion of the two degree limit. I limit my analysis to the WBGU reports, focussing in particular on the 1995 paper; this is because the papers from 1997 and 2003 reproduce the claims made in the 1995 publication. Following Tol (2007) and the scientists interviewed for this study, I suggest that these papers are central to the shaping of the two degree limit. In addition, they have been key in shaping EU climate change policy. The WBGU reports of 1995, 1997 and 2003 were commissioned by the German government at the behest of the EU and fed directly into the creation of the Kyoto Protocol (WBGU, 1995; 1997) and current EU policy (WBGU, 2003).

The 1995 WBGU report was produced for the First Conference of the Parties to the Framework Convention on Climate Change in Berlin. This conference is an important one because it brought together the signatories to the UNFCCC for the first time, the purpose being to clarify the definitions of dangerous climate change which featured in the UNFCCC. The WBGU report was intended to propose some definitions of dangerous which could be used to develop policy.[2]

The primary purpose of the report was to answer the question 'How quickly, and by how much, do we need to reduce emissions of carbon dioxide in order to avoid dangerous climate change?' Answering that question required the definition of two points:

i) How much warming is dangerous?
ii) How much carbon dioxide will cause this dangerous warming? (Climate sensitivity).

Table 1: *Discussions of two degrees following the United Nations Framework Convention on Climate Change*

Year	Event	Notes
1994	Dutch National Research Programme	Identified 2 degree limit
1995	German Advisory Council on Global Change (WGBU) – Statement on the occasion of the First Conference of the Parties to the Framework Convention on Climate Change in Berlin	Simultaneous application of several criteria to limit choice of emissions pathways (Tolerable Window Approach). Calculates 2 degrees as tolerable limit
1995	Intergovernmental Panel on Climate Change (IPCC) Second Assessment Report	Generates range of emission scenarios, mid-range assumes 2 degrees warming by 2100
1997	WBGU – A Study for the Third Conference of the Parties to the Framework Convention on Climate Change in Kyoto	Reconfirms 2 degree limit
2001	IPCC Third assessment report	Saw attempts to define 'dangerous' as beyond its legal remit, organized vulnerabilities in 5 categories
2003	WBGU – Climate Protection Strategies for the 21st Century. Kyoto and Beyond	Calls on EU to set the lead by committing to limiting warming to 2 degrees
2005	Kyoto Protocol ratified	First step towards emission cuts required to avoid dangerous climate change
2005	The International Symposium on Stabilisation of Greenhouse Gas Concentrations	Conference called by Tony Blair to quantify a dangerous limit to climate change
2007	IPCC Fourth assessment report	Increased detail on likely impact of various scenarios.
2007	EU Climate and Energy strategy	Legal instruments for avoiding breaching of 2 degree limit

Our interest is in the former question. To avoid dangerous climate change, the report argued, the warming should be limited so that we can be assured of the 'preservation of Creation in its current form' (WBGU, 1995: 13). This has been described as a 'peculiar' goal for a secular government to support (Tol, 2007: 246). The sort of temperature range that might allow for the preservation of Creation was derived from the same premise as that which informed Nordhaus's analysis from 1979. The WBGU report identifies the highest global average temperatures during the previous 10,000 years (the period in which human civilization developed) as being around 16.1 degrees centigrade. The report suggests that if this temperature is exceeded then 'dramatic changes in the function and composition of today's ecosystems can be expected' (WBGU, 1995: 13). Today's global average temperature is calculated by the WBGU to be around 15.3 degrees centigrade, leaving only 0.8 degrees of warming before the climate warms dangerously. However, the WBGU report adds 0.5 degrees centigrade of warming to the assumed tolerance range on the basis of humanity's 'improved adaptive capacity' (WBGU, 1995: 13). That allows for 1.3 degrees of warming before change becomes dangerous. The earth has warmed by 0.7 degrees since the pre-industrial average. The 1.3 and the 0.7 give us the two degree limit.

The report does not provide any rationale for assuming that industrial humanity is more adaptable to climate change than our hunter-gatherer forebears nor why, if such adaptability did exist, it would equate to 0.5 degrees of warming. In addition, the desire to preserve Creation mentioned above was one of two principles used to calculate the emissions cuts required, the other being 'the prevention of excessive costs'. Thus, rather than being an expression of the precautionary principle, which one might expect given that it was commissioned at the behest of the EU, this report is a simple cost-benefit analysis.

The 1997 WBGU report to the Kyoto Conference reaffirms the basic premise which informed its 1995 report, a premise which underpins the adoption of a two degree limit in the EU's current Climate and Energy Strategy, released in 2007. The spirit of precaution seems absent from the rather cavalier attitude adopted in the calculating of a two degree limit in the WBGU reports, a process described by one academic as based on a 'sloppy' methodology and 'inadequate' reasoning (Tol, 2007: 424). The EU has not seen fit to re-examine the two-degree limit despite the supposed incorporation of the precautionary principle into its environmental policy and despite the fact that even before the EU released its Energy and Climate Strategy, the two-degree consensus was beginning to break.

Doubts about the dangerous limit

Agreement on the idea of a two degree limit has, until recently, been widespread, but not universal. The most significant challenge to the consensus came from the US president George W. Bush who said '...no one can say with any certainty what constitutes a dangerous level of warming, and therefore what level must be avoided' (US President George W. Bush, 11 June 2001, cited in Singer and Avery, 2007: 223).

But for all those actors concerned about the impacts of climate change, whether political, corporate or environmental, the response has almost always been framed within the rubric of a two-degree limit.

Since 2005 however, faith in the idea that the dangerous limit lies at two degrees of warming has been shaken. Table 2 outlines some significant statements and reports challenging the two degree idea.

The table shows that questions about the validity of the two-degree limit have come mainly from climate scientists. This raises questions about how scientists, the media and NGOs understand their varying perspectives on the two degree limit. In the next part of the chapter I draw on a range of secondary and primary sources to explore those perspectives in more depth.

Two degrees and the media, NGOs and climate scientists

Printed Media

Criticism of media coverage of climate change has focussed mainly on the willingness to provide space to positions which deny either that the climate is changing or that any changes can be attributed to human activity. The media have also been accused of being alarmist in their depiction of 'apocalyptic' climate change impacts, these accusations coming from some climate scientists as well as those challenging the existence of anthropogenic climate change. My analysis differs from these established criticisms, and addresses representations of climate change which, in the process of accepting the validity of anthropogenic climate change, reproduce the idea of a two degree dangerous limit. My discussion uses commentary from two UK broadsheet newspapers.

The first text comes from a columnist with *The Independent*, a UK newspaper with a left-leaning liberal agenda similar to that of the longer established *Guardian* newspaper. In discussing the need to avoid exceeding the two degree limit the columnist writes

> This sounds, at first glance, hysterical, I know. What's three degrees of warming? A little extra sunscreen and a new pair of Gucci sunglasses, surely. But the overwhelming scientific evidence tells us something very different. The maximum figure of two degrees of warming on the global thermostat was not plucked randomly by Angela Merkel, the German Chancellor who tried to drag the other leaders towards it. No – it is calculated by virtually all the world's scientists to be the threshold beyond which our planet's fragile natural systems will begin to unravel rapidly. (Hari, 2007)

Permission to warm the earth by two degrees is here given by identifying two degrees as a limit *beyond* which things begin to go wrong. That we can be certain of this is apparent because it wasn't plucked 'randomly', but was calculated by 'virtually all the world's scientists.'

Fiona Harvey, Environment Correspondent for the *Financial Times* also invokes the scientist as a symbol that can be used to communicate certainty about the two-degree limit. Harvey argues the target to halve carbon dioxide emissions by 2050 has been '…established on the basis of scientific advice, aimed at preventing a rise of more than 2oC (sic) in global temperatures, which scientists say is the limit of safety' (Harvey, 2008).

Table 2: *Recent statements casting doubt on the two degree limit*

Statement	Author	Date
'The two degree scenario cannot be recommended as a responsible target, as it almost surely takes us well into the realm of dangerous anthropogenic interference with the climate system.'	Hansen, J. Director NASA Goddard Institute for Space Studies	2007
'People are actually questioning if the 2 degrees centigrade benchmark that has been set is safe enough,'	Pachauri, R. Head of the Intergovernmental Panel on Climate Change, cited Reuters, 2007	2007
'I think that 2 degrees is rather arbitrary. It's not clear to me that the answer shouldn't be three degrees, or more, or less. We don't have a scientific basis for selecting the two degree number – it's a hunch, a guess.'	Marburger, J. President of the American Association for the Advancement of Science	2008
New NGO formed on basis that scientists saying already dangerous levels of carbon dioxide in the atmosphere	www.350.org	2008
'The two degree threshold does not have a scientific basis and is likely to lead to dangerously misguided policies. It is increasingly unlikely that any global agreement will keep warming below two degrees of warming.'	Anderson, K. Professor of Energy and Climate Change, Director of the Tyndall Energy Programme. Bows, A. Core Researcher, Tyndall Centre, University of Manchester	2008
'Current levels of carbon dioxide have likely already commited us to 2.4 degrees centigrade of warming.'	Ramathan, V. Professor of Applied Ocean Sciences, Distinguished Professor of Climate and Atmospheric Sciences, Scripps Institution of Oceanography. (Co-authored with Feng, Y.)	2008
'No policy scenario has a greater than 90% chance of not going above the two degree ceiling currently seen as the basis for climate "success". Little chance of even staying below three degrees of warming.'	Stockholm Network Carbon Scenarios	2009

Climate scientists

The climate scientists I interviewed did not share the belief in the calculability of a dangerous limit that has been attributed to them by the journalists. Only one interviewee, from a German science institute, even supported the idea of climate science as somehow separate from policy. Whilst, in common with all other interviewees from the science community, he held no belief in the ability to stay under two degrees of warming, this interviewee maintained a favourable attitude to the processes. The skeletal definition of danger provided by the UNFCCC was unproblematic for this interviewee.

> The UNFCCC has defined what is dangerous so scientists don't have to make that definition, but to elaborate on the elements which constitute the definition of danger-ous. It is in the end the role of scientists to quantify the dangers, the background idea is that the UNFCCC definitions should be inherently quantifiable. (German climate scientist, November 2008)

The scientist did not, however, make any claim that climate science has success-fully completed the work of quantifying a dangerous limit. For this scientist, defining danger was very much still a work in progress.

This reference to the UNFCCC statement of 1992 was unique. Other scien-tists felt the world had moved on since then, and these scientists were happy to adopt a much more value laden approach to the idea of a dangerous limit:

> I do often point out I use 2 degrees centigrade and I haven't come up with the defini-tion. It is one certain people in the UK and EU have come up...it's a socially politi-cally constructed number, it's not a scientifically derived number. (UK climate scientist, September 2008)

Another UK climate researcher described the idea of dangerous warming as 'fluffy' (UK climate academic, August 2008), whilst a prominent US climate scientist considered the climate numbers as 'meaningless' (First US climate sci-entist, February 2009).

In the face of worries about the moral implications of attempting to define a dangerous limit, concern was also expressed about how those external to the science community were talking about the two degrees with an unjustified level of certainty. This was often described as an inevitable response to the demands of policy.

> I don't think it's got any scientific legitimacy...I don't think it ever had any scientific legitimacy...I find that really quite worrying that there are a lot of pontificators out there sharing their views one way or another without any real grasp of what the science is telling them – they simply haven't engaged. (UK climate scientist, Septem-ber 2008)

> ...back in 1988 environmental groups were arguing we must have a 20% reduction in our emissions...and I said wait a minute guys...you can't just pluck a number out of your head and they said no, we have to have a number because without a number we can't get their [politicians] attention; so I understand there is a political strategy in approaching this in terms of number. (Second US climate scientist, Decem-ber 2008)

Everyone seems to have latched on to the 2 degree idea... I think when you are trying to have some sort of policy impact you have to be fairly pragmatic about the targets you are using and to have some point at which you can begin to engage. (UK government business advisor, January 2009)

Back in about 97 when I actually went to one of these NERC meetings and the scientists were all there deliberating about... the policymakers have asked us to give them, you know, some definition of what would count as safe or unsafe climate change, where the limit is and I asked are you sure that you can actually pretend to answer that question? Why don't you say to the policymakers we can't answer that question? Wouldn't that be a scientifically sound and reasonable thing to say on the basis of existing science and probably based on future science as well? And they didn't want to do that at all because they were scared it would undermine their funding and influence so they are already operating with assumptions about what policymakers would take on board. (UK science academic, June 2008)

It is apparent from these statements that, contrary to the media discourses, scientists have not calculated two degrees to be a safe limit, and have deep misgivings about other actors proposing simplistic solutions based on incorrect targets. How do NGOs understand their use of the two degree limit?

NGOs

Effective application of the precautionary principle is understood to require a broadening of the peer review process to include non-expert opinion. This echoes an aspect of the 'post-normal science' methodology Funtowicz and Ravetz have proposed for dealing with complex environmental problems. In their model of a post-normal science, Funtowicz and Ravetz see scientific data as just one part of the evidence used to make a decision about environmental policy. An extended peer-review network is employed to evaluate the science alongside a range of other values and considerations, so that the final judgement is of a sufficiently high quality rather than simply right or wrong (Funtowicz and Ravetz, 1994).

The absence of a formal extended peer–review network for climate change policy has led to the development of an informal peer–review network, made up of, amongst others, NGOs and the media. This informal peer-review network has mediated the findings of scientific papers into a coherent narrative about climate change. However, the informal nature of this peer-review process has resulted in the reproduction and legitimation of what climate scientists consider to be a rather arbitrary and unscientific definition of dangerous climate change.

Mark Lynas, a prominent environmental journalist and campaigner, examined the impacts that might arise from various levels of warming, from one degree through to six degrees. He concludes with a plea for us all to '... work eagerly and collectively to achieve the two degrees target...' (Lynas, 2007: 299).

This plea has been heard by a wide range of climate activists. The authors of a recent report entitled 'Zero Carbon Britain', speaking before a large audience at a week-long protest at Heathrow Airport in 2007 remarked, apropos exceeding two degrees of warming '…it does lead to unthinkable consequences. For any of you who haven't read Mark Lynas' book, I do recommend it'. (UK climate activist, August 2007)

When I asked a campaigner with the Climate Camp movement where she thought the idea of two degrees came from, she replied,

I haven't a clue but the temperature and the parts per million are related and umm (laughing) (long pause) the other person who has most impressed me is Mark Lynas who has this 6 degrees book and I have found that really useful in talking about climate change to people. (Climate activist, March 2008)

A worker from Oxfam said they used the two degree limit in their campaigning because 'Everyone else is using it' (Climate campaigner, Personal communication, 18th September 2008). This unreflective adoption of the two degree dangerous limit was shared by a senior campaigns officer for Friends of the Earth, who revealed that she did not know the origins of the two degree limit but instead 'I just kind of take it on trust' (Environmental campaigner, Personal communication, June 2007).

That the origin of the two degree limit has an almost mythical status for many in the NGO community was made clear to me by an ex-member of Margaret Beckett's team from her time as Environment Secretary for Tony Blair's government. Now director of a government funded green consultancy, he described the two-degree number as 'theological' and was unable to recall why they had started using it as a target (Environmental consultant, Personal communication, November 17th 2008).

However, many campaigners and activists also recognize the two-degree limit as a compromise. For these actors, two degrees is used as target for the pragmatic reasons outlined above, and because climate impacts are believed to be so much worse beyond two degrees of warming.

We're already in the 'dangerous impacts' zone of global warming but the dangers we're trying to avoid are the ones we can't normalize further down the line. There's no bringing back the Greenland ice sheet once it goes. (US climate activist, July 2008)

Two degrees is a compromise in itself and with that target we are probably negotiating thousands of species and millions of lives but having said that it is a tipping point and it does lead to unthinkable consequences. (UK climate activist, June 2007)

There are few who, in conversation, identify the two-degree limit as being a realistic marker between safe and dangerous climate change. Rather, for both the media and NGO communities, the two degrees has become a convenient trope, a 'necessarily simple abstraction' (Scott, cited in Shotter, 2006: 118), which turns the problem into 'a viable object of decision making' (Lahde, 2006: 87). The data presented above supports the theory that climate science, climate campaigning goals and policy are constructed in tandem, within a framework defined by policy. Actors within the science and activist community shape findings and recommendations in ways that will avoid a hostile reception from the policy community (Newell, 2000; Boehmer-Christiansen, 1994). There is little evidence to support the belief that this policy framework, in assuming a two degree limit to warming, has been shaped by the precautionary principle.

Discussion and conclusion

It has been argued that climate change is an appropriate case for the application of the precautionary principle (Brown, 2003: 142). Yet the evidence presented here shows that European climate policy never has been precautionary. Instead policy has been shaped around an end point target derived from rather arbitrary and limited assumptions about how much warming humanity could tolerate. Media and NGO discourses have largely taken their lead from this policy framework, and used spurious interpretations of climate science to legitimate the adoption of a two degree target.

If the descriptions of the precautionary principle as a cost-benefit analysis are correct, then the precautionary principle probably never was an appropriate policy response to climate change. The UK government commissioned the economist Nicholas Stern to produce a cost-benefit analysis of the case for reducing carbon dioxide emissions in line with the government's own targets (Stern, 2006). The conclusions of the report were well publicized, and treated very favourably by the mass media, who consider Nicholas Stern the 'rock star' of the modern climate change movement. 'When he speaks the whole world listens' (Aitkenhead, 2009). However, the costings used in his report assumed cuts in atmospheric concentrations which leave a 50 per cent probability of the climate warming by more than three degrees centigrade (Baer, 2007: 2), significantly more than the two degrees deemed tolerable by the WBGU. Therefore within the framework of a cost-benefit analysis, precautionary or otherwise, it has not yet proved possible to make the case for the reductions in carbon dioxide required to avoid the EU's definition of dangerous change. Whatever the historic case for developing climate change responses under the rubric of the precautionary principle, current climate science (Harvey, 2007a, 2007b) indicates that the precautionary window of opportunity has now passed.

What remains is to find a policy framework that will allow for the development of responses that will move humanity out of the danger zone rapidly, thereby reducing the amount of damage and harm that ensues. A concurrent need is to understand what prevented the necessary action being taken when it mattered. Funtowicz's and Ravetz ideas of a post-normal science (1993) assume that we are no longer in a situation of puzzle solving science, which Kuhn considered normal (1970). Instead we must learn to live with irreducible uncertainty, learn to ask and answer questions to which science can only provide partial answers. With post-normal science, the environmental problems confronting humanity require science to sit alongside a range of other considerations as part of a democratic decision-making process with a formalized and consciously structured extended peer review network. This requires us to begin the process of trying to tame technology and science. Ellul understood industrial technology, and the ideologies used to legitimate its dominance of human aspirations, to be a force without limits. The centrality of technology to human existence is justified by the goal of ever increasing efficiency. All areas of human life are subject to this goal. Further, increased efficiency is a goal without ends; there will always be room for greater efficiency, and all other ends are to be subservient to this goal (Ellul, 1965). Consequently any attempts at developing an effective and democratic climate change policy must take account of the negative impacts that result from deferring to the demands of science and technology. Taming science and technology so that they co-exist alongside other considerations will require that we rethink where the boundaries to the climate change problem lie. Is it simply a technical problem of too much carbon dioxide in the atmosphere? Hoppe asks 'How do people, scientists, stakeholders, policy workers or politicians, arrive at 'closure' about the boundaries to be drawn around 'problematic' systems? How do they frame the scientific and policy problem?' (Hoppe, 2008: 27). Without extending the boundaries of the problem beyond the limits of technology are we not doomed to forever stumble from one global crisis to another, as has been humanity's lot since the middle of the 20th century? Extending the boundaries of the climate change problem is made possible by O'Brien's suggestion of a more positive application of the ideas which are meant to inform the precautionary principle. Rather than simply being content to avoid harm, we might instead begin developing positive goal-based visions of the future. The precautionary principle is thus reconstructed as something other than a process which is triggered by a crisis. Instead the precautionary principle becomes an omnipresent, value-based, decision-making screen, which continually guides our decision-making process away from potential harms. Such an approach helps reduce our reliance on science as we are no longer quibbling about credible evidence and safe levels. Avoidance of these technical discussions means that the public are not marginalized from the debates, and a more democratic process is made possible (O'Brien, 2003: 278–281). A positive future requires us to recognize that existing policy frameworks, such as the precautionary principle, have failed; acceptance of this failure may open the way to a less technocratic vision of our collective future.[3]

Notes

1 Tol (2007) challenges the summary that Petsonk and Oppenheimer offer, saying that Nordhaus has a different opinion on the matter. Tol cites a 1991 paper by Nordhaus (Nordhaus 1991) in support of this claim. I cannot see where in this 1991 paper that Nordhaus makes reference to his 1979 paper.

2 The German Advisory Council on Global Change (WBGU) was set up by the German government in 1992 at the behest of the EU. Its purpose is to provide information that can be used to guide policy on large scale environmental issues such as climate change. The work of the WBU supplements and extends the reports produced by the Intergovernmental Panel on Climate

Change (IPCC). Whilst the IPCC is the foremost global body for the co-ordination and dissemination of climate change science it has no advocacy role, and cannot make policy recommendations. The WBGU however is not so constrained, and thus can provide recommendations about appropriate courses of action.

3 A landmark publication 'Late lessons from early warnings: the precautionary principle 1896–2000' provides an extremely useful history of policy responses to a range of environmental problems. Though the report does not address the issue of climate change, its findings on reasons why the precautionary principle hasn't been applied successfully to other environmental problems have informed this study.

References

Adger, W. N., Dessai, S., Hulme, M., Kohler, J., Turnpenny, J., and Warren, R., (2003), Tyndall Centre for Climate Change Research. *Defining and experiencing dangerous climate change: an editorial essay*, http://www.tyndall.uea.ac.uk/publications/working_papers/wp28.pdf Accessed 12 February 2007.

Aitkenhead, D., (2009), 'We're the first generation that has had the power to destroy the planet. Ignoring that risk can only be described as reckless', *The Guardian* March 30th. http://www.guardian.co.uk/environment/2009/mar/30/climate-change-nicholas-stern-interview Accessed 30 March 2009.

Anderson, K. and Bows, A., (2008), Reframing the climate change challenge in light of post-2000 emission trends, *Philosophical Transactions of the Royal Society*, 13 November 2008 vol. 366 no. 1882 3863–3882.

Baer, P., (2007), *The worth of an ice sheet. A critique of the treatment of catastrophic impacts in the Stern Review*, http://www.ecoequity.org/docs/WorthOfAnIceSheet.pdf Accessed 12 November 2008.

Black, R., (2006), *Carbon emissions show sharp rise*, BBC News Website, 27 November 2006 http://news.bbc.co.uk/1/hi/sci/tech/6189600.stm Accessed 26 March 2009.

Boehmer-Christiansen, S., (1994), Global Environmental Protection Policy: The limits of scientific advice, Part 1, *Environmental Change* 4 (2): 140–159.

Bookchin, M., (1987), *The modern crisis*, Black Rose Books.

Bray, D. and Shackley, S., (2004), Working Paper 58: *The Social Simulation of the Public Perception of Weather Events and their Effect upon the Development of Belief in Anthropogenic Climate Change*, Tyndall Centre for Climate Change Research.

Brown, D., (2003), The precautionary principle as a guide to environmental impact analysis: lessons learned from global warming in *Precaution, Environmental Science and Preventive Public Policy*, J. Tickner (ed.), London: Island Press: 141–156.

Christoforou, T., (2003), The precautionary principle in European community law and science in *Precaution, Environmental Science and Preventive Public*, J. Tickner (ed.), London: Island Press: 241–262.

Douglas, M. and Wildavsky, A., (1982), *Risk and Culture: An Essay on the Selection of Technological and Environmental Dangers*, University of California Press.

Eckersley, R., (2006), *Green Theory*, http://www.oup.com/uk/orc/bin/9780199298334/dunne_chap13.pdf Accessed 11 March 2009.

Ellul, J., (1965), *The Technological Society*, London: Jonathan Cape.

Europa, (2009), EU Energy and Climate Policy, Speech at the 7th Doha Natural Gas Conference, http://europa.eu/rapid/pressReleasesAction.do?reference=SPEECH/09/102&format=HTML&aged=0&language=EN&guiLanguage=en Accessed 30 March 2009.

European Environment Agency, (2002), *Late lessons from early warnings: the precautionary principle 1896–2000*, http://www.eea.europa.eu/publications/environmental_issue_report_2001_22/Issue_Report_No_22.pdf Accessed 12 February 2009.

Funtowicz, S. and Ravetz, J., (1993), Science for the Post-Normal Age, *Future*, 25/7: 735–755.

Funtowicz, S. and Ravetz, J., (1994), The worth of a songbird: ecological economics as a post-normal science, *Ecological economics* Vol: 10 197–207.

Gerhardsa, J. and Lengfeldb, H., (2008), Support for European Union Environmental Policy by Citizens of EU-Member and Accession States, *Comparative Sociology* 7: 215–241.

Hansen, J., Sato, M., Kharecha, P., Beerling, D., Berner, R., Masson-Delmotte, V., Pagani, M., Raymo, M., Royer, D., and Zachos, J., (2007), *Clarion Caller; An interview with renowned climate scientist James Hansen* Grist, http://www.grist.org/news/maindish/2007/05/15/hansen/ Accessed 24 May 2007.

Hansen, J., (2008), *Target atmospheric CO_2: Where should humanity aim?*, arXiv.org, http://arxiv.org/abs/0804.1126 Accessed 3 September 2008.

Hari, J., (2007), 'What Makes Us Think We Can Entrust The Future of The Human Race to These People?' *The Independent*, June 11th http://www.commondreams.org/archive/2007/06/11/1801/ Accessed 17 February 2008.

Harvey, F., (2008), 'Divided we stand', *Financial Times*, September 15th http://www.ft.com/cms/s/0/232915f4-7aff-11dd-adbe-000077b07658.html Accessed 30 March 2009.

Harvey, L. D. D., (2007a), Dangerous anthropogenic interference, dangerous climatic change, and harmful climatic change: non-trivial distinctions with significant policy implications, *Climatic Change* 82: 1–25.

Harvey, L. D. D., (2007b), Allowable CO_2 concentrations under the United Nations Framework Convention on Climate Change as a function of the climate sensitivity probability distribution function, *Environmental Research Letters 2*.

Hoppe, R., (2008), Lost in translation? A boundary work perspective on making climate change governable in *Workshop: Climate change and the science policy interface*, Personal communication, 30th January, 2009.

Hulme, M., (2007), Understanding climate change – the power and the limit of science. *Weather*, September 2007, Vol. 62, No. 9: 243–244.

Jordan, A., (2008), 'An ever more environmental union amongst the peoples of Europe?', *Environmental Politics*, 17: 3: 485–491.

Kaiser, M., (2003), Ethics, Science and Precaution: a view from Norway in Tickner, J., (ed.), Precaution, Environmental Science and Preventive Public Policy, London: Island Press; 39–53.

Khun, T., (1970), *The structure of scientific revolutions*, Chicago: Chicago University Press.

Lahde, V., (2006), Gardens, climate changes and cultures in Y. Haila, and C. Dyke (eds), 2006 *How Nature Speaks: The Dynamics of the Human Ecological Condition*, Durham and London: Duke University Press.

Latour, B., (2004), Why has critique run out of steam? From Matters of Fact to Matters of Concern, *Critical Inquiry* 30.

Lynas, M., (2007), *6 degrees: Our future on a hotter planet*, London: Fourth Estate.

Marburger, J., (2007), *US Chief Scientist says world could become 'unliveable' under global warming*, The Ecologist, http://www.theecologist.org:80/news_detail.asp?content_id=1068 Accessed 22 October 2008.

Moss, R., (1995), Avoiding 'dangerous' interference in the climate system: the roles of values, science and policy, *Global Environmental Change*, Vol 5, No.1: 3–6.

Newell, P., (2000), *Climate for Change: Non-state actors and the global politics of the greenhouse*, Cambridge: Cambridge University Press.

Nordhaus, W. D., (1991), To Slow or Not to Slow: The Economics of the Greenhouse Effect, *The Economic Journal* 101: 920–937.

O'Brien, M., (2003), Science in the service of good: the precautionary principle and positive goals in J. Tickner, (ed.), *Precaution, Environmental Science and Preventive Public Policy*, London: Island Press: 279–296.

Oppenheimer, M., (2005), Defining Dangerous Anthropogenic Interference: The role of science, the limits of science, *Risk Analysis*, Vol. 25, No. 6: 1399–1407.

Oppenheimer, M. and Petsonk, A., (2005), Article 2 of the UNFCCC: Historical origins, recent interpretations, *Climatic Change* 73: 195–226.

Pachauri, J., (2007), *Even Tougher Warming Curbs May Be Needed*, Reuters News Service, October 2nd 2007.

Pearce, F., (2007), *The last generation. How nature will take her revenge for climate change*, Eden Project Books.

Pettenger, M., (2007), The Netherlands Climate Change Policy: Constructing themselves/constructing climate change in M. Pettenger (ed.), *The social construction of climate change. Power, Knowledge, Norms, Discourses (Global Environmental Governance)*, Aldershot: Ashgate Publishing Limited: 51–74.

Quijano, R., (2003), Elements of the precautionary principle in *Precaution, Environmental Science and Preventive Public Policy*, J. Tickner (ed.), London: Island Press: 21–28.

Ramathan, V. and Feng, Y., (2008), On avoiding dangerous anthropogenic interference with the climate system: Formidable challenges ahead, *Proceedings of the National Academy of Sciences*, Vol. 105, No. 38: 14245–14250.

Raino, M., (2008), Climate science and the way we ought to think about danger, *Environmental Politics*, 17: 4660–4672.

Ravetz, J., (2006), Post-normal science and the complexity of transitions towards sustainability, *Ecological Complexity*, 3(4): 275–284.

Roberts, J., (2004), *Environmental Policy*, London: Routledge.

Schlosberg, D. and Rinfret, S., (2008), Ecological modernisation, American style, *Environmental Politics*, Vol. 17, No. 2: 254–275.

Schneider, S., (2008), 'Dangerous' Climate Change: Key Vulnerabilities in E. Zedillo, (ed.), *Global Warming: Looking Beyond Kyoto*, Brookings Institution Press and Yale Center for the Study of Globalization.

Shotter, J., (2006), 'Participative Thinking: "Seeing the Face" and "Hearing the Voice" of Nature' in Y. Haila, and C. Dyke (eds), *How Nature Speaks: The Dynamics of the Human Ecological Condition*, Durham and London: Duke University Press.

Singer, F. and Avery, D., (2007), *Unstoppable Global Warming*, London: Rowman & Littlefield Publishers.

Smith, H., (2007), Disrupting the global discourse of climate change: the case of indigenous voices in M. Pettenger, *The Social Construction of Climate Change: Power, Knowledge, Norms, Discourses (Global Environmental Governance)*, Aldershot: Ashgate Publishing Limited: 149–172.

Stern, N., (2006), *Stern Review on the Economics of Climate Change*, HM Treasury, http://www.hm-treasury.gov.uk/independent_reviews/stern_review_economics_climate_change/sternreview_index.cfm Accessed 21 February 2007.

Stipple, J. and Paterson, M., (2007), Singing Climate change into existence: on the territorialization of climate policymaking in M. Pettenger (ed.), *The Social Construction of Climate Change: Power, Knowledge, Norms, Discourses (Global Environmental Governance)*, Aldershot: Ashgate Publishing Limited.

Stockholm Network Carbon Scenarios, (2009), http://www.stockholm-network.org/downloads/publications/CS_WEB.pdf Accessed 27 February 2009.

Tickner, J., (ed.), (2003), *Precaution, Environmental Science*, London: Island Press.

Tol, R., (2007), Europe's long-term climate target: A critical evaluation, *Energy Policy*, 35 424–432.

United Nations Framework Convention on Climate Change, (1992), http://unfccc.int/resource/docs/convkp/conveng.pdf Accessed 27th January 2009.

Van der Sluijs, J., van Eijndhoven, J., Shackley, S., and Wynne, B., (1998), Anchoring Devices in Science for Policy: The Case of Consensus around Climate Sensitivity, *Social Studies of Science* 28: 291–323.

Walker, G. and King, D., (2008), *The hot topic. How to tackle global warming and still keep the lights on*, London: Bloomsbury.

WBGU, (1995), *Scenario for the derivation of global CO$_2$ reduction targets and implementation strategies. Statement on the occasion of the First Conference of the Parties to the Framework Convention on Climate Change in Berlin*, http://www.wbgu.de/wbgu_sn1995_engl.pdf Accessed 28 January 2007.

WBGU, (1997), *Targets for Climate Protection, 1997. A Study for the Third Conference of the Parties to the Framework Convention on Climate Change in Kyoto*, http://www.wbgu.de/wbgu_sn1997_engl.pdf Accessed 28 January 2007.

WBGU, (2003), *Climate Protection Strategies for the 21st Century. Kyoto and Beyond*, http://www.wbgu.de/wbgu_sn2003_engl.pdf Accessed 11 March 2009.

Weart, S., (2003), *The Discovery of Global Warming*, London: Cambridge University Press.

Wellmer, A., (1983), The critique of critical theory: Reason, utopia and the dialectic, *Praxis International*, Vol 3, No 2: 83–107.

Willig, C., (1998), Social constructionism and revolutionary socialism: A contradiction in terms? in I. Parker (ed.), *Social constructionism, discourse and realism*, London: Sage: 91–104.

A stranger silence still: the need for feminist social research on climate change

Sherilyn MacGregor

If the scientific consensus is correct, then humanity faces an impending climate crisis of catastrophic proportions. It is no longer a question of whether it is really happening, but what will be the impacts of climate change on societies around the world and how governments and individuals will adapt to the troubles they will bring. In the light of frightening predictions, it might reasonably be asked, what is the point of suggesting that greater attention should be paid to gender? Feminist scholarship on environmental problems must always be ready for such questions, to defend the relevance of gender analysis in the face of dominant tendencies to see humanity as homogeneous, science as apolitical, and social justice as a luxury that cannot be chosen over survival. In this essay, I make the case for feminist social research on climate change with the following argument: shedding light on the gender dimensions of climate change will enable a more accurate diagnosis and a more promising 'cure' than is possible with a gender neutral approach. My argument is that any attempt to tackle climate change that excludes a gender analysis will be insufficient, unjust and therefore unsustainable.

Supporting this argument with evidence is challenging because there is a worrying lack of research on which to draw. Social research on climate change has been slow to develop; feminist research into the gender dimensions has been even slower. After briefly taking stock of the small amount of research that currently exists on these issues, I take a critical look at the ways in which gendered discourses, roles and identities shape the political and material aspects of climate change. I consider the ways in which gender plays a role in three broad areas: i) the construction of climate change, ii) experiences of climate change in everyday life and iii) institutional and individual responses to climate change. Where possible I discuss what is already known in the available research; but it is also possible to draw on traditions of feminist theorizing in the field of 'gender and environment'. In many ways climate change raises issues that are no different from the environmental challenges we have been facing for the past 40 years. My intention is to highlight gaps where more research is needed now, and so I conclude with a call for more feminist-informed sociological research into the ways in which the material and discursive dimensions of climate change are deeply gendered. If these can be made more obvious, then perhaps the need for feminists constantly to make the case for gender analysis can be diminished and we might turn our attention to developing critical social theories for a post-carbon world.

Gender and environmental social science: from the margins of the margins

While billions of pounds worth of funding have been spent on climate research in the natural sciences, until recently social research in this area has been minimal. Lever-Tracy (2008: 450) observes that there has been a 'strange silence' about global warming in mainstream sociology. Since sociologists have given little attention to the environment in general, the silence on climate change is not surprising. Exceptions are found in the subfields of environmental and rural sociology, which have examined the social dimensions of environmental problems for decades. Most agree that these subfields have been marginalized within the discipline (Lever-Tracy, 2008). Things move quickly, however, and as I write this I am aware that there are probably several new books on the sociology of climate change going to press. In 2008 Lever-Tracy noted the lack of attention (even the degree of scepticism!) that Britain's leading sociologist Anthony Giddens paid to the existence of global warming; in 2009 he has published *The Politics of Climate Change*. As the topic 'hots up' academically, it is to be expected that more sociological research and theorizing will consider the complex social and political dimensions of climate change. Will gender be included as a relevant category of analysis within this sociological climate change research? As things stand now, it seems unlikely.

At the time of writing there is very little work on gender and climate change in sociology or any other field. Given that feminist perspectives in the marginalized field of environmental sociology are marginalized further still, it is difficult to imagine that this even stranger silence will be broken and knowledge gaps filled, without a great deal of effort by a small number of feminist researchers who face a gruelling uphill battle. Banerjee and Bell (2007) have noted the lack of attention to gender in the environmental social sciences, pointing to the 'shockingly low' number of articles on gender, sex or feminism in the top journals in the field over the past 25 years. They affirm something that feminists who have been involved in interdisciplinary environmental research have been arguing for decades: that there is a pervasive blindness to gender within mainstream (ie non-feminist) environmental disciplines. Whereas class and poverty, 'race' and ethnicities seem to have been easily integrated into sociological analyses of environmental politics – in new literatures on 'environmental justice' and 'climate justice' – the same cannot be said for gender. When Giddens (2009) raises social justice concerns in his analysis of climate change, he appears to be interested only in the relative impacts on poor versus affluent groups in society. He does not mention gender as a relevant category, nor does he mention women other than to remind us that they too drive SUVs (Giddens, 2009: 3).

Given the track record, it is not surprising that there is a lack of attention to the gender dimensions of climate change within sociology and other social sciences. What is somewhat surprising (to me, at least) is that there has been an almost total avoidance of climate change by feminist social scientists in recent years. If conference themes and journal articles are anything to go on, climate change is not on the academic feminist agenda. This may be for reasons similar to those given for mainstream sociology's avoidance of issues that have been defined by the natural sciences (Lever-Tracy, 2008; Rosa and Dietz, 1998). Feminists too have maintained a sceptical stance toward 'nature' for fear of treading into dangerous essentialist territory. Ecofeminism, the one scholarly field that is concerned with the links between gender oppression and the exploitation of nature (or the environment), has been plagued by a negative reputation as being spiritualist, essentialist, and downright 'fluffy' and so arguably has kept feminist-environmental scholarship confined to a ghetto. Banerjee and Bell (2007) suggest that the low status of ecofeminism is partially to blame for the avoidance of environmental issues by mainstream feminist scholars. I shall not review the debate here (but see MacGregor, 2009).

The small amount of research that exists on gender and climate change has been conducted by gender, environment and development (GED) scholars and by feminist researchers working for the UN, government ministries and women's environmental organizations. The bulk of the scholarly work has appeared in two special issues of the journal *Gender and Development* (published in 2002 and 2009), and these are written from a development policy and practice perspective. There are gestures toward feminist and social theory (feminist political ecology in particular); but the work is primarily aimed at development-related issues and takes a materialist approach. A theme running throughout both special issues is that more research into the implications of climate change for women and men as gendered beings is needed. As Geraldine Terry writes in her opening commentary to the 2009 issue, 'academics, gender and development practitioners, and women's rights advocates are still only starting to grapple with [the] many gender dimensions [of climate change]' (Terry, 2009: 5).

I argue that there ought to be a broader agenda for researching and theorizing the gender dimensions of climate change than that presented from a development perspective. At present, the dominance of development scholarship on climate change in the 'South' has resulted in a disproportionate emphasis on vulnerable victims 'down there', when it is the affluent in the sociological 'North' whose large carbon footprints are to blame for global warming. It is also necessary to avoid making the mistake that many outside of the development field have made (eg Giddens, 2009) in presenting climate change as a *future event*. For most of the people living on this planet it is a process whose effects are being experienced *now* (Dankleman, 2002). To broaden the scope of analysis, therefore, my agenda includes three areas in which the workings of gender are apparent in the way climate change is framed (or 'constructed'), in the way climate change is and will be experienced in everyday life, and in the way states and individuals are responding to the challenge of 'tackling' climate change. In each of these three areas, I am particularly interested in considering examples from within the social and political contexts of overdeveloped, affluent societies.

Constructing climate change: science and security

The first place where gender analysis is possible and necessary is in the very construction of the problem of climate change. Rosa and Dietz (1998: 429) argue that one of two sociological responses to climate change is to ask 'what *social conditions* and what *social actors* created this global concern?' (my emphasis). Bringing a social constructivist perspective to the issue is not meant to deny the existence of anthropogenic climate change but to enable critical interrogation of the social and political forces that shape dominant understandings of it. From a *feminist* social constructivist perspective, it is important to examine the ways in which gendered environmental discourses frame and shape dominant understandings of the issue. Gender here is not just an empirical category (ie men/women), it is also a discursive construction that shapes social life. Gender analysis should involve the analysis of power relations between men and women and the discursive and cultural constructions of hegemonic masculinities and femininities that shape the way we interpret, debate, articulate and respond to social/natural/techno-scientific phenomena like climate change.

While scientists have suspected that human activities are changing the earth's climatic systems for many decades, the rise of climate change to the top of the political agenda at the start of the 21st century can be attributed to some particular social conditions. One obvious social condition is the increasing awareness, thanks to unprecedented amounts of scientific evidence disseminated in the popular media, that the climate is changing. Lever-Tracy (2008) identifies the year 2005 as a social 'tipping point' brought about by the Asian tsunami and Hurricane Katrina, among other extreme environmental catastrophes. A related social condition, which has been theorized by Bauman (2006) and others, is the generalized sense of fear and anxiety about the future that characterizes late, 'liquid' modernity, a condition that has been shaped by threats of terrorism, natural disasters and economic collapse in the 2000s. It is within this context that climate change has been presented not only as a largely scientific problem (one might say it has been '*scientized*'), but also as a threat to national and international security (ie it has been '*securitized*').

Better known in the field of international relations than in sociology, the discourses of environmental security, and 'its most powerful and neo-liberal off-spring, "climate security"' (Doyle and Chaturvedi, 2009: 3), are premised on Hobbesian predictions that climate change will lead inevitably to conflict over scarce resources (especially energy) between and within states (Homer-Dixon, 1999; see also Giddens, 2009: 204–5). Since the early 1990s, defence ministries (traditionally the domain of men) have been interpreting environmental 'insecurities' in ways that call for armed and militaristic readiness, alliances and responses (Elliott, 2004). There has been growing interest in recent years in presenting climate change as a serious threat to national and global security. For example in 2004 the UK's Chief Scientist Sir David King made the connection clear, saying that climate change is a worse threat than terrorism (Connor, 2004). Conflicts in some regions of the developing world are attributed to climate change (Darfur is the classic example). These are seen to have knock-on effects for affluent countries such as the influx of environmental refugees from impoverished countries. The security threats posed by climate-related mass migration are met with calls for the tightening up of borders and the increasing of aid budgets (for 'selfish reasons' [Giddens, 2009: 212]) so that 'we' do not have to face the social problems 'they' will import from the South.

A feminist response is to point out that by 'scientizing' and 'securitizing' it, climate change is constructed as a problem that requires the kinds of solutions that are the traditional domain of men and hegemonic masculinity. Whereas the environment was once considered a 'soft politics' issue (Peterson and Runyan, 1999: 59–60) in the field of international relations, it has become 'hardened' by the threats to national and international order that are predicted to come with climate change. This securitizing move has framed the issue in a way that justifies both military responses and exceptional measures that depend on a downgrading of ethical concerns that were once central to environmentalism. Interestingly, climate change is used to 'trump' some of the issues about which women have traditionally expressed concern. For example, fears about the health risks of radiation from nuclear waste, significantly higher among women than men (Solomon, Tomaskovic-Devey and Risman, 1989; Kiljunen, 2006; Freudenberg and Davidson, 2007), have been put aside because nuclear power is allegedly a low-carbon emitting form of energy production. The potential health risks and the ethical uncertainties associated with genetically-modified organisms, again expressed more by women than men (GM Nation Report, 2003; Moon and Balasubramanian, 2004), have been put to one side in the face of climate-related crop failures and the need for biofuels. Finally, the contemporary climate change debate is increasingly framed as one that involves dangerous population growth. The reproductive freedom of women, for which feminists have long fought, is therefore being questioned again by neo-Malthusian environmentalists who argue that population growth is a key driver of climate change (Guillebaud, 2007).

With respect to the social actors involved in bringing climate change to the top of the political agenda, it is uncontroversial to note that men are in the majority. After several decades of women carving out a niche as advocates and exemplars of more sustainable ways of living, climate change has brought about a *masculinization* of environmentalism. Men dominate the issue at all levels, as scientific and economic experts, entrepreneurs, policy makers and spokespeople. Since the 1970s climate change had been identified and explained by natural scientists. As Rosa and Dietz (1998: 442) write, '[s]cience provides the framing and discourse for the problem and scientific elites promote the discourse.' It is not irrelevant that the majority of climate scientists are men. The Intergovernmental Panel on Climate Change (IPCC) is mostly made up of male scientists, with 'chairman' Rajendra Pachauri leading at the global level. Men also dominate in the climate policy arena and as prominent spokespeople whose worldviews and personalities serve to construct the issue in gender-specific ways. International environmental delegations are mostly made up of and led by men (Dankelman, 2002). The most prominent politicians associated with the issue are male. In the USA the issue has been popularized by former Vice President Al Gore, Governor of California Arnold Schwarzenegger, and Senator Robert Kennedy Jr. In the UK political awareness about climate change has been aroused in various ways by such men as Sir Jonathon Porritt (chair of the Sustainable Development Commission), Lord Nicholas Stern (economist and author of the Stern Review); the Miliband brothers (David, the former Secretary of State for Environment and Ed, the new Secretary of State for Energy and Climate Change) and the Prince of Wales (who won the title of Global Environmental Citizen in 2007 [Milmo, 2007]). In 2007 an Internet survey of 'global consumers' in 47 countries conducted by The Nielsen Company and Oxford University found that 18 out of the 22 'most influential spokespeople on climate change' are men, among them Al Gore, Kofi Annan, Nelson Mandela and Bill Clinton (Nielson Company, 2007). The five women on the list are not politicians or scientists, but models and actresses with highly questionable connections to climate change policy.

Why are women largely absent as framers and shapers of climate change as a political issue? One answer is that women make up a small minority in fields that have influence over climate change policy-making; in the UK they represent just 18 per cent of MPs and 22 per cent of MEPs (WEN and NFWI, 2007: 11). Another is that the climate change debate has been shaped by stereotypically masculinist discourses (ie of science and security) that work to invisibilise women and their concerns. It is possible that one of the consequences of the scientific framing is that women have become alienated from the climate change debate because they are less inclined than men to engage with science and technology. It is well known that hegemonic femininity does not encourage women's aptitude for maths and science, and the underrepresentation of women in these fields provides convincing evidence. In the UK, it is estimated that women make up just 19 per cent of scientists and engineers (WEN and NFWI 2007:11). When it comes to a highly scientized issue like climate change, it is quite possible that many women simply 'switch off'. According to survey data collected in the UK '...men are better informed about climate change science than women' (Hargreaves *et al.*, 2003 quoted in Shackley, McLachlan and Gough, 2004: 33). Reflecting on her experience of high-level climate meetings, Ulrike Rohr, director of the German gender and environment project Genanet, attributes the low participation of women to the exclusively scientific and technical approach to global warming. 'Women feel like they can't enter the discussions,' she says (quoted in Stoparic, 2006).

Experiencing climate change: impacts and perceptions in everyday life

A second area that is ripe for gender analysis is the impacts of climate change on the everyday lives of men and women. Impacts are predicted to include an increase in extreme weather events like hurricanes and tsunamis, droughts, floods and heat waves, sea level rise, food shortages, displacement and homelessness. There are gender differences in the way people think about, experience and adapt to these impacts. 'Everyday life' is the area in which there has been the most feminist-informed research to date, probably because the gender dimensions are fairly obvious. Even though it has largely omitted gender from its analyses, the IPCC (Intergovernmental Panel on Climate Change) acknowledges (in its Fourth Assessment Report, 2007) that people's capacity to adapt to climate change will be shaped by their gender roles (Terry, 2009). As noted earlier, there is a body of research on the material impacts of climate change on vulnerable women and men in the Global South. This research takes a materialist (or 'neo-realist' in Rosa and Dietz's 1998 terms) perspective, in that it accepts the scientific predictions as given and focuses on the impacts that will be experienced by individuals and communities. The overarching theme in this work is that climate change is not gender-neutral (as per popular belief) but has gender-differentiated causes and effects (Dankleman, 2002: 24). I shall not go into detail about the many ways people are now, and will be, hurt as a result of the crisis; rather I will identify three key themes that are important in considering the impacts of climate change on everyday life from a feminist perspective.

There is widespread agreement among climate change analysts and policy makers that the more socially and economically marginalized people are, the more vulnerable they are to the effects of global warming. The poor will be hurt the most. However, few other than feminists put the *global feminization of poverty* into the frame. In his analysis, for example, Giddens (2009) refers to 'the poor' as a homogenous group, with no attention to the fact that women are more likely to be poor, and to be responsible for the care of poor children, than men. This is a problematic blindness. Approximately 70 per cent of the world's poor are women; rural women in developing countries are among the most disadvantaged groups on the planet. They are therefore unlikely to have the necessary resources to cope with the changes brought by climate change, and very likely to suffer a worsening of their everyday conditions. Research has found that poor women are more likely to be hurt or killed by natural disasters and extreme weather events than men (Nelson *et al.*, 2002). There is also evidence to suggest that when households experience food shortages, women tend to go without so that their children may eat, with all the health implications this brings for them (Buckingham-Hatfield, 2000). Economic and social breakdown caused by displacement will bring about a worsening of women's already low status and vulnerability. Their poverty and low social status also makes it less likely that they will be involved in decision-making. Drawing on specific case studies from developing countries, the contributors to the special issues of

Gender and Development provide a long list of such gender differences in vulnerability to climate change due to poverty.

Secondly, ecofeminists and GED scholars have been claiming for decades that women are more dramatically affected by environmental degradation than men, due to their social roles as provisioners and carers (Buckingham-Hatfield, 2000; Mellor, 1997; Jackson, 1994). Much of this work draws on analyses of social reproduction and *the gendered division of labour*, which have been central to feminist political economy for decades. Attention to women's gender-ascribed responsibility for social reproduction allows for recognition of the ways in which men and women will be affected differently by climate change. Di Chiro (2008: 281) gives a useful ecofeminist definition of social reproduction as 'the intersecting complex of political-economic, socio-cultural, and material-environmental processes required to maintain everyday life and sustain human cultures and communities on a daily basis and intergenerationally'. She notes that social reproduction, a feminized sphere of activity, has been 'ignored or trivialized' in mainstream (ie non-feminist) scholarship, even though it has been affected in important ways by neoliberal capitalist globalization and ecological degradation. In developing countries, women's everyday provisioning work will be made more difficult due to climate change-related impacts such as drought (eg walking further for clean water and firewood, spending more time growing food for household consumption). Little research has been done on how the gender division of labour will shape women's and men's experiences of climate change in affluent, overdeveloped societies, but it is reasonable to suggest that there will be gender-differentiated implications for both formal employment (eg job losses in the traditional energy and manufacturing sectors) and paid and unpaid reproductive work (eg increases in amount of care required for people hurt by climate change). Policies aimed to achieve a drastic reduction in greenhouse gas emissions, such as carbon rationing, are likely to affect those with greater responsibility for household consumption and transportation. Later in the chapter I comment on how the need for lifestyle changes in the private sphere disproportionately implicate women and their gendered sense of duty.

A third area for feminist research into everyday life is *gender differences in perception of climate change-related risks*. There is an established body of work on risk perception in environmental sociology and social psychology that tends to find differences in men's and women's levels of concern about environmental risk (Slovic, 1999; Finucane *et al.*, 2000). Generally speaking, there is evidence to suggest that women express higher levels, and men lower levels, of concern, and this has been attributed to differences in gender roles and social status (including class). Just as women's socially ascribed roles as carers and provisioners make them more vulnerable to the impacts of climate change, women tend to feel more responsible for and more concerned about the quality of the environment (Zelezny *et al.*, 2000; Dietz *et al.*, 2002; Hunter *et al.*, 2004). Thomas Dietz, who specializes in social psychological research into environmental attitudes, reports that 'generally, women are more concerned about environmental issues [than men]...' (Dietz, Dan and Shwom, 2007). Terry (2009) notes that there has been very little research on gender differences in perceptions of climate risks, but preliminary evidence collected in South Africa, in a survey of male and female farmers, suggests that women feel more worried than men about the likelihood of increased climate-related drought. She suggests that this is due to women farmers' heightened sense of responsibility for household survival: drought means crops fail and families go hungry. Men, on the other hand, tend to be more involved in livestock rearing, which is slightly less sensitive to climate change (Terry, 2009: 8). In the UK, a survey conducted in 2007 by the Women's Environmental Network (WEN) and the Women's Institute (WI) found that women are more concerned about climate change than men and have stereotypically gendered (ie feminized) priorities in response to this concern. Women in the survey were far more concerned about the risk of climate change to future generations (85 per cent), to animal life (81 per cent), and to food security (81 per cent) than they are about threats to the economy (39 per cent) (a stereotypically masculine concern) (WEN and NFWI, 2007: 14).

Tackling climate change: institutional and individual responses

The final area in which there is scope – and need – for a feminist analysis is in the types of responses to climate change that are made by institutions and individuals in different spheres of social life. Echoing much of what I have discussed thus far, Masika alludes to a gendering of responses to climate change when she writes:

> Predominant approaches and policy responses have focused on scientific and techno-logical measures to tackle climate change problems. They have displayed scant regard for the social implications of climate change outcomes and the threats these pose for poor men and women, or for the ways in which people's political and economic environments influence their ability to respond to the challenges of climate change.' (Masika, 2002: 3)

As noted earlier, the scientizing and securitizing discourses that construct climate change as a social problem are informed by stereotypically masculine concerns; it follows that it should be possible to theorize a masculinization of the dominant responses.

There are two main policy responses to climate change: some that aim towards *mitigation* and others that focus on *adaptation*. Mitigation refers to policies aimed at reducing CO_2 emissions in order to slow the speed of climate change. Setting targets for the reduction of CO_2, such as an 80 per cent reduction in emissions by 2050, is now common in most overdeveloped countries and a goal of international environmental negotiations. Achieving these targets will involve social and economic changes that will be slow and politically difficult to make, so at the same time as working toward mitigation, policy-makers also need to think about how to prepare for the likely impacts that will come with climate change in the next 50 years. If people are not prepared, they will not be able to adapt, and the consequences for governments will be serious. So there is a growing focus on improving people's capacity to adapt to things like water shortages, extreme weather and coastal erosion.

Mitigation and adaptation policies are informed by the dominant discourse of ecological modernization which advocates the use of 'technological advancement to bring about [both] better environmental performance' (Schlosberg and Rinfret, 2008: 256) and economic efficiency in a win-win situation. Largely replacing the contested notion of 'sustainable development' in green policy circles, ecological modernization has a supply-side focus and depends on cooperation between government and business to solve environmental problems (Hajer, 1995). It has brought about the development of all sorts of complex technologies and systems that are (or promise to be) highly profitable, such as carbon trading and offsetting, carbon capture and storage, carbon sequestration, renewable energy (wind, solar, wave and geothermal power, biofuels), patented genetically modified crops – the list could go on. Many of the proposed solutions to climate change come in the form of innovations and gadgets, or 'lots of neat green stuff' (Schlosberg and Rinfret, 2008: 268). Giddens (2009) endorses the ecological modernization approach in *The Politics of Climate Change*, arguing that technological innovation and risk-taking is our best hope for ending fossil fuel dependency. His enthusiasm is nicely displayed when he writes:

> Taking risks adds edge to our lives, but much more importantly is intrinsic to a whole diversity of fruitful and constructive tasks. Risk-taking is essential to new thinking in all spheres, to scientific progress and to wealth-creation. We have no hope of responding to climate change unless we are prepared to take bold decisions. It is the biggest example ever of *he who hesitates is lost*. (2009: 57, my emphasis)

With his use of 'he' in this quotation Giddens may not intentionally be making a comment on the gendered nature of ecological modernization, but I think one reasonably can be inferred. While many green techno-scientific innovations will no doubt be important for a sustainable future, it is also true that ecological modernization amounts to more searching for the new rather than improving the old; more omnipotence rather than humble reflection on the benefits *and the costs* of male-dominated scientific ingenuity to date. It is arguably masculine risk-taking and the quest for progress that got us into our ecological mess.

Feminist critics have suggested that the dominant responses to climate change mitigation and adaptation display a stereotypically masculine focus on supply side, technical solutions and militaristic 'muscle-flexing' (Denton, 2002: 18; see also Terry, 2009: 6). Meanwhile feminists argue that women have tended to focus their responses on the social dimension rather than looking to technical fixes for environmental problems (Johnsson-Latham, 2007: 6). The discourses of sustainable lifestyles, ethical consumption, and the precautionary principle seem to reflect a stereotypically feminine set of concerns. The Women's Environment and Development Organization (WEDO), for example, have called for a 'human security' approach, possibly to distinguish it from the dominant environmental security discourse. Human security has been defined as the protection of 'the vital core of all human lives in ways that enhance human freedoms and fulfilment' (Ogata and Sen, 2003). This is a theme in the GED research on women's responses to climate change in the Global South. In order to counter the image of women as powerless victims of climate stresses and natural disasters, feminist researchers have documented the various short- and long-term strategies that women have used to adapt to – and resist – harsh environmental conditions and political marginalization. There tends to be a desire in this literature to theorize women's 'gendered indigenous knowledge' (Terry, 2009: 13) that stems from their close proximity to the natural world through everyday agricultural practices. There is also some work on international women's environmental organizations and the modest success they have had in their efforts to put gender on the agenda of UN policy makers, such as at the Bali Conference in 2007 (Terry, 2009).

It has always been somewhat dangerous for feminists to celebrate women's responses to environmental problems when they are connected to their gender-specific responsibilities for social reproduction (MacGregor, 2006). In the Global South, gender analyses have sometimes led to development programmes that are explicitly designed to be carried out by unpaid women volunteers, based on the assumption that rural women are predisposed to taking an environmental care-taking role (Jackson, 1994). This assumption, writes Maskia (2002: 6) '... continue[s] to translate into initiatives that place greater burdens on women's time and labour without rewards, and do not provide them with the inputs (education, information, and land rights) they require'. In the affluent North, the assumption is subtler. Thus far there have not been any programmes that overtly target women as they do in the South. But governments and environmentalists place emphasis on the role of individuals as consumers to tackle climate change by conserving energy, taking public transit, recycling waste, growing food and foregoing flights. Households contribute about 40 per cent of emissions in the UK and so are under pressure to change their behaviour and 'lifestyles'. Giddens (2009) claims to be 'hostile' to efforts aimed at making people adopt green lifestyles because they are unrealistic, punitive and possibly counterproductive – in short, they might put people off. A feminist objection is to point out that there are unfair gender asymmetries involved in greening the household, which stem from the traditional division of labour.

In so far as consumption is a private sphere activity, and women tend to be principally responsible for household consumption, it is likely that exhortations to 'live green' are directed at (and will be received primarily by) women. Men may hear them, but expect women to do the work. There is evidence to suggest that women are more likely than men to take on green housework (Schultz, 1993; MacGregor, 2005; Vinz, 2009). It is therefore not surprising that women tend to respond to the climate change crisis with increased green diligence in the private sphere and public announcements of gender-specific concern through forms of activism. For example, the EcoMom Alliance, an American non-profit organization that was established in 2006, has the expressed aim of 'inspiring and empowering women to help reduce the climate crisis and create a sustainable future'. It has over 6,000 members and a trademarked motto: *Sustain Your Home, Sustain Your Planet, Sustain Your Self*™. The EcoMom Alliance pushes all the right buttons of hegemonic femininity in the effort to convince women that it is their duty as mothers to save the planet. Their website sums up the organization's *raison d'etre* like this:

> Throughout history, during times of fever, flood, famine or flu, women step up and do what must be done...As both role models and a market force, we believe mothers (and earth mothers alike), can help propel an environmentally, socially and economically vibrant and healthy future. (http://ecomomalliance.org/about)

The website also invites women to 'take the ecomom challenge', which entails taking ten well known steps toward tackling climate change by changing household practices and making the right consumer choices. All of these steps are promoted by government and environmental campaigns; the difference is that whereas masculinist greens do not address who will take the steps, here there is an explicit acknowledgement that this is *women's work*, indeed work that most 'good moms' already do. The same may be said for one of the very few women's organizations that campaign on climate change in the UK, the Women's Institute. The WI traditionally has been associated with stereotypically feminine pursuits and concerns about domestic life. In recent years, it has become involved in expressing a 'women's perspective' on such political issues as European agricultural policy, prostitution and the environment. In 2007, the WI paired up with the Women's Environmental Network (WEN) to publish the Women's Manifesto on Climate Change, the preamble of which states: '[w]omen in the UK have a key role in tackling climate change as consumers, educators and 'change agents' in our homes, encouraging the adoption of lower carbon lifestyles and passing on green values to the next generation. We are also far more concerned about environmental issues than men' (WEN and NFWI, 2007: 2). The WI celebrates women's 'power' to tackle climate change by making good decisions in the supermarket and in the household. 'As household managers, [women] are also key to controlling the 30% of UK carbon emissions that are produced in the home' (WEN and NFWI, 2007: 9). The Manifesto contains a list of 'what women want' the government to do about climate change, a list of demands that is justified by the argument that not only are women in a better position to take action on climate change than men, they are also more concerned about it than men. Rather than questioning the traditional gender division of labour (where women take on all the unpaid housework while men are exempt from such domestic drudgery), the EcoMom and the WI campaigns accept and affirm the gendered status quo – and want to put it good green use.

An ecofeminist critique of environmental politics is that it pays insufficient attention to the politics of gender in general and the gender division of labour in particular (Shultz, 1993; Sandilands, 1993; Littig, 2001; MacGregor, 2006;

Vinz, 2009). Because women's responsibility for social reproduction is *assumed-yet-ignored,* no one stops to raise questions of equity and fairness in a green agenda that depends on it. Ecofeminists have criticized this as a form of environmental privatization that is consistent with neoliberalism (Sandilands, 1993). Women have internalized the sense of responsibility to 'do their bit' for the environment and have taken up the duties promoted by the 'green agenda' quite willingly and publicly. Invoking a Foucauldian analysis, some theorists have referred to this internalization as a form of 'environmentality' (Agrawal, 2005) whereby people are made into good green subjects by adopting the values of government. As I have analysed at length elsewhere (MacGregor, 2005, 2006) many women have become 'environmental subjects' who wear their green duty with feminine pride. Similarly, Sandilands (1999: xiii) describes what she calls 'motherhood environmentalism,' arguing that women's environmental concerns tend to 'boil down to an obvious manifestation of natural protective instincts towards home and family.' Women's maternal role is often used as a justification for their involvement in environmentalism. I have called this 'ecomaternalism' (MacGregor, 2006) in relation to women's 'quality of life activism'; I now recognise it in women's private and public responses to climate change.

Conclusion: the need for feminist social research on climate change

It remains to provide an answer to the question: why call for an end to the strange silence that exists on gender and climate change within the social sciences? Why is feminist research in this area necessary? After decades of feminist scholarship it is regrettable that the onus is still on those of us who want to include gender as a relevant social category rather than those who regularly ignore it.

A great deal of energy is devoted to making the case for gender analysis, energy that might be better spent on other things – like theorizing the social conditions necessary for a low-carbon society. It is tempting to give in to paranoia when one searches in vain for the incorporation of feminist insights on environment-society relations in newly published books and journal articles on climate change. I shall conclude by turning the question around: what are the implications of leaving gender analysis out of sociological investigation into a crisis that threatens to 'undermine the very basis of human civilisation' (Giddens, 2009: 1)?

Gender and development researchers make the instrumental argument that, because it is undeniable that the impacts of climate change are and will be gendered, 'policies need to ensure that gender analysis is fully integrated to avoid exacerbating gender inequalities' (Nelson *et al.*, 2002: 58). Feminist lobbyists at the Bali Climate Conference in 2007 used the slogan 'No climate justice without gender justice' to make their position clear. Empirical research on gender dimensions of climate change, such as that produced by feminist development specialists, will enable a more accurate diagnosis of the problem and thus a more promising 'cure' (if there is one) than is possible with a gender neutral approach.

But those in the field are unanimous in calling for more case studies and more evidence that will contribute to a thorough understanding of gender differences in perceptions, impacts, and responses in developing and overdeveloped regions of the world. Attempts to tackle climate change that proceed without the benefit of this knowledge will be insufficient, unjust and hence unsustainable.

It is also important that materialist-informed empirical research be complemented by critical feminist theorizing of non-material and discursive aspects of climate change. Sociologists have a long tradition of interpreting the processes through which social issues are constructed and framed, and this approach is highly useful in the climate change arena. As I have shown above, the dominant discourses that shape climate change as a social issue, the kinds of responses that are deemed appropriate for it, and the kinds of concerns that are displaced by it, are ripe for feminist analyses of hegemonic gender codes. The case for developing this kind of constructivist analysis is simply 'intellectual opportunity' (Rosa and Dietz, 1998: 446): it will allow deeper, better sociological understanding of an issue that dominates social life in the 21st century. Feminist social constructivist analyses of climate change will not yield solutions per se and so perhaps will be regarded as frivolous at a time like this. But if the social sciences are to contribute to climate change research on an equal footing with natural sciences (as Rosa and Dietz hoped would happen back in 1998), then there must be space for non-instrumental goals and critical interrogation of scientific knowledge claims from a range of perspectives.

In *The Politics of Climate Change* Anthony Giddens's aim is to understand in order to solve: to analyse the root causes, survey the available technologies, calculate the costs, weigh up the risks and benefits, and propose viable solutions. Despite the book's title, its starting point is the claim that '*we have no politics of climate change*' (2009: 4) (many of us who have been working on environmental political issues for a lot longer than he has would beg to differ with his assessment). 'In other words,' he continues, 'we do not have a developed analysis of the political innovations that have to be made if our aspirations to limit global warming are to become real. It is a strange and indefensible absence...'. From a feminist perspective, it is unlikely that 'our aspirations' can be realized without an accurate understanding of the social and political relations that have brought about the crisis of climate change or of the social conditions under which potential solutions will enhance rather than entrench existing injustices. So perhaps a more interesting question for him and others gripped by the present ecological crisis is: when will we have a *sociology of climate change*? Until there is an end to the strange silence on the gender dimensions of climate change, this will remain an elusive goal.

References

Agrawal, A., (2005), *Environmentality: Technologies of Government in the Making of Subjects*, Durham: Duke University Press.

Banerjee, D. and Mayerfeld Bell, M., (2007), Ecogender: locating gender in the environmental social sciences, *Society and Natural Resources* 20: 3–19.

Bauman, Z., (2006), *Liquid Fear*, London: Polity Press.

Buckingham-Hatfield, S., (2000), *Gender and Environment*, London: Routledge.

Connor, S., (2004), US climate policy bigger threat to world than terrorism, *The Independent*, Friday, 9 January 2004. On line at: http://www.independent.co.uk/news/world/americas/us-climate-policy-bigger-threat-to-world-than-terrorism-572493.html Accessed 24 May 2007.

Dankleman, I., (2002), Climate change: learning from gender analysis and women's experience of organizing for sustainable development, *Gender and Development* 10 (2): 21–29.

Denton, F., (2002), Climate change vulnerability, impacts and adaptation: why does gender matter? *Gender and Development* 10 (2): 10–20.

Di Chiro, G., (2008), Living environmentalisms: coalition politics, social reproduction and environmental justice, *Environmental Politics* 17 (2): 276–298.

Dietz, T., Kalof, L. and Stern, P., (2002), Gender, values and environmentalism, *Social Science Quarterly* 83 (1), 353–364.

Dietz, T., Dan, A. and Shwom, R., (2007), Support for climate change policy: social psychological and social structural influences, *Rural Sociology* 72 (2), 2007: 185–214.

Doyle, T. and Chaturvedi, S., (2009), Securitizing the wind: climate security in the Global South, Unpublished paper presented at the British International Studies Association (BISA) Conference, December 2008, University of Exeter, UK. http://ecomomalliance.org/about Accessed 24 November 2008.

Elliott, L., (2004), *The Global Politics of the Environment* (Second edition), London: Macmillan.

Finucane, M. L., Slovic, P., Mertz, C. K., Flynn, J. and Satterfield, T. A., (2000), Gender, race, and perceived risk: The 'white male' effect, *Health, Risk, & Society* 2 (2): 159–172.

Freudenberg, W. and Davidson, D., (2007), Nuclear families and nuclear risks: The effects of gender, geography, and progeny on attitudes toward a nuclear waste facility, *Rural Sociology* 72 (2) 215–243.

Giddens, A., (2009), *The Politics of Climate Change*, London: Polity.

GM Nation? Findings of the public debate. UK Department of Trade and Industry (2003).

Guillebaud, J., (2007), Youthquake: Population, fertility and environment in the 21st century. Optimum Population Trust. Online at: http://www.optimumpopulation.org/Youthquake.pdf Accessed 15 June 2009.

Hajer, M., (1995), *The Politics of Environmental Discourse: Ecological Modernization and the Policy Process*, Oxford: Oxford University Press.

Hargreaves, I., Lewis, J. and Speers, T., (2003), *Towards a Better Map: Science, the Public and the Media*. Economic and Social Research Council, Swindon, UK.

Homer-Dixon, T. F., (1999), *Environment, Scarcity, and Violence*, Princeton, NJ: Princeton University Press.

Hunter, L., Hatch, A. and Johnson, A., (2004), Cross-national gender variation in environmental behaviours, *Social Science Quarterly* 85 (3), 677–694.

Intergovernmental Panel on Climate Change, (2007), Fourth Assessment Report *Climate Change 2007*.

Jackson, C., (1994), Gender analysis and environmentalisms In M. Redclift and T. Benton, (eds), *Social Theory and the Global Environment*, London: Routledge: 113–149.

Johnsson-Latham, G., (2007), A study on gender equality as a prerequisite for sustainable development. What we know about the extent to which women globally live in a more sustainable way than men, leave a smaller ecological footprint and cause less climate change. Report to the Environment Advisory Council, Ministry of the Environment, Sweden.

Kiljunen, P., (2006), Energy Attitudes 2006: Public Opinion in Finland. Results of a follow-up study concerning Finnish attitudes towards energy issues 1983 2006. http://www.sci.fi/~yhdys/eas_06/english/eng_luku2–4.htm Accessed 02 December 2008.

Lever-Tracy, C., (2008), Global warming and sociology, *Current Sociology* 56 (3): 445–466.

Littig, B., (2001), *Feminist Perspectives on Environment and Society*, Harlow: Prentice Hall.

MacGregor, S., (2005), The Public, the Private, the Planet and the Province: Women's Quality of Life Activism in Urban Southern Ontario In M. Hessing, R. Raglan and C. Sandilands (eds), *This Elusive Land: Women and the Canadian Environment*, Vancouver: University of British Columbia Press.

MacGregor, S., (2006), *Beyond Mothering Earth: Ecological Citizenship and the Politics of Care,*. Vancouver: University of British Columbia Press.

MacGregor, S., (2009), 'Natural allies, perennial foes? On the trajectories of feminist and green political thought' in *Contemporary Political Theory*, 8 (3): 329–339.

Masika, R., (2002), Editorial, *Gender and Development* (Special issue on climate change) 10 (2): 2–9.

Mellor, M., (1997), *Feminism and Ecology*, Washington Square, NY: New York University Press.

Milmo, C., (2007), Prince Charles jets in to US to collect environment award, *The Independent*, Saturday, 27 January 2007. Online at: http://www.independent.co.uk/environment/prince-charles-jets-in-to-us-to-collect-environment-award-433823.html Accessed 04 February 2007.

Moon, W. and Balasubramanian, S., (2004), Public attitudes toward agrobiotechnology: the mediating role of risk perceptions on the impact of trust, awareness, and outrage, *Review of Agricultural Economics* 26 (2): 186–208.

Nelson, V., Meadows, K., Cannon, T., Morton, J. and Martin, A., (2002), Uncertain predictions, invisible impacts, and the need to mainstream gender in climate change adaptations, *Gender and Development* 10 (2): 51–59.

Nielsen Company, (2007), Climate change and influential spokespeople: a global Nielsen on-line survey. June 2007. The Nielsen Company and the Oxford University Environmental Change Institute. Availble online at http://www.eci.ox.ac.uk/publications/downloads/070709nielsen-celeb-report.pdf Accessed 12 November 2008.

Ogata, S. and Sen, A., (2003), Human security now: final report of the Commission on Human Security, New York: United Nations.

Peterson, V. S. and Runyan, A. S., (1999), *Global Gender Issues*, Boulder, CO: Westview Press.

Plumwood, V., (2002), *Environmental Culture: The Ecological Crisis of Reason*, New York: Routledge.

Rosa, E. and Dietz, T., (1998), Climate change and society: speculation, construction and scientific investigation, *International Sociology* 13 (4): 421–455.

Sandilands, C., (1993), On 'green consumerism': Environmental privatization and 'family values', *Canadian Women's Studies/Les Cahiers de la Femme* 13 (3), Spring: 45–7.

Sandilands, C., (1999). *The Good-Natured Feminist: Ecofeminism and the Quest for Democracy*, Minneapolis: University of Minnesota Press.

Schlosberg, D. and Rinfret, S., (2008), Ecological modernization, American style, *Environmental Politics* 17 (2): 254–275.

Schultz, I., (1993), Women and waste, *Capitalism, Nature, Socialism* 4 (2): 51–63.

Shackley, S., McLachlan, C. and Gough, C., (2004), The Public Perceptions of Carbon Capture and Storage, Tyndall Centre for Climate Change Research Working Paper 44. Online at: http://www.tyndall.ac.uk/publications/working_papers/wp44.pdf Accessed 14 October 2008.

Slovic, P., (1999), Trust, emotion, sex, politics, and science: surveying the risk-assessment battlefield, *Risk Analysis* 19 (4): 689–701.

Solomon, L. S., Tomaskovic-Devey, D. and Risman, B. J., (1989), The gender gap and nuclear power: attitudes in a politicized environment, *Sex Roles* 21:5/6, 401–414.

Stoparic, B., (2006), Women push for seats at climate policy table, *Women's e-news* [Online] http://www.womensenews.org/article.cfm/dyn/aid/2804 Accessed 9 Nov 2008.

Terry, G., (2009), No climate justice without gender justice: an overview of the issues, *Gender and Development* 17 (1): 5–18.

Vinz, D., (2009), Gender and sustainable consumption: a German environmental perspective, *European Journal of Women's Studies* 16 (2): 159–179.

Women's Environment and Development Organization, (2005), Beijing betrayed [online], New York: WEDO (Women's Environment and Development). Online at: http://www.wedo.org/library.aspx?ResourceID¼31

Women's Environmental Network and the National Federation of Women's Institutes, (2007), Women's Manifesto on Climate Change. Online at: http://www.wen.org.uk/general_pages/reports/manifesto.pdf

Zelezny, L., Poh-Pheng Chua, P. and Aldrich, C., (2000), Elaborating on gender differences in environmentalism, *Journal of Social Issues* 56: 443–457.

Broadcasting green: grassroots environmentalism on Muslim women's radio

Daniel Nilsson DeHanas

In 1967, Lynn White published a wide-ranging essay in *Science* arguing that the causes of the world's ecological crises are, at their roots, spiritual. He wrote that Abrahamic thought has always been profoundly anthropocentric, beginning with the creation account in Genesis in which God gives humanity full dominion over the earth and over animals. According to White, Western Christianity and related traditions, such as Islam, have seen nature as instrumental to human needs. These branches of thought have therefore justified the exploitation of nature. White concluded that '[s]ince the roots of our trouble are so largely religious, the remedy must also be essentially religious, whether we call it that or not'. Using St. Francis of Assisi as a model, White called for a re-envisioning of the modern human relationship with nature that reached to the depth of the soul.

Though perhaps not quite what White had in mind, a religious reshaping of environmental ethics *is* at work in the West within some of its Muslim communities. In this paper I will investigate the particular case of the Muslim Community Radio (MCR, 87.8 FM) environmental broadcasting campaign in the East End of London during Autumn 2007. The radio campaign is an instance of a small but significant set of Muslim environmental collective action campaigns emerging in Britain. I focus the paper on the women's radio programming during the MCR radio campaign. I argue that the women's radio broadcasts were intended to 'sacralize' environmentalism in the minds of the female Muslim listening audience, imbuing environmental ethics with religious meaning. Though the primary overt discourse in the campaign was this sacralized environmentalism, I will also point out two underlying discourses: 1) The assertion that Islam is modern and compatible with selected western values and 2) the call for Muslim women to take up a carefully gender-structured community activism. Therefore, the radio campaign was in reality three simultaneous campaigns: for environmental activism, for the justification of Islam in modern Britain, and, in a more veiled form, for women's empowerment. These interconnected layers of meaning reveal something of the complexity of concerns within Muslim communities in Britain. As I will argue in the conclusion, the case also contributes to our general understanding of religious influences on environmental behaviours and of the agentic role of women in sacralization processes in the modern West (Aune, Sharma and Vincett, 2008).

Religion and environmental attitudes

The role of religion on environmental attitudes has been an intriguing topic of research since the publication of Lynn White's essay. Several nationally representative studies in the USA have empirically compared the ecological attitudes of members of different Christian religious traditions. Some of this work finds an inverse relationship between ecological interest and either biblical literalism or general religious conservatism (Guth *et al.*, 1995; Greeley, 1993). The main British contribution finds that Catholics are more sceptical of environmentalism than other British Christians (Hayes and Marangudakis, 2001). The consensus in most recent work, however, is that religiosity and affiliation have complex, nuanced, and generally small effects on environmental attitudes that are difficult to gauge quantitatively (Ignatow, 2006; Nooney *et al.*, 2003; Kanagy and Nelson, 1995). For example, Ignatow (2006) questions religio-cultural generalizations based on his broad sample of 21 nations from the International Social Survey Programme. Instead, he argues that 'the public adoption of an ecological worldview is predicated on modern, secular, Western-style mass education' (Ignatow, 2006: 457).

Quantitative work comparing ecological attitudes in contemporary religious traditions has been informative. But in some ways it misses the spirit of White's original provocative thesis. White's thesis was about a religious idea – biblical anthropocentrism – that he argued had been an historical precondition for modern anti-ecological ways of thinking. His style of argument was akin to Max Weber's theses on the elective affinities between religious ideas and cultural or economic outcomes (Weber, 2002 [1905], 1968 [1915]). White was not necessarily arguing that the Biblicism of contemporary religious groups would predict their current ecological commitment, but rather that a certain religious idea had influenced general western environmental practices through the course of centuries. In Weberian terms, White was suggesting that religious ideas might again serve as 'switchmen' to set western societies back on track.

Andrew Greeley's (1993) empirical study may be the best match with White's mode of cultural analysis. With a US national sample, Greeley finds that being Roman Catholic and having a gracious image of God are positively correlated with spending money on the environment, while biblical literalism was negatively correlated with such spending. He suggests that the positive environmental consciousness of certain subsections of American Christianity results from the development of a less rigid and more generous religious imagination. Though his analysis is not as comprehensive as the most recent studies, Greeley's framing of the problem in terms of 'religious imagination' is provocative and helpful.

Recasting the question of religion and the environment in terms of the religious or spiritual imagination, it becomes theoretically important to identify the ideas available in a religious system to envision the human relationship with the natural world. Creation narratives, theologies of human nature, and similar concepts can be seen as religious resources that enable or restrict the capacity for adherents to live in a harmonious relationship with nature.

Certain forms of spirituality seem to have especially rich imaginations of the natural world. Recent work in the sociology of religion has brought to the fore 'spiritualities of life,' particularly those connected to the new age movement (Heelas and Woodhead, 2005). Spiritualities of life emphasize nature and self over other forms of authority. These forms of spirituality tend to be grounded in a nature-related language and ethos and therefore might be expected to develop spiritual imaginations teeming with ecological ideas. A key case is ecofeminism, a combination of feminist ideology, ecological thinking, and (in some of its forms) a nature-spirituality (Eaton, 2005; Diamond and Orenstein, 1990). Ecofeminists emphasize the dual historical role of patriarchy in degrading women and exploiting the environment, seeking to raise consciousness for both environmental and feminist activism.

Islamic religious resources for environmentalism

What of Islam and the environment? In Heelas and Woodhead's typology, Islam can be identified as a form of 'life-as religion,' meaning that it provides for the total orientation of life around religious truth claims. In comparison with the spiritualities of life, 'life-as religion' may at first glance seem to engender an impoverished imagination for environmental action. Some ecofeminists have indeed been critical of the Islamic religious imagination, characterizing the system of practice and belief as one that stifles women's freedom of expression. Following this line of argument, one would expect Muslim women's radio programming to have little to offer to a proactive environmentalism.

Yet there is significant theoretical and theological literature to suggest that as a religious system and historical tradition, Islam has rich potential resources for an engaged ecological perspective. Analogous to the 'dominion' over the environment described in Genesis, in an Islamic perspective God has assigned humanity to be the *khalifa*, or vice-regent, responsible for the natural world (Mohamed, 2007). In both Islamic and Judeo-Christian perspectives, the role of humanity on Earth can potentially be seen more in terms of responsible 'stewardship' rather than property ownership (see Gelderloos, 1992).

The core principle of Islam is *tawheed*, or the oneness of God, whereby everything in creation is under God's unified sovereignty. According to Khalid (2002: 337) the concept of *tawheed* is 'testimony to the unity of all creation and the fabric of the natural world of which humankind is an intrinsic part. . . . This is the bedrock of the holistic approach in Islam as this affirms the interconnectedness of the natural order'.

The *Sunnah*, or example of the Prophet Muhammad's life, is a major source of Islamic ecological thought. According to journalist Francesca De Chatel (2003), 'based on accounts of his life and deeds, we can read that Muhammad had a profound respect for the fauna and flora, as well as an almost visceral connection to the four elements – earth, water, fire, and air'. De Chatel argues that Muhammad's actions were particularly forward-looking in the sustainable usage of land, the conservation of water, and the humane treatment of animals. For example, Muhammad's early followers established publicly-owned wildlife refuges, known as the *hima* system, a practice which continues today in some Muslim majority countries (IUCN 2007).

The Qur'an places great emphasis on the natural world as displaying evidence of God. Indeed, the natural world is sometimes referred to as the 'book of nature', a form of revelation complementary to the Qur'an (see Helminski, 2006). For example, in Sura 13, Verse 3:[1]

> It is He who spread out the earth, placed firm mountains and rivers on it, and made two of every kind of fruit; He draws the veil of night over the day. There truly are signs in this for people who reflect.

The repeated emphasis on creation as a sign in the Qur'an potentially provides a less anthropocentric perspective than Judeo-Christian traditions. The Qur'an expresses a high value for animal life and a doctrine that natural creation, rather than humankind, is God's crowning achievement:

> All the creatures that crawl on the earth and those that fly with their wings are communities like yourselves. (Sura 6, beginning of Verse 13)

> The creation of the heaven and the earth is greater by far than creation of humankind, though most people do not know it. (Sura 40, Verse 57)

The Qur'an even dramatically personifies the natural world, suggesting that God offered the role of earth's 'vice-regent' to nature first, which refused:

> We offered the Trust to the heavens, the earth, and the mountains, yet they refused to undertake it and were afraid of it; mankind undertook it – they have always been inept and foolish. (Sura 33, Verse 72)

The radical emphasis on nature in Islamic scripture has a surprising affinity with certain contemporary developments in social theory. It resonates with the move away from anthropocentric perspectives by current theorists such as Bruno Latour and John Gray. Also, intriguingly, the high Islamic valuation of nature is a common ground with ecofeminist theory.

Potential environmental effects of Islam in Britain

Islam has scriptural and historical resources for a proactive environmentalism. Yet in the contemporary world, Muslim nations and communities are not particularly known for eco-ethical practices. Muslim philosopher Seyyed Hossein Nasr (2003) reasons that Muslim ecological thinking has remained dormant while Muslim societies have been eager to modernize and raise their standards of living. A related argument could be that many nations with significant Muslim populations are poor or face internal strife, while environmentally conscious policy is more feasible in highly developed and secure nations. According to a study by Geoff Dench and coauthors (2006: 174), Bangladeshi Muslims in East End London, the focus case in this paper, are frequently subject to complaints from other local residents for leaving rubbish on the streets. The authors learn from a Bangladeshi informant that this habit matches with practices in the many Bangladeshi villages that do not have rubbish collection. Rather than Islam in particular, neglectful environmental practices are the result of lifestyles from an impoverished nation being transplanted to London.

Environmentalism among East End Bangladeshi Muslims has only recently risen to the surface as a possible topic of research. Bangladeshis in the East End of London have experienced significant generational transitions in the past few decades, opening the way for a first wave of environmental activism. The original migrants from Bangladesh came for economic reasons, sending remittances back to their home country and intending to return eventually (Gardner, 2002). Second and third generations, however, which were educated and socialized in this country, have tended to identify more strongly with Britain and are more likely to be politically active. East End Bangladeshis in recent years have developed an activist culture, primarily focused on asserting a strong Muslim identity and protesting against interventionist British and American foreign policy in Muslim majority countries (Birt, 2005). Yet there is evidence that Muslims in East End London, and the UK in general, are gradually adopting the environment as an important issue of concern.

A nascent Muslim environmentalism has been developing through the growth and activities of particular organizations. The largest Muslim environmental organization in Britain, the Islamic Foundation for Ecology and Environmental Sciences (IFEES), has campaigned at the East London Mosque for the environment and distributed *khutbah* (sermon) notes to various Imams who are willing to preach on the subject (EcoIslam, 2006). The community-based London Islamic Network for the Environment (LINE) has engaged in several innovative activities, including a protest along 'curry avenue', Brick Lane, where LINE demonstrators wore snorkels and flippers to highlight the dangers of flooding caused by climate change. The founder of LINE, Muzzamal Hussain, says of Muslim environmental activism in London:

> It's a bit of an uphill struggle....What we have now, though, is a small group of people who are ready to take action. Global issues such as climate change are very important, especially with their impact on Muslim society. When an Imam does give a Friday sermon on the environment, it always goes down well. (Quoted in Vidal, 2007)

The environmental focus of Muslim Community Radio in 2007 may be best comprehended in the light of the small but active minority of Muslims engaged in environmental advocacy through organizations such as LINE and IFEES. The MCR radio station is a grassroots effort, able to tap into a pre-existing activist culture among young Bangladeshi Muslims in the East End. Islamic scripture and tradition, as briefly reviewed here, provide a substantial foundation for this new environmental advocacy.

Research methods

This paper considers Muslim environmentalism in the specific case of the Muslim Community Radio broadcasts from the London Muslim Centre during Ramadan 2007. The London Muslim Centre (LMC) is a community centre and a public advocacy organization for Islam in Britain, located on Whitechapel Road in Tower Hamlets, London. The LMC is an extension of the prominent East London Mosque (ELM). The ELM and LMC buildings are large and symbolic structures centred near the 'heartland' of London's Bangladeshi community (Dench, Gavron and Young, 2006: 54). The impressive LMC complex was completed in 2004 and includes a primary school, housing, a library, a sex-segregated gym, large event and prayer spaces, and a restaurant. Two influential Muslim organizations in Britain – Muslim Aid are headquartered – and Islamic Forum Europe in the business wing of the LMC. Muslim Community Radio was produced in this business wing, in a well-equipped professional recording studio that I visited once after the Ramadan broadcasts had finished. I interviewed the director of MCR English language programming, Muhammad Abul Kalam, during this visit (March 2008).

Muslim Community Radio (MCR) ran from September 12th through October 13th 2007, covering the entire Islamic month of Ramadan. It marked MCR's tenth year of Ramadan broadcasts, which had grown in scope with each year. A major theme for 2007 was the environment, including topics such as global warming and recycling. MCR received sponsorship funding from the Tower Hamlets Council because of its commitment to environmental broadcasting and because it also advocated a Tower Hamlets school attendance initiative.

I listened to MCR throughout the month of Ramadan. Over time I made digital recordings, or was granted them by the radio station, for approximately fifty hours of programming. My research work on MCR is part of a larger project in which I have been investigating the role of religion in identity and citizenship formation among second generation Bangladeshi and Jamaican young people. While listening for citizenship and identity-related discourse on MCR, I found myself interested in the way in which the environmental theme was presented. Because my radio research is part of a larger study in which I frequently visit the London Muslim Centre and East London Mosque, I have been able to place the environmental broadcasting in larger context.

I chose to focus my attention for this paper on the 'Women's Hour', an hour-and-a-half radio show hosted by women throughout Ramadan on Tuesday mornings and on Monday, Wednesday, and Friday evenings. There are good practical and theoretical reasons for this choice of focus. The Women's Hour had a substantially higher proportion of environmental content than the other programmes to which I listened. Also, the programme provided a unique window into the thoughts and attitudes of religiously conservative Muslim women, whom I as a male non-Muslim researcher could not have accessed to the same depth. The choice of the Women's Hour is significant, furthermore, because it allows me to consider the gender dynamics of Muslim female radio broadcasting and environmental advocacy.

While listening to live MCR broadcasts, I took notes on segments and phrases relating to nature and the environment. I developed initial conjectures and hypotheses from this stage of listening. When Ramadan ended, I went back to the recordings and listened through them again more closely, transcribing all nature-related references and noting their locations in the recordings. During this process I was able to code references to the environment, gender, and religion in these nature-related sections. I communicated with the organizers of MCR, who graciously agreed to provide copies of all Women's Hour recordings, including some that I did not yet have. I applied the same listening, transcribing, and coding procedure to this set of recordings. Based on the codes produced and on re-listening to segments, I conducted an inductive analysis to address the Islamic framing of environmentalism and the role of gender.

Findings

Each Women's Hour show on Muslim Community Radio was hosted by a team of two or three women in their 20s or 30s. The themes of broadcasts were generally based on the interests expressed by focus groups of female listeners organized at the end of the MCR season the previous year. Even so, hosts had significant artistic freedom in choosing their topics and approaches. For example, one set of hosts chose to focus on the spiritual disciplines of the month of Ramadan, while another set dedicated their shows to discussing the benefits of international travel. Regardless of the chosen topic, most episodes included the environmental theme in a significant way. Two episodes focussed on the environment entirely. The format of shows varied, but usually consisted of conversation between the hosts, interviews with guests, and opportunities for the listening audience to call or send text messages to join the discussion.

The most regular and recognizable feature of The Women's Hour – and all shows on Muslim Community Radio – was a recurrent musical jingle broadcast about every ten minutes. During the Women's Hour, some hosts referred to the jingle as a 'drop' because it 'dropped in' almost unexpectedly during the broadcast. The jingle had been pre-recorded with two youthful male voices and was delivered in a street rap style:

> M C R
> *Authu bilahi minash shaitanu rajeem*
> *Bismillah ir-rahman ir-raheem*[2]
> Keep your *deen*[3] clean
> Keep your scene clean
> Drop your rubbish in the bin[4]
> Yo!
> This is Muslim Community Radio!'

The jingle was a regular reminder of the environmental theme of MCR. Even if a specific Women's Hour programme never directly mentioned nature or ecology, listeners would hear the encouragement to be environmentally minded in the jingle several times in the course of a programme. Importantly, the ubiquitous rap jingle communicated something of the philosophy behind the environmental campaign. First, it expressed the idea that positive environmental activities are deeply Islamic. The opening Arabic lines of the jingle are the words with which Muslims initiate prayer – words which cast away evil and prepare the worshiper to enter the presence of Allah. These words held an immediate significance for MCR's listener base and added a sacred quality to the environmental message.[5] The Arabic word *deen* later in the jingle refers to the religious practices, or religious way of life of Islam. The implication of this word choice is that environmental behaviour is an expression of Muslim piety – to be a good Muslim is to be environmentally conscious on a practical, everyday level.

Second, because the jingle was in a rhyming rap style, it communicated with youthful energy MCR's assertive challenge to cultural assumptions about Muslims and their place in modern Britain. These two themes – that environmentalism is Islamic and that Islam is modern – were major emphases in MCR broadcasting on the Women's Hour. I will explain how each of these themes was conveyed, and then address gender issues within the radio discourse.

Sacralizing environmentalism

As noted above in the analysis of the main jingle, MCR radio programming emphasized the connection between daily Islamic practice, or *deen*, and environmental ethics. Women's Hour environmental broadcasting frequently suggested incorporating ecological habits into one's regimen of Islamic self-discipline. For example, one broadcaster said: 'Remember recycling, sisters! You can write your [Qur'an memorization] verses on old scraps of paper lying around the house'. The broadcasts regularly encouraged listeners to develop habits that would conserve energy, minimize waste, and improve the health of their lifestyle and of the local environment: eg 'We are encouraging a waste-free society, which is what Islam teaches us – to use as much as we need and not more than that'. Ecologically friendly and fairtrade products were supported in a melding of the environmental theme with Islamic concerns for global justice.

The message of self-discipline in everyday actions was particularly relevant because the broadcasting took place during Ramadan. Listeners were engaged in daily fasting and prayer and were expected to be closely attuned to the ethics of even seemingly small actions.

The primary rhetorical strategy for motivating ecological actions was through tying them into habits of Islamic practice. In this way the Women's Hour broadcasting took many mainstream environmental activities, like recycling and water conservation, and imbued them with religious significance. It was a process of sacralizing environmentalism: extending the boundaries of the Islamic sacred and profane to subsume the categories of the environmental movement and grant them spiritual depth.

The sacralization of environmental discourse was evident on the Women's Hour not only in discussions of practical actions, but also in broader reflections on nature, beauty, and humanity. In one episode, Nazeema read her favourite section from Lord Byron's poem *Childe Harold's Pilgrimage*. In the poem, Byron reflects on how the 'torture' of human cities leads to a desire to seek sanctuary in nature. Nazeema discussed the poem and her own feelings about London city life with her co-host Farida:

> Nazeema: 'Seeing concrete all day, I don't know, after a while you get bored of it. It gets to you and you feel a bit claustrophobic. And that's why you appreciate seeing scenery and things like that.'

> Farida: 'One thing [Lord Byron] said that was quite interesting, you know he was talking about the torture of humans in cities, and it's quite interesting because when you go, when you're in nature and when you're surrounded by nature that's when you kind of reflect on life. You kind of reflect on the Creator and the Creation. And that's how the Prophet reflected on Creation, that's how the message came to him.'

There is a certain irony in recalling the life story of the Prophet Muhammad through the touchstone of the reckless Romantic poet and paramour Lord Byron. Yet more than anything, the example demonstrates the radio hosts' ability to subsume a wide range of references to natural beauty and human yearning into an Islamic meta-narrative.

Sacralization of environmental discourse at times arose spontaneously in Women's Hour discussions. For example, on two separate occasions in an episode about international travel, hosts and guests were caught up in worshipful wonder at natural beauty:

> Rupa: '...Traveling is a way to ponder on Allah's creation.'
> Asma: 'We saw some beeaauutiful sights while we were driving down!'
> Rupa: '*Mashallah!*[6] Absolutely.'
> Asma: 'We got pictures of those. Loads!'
> Shareen: 'I think that for my argument's sake, that you can just look at pictures.'
> Asma: 'No, it's nothing compared to – I've seen pictures of Mont Blanc, for example, and when we saw it, it was just like: Wow am I really standing here and looking upon this mountain!'

> Shareen: 'One of the street interview people was talking about how Italy is really romantic, and you've got places like Venice and stuff. Well, you've got Little Venice in Oxford don't you? So you can always make your alternative as well in this country. And there is some really really beautiful places.'
> Rupa: 'Beautiful green places.'
> Shareen: 'If you want to ponder upon the creation of Allah, go to places like Wales –North Wales – or Bangor and Ben Nevis areas or Scotland or places like that.'

Asma: 'I have to say that I once did travel to Wales and the most *amazing* sight I saw was actually being in the same sea as dolphins! You know you don't think dolphins are in England, but it was just so surreal, so unreal seeing them!'

Natural beauty was understood to invoke wonder and reflection on the majesty of God's creation. Islamic reflection of this kind could remind the radio listener of a utopian vision of Islam's beginnings or of abstract principles beyond time. Even so, many references to natural beauty – whether citing Lord Byron or Ben Nevis – remained within the knowable, worldly bounds of British culture or geography. Sacralization was the process of attaching everyday places, ideas, and environmental practices to something greater.

Presenting a modern Islam

The theming of the MCR radio season in Ramadan 2007 was described on the official website in this way:

'One of our themes this year is *Presenting Islam* and our focus will be on the environment, global warming, recycling, etc.'

This description of the broadcasting theme reveals the somewhat awkward pairing of an environmental message with the promotion of Islam.

An Islamic positive public relations agenda came across very directly in a Women's Hour episode in which the hosts interviewed a local Muslim environmental activist. The activist explained her organization's purpose for environmental activism, at least in part: 'We use the environment agenda as a diplomatic [tool] to forward various issues'. For this activist, environmental goals were secondary – environmentalism was an admirable agenda that proved diplomatically useful in building community partnerships and improving the public perceptions of Islam.

If an underlying goal of the radio campaign was to present Islam, what image of Islam was being presented? The first episode of the Women's Hour set the tone. In this episode, a special pre-recorded radio segment profiled Muhammad as a pioneer of environmentalism. The segment included Women's Hour hosts reading examples of Muhammad's environmental ethics from *ahadith*[7] and from Tariq Ramadan's *In the Footsteps of the Prophet* (2007). The overall message of the segment was that environmentalism has been integral to Islam since its inception. Islam is not only compatible with the best principles in modern western environmental ethics, but had in fact *anticipated* these principles centuries earlier. Rather than in need of modernisation, Islam was presented as timeless.

In their presentation of Islam, broadcasters on the Women's Hour seldom used the word 'modern'. Their implicit understanding was that Islam transcended historical time. Nonetheless, their discussions were shaped in countless ways by the socio-historical context of contemporary London, where most of the broadcasters had spent their lives. The episode that profiled Muhammad as environmental activist paired this profile with a more down-to-earth contemporary example of Body Shop founder Anita Roddick. Samia and Nilufar expressed their admiration for this well-known advocate of 'green' cosmetics:

> Samia: 'I think it fits in quite nicely to look at somebody who's dedicated their life to doing things that are anti-animal testing and pro-nature. And she's one of those people who's made it fashionable to be pro-climate and pro-environmentalism.'
> Nilufar: 'And she started at the time, back in the '70s, you know, when the idea of ethics or environmental issues was more of a hippy thing.'

As the hosts explained the move of Anita Roddick's environmentalism from 'more of a hippy thing' to something 'more fashionable now' they identified themselves with the mainstreaming of the modern environmental movement. They therefore in the same episode connected the lineage of their Islamic environmentalism to both Muhammad and the modern mainstream environmental movement.

Overall, the radio campaign involved a balance of portraying Islamic environmentalism as timeless while recognizing that its current incarnation had developed within the modern west. This balance was key to the radio programme in fulfilling their aims of an attractive presentation of Islamic environmentalism, and of Islam itself.

Gendered activism

A third and final theme of the Women's Hour environmental campaign – the empowerment of women into activism – was expressed in more circumscribed and subtle ways.

Women's Hour presenters frequently expressed that women had specific Islamic roles with certain limitations. In doing so, they were 'on message' with the complementarian perspective[8] on gender held by the London Muslim Centre, the producers of the programme. For example, hosts on one episode spoke of the impropriety of shaking hands across gender lines, including the potential dilemma that would arise if receiving a diploma from a man at a graduation ceremony. Though radio conversations were generally very free and open, this freedom was in part achieved by assuming a Muslim female listening audience. In some instances when female hosts received a challenging question from the listening audience they explained that they could not provide *fiqh* (Islamic jurisprudence) and callers should address their questions to the MCR *fiqh* radio show.

Though in their rhetoric Women's Hour hosts recognized limited roles for women, their very act of radio broadcasting problematized such limits. Pious Muslim Women in Tower Hamlets typically have more private, domestic roles. Radio was a strikingly public platform. Gatherings at the London Muslim Centre are consistently gender segregated, and some women believe that they should conscientiously control their tone of voice in the presence of men to avoid the possibility of temptation. Yet the Women's Hour broadcast female voices unguarded throughout East London, at times speaking about sensitive and personal subjects. Women took an unusually powerful and public role as radio personalities. A wide listening audience called in and sent text messages in a boldly open setting. If Women's Hour presenters were role models for their female listening audience, one might expect this audience to grow in its interest in participating in the public sphere.

Women's Hour presenters encouraged their listeners to environmental collective action in ways that matched with local Islamic social structures. One episode profiled the Muslim Women's Collective, a local network of Muslim women with an environmental purpose. The Collective organizes activities that gather local women together, such as garden projects. They are developing environmentally friendly initiatives for children, including a football programme that provides fair trade, organic, healthy snacks and teaches Islamic perspectives on fitness and the environment in rest breaks. During the radio episode on the Collective, the presenters discussed various ways to involve children and families in environmental action:

> Do we actually have transparency in our actions as adults? Because sometimes we do lots of things. I do a lot of recycling. But are my children involved in it at all? They just see the pink bags come in and out. But what goes in there, why they go in there, what will happen to them, how they'll be recycled – it's such an amazing discussion topic! We can actually have a whole discussion within the family about these things.

The structure of environmental activism advocated by Muslim Community Radio was highly relational and distinctly gendered. Women were encouraged to utilise more fully their relationships in families and in friendships with other women. The Women's Hour accepted scripturally complementarian gender roles, yet sought to empower women to work effectively and creatively within those roles and their networks.

Conclusion

The multi-layered messaging on the Women's Hour of Muslim Community Radio allows a view into the complexity of concerns faced by Muslims in Tower Hamlets. As previously noted, the local Muslim community has been questioned over its integration into British society, with the perception that Bangladeshis are neglectful of their environment being one of many touch points. Muslims are faced with an array of choices as they work out identities that are western, Islamic, or perhaps some hybrid combination of these (Jacobson, 1998). Women are in a particular point of tension as many seek to fulfil their potential both in terms of worldly achievement and Islamic piety (Ramji, 2007).

One solution to many of these problems, as advocated by the Women's Hour broadcasting, is to sacralize them. By subsuming seeming cultural oppositions under an all-encompassing religious framework, one can find an answer that both fits with the times and transcends them. Of course, the success of this strategy can be debated. The gender limits to the solution are quite tangible. It must be remarked, however, that for the female presenters on the Women's Hour, the integration of complex and seemingly contradictory viewpoints into an Islamic perspective appeared natural, and almost effortless.

In reference to sociology of religion, this study complements other recent work that finds sacralization and secularization to be gendered processes (Aune, Sharma and Vincett, 2008; Brown, 2001). The female broadcasters on the Women's Hour sought to broaden the religious imaginations of their listening audience to adopt environmental actions as expressions of piety. Mirroring Penny Long Marler's (2008) remarks, the case confirms that to understand the process of sacralization it is essential that we 'watch the women'.

Finally, the Women's Hour environmental campaign and similar mobilization efforts have a significant potential to motivate ecological collective action. Sociological research has demonstrated the force of religion in motivating and structuring social movement activism (Smith, 1996; Wood, 2002). If large-scale environmental action is to be catalysed in Tower Hamlets, Muslim women are well positioned to play a leading role. Muslim females currently have the highest levels of academic achievement of any subgroup in Tower Hamlets schools (Dench, Gavron and Young, 2006: 142). Muslim mothers are typically the predominant influence in the socialization and values education of their next generation. Based on the high profile of environmentalism in Women's Hour programming and the apparent enthusiastic response among listeners, there is room for healthy optimism that an Islamic environmentalism can take root, if it is not underway already.

There is an irony to Lynn White's original thesis about religion and the environment. White found religion at fault in the present ecological crisis because it gave people a greater sense of agency over their environment. White's concept of human agency, however, was deterministic, giving his thesis a static character. As the Muslim Community Radio case demonstrates, religion does indeed provide resources and motivation to take action on nature – but this agency can just as readily take the form of an activist environmentalism.

Notes

1 For all Qur'anic references in this paper, I use the elegant and highly readable M. A. S. Abdel Haleem (2004) English translation.
2 These are the words said by Muslims before initiating prayer. Translated from the Arabic they mean: 'I seek refuge with God from Satan the rejected; In the name of God most compassionate, most merciful'. Having these words said throughout the MCR broadcast was a way of dedicating the radio time to God while at the same time bringing Islamic phrases into youthful rap lyrics.
3 *Deen* is the Arabic word for religious practice, or religious way of life.
4 'Bin' is pronounced like 'bean' so that it rhymes with 'clean' in the earlier lines of the rap.

5 The use of these words of prayer may have been controversial for some listeners. When presenting this paper at a conference, another conference participant who is Muslim expressed his discomfort with the use of such holy language in this way.

6 *Mashallah* is an Arabic phrase which means 'God has willed it'. It is used as an expression of delight and praise of God.

7 *Ahadith* (singular: *hadith*) are accounts of Muhammad's life and actions. Schools of Islamic thought vary in the weight of authenticity they give to individual accounts.

8 Complementarianism is the religious view that God has created women and men to fulfill 'distinct, complementary roles in family and society' (Joseph, 2003: 211).

References

Abdel Haleem, M. A. S., (2004), *The Qur'an: A New Translation*, Oxford: Oxford University Press.

Aune, K., Sharma, S. and Vincett, G., (eds), (2008), *Women and Religion in the West: Challenging Secularization*, Aldershot: Ashgate.

Birt, J., (2005), 'Lobbying and Marching: British Muslims and the State', in T. Abbas (ed.), *Muslim Britain: Communities under Pressure*, London: Zed Books.

Brown, C., (2001), *The Death of Christian Britain: Understanding Secularisation, 1800–2000*, London: Routledge.

Byron, Lord G. G., (2004 [1818]), *Childe Harold's Pilgrimage*, Whitefish, MT: Kessinger.

De Chatel, F., (2003), 'Muhammad: A Pioneer of the Environment', *IslamOnline*, http://www.islamonline.net/english/Contemporary/2003/02/Article02.shtml.

Dench, G., Gavron, K. and Young, M., (2006), *The New East End: Kinship, Race and Conflict*, London: Profile Books.

Diamond, I. and Orenstein, G., (eds), (1990), *Reweaving the World: The Emergence of Ecofeminism*, San Francisco: Sierra Club Books.

Eaton, H., (2005), *Introducing Ecofeminist Theologies*, London: Continuum.

EcoIslam, (2006), 'Eco-Friendly East London', 1:8, http://www.ifees.org.uk/newsletter_1_small.pdf.

Gardner, K., (2002), *Age, Narrative, Migration: The Life Course and Life Histories of Bengali Elders in London*, Oxford: Berg.

Gelderloos, O. G., (1992), *Eco-Theology: The Judeo-Christian Tradition and the Politics of Ecological Decision-Making*, Glasgow: Wild Goose.

Greeley, A., (1993), 'Religion and Attitudes toward the Environment,' *Journal for the Scientific Study of Religion*, 32(1): 19–28.

Guth, J., Green, J. C., Kellstedt, L., and Smidt, C., (1995), 'Faith and the Environment: Religious Beliefs and Attitudes on Environmental Policy', *American Journal of Political Science*, 39(2): 364–382.

Hayes, B. C. and Marangudakis, M., (2001), 'Religion and Attitudes towards Nature in Britain', *British Journal of Sociology*, 52(1): 139–155.

Heelas, P. and Woodhead, L., (2005), *The Spiritual Revolution: Why Religion is Giving Way to Spirituality*, Oxford: Blackwell.

Helminski, C., (2006), *The Book of Nature: A Sourcebook of Spiritual Perspectives on Nature and the Environment*, Watsonville, CA: The Book Foundation.

Ignatow, G., (2006), 'Cultural Models of Nature and Society: Reconsidering Environmental Attitudes and Concern', *Environment and Behavior*, 38(4): 441–461.

IUCN (International Union for Conservation of Nature), (2007), 'Al-Hima Revives Traditional Methods of Conservation and Poverty Reduction', *IUCN News – Fact Sheet*, 8/4/07, http://www.iucn.org/where/asia/index.cfm?uNewsID = 255.

Jacobson, J., (1998), *Islam in Transition: Religion and Identity among British Pakistani Youth*, London: Routledge.

Joseph, S., (ed.), (2003), *Encyclopedia of Women and Islamic Cultures*, Leiden and Boston: Brill.

Kanagy, C. L. and Nelson, H. M., (1995), 'Religion and Environmental Concern: Challenging the Dominant Assumptions', *Review of Religious Research*, 37(1): 33–45.

Khalid, F. M., (2002), 'Islam and the Environment', In T. Munn (ed.), *Encyclopedia of Global Enviromental Change*, Chichester: John Wiley & Sons.

Marler, P. L., (2008), 'Religious Change in the West: Watch the Women', in K. Aune, S. Sharma and G. Vincett (eds), *Women and Religion in the West: Challenging Secularization*, Aldershot: Ashgate.

Mohamed, N., (2007), 'Islamic Ecoethics: From Theory to Practice', Paper presented at the World Environmental Education Congress, Durban, 4 July 2007.

Nasr, S. H., (2003), 'Islam, the Contemporary Islamic World, and the Environmental Crisis', in R. C. Foltz, F. M. Denny and A. Baharuddin (eds), *Islam and Ecology: A Bestowed Trust*, Cambridge, MA: Harvard University Press.

Nooney, J. G., Woodrum, E., Hoban, T. J., and Clifford, W. B., (2003), 'Environmental Worldview and Behavior: Consequences of Dimensionality in a Survey of North Carolinians', *Environment and Behavior*, 35(6): 763–783.

Ramadan, T., (2007), *In the Footsteps of the Prophet: Lessons from the Life of the Prophet Muhammad*, New York: Oxford University Press.

Ramji, H., (2007), 'Dynamics of Religion and Gender amongst Young British Muslims', *Sociology*, 41(6): 1171–1189.

Smith, C., (1996), 'Correcting a Curious Neglect, or Bringing Religion Back In', in C. Smith (ed.), *Disruptive Religion: The Force of Faith in Social Movement Activism*, New York: Routledge.

Vidal, J., (2005), 'The Greening of Islam', *The Guardian*, 30/11/05.

Weber, M., (2002 [1905]), 'The Protestant Ethic and the Spirit of Capitalism', in P. Baehr and G. C. Wells, (eds, trans.), *The Protestant Ethic and the Spirit of Capitalism and Other Writings*, New York: Penguin.

Weber, M., (1968 [1915]), *The Religion of China: Confucianism and Taoism*, H. H. Gerth, (trans.), New York: Free Press.

White, L., Jr., (1967), 'The Historical Roots of Our Ecological Crisis', *Science*, 155: 1203–1207.

Wood, R. L., (2002), *Faith in Action: Religion, Race, and Democratic Organizing in America*, Chicago: University of Chicago Press.

Part Three
Sociological Futures

The 'value-action gap' in public attitudes towards sustainable energy: the case of hydrogen energy

Rob Flynn, Paul Bellaby and Miriam Ricci

There is now increasing evidence that the public has become much more aware of global warming, climate change and environmental risks. This has been repeatedly demonstrated in a number of official surveys and other research. However, the salience of these issues varies; for some social groups, there are other more significant problems and urgent priorities. It has also been found that while expressing strong beliefs about the negative consequences of global warming, or dependence on fossil fuels, or more positive approval of alternative and renewable energy sources, people do not seem to have translated those opinions into practical actions to limit their energy use in their domestic consumption, lifestyles, or travel patterns, for example. It is this apparent 'discrepancy' between stated beliefs (and values) and behaviour, which comprises the so-called 'value-action gap'. Various writers have observed this in different contexts previously, as will be discussed below. In this chapter, we examine the importance of the value-action gap in relation to hydrogen energy and the emerging hydrogen economy. Qualitative and quantitative data are presented from a series of focus groups and a telephone questionnaire survey of selected samples in seven different areas of England and Wales[1]. The chapter first gives a very brief outline of the nature of hydrogen energy and its potential uses as an innovative technology. Secondly, it reviews selected literature about public attitudes towards environmental and energy issues and the apparent value-action gap. Findings from our recent research are then discussed. Finally, some general conclusions are offered to account for the ambivalence revealed in this case of hydrogen energy, and the disjunction between people's awareness of an energy crisis and their reluctance to change behaviour.

Hydrogen energy and the 'hydrogen economy'

With the rapid depletion of fossil fuels (coal, natural gas, oil), governments and energy corporations have been increasingly investing in research and development in alternative and sustainable (renewable) energy sources. The Stern

Review (2007) on the economics of climate change gave a stark warning to the industrialized economies about the need to reduce reliance on carbon and to develop alternative energy technologies. In the UK, the government's energy 2007 White Paper (DTI, CM7124, 2007) highlighted the necessity of reducing greenhouse gases (especially carbon dioxide) and stressed the need to find other, more secure supplies and sources of energy which are not as vulnerable to external (international) instability. Support was given for energy-saving measures as well as greater investment in low carbon technologies, including renewable energy systems (biomass, hydro, solar, wind, wave) and carbon-capture and storage. The position of nuclear energy in this 'renewable' category is controversial, but the British government has effectively endorsed its expansion. The UK Committee on Climate Change (2008) also noted that climate change resulting from carbon dioxide and other greenhouse gases posed a threat to human welfare, and recommended that the UK reduced its emissions by at least 80 per cent of the 1990 levels by 2050.

As part of these developing scenarios, a high level of commitment has been given to develop hydrogen energy and hydrogen energy technologies. Comparatively, far greater levels of investment in hydrogen have already been made in Japan and the USA (and several other countries) but the British government has recognized the potential benefits of a shift to hydrogen as part of its broader strategy. The European Union has strengthened its support for the commercialization of hydrogen technologies, especially in transport, through its 'HyWays' project (HyWays, 2008).

Hydrogen is the most abundant element in the universe and is an *energy carrier* (and an energy *store*) not an energy source in itself. It can be produced by splitting water into hydrogen and oxygen; it can be produced from 'reforming' gas (both natural gas and methane from biogas) as well as from electricity derived from any source (wind, solar, wave, nuclear). Various proponents have described hydrogen as 'green', 'clean' and non-polluting. It is likely to be most extensively used in fuel cells for vehicles, but can also be used in larger-scale combined heat-and-power systems, and other smaller portable devices (such as to power laptops or other electronic equipment). Currently, most of these technologies are at the advanced research and development or prototype stage, but there are already hydrogen fuel cell cars and buses on trial, some experimental refuelling stations, and also some combined heat-and-power systems in public buildings (see Ekins and Hughes, 2007; European Hydrogen and Fuel Cell Technology Platform, 2005; Ricci *et al.*, 2007a; United Nations, 2006).

Ambitious claims have been made regarding the innovative potential of this emerging hydrogen energy system. Rifkin (2002) claimed that the widespread adoption of hydrogen energy would transform the economy and society, as it offers the prospect of radically democratizing energy production as well as supply. Consumers could become their own energy producers through decentralized electricity production from hydrogen. Of course it must also be noted that there are many critics and sceptics who question the costs, desirability and feasibility of a shift towards hydrogen energy. Some raise doubts about its safety

– it is a highly explosive gas which must be stored at very high pressures, and it must be stored at extremely low temperatures when in liquid form. There may be problems with its storage and transportation; there are unresolved problems with the materials used to store hydrogen. The most fundamental question concerns how the hydrogen is *produced*, and whether this is from genuinely sustainable or carbon-neutral sources: currently most hydrogen is derived from fossil fuels (natural gas) and is already used in a variety of industrial applications. Nevertheless, while among expert stakeholder groups there is some consensus that there are a limited number of 'hydrogen futures' with differing infrastructures, there is some divergence in the speed at which this emergent technology will develop (McDowall and Eames, 2006).

Hydrogen offers an interesting case to examine public attitudes towards an ostensibly 'environmentally-friendly' set of solutions to the energy crisis and climate change. It is argued here that it is important to investigate social attitudes towards hydrogen while it is still an *emergent* technology (Flynn *et al.*, 2006). These can then also be compared with other evidence about people's environmental beliefs and behaviour.

Environmental attitudes and behaviour: the 'value-action gap'

There is a diverse and very extensive literature about social attitudes concerning environmental matters, spanning economics, environmental studies, geography, politics, psychology and sociology. Here we highlight, only selectively, some aspects of this literature that have very direct relevance to the sociological debate about environmentalism and sustainable energy (but for wider discussion of the issues, see Dickens, 1992; Irwin, 2001; Newby, 1991; Urry, 2008; Yearley, 2005).

Awareness of environmental and related questions in Britain has been the subject of large-scale longitudinal national questionnaires for the British Social Attitudes surveys (see Park *et al.*, 2002, 2008). Christie and Jarvis (in Park *et al.*, 2002) found that while the level of awareness of environmental problems, such as global warming, climate change and pollution, was relatively high, it was lower in Britain than in other European countries. They also found that 'environmentally-friendly' behaviour was far lower than the level of environmental concern. More generally, only 16 per cent of the sample believed that economic growth always harms the environment, whereas 42 per cent believed that to protect the environment, economic growth was necessary. They observed that there was a 'broad base of environmentally well informed people in Britain' (Christie and Jarvis, 2002: 137). Nevertheless, they found little evidence of a breakthrough in willingness to make sacrifices to protect the environment. Regarding 'green' activism (such as signing petitions, membership of environmental pressure groups) there had been a reduction since 1993. When asked about individual participation in recycling, or reducing car use, substantial numbers claimed to have participated in those actions, but these were far from a majority of the respondents. Overall, Christie and Jarvis noted a 'plateauing' of attitudes and a disconnection between awareness of environmental attitudes and personal actions to tackle them.

More recently the British Social Attitudes survey focused specifically on car use and climate change (Stradling *et al.*, 2008). They found that the vast majority (four fifths) agreed that car use has a serious detrimental impact on climate change. Two thirds of drivers and non-drivers think that everyone should reduce how much they use their cars, for the sake of the environment. But almost a quarter of the sample believed that people should be allowed to use their own cars as much as they like, even if it causes damage to the environment. Furthermore, 16 per cent agreed with the statement that 'anyone who thinks reducing their own car use will help the environment is wrong, because one person does not make any difference'. Stradling and colleagues note that there are major difficulties in persuading people to change their behaviour, irrespective of their beliefs about the environment and climate change. Similarly, regarding flying, Butt and Shaw (2009) found that while 70 per cent of people agree that air travel has a serious effect on climate change, 63 per cent also agree that people should be able to travel by plane as much as they like. As Urry (2008) observed, we are evidently 'locked-in' to current modes and patterns of travel and communications, and reluctant to accept limitations on personal mobility and freedom.

These findings reveal what has been frequently identified in many other studies – the 'gap' between attitudes and action. People express strong support for environmentally sustainable policies, but display little commitment to alter their own behaviour. What such findings also implicitly suggest is acceptance of a model of behaviour in which, if only individuals are supplied with appropriate information, they will modify their behaviour to meet some preferred goal. Numerous commentators have pointed out the difficulties with this approach, but it is necessary to consider some of the background assumptions associated with it.

The 'value-action gap' has been defined in generic terms by the Sustainable Development Commission (2006: 63) as 'the observed disparity between people's reported concerns about key environmental, social, economic or ethical concerns and the lifestyle or purchasing decisions that they make in practice'. Probably the first most explicit use of the 'value-action gap' idea was in the field of environmental psychology and particularly in connection with pro-environmental behaviour (see Kollmuss and Agyeman, 2002). Blake (1999: 275) referred to the 'value-action gap' – 'to signify in general terms the differences between what people say and what people do'. He also cogently added that 'terminological confusion is rife in this area, with different researchers variously referring to 'attitudes', 'opinions', 'concerns', 'worries', 'values', beliefs', 'actions', and 'behaviour' ' (Blake, 1999). Blake was critical of theories and policies using the 'value-action gap' paradigm, as they are based on an information-deficit and rational choice model of human behaviour, which is inadequate. As he notes, purely cognitive or social-psychological theories of decisions fail to take account of cultural, institutional and structural constraints on people's capacity and willingness to take action.

Among other environmental psychologists studying 'environmentally significant behaviour', it has been found that there are numerous types of such behaviour and numerous causal factors. These factors are associated with different patterns of beliefs, norms and values. Stern (2000) refers to 'Value-Belief-Norm Theory' and suggests that personal moral norms are an important basis for individuals' predisposition to pro-environmental action. However, he also acknowledged that personal habits and household routines, as well as infrastructural constraints, may affect people's decisions. Stern's conclusion (2000: 421) is that 'environmentally significant behaviour is dauntingly complex, both in its variety and in the cultural influences on it'.

Darnton (2004), in a systematic literature review, observed that the 'value-action gap' approach must be supplemented – or even replaced – by models which reflect the complexity and multiplicity of factors influencing pro-environmental behaviour. Poortinga *et al.* (2004) studied household domestic energy use and transport, and found that pro-environmental behaviour was associated with socio-demographic variables (eg age, income, household size) rather than attitudinal variables *per se*. Environmental behaviour was, they argued, determined by contextual factors rather than motivational factors alone. Similarly, Anable *et al.*, (2006), in their review of the evidence about public attitudes to climate change and transport behaviour, stressed that the relationship between attitudes and behaviour is mediated by social (and moral) norms and other factors. They argue that there are competing theories of behaviour and behaviour change, with different explanations of the apparent 'disconnection' between holding pro-environmental values and taking pro-environmental action. Those theories can be broadly grouped into three categories: dealing with the individual, interpersonal and community levels. None is comprehensive and sufficient by itself, and each entails quite different prescriptions for policy and policy-makers.

Barr and Gilg (2006) examined the value-action gap among citizens adopting sustainable lifestyles (energy saving, waste recycling, water conservation, 'green' consumption). Their findings showed important differences not only between separate groups (committed environmentalists; mainstream environmentalists; occasional environmentalists; and non-environmentalists) but also in their level or degree of commitment, which was affected by much deeper social values. They also point out that people's preparedness to take environmental action is embedded in, and constrained by, their existing domestic lifestyle and everyday experience.

Thus it is evident that in attempting to explain the apparent paradox of a mismatch between people's opinions and views about environmental problems, and their ability and willingness to take action to ameliorate those problems, there are major conceptual and methodological challenges. Notwithstanding these difficulties, governments and other bodies continue to seek ways of educating, informing and persuading the public to modify their behaviour (see

DEFRA, 2008). These questions have been specifically addressed by the ESRC Sustainable Technologies Programme and their review of measures to stimulate behavioural change in sustainable consumption (Jackson, 2004). The Sustainable Development Commission in the UK is one of the most active agencies promoting 'behaviour change' across the widest range of human activities. Their goal is to facilitate lifestyle changes by programmes (through 'encouragement, example, enabling and engaging') which assist people to overcome inertia or reluctance – 'to make sustainable choices easier to take up' (Sustainable Development Commission, 2006: 1). They observe that people are often 'locked-in' to currently unsustainable consumption practices, due to economic constraints, inequalities or institutional barriers to change. This 'lock-in' may also be due to cultural norms and social expectations, and in combination, these may be the most cogent explanation of the value-action gap. To begin to break out of this lock-in, and as part of the process of enabling people to adopt more sustainable lifestyles, and to make it meaningful for individuals, the Sustainable Development Commission (2006: 34) has an explicit commitment to involve and *engage* people in deliberative debates – and community-based action – about sustainability.

This approach has some parallels with wider efforts to 'engage' the public in consultations about other major developments in planning, transport and scientific and technological innovation. It is assumed that by incorporating citizens in early discussions about the scale of a problem and alternative future scenarios and policies, greater awareness and understanding of the issues will emerge, and acceptance of strategic change can be secured (Flynn, 2007; Mohr, 2007). This, of course, resonates with the much criticized information-deficit model in the public understanding of science literature (Irwin and Wynne, 1996; Irwin and Michael, 2003). Irwin (2007) has identified many of the failures of attempts to engage scientific citizens in public dialogue. In many different policy areas, the framing of debate is dominated by experts and technocrats, and the forms of citizen deliberation and engagement are restricted. Grove-White *et al.* (2000) showed that although moves towards greater transparency and openness may be welcomed by the public, in the case of the controversy over Genetically Modified crops, there was still a one-way communication of information to 'assist' people's 'choices' and decisions. Other attempts to evaluate the effectiveness of schemes to engage the public in decisions about Genetically Modified Organisms have also proved problematic and provoked criticism of the exercise (Rowe and Frewer, 2004). Advocates of 'upstream' public engagement have forcefully argued for governments to use more deliberative processes to actively involve consumers and citizens at the earliest possible stage of policy formation associated with new scientific and technological developments (Wilsdon and Willis, 2004). However, Wynne (2005) has criticized the current fashion for public engagement as a 'mirage', and Stirling (2005) has argued that, in the case of the social appraisal of technology, it is questionable as to whether the participatory mechanisms (such as citizens' juries, consensus conferences, etc) 'close down' rather than 'open up' public debate.

While acknowledging these important *caveats* and strictures about the validity and effectiveness of such public consultation and engagement exercises, it is argued here that it is still worthwhile to try and assess people's awareness of, and attitudes towards, new energy systems and future hydrogen energy infrastructures, for example, and to attempt to gauge their opinion about the desirability and likelihood of their adoption. Although 'consultation' remains problematic, significant change of the kind envisaged in future energy systems depends substantially on consumers and citizens seeking benefits from it at acceptable costs and manageable risk. The next section of the chapter presents findings from two recent studies by the authors (in collaboration with colleagues in the UK Sustainable Hydrogen Consortium and others) about public perceptions of the potential risks, costs and benefits of a hydrogen energy system and also their views about the uses of hydrogen (and its supporting infrastructure) in transport.

Public attitudes towards hydrogen energy and the environment

Before considering in detail the methods and results of our research on public attitudes to hydrogen energy, it is necessary to outline briefly what is already known about attitudes to renewable energy generally. Various official and academic studies have been carried out which seem to suggest that there is, overall, strong support for *renewable* energy sources. For example the UK Department of Business, Enterprise and Regulatory Reform commissioned research about awareness of and attitudes towards renewable energy in March 2006 and March 2007, through a telephone survey of a nationally representative sample of 1,870 respondents. The report (BERR September 2007) found that awareness and support for renewable energy was high. For example, over 80 per cent had heard of solar, hydroelectric and wind energy, almost 60 per cent had heard of tidal and wave energy, and over 50 per cent had heard of bio-mass energy. However, 35 per cent believed that renewable energy sources were too costly and this outweighed any environmental benefits. There were some gender and socio-economic differences in the levels of support: men and higher socio-economic groups were more likely to support renewables. When asked their overall opinion of renewable energy as an alternative to fossil fuels only a quarter of respondents were totally in favour, whereas almost one fifth were against or totally against.

Other research commissioned by BERR (2008) similarly found that 83 per cent of the public support the use of renewable energy; 82 per cent are in favour of wind power, and 59 per cent said they would be happy to live within 5 km of a wind power development. Their review of over forty different studies between 1990 and 2002 indicated that, on average, 74 per cent of those surveyed supported wind energy.

Generally, it can be observed that while people's stated beliefs about renewable energy (and pro-environmental behaviour) are positive, and substantial numbers claim to have adopted some energy-saving measures and recycling, there is still a degree of ambivalence. More broadly, for example, while there are relatively high levels of support for wind energy, opposition to wind farms is extensive (Bell *et al.*, 2005). In August 2007, the Department for Environment, Food and Rural Affairs published a report on a national survey of public attitudes and behaviours towards the environment (DEFRA, 2007). The results indicated first that the environment was *fourth* in a list of priorities for most people (behind crime, health and education). About one quarter agreed with the statement 'It takes too much effort to do things which are environmentally friendly' and 'I don't believe my behaviour and everyday lifestyle contribute to climate change'. While a majority believed that if people used a car less or flew less, it would contribute to reducing carbon emissions, few respondents thought that many people were willing to do this: moreover, 24 per cent said they 'don't really want to' use a car less or fly less frequently (see also Butt and Shaw, 2009).

Evidence about people's awareness of hydrogen energy is very limited, principally because it is such a new and emergent technology. There are few official or academic studies of public perceptions of hydrogen (for reviews, see Flynn *et al.*, 2006; O'Garra *et al.*, 2007; Ricci *et al.*, 2007b, 2008). In general, there are low levels of awareness of hydrogen energy and energy systems; perceived safety and risk issues are not specifically regarded as highly important; and people are interested in obtaining more information about, and practical experience of, hydrogen technologies.

To investigate people's knowledge of and attitudes towards hydrogen and hydrogen energy technologies, the authors have carried out a series of focus groups in three areas of the UK where there are already hydrogen production infrastructures in operation and/or there are demonstration projects and experimental uses of hydrogen. The areas were Teesside (3 groups), south west Wales (2 groups) and London (2 groups). The focus groups were recruited from existing local authority public consultation panels (which themselves were drawn from locally representative samples) and had a mixed social composition in terms of age, gender and socio-economic group.[2] There were two 'waves' of focus group meetings in these areas with the same members. Members of the research team facilitated these meetings; the discussions were digitally taped, transcribed and analysed thematically.

The findings reported in the next section of the chapter are drawn from the second round of focus groups, conducted between October and November 2006. During the first phase of focus groups, people discussed ideas about the environment and energy and were only introduced to information about hydrogen after open-ended debate. In the second-round meetings, information sheets and graphic images of possible applications of hydrogen energy were shown, and 'Powerpoint' and other visual materials were used to illustrate demonstration projects and infrastructure developments. People were asked to discuss their current uses of energy and whether they thought other people (and themselves) were willing to change their behaviour. They were also asked for their opinions about hydrogen, what criteria they would use to evaluate the case for widespread adoption of hydrogen technologies, and how they thought people should be involved in decision-making about hydrogen's role in future energy policy. The next section of the chapter presents collated summaries of the discussions in the groups, together with some typical illustrative quotations, around the themes of energy use and behaviour change; attitudes to hydrogen technologies; and public engagement.

1. Environmental values and current behaviour in energy use

a) Connecting the global to the local

When discussing the impacts of using fossil fuels to produce energy, people acknowledged that these are global issues and as such they need to be tackled on a global scale. Some people showed quite detailed knowledge of, and interest in, environmental and energy issues, and could relate them to international politics and economic phenomena. However, a recurrent claim was made in all groups that, even when people are aware of energy and environmental problems and consider them relevant as political issues, they find it difficult to connect them with their daily life and preoccupations. The lack of saliency and immediacy of issues around energy and the environment in people's everyday experience has been found in several surveys (for a review see Ricci *et al.*, 2006; Ricci *et al.*, 2008), which also indicate that social issues such as health, crime and education are the predominant concerns. The effects of climate change are generally considered distant, both in space and time, and are not easily linked to individual behaviours in areas such as using electricity, providing heating and cooling in the home, getting around and travelling.

b) Blame and responsibility

We found a tendency, in all groups, to place both blame and responsibility on 'others'. In the London groups, people thought that industry and business are the biggest contributors to energy consumption and global warming, and that citizens have a negligible role. In the other groups, people blamed the USA and rapidly growing economies, such as China and India, for not complying with environmental standards and international agreements. Most people felt those countries, and industry and business, should make the greatest sacrifices to avert energy and environmental crises, rather than individual consumers. There were a few people, however, who felt that taking personal responsibility for the environment in a global sense was almost a moral obligation. Some of our participants felt that any unilateral attempt by the UK Government to act alone would be useless or, at worst, counterproductive. At the same time, however, the role of Government was advocated as a leader in building commitment, among the citizens as well as internationally, and driving the change.

In one of the Teesside groups, for example, one man expressed a feeling of frustration and powerlessness:

> I think a lot of people think that the changes that they make individually are very small, compared to the total picture which they believe is really serious and therefore needs something large doing, something on a big scale rather than a few people turning their tellies off rather than being on standby. (Guisborough, Teesside)

Similarly a woman in a different Teesside group commented:

> I think as individuals we are trying to do our little bit towards it but I think there is an awful lot like the Americans who have so much pollution. The Chinese, the Koreans and... our little bit, is it doing any good? We do try we use low energy lights and we switch the television off and we take the bus wherever we can because we have got a free bus pass. But we do all that, but is it doing anything to help when we have got these big nations just shoving it all out there, you know? But yes as individuals we do try to help. (Eston, Teesside)

c) The value-action gap

One key finding from all the focus groups is that, despite their self-proclaimed concerns about the environment and energy futures, and pro-environmental attitudes, people do <u>not</u> seem to be actively and radically changing their behaviour with the primary purpose of tackling problems such as energy shortages or global warming. Behavioural changes (such as switching off lights when not used, avoid leaving appliances on stand-by, buying more efficient products, etc) appear to be marginal rather than radical, and are dominated, in people's narratives, by recycling. Such actions may well reflect a genuine willingness to take personal responsibility for the environment. However, we need to take into account the possible bias of social desirability in people's statements and that other intentions may motivate environmentally friendly behaviour. In the first focus group series (Ricci *et al.*, 2006), it emerged that positive attitudes towards the environment are not generally a sufficient condition to motivate energy-conscious behaviour. In some cases, they are not even necessary: many people admitted that financial incentives or cutting down bills can be stronger drivers of reducing energy consumption.

Energy consumption encompasses many different behaviours, most of which are taken for granted as part of people's routines and are not usually understood in terms of their impacts on the environment. When participants in our groups were asked to discuss how behaviours could be changed, in the light of the problems with energy availability and its impact on the environment, they talked about the difficulty of, and their aversion to, changing certain behaviours (chiefly the use of private transport) because it would diminish the levels of comfort and convenience people are used to. Such behaviours are deeply ingrained in the lifestyles through which citizens construct their identities, status, and social affiliations.

When asked directly about their willingness to change behaviour, people were ambivalent. For example, as one woman expressed it:

> I think we tend to make the changes that are more convenient to us, like we are all very keen on energy efficient light bulbs and that sort of thing, turning the thermostat

down, putting insulation in, but we are also quite keen on going abroad for our holi-
days and I think we have to almost be forced by some kind of price or having to pay
some kind of tax in to being deterred against that at the moment, otherwise I think
it would be hard to make that decision. (Guisborough, Teesside)

The urgency of other pressing priorities was also featured as a constraint on
change:

To be fair, you know, if you know you go up to a woman in, you know, five kids in
a deprived area or something, the top concerns are maybe making sure the kids get
a good meal, good schooling etc. etc. How they save the planet from destruction is
probably very low on their list, so you can't lecture. (Woman, London, Group 1)

Across all groups we found a consensus that in many circumstances people
are actually 'locked' into certain types of behaviours and activities because of
the limitations available due to infrastructure (in terms of technological options,
design, etc.) and institutional setting (such as regulations, standards, laws, etc),
which citizens feel unable to change. A frequently cited example in the groups
was building regulations and house design as strong barriers to the diffusion of
energy-saving and renewable energy technologies. One group in London complained about the large amount of unnecessary packaging used by supermarkets, while in rural areas some people pinpointed the lack of an efficient public
transport network as a cause of car dependency. In sum, people acknowledged
that there are many cases in which personal choices are in fact dictated by what
is available and affordable to them.

In all the focus groups people discussed the personal costs of changing behaviour and taking up new energy efficient or renewable technologies. There was
a general agreement that a shift towards energy-conscious behaviour should not
entail higher costs to consumers because people on low income, such as pension-
ers and the unemployed, would not be able to afford it. Issues related to fairness
appear to be important in how people think about behavioural change.

In general, across the groups, behavioural change was always conceptualized
as a collective initiative that could only occur within broader changes in the way
technologies are designed and become embedded in people's everyday lives. It
was also seen as inseparable from regulatory and institutional approaches to
energy saving, efficiency and environmental protection in all sectors, from
private business to government.

d) People as 'consumers' and 'citizens'

When participants in our groups discussed their willingness to change behaviour
in energy use, a further conflict emerged between the short-term economic and
social interests of 'consumers' and the long-term environmental and social
concerns of 'citizens'. On the one hand, people were reluctant to take radical
steps to alter significantly the way they used energy, in the home and in personal
transport, because they felt that such a change would not be effective in a global
picture and it would diminish their freedom, comfort and convenience. Most

people stressed that they would need to have private benefits from a shift in behaviour, for it to become sustained over time. On the other hand, environmental values and concerns for the next generation(s) could encourage people to change. In our groups, people frequently mentioned family members (such as children and grandchildren) when identifying cogent reasons to change behaviour as individuals.

2. Attitudes to hydrogen technologies

People expressed neither full support for, nor outright opposition to, hydrogen energy and its associated infrastructure and technologies. Here it must be noted that 'acceptability' of new technologies should be conceptualized as a *continuum*. There are likely to be differing degrees of acceptability (or acceptance), and different reasons for acceptability, among different groups (see Flynn, 2007). Discussions in the focus groups suggest that acceptability is mediated by, and is contingent upon, numerous complex factors, including cost, safety, effectiveness in tackling climate change and improving energy security, performance and convenience. Focus group members repeatedly pointed out that the acceptability of hydrogen technologies can only be assessed in relative terms, ie comparing benefits, costs and risks with existing and other alternative energy systems and applications. In each area, members spontaneously posed questions about the entire cycle of hydrogen production, distribution and use, effectively adopting a 'whole systems' approach. They were interested and quizzical, and expected to be provided with much more information (especially on costs, efficiency and safety) in order to offer their assessment.

> But which one [hydrogen production method] has the most potential? Because I think that is the one people want to know about, which is the one we should be going for because it is the cleanest, because it is reasonably cheap and less impact on the environment you know? (Man, Guisborough, Teesside)

> I do think historically hydrogen generally has bad press though. I mean I had no idea that hydrogen could be used in the sort of way that you know would provide an efficient energy source. I just always assumed that hydrogen is bad and we should stay away from it. So in terms of safety then you know people need to be made aware that it can be safe, it can be manufactured safely. (Woman, Carmarthen, Wales)

> It's like swapping electrical appliances, if you said to someone there's hydrogen, there's there and they would say – well, what's the cheapest? And that is what most people do. (Man, Llanelli, Wales)

> [People] will either pay more for the greener ways of powering things or they will pay even more for the even less green ways of powering things. There will just be more tax on petrol in order to evaluate the costs and perhaps make the hydrogen economy slightly cheaper. (Man, London, Group 2)

Becoming small-scale energy producers by using hydrogen fuel was for most participants something rather unfamiliar, whereas most people had already heard about solar panels and micro wind turbines. Cost, availability, ease of use and other practical aspects were the most cited barriers to adoption. All groups agreed that people need to have incentives to adopt renewable energy in their homes and installing such systems should be a collective initiative, led by the government through building regulations, instead of an isolated choice left to the goodwill (and financial resources) of the individual consumer. Many questions were asked about domestic combined heat and power (CHP) systems fuelled by hydrogen: how would it be regulated? Would the system take a lot of space? Would it be safe? Would it be difficult to run and require lots of maintenance? Would it create tensions with neighbours? How about if a part was stolen or vandalized?

Most people spontaneously identified as criteria for assessment the following: cost (especially to the individual consumer), safety, effectiveness in tackling environmental and energy security problems, performance and convenience. People needed to be reassured that hydrogen production was sustainable in the longer term and cost-effective in tackling climate change and that the whole spectrum of new infrastructure, technologies and applications would be safe. People expected that, to be fully accepted and adopted, hydrogen applications need to perform at least as well as conventional technologies (such as cars, buses and domestic heat and electricity) and provide at least the same level of comfort and convenience people are used to.

People in Teesside and Wales were asked in particular whether they would be more supportive of a large-scale hydrogen development if it brought jobs and improved the local economy. Most people acknowledged that hydrogen could bring new jobs, improve the economy and help regenerate obsolete industrial sites. However, people would need to be consulted if new facilities were being planned. They stressed that being used to living near big chemical complexes did not imply they would unconditionally accept new installations.

Overall, most people were not at ease in expressing criteria, as they felt they did not have any practical experience of any new hydrogen development. Most people knew little about local hydrogen projects and felt they could have been publicized more. Focus group members pointed out that decisions on acceptability can only be gauged when there are real demonstration projects available for inspection, which enable people to evaluate how the new technology connects with their everyday lives, needs and aspirations. It was also made clear that how people make sense of hydrogen depends not only upon the specific technologies and their characteristics, but also on the context in which they will be developed and the process by which they will be introduced. People do not expect to become 'experts' in hydrogen use: they expect to be able to manage their lives with no additional worries and concerns, and to be able 'to forget' (as one of the participants put it) that the fuel they may be using is hydrogen, as they have done with other technological innovations (new types of fuels, mobile phones, etc).

3. Public engagement

When people were asked about involving the public in decisions about hydrogen and energy, most of them understood 'involvement' as a form of one-way communication, advertising (by using TV, radio and newspapers) or education (especially of new generations). People supported more active types of engagement as reflecting democratic ideals, but at the same time they questioned the assumptions underpinning public participation, such as the actual willingness to 'engage' and 'participate'.

There was also a diffuse feeling of distrust of 'other people'. While participants claimed *they* were interested and willing to participate in debates about energy, *'others'* would be unaware of the problems associated with energy and the environment, and too busy dealing with their everyday problems (keeping their jobs, making ends meet, etc).

All groups agreed that people need to be better informed on the choices available to them and needed guidance on what actions to take to combat climate change effectively and save energy. The demand for more information may reflect a 'knowledge deficit' that people feel. However, participants indicated that such a 'deficit' is not about information as a collection of facts, but rather of practical advice people can trust and credible examples they can follow.

People expressed a clear distrust of most politicians (with the exception of certain charismatic local politicians). Distrust of national politicians caused suspicion when issues like climate change and energy saving were seen to become priorities suddenly in the political agenda or during elections. People also did not trust industry and business to take environmental problems seriously. Moreover, they also distrusted 'other people' to become committed towards the environment and energy saving.

Although public participation in decision-making over energy futures was generally favoured and expected, people emphasized the barriers rather than the benefits. Many participants noted that it would be difficult, for example, to involve people who are not interested, or those who think that energy issues are not their immediate and most relevant concern.

For example:

> The problem is people who care will get involved in whatever format is suggested and people who couldn't give a hoot would have to be dragged into it. (Woman, Redcar, Teesside)

> Not everybody wants to be consulted on these things though, a lot of other people have got more important things in their lives or they consider more important things. Nearly everybody I know, I can't think of one person who would come to something like this. The people that I work with are just not interested, there's other people looking into those things and I would say the vast majority of people aren't bothered about being consulted. (Man, Guisborough, Teesside)

> In answer to the last question you posed if you actually make information readily available to anyone who wants it, that's good. But I think you will find most people

will just accept whatever they are given as long as it doesn't discommode them in any way. If it is not too expensive they don't mind. As long as they can live a comfortable life then they are not bothered. That's really it, we are all being selfish. (Man, Carmarthen, Wales)

In all of the groups in each of the three areas, it was acknowledged that reaching consensus on decisions about hydrogen and future energy technologies would be a complex task, as it would require the negotiation of different and conflicting interests and agendas.

Public engagement in hydrogen infrastructures in transport

As an extension of this study of public attitudes towards hydrogen energy, and to investigate them specifically in relation to transport infrastructures, another series of focus groups, and a telephone survey, was carried out as part of a Department for Transport-funded (DfT) project (Bellaby and Upham, 2007). The next section of the chapter presents a very short summary of results from that report. In addition to some 'headline' findings from the survey questionnaire, general observations from focus groups are presented.

First, some important methodological points must be noted. The case-study research design for this DfT project deliberately selected certain areas of England because of their labour market and transport system characteristics and because there are no existing or embryonic hydrogen infrastructures there or immediately planned. The cities and travel-to-work areas were Norwich, Sheffield and Southampton. A commercial social research company (BMRB) carried out a telephone poll of a representative sample of the local populations (n = 1,003), and having administered a questionnaire, then recruited 12 focus groups, four in each area, during May and June 2007. These groups (each of between 8 and 10 participants) were differentiated by social grade, age and gender (for full details of the composition of groups, see Bellaby & Upham, 2007). A professional facilitator convened the group discussions in line with a script prepared by the research team, and a specially commissioned DVD film about hydrogen energy and its applications in transport (designed by the research team) was shown to participants. All the meetings were digitally recorded, transcribed, and analysed thematically (including using 'NVivo').

Secondly, some summary results from the sample survey are worth noting. Concern about climate change was high: 73 per cent of the sample said they were very worried or fairly worried about it. But 26 per cent said they were not worried. In terms of willingness to change travel behaviour, 53 per cent said they 'might' or 'would' be prepared to fly less; and 61 per cent said they 'might' or 'would' be prepared to drive less. Interestingly, about 21 per cent would not be prepared to do either. People's knowledge about hydrogen was varied: men, those in higher social grades, and those in full time employment, had a better knowledge of hydrogen and its characteristics. There was a noticeable gender dimension in responses to a number of different environmental and transport questions: women were 'greener' than men, although knowledge of hydrogen and its uses was higher among men.

There were twelve focus groups (four in each area) held in Norwich, Sheffield, and Southampton. Thematically, three broad issues emerged across all the areas: personal mobility and the environment; questions about the uses of hydrogen as a fuel in transport; and concerns about communication, trust and public consultation. Here, for reasons of space, only a highly abbreviated account can be given, and this is based on a synthesis of the qualitative data from each group.

(i) Personal mobility and the environment

At the start of discussions, it was evident that appearing environmentally conscious was socially desirable. But deeper concerns emerged with the showing of the film, when broader transport and environment issues were raised. Participants tended to be worried most about impediments to mobility, and climate change featured rarely. Travel behaviour was clearly dictated by participants' personal lives, networks of family and friends, and jobs. If there was to be change in mobility patterns, people indicated that there has to be accompanying personal benefits. Occasionally a sense of responsibility for future generations – eg ties to grandchildren – emerged. Air pollution and its public health impact was often emphasized in these discussions.

Blame was attached to mobility habits but responsibility was laid not so much on individual conduct as on government – to take a lead. It seemed that science and technology were looked to for supply of cleaner fuels, but individuals had a sense of powerlessness, since political and commercial interests seem still to revolve around polluting technology.

(ii) Hydrogen as a fuel for transport

The documentary film and the accompanying script of the focus group addressed the 'whole system' (or infrastructure) of which the use of hydrogen energy in transport vehicles is but a small part. Thus, production of hydrogen, its storage prior to distribution, and how it might be distributed were featured, and then discussed by the groups.

Production: Participants were often critical of the use of non-renewable primary sources to generate hydrogen (especially nuclear power and coal) and wanted government to give more support to renewable energy. This discussion drew on broader concerns about energy policy than the specifics of a hydrogen economy. One of these concerns was the relative risk of centralized and of distributed production. The aesthetics of large industrial-like installations – whether of wind farms or of processing plants – were also debated.

Storage: Bulk storage of hydrogen in underground caverns was referred to in the film but was clearly unfamiliar to participants. People demanded more information about the risks, such as from undetected leaks.

Distribution: Participants were interested in what might be the most efficient and cost-effective way of distributing hydrogen, also the safest. If the benefits were clear, people would probably accept it, but there were concerns about pipelines in built-up areas and numerous tankers on the roads.

Transport applications: Participants valued the absence of carbon emissions, polluting fumes and quiet engines in hydrogen fuel cell vehicles. There was general agreement that longer filling-up time, larger tank and shorter range than for petrol/diesel were not major inconveniences and that hydrogen technologies would eventually be improved. Hydrogen as a fuel for bus fleets would increase awareness and build familiarity.

Risks: People needed to know what changes in their behaviour would be required to deal with the different 'risk profile' of hydrogen. Yet, overall, no significant opposition was found on the basis of safety concerns.

(iii) Communication, trust and public participation

In response to questions about how the public can be persuaded to engage with these issues, it was apparent that people's attitudes towards hydrogen energy are not yet fully formed. Their attitudes will be conditional upon knowing more about the technologies, the process of change and the context in which the infrastructure is developed – and also the other actors that are involved. However, there was scepticism about how far public opinion would be actually fed into decision-making.

(iv) General issues

Most people were concerned about global warming and climate change, but for many it still seems a remote not an imminent threat. Traffic-related imminent threats were viewed as air pollution and (for rather fewer) noise – issues in which hydrogen energy might bring benefit. But both the problems hydrogen might address, and the prospect of a solution, still seem remote to the public.

There were also acknowledged gaps between perception and attitude (willingness to 'sacrifice' convenience, pay more etc) as well as attitude and behaviour (what people actually do).

Most people think science will come up with solutions, including safe handling of hydrogen. But while they look to government to give a lead, they do not trust business or government to act in a disinterested way or have long term vision. People assessed hydrogen not in isolation but in context: including in terms of its potential role in their daily lives, its substantial energy supply requirement and alternative energy sources.

Conclusion

Evidence from these two studies of attitudes to hydrogen energy suggests that the apparent disconnection between values and action is still significant.

However, what the focus group material also indicates is that the reasons for such a 'gap' are complex and not reducible to lack of information or motivational factors. A number of consistent themes emerged, both in the areas where there were already hydrogen facilities or demonstration projects in place (or planned) <u>and</u> where there were none. Many people were reluctant to commit to changing their behaviour in relation to energy use or transport because they believed that their personal lifestyles were of marginal importance compared with industry's impact on the environment. This view was also connected with a widespread distrust of claims by business and industry, and information campaigns by government. They also believed that international and national changes in policy (in reduction of carbon emissions) had to be seen to occur in order for citizens and consumers seriously to consider radical changes in their behaviour. Individuals felt that their own actions were insignificant unless there was a wider set of transformations in energy use. Related to this, another recurrent theme was that while people are alert to global climate change, the crisis over fossil fuels and environmental problems, these are still perceived as distant and remote from their everyday lives, both in time (as problems affecting future generations) and in space (affecting other regions or countries). Focus group members in all areas believed that until there were substantial economic incentives or financial penalties (such as higher energy prices, road charging, higher costs of flying, etc) most people would maintain their current lifestyles and energy uses. Specifically in relation to hydrogen energy, most people were 'agnostic' about its desirability and feasibility, and expected to be shown practical demonstrations of how it would improve their own lives or avoid current environmental problems. If hydrogen energy systems were to be implemented on a large-scale, people required that this would not be too disruptive of existing behaviours, and must match current levels of cost and convenience.

These findings are consistent with, and support, much previous sociological evidence about the relationship between environmental values and behaviour.

Over a decade ago, Burningham and O'Brien (1994) showed that environmental problems, and individuals' decisions to address them, are only meaningful for people when they are connected with people's everyday routines and problems, and when they are locally contextualized. Macnaghten and Urry (1998) found that while there were expressions of environmental concern, there was little evidence that people were restructuring their lifestyles to conform with ideas about sustainability. They cogently observed that: 'People's responses to, and engagement with nature and the environment are...diverse, ambivalent, embedded within daily realities, and contested.' (Macnaghten and Urry, 1998: 232). The lack of action was attributed to ambivalent attitudes, individuals' perceived lack of personal responsibility, and a distrust of official institutions. Similarly, Macnaghten (2003) highlighted people's sense of a lack of agency in connection with sustainability and found that environmental problems only become salient for people when their families and immediate localities are directly affected. Hobson (2001, 2003) showed how people's domestic lifestyles are deeply embedded in cultural contexts and complex practicalities, which themselves may serve as 'barriers' to change. Environmentally-detrimental behaviour is built into 'the infrastructures and technologies of daily lives… unquestioned habits and contextual norms' (Hobson, 2003: 102) so that irrespective of people's attitudes and values, they may be cautious about, and even incapable of, changing their way of life to a more sustainable one.

These and other studies (see Flynn *et al*., 2008), and our findings about hydrogen energy, suggest that while the 'value-action gap' has some validity, its explanation requires a different and multi-layered, multi-factorial, approach. Focusing on beliefs and values as phenomena separately from context and practices is too limited. If we wish to understand why people's capacity and willingness to alter their behaviour – and in this case to consider adopting an emergent or unknown technology like hydrogen – is constrained, then we must recognize the importance of the inter-relationship between their experiences and the wider social contexts and processes which influence them. Public engagement initiatives which simply rely on providing more or better information – and generalized exhortations to adopt 'greener' low carbon lifestyles – are unlikely to resonate with many citizens or consumers.

Notes

1 The findings reported in this chapter are derived from two inter-related research projects, one funded by the EPSRC through the Sustainable Hydrogen Energy Consortium ('UKSHEC': see www.uk-shec.org.uk), the other funded by the Department for Transport 'Horizons' research programme (PPRO 4/54/2).

The views expressed in this chapter are those of the authors alone.

2 Seven focus groups were conducted in the period October – November 2006, in different localities in Teesside in the North East of England, South West Wales and London. A total of 47 people were involved. The groups were mixed in terms of age, gender and socio-economic background, however, especially in Teesside, there was a predominance of middle-aged people. The London groups were also mixed in terms of ethnic origin. The focus groups were composed as follows:

Focus Groups Location	Number of people	Age range	Facilitators
Redcar, Teesside	7 (2 W + 5 M)	34–65	R Flynn & M Ricci
Guisborough, Teesside	6 (3 W + 3 M)	32–72	R Flynn & M Ricci
Eston, Teesside	10 (5 W + 5 M)	25–71	R Flynn & M Ricci
Carmarthen, SW Wales	8 (4 W + 4 M)	23–71	P Bellaby & M Ricci
Lllanelli, SW Wales	5 (4 W + 1 M)	31–55	P Bellaby & M Ricci
London, group 1	8 (5 W + 3 M)	28–76	J Tomei & N Hughes
London, group 2	3 (1 W + 2 M)	28, 47, 77	J Tomei & N Hughes

References

Anable, J., Lane, B. and Kelay, T., (2006), *An evidence base review of public attitudes to climate change and transport behaviour*, Final Report to Department of Transport, London, Contract PPRO 004/006/006; http://www.dft.gov.uk/pgr/sustainable/climatechange/areviewofpublicattitudestocl5730

Barr, S. and Gilg, A., (2006), 'Sustainable lifestyles: framing environmental action in and around the home', *Geoforum*, 37: 906–920.

Bell, D., Gray, T. and Haggett, C., (2005), 'The "social gap" in wind farm siting decisions', *Environmental Politics*, 14(4): 460–477.

Bellaby, P. and Upham, P., (2007), *Public Engagement with Hydrogen Infrastructures in Transport*, report for the Department for Transport Horizons Research programme, contract number PPRO 4/54/2, December 2007. Available from http://www.iscpr.salford.ac.uk

BERR, (2007), *Renewable Energy Awareness and Attitudes Research – management summary*, URN 07/706, September, from: http://www.berr.gov.uk/files/file41239.pdf Accessed 25 February 2008.

BERR, (2008), *'Public perception'*, Department for Business, Enterprise and Regulatory Reform, summary report, from: http://www/berr.gov.uk/energy/sources/renewables/planning/public-perception Accessed 23 February 2008.

Blake, J., (1999), 'Overcoming the 'value-action gap' in environmental policy', *Local Environment*, 4(3): 257–278.

Burningham, K. and O'Brien, M., (1994), 'Global environmental values and local contexts of action', *Sociology*, 28(4): 913–932.

Butt, S. and Shaw, A., (2009), 'Pay more, fly less? Changing attitudes to air travel', in A. Park, J. Curtice, K. Thomson, M. Phillips and E. Clery, (eds), *British Social Attitudes: the 25th Report*, London: Sage.

Christie, I. and Jarvis, L., (2002), 'How green are our values?' in A. Park, J. Curtice, K. Thomson, L. Jarvis and C. Bromley, (eds), (2002), *British Social Attitudes: the 18th Report*, London: Sage.

Darnton, A., (2004), *The Impact of Sustainable Development on Public Behaviour*: report 1 of desk research commissioned by COI on behalf of DEFRA, May, from: http://www.sustainable_development.gov.uk/publications/pdf/desk-research1.pdf Accessed 13 Feb 2008.

DEFRA, (2007), *2007 Survey of Public Attitudes and Behaviours toward the Environment*, Department for Environment, Food and Rural Affairs, August 2007, from: : http://defra.gov.uk/environment/statistics/pubatt/download/pubattsum07.pdf Accessed 25 Feb 2008.

DEFRA, (2008), *A Framework for pro-Environmental behaviours*: Report, January 2008, from: http://www.defra.gov.uk/evidence/social/behaviour/pdf/behaviours-jan08-report.pdf Accessed 17 March 2009.

Dickens, P., (1992), *Society and Nature: towards a Green social theory*, Hemel Hempstead: Harvester-Wheatsheaf.

DTI, (2007), *Meeting the Energy Challenge: a White Paper on Energy*, Department of Trade and Industry, May 2007, CM 7124, London.

Ekins, P. and Hughes, N., (2007), 'The prospects for a Hydrogen Economy', UKSHEC Social Science Working Paper, June, Policy Studies Institute, London; http://www.psi.org.uk/ukshec/publications.htm

European Hydrogen and Fuel Cell Technology Platform, (2005), *Strategic Research Agenda*, July, Report from: http://www.HFPeurope.org/uploads/677/686/HFP_SRA004_SRA-report-final_22JUL2005.pdf Accessed Jan 2006

Flynn, R., (2007), 'Risk and the public acceptance of new technologies', in R. Flynn and P. Bellaby (eds), *Risk and the Public Acceptance of New Technologies*, Basingstoke: Palgrave-Macmillan.

Flynn, R., Bellaby, P. and Ricci, M., (2006), 'Risk perception of an emergent technology: the case of hydrogen energy', *Forum for Qualitative Social Research*, 7, 1, art 19, at: http://www.qualitative-research.net/fqs-texte/1-06-1-19-e.htm.

Flynn, R., Bellaby, P. and Ricci, M., (2008), 'Environmental citizenship and public attitudes to hydrogen energy technologies', *Environmental Politics*, 17(5): 766–783.

Grove-White, R., Macnaghten, P. and Wynne, B., (2000), *Wising Up: the public and new technologies*, Research Report by the Centre for the study of Environmental Change, Lancaster University.

Hobson, K., (2003), 'Thinking habits into action: the role of knowledge and process in questioning household consumption practices', *Local Environment*, 8(1): 95–112.

Hobson, K., (2001), 'Sustainable lifestyles: rethinking barriers and behaviour change', in M. Cohen and J. Murphy (eds), *Exploring Sustainable Consumption: environmental policy and the social sciences*, Oxford: Elsevier/Pergamon.

Hyways, (2008), *The European Hydrogen Roadmap: roadmap and action plan: executive summary*: http://hyways.de/docs/Brochures_and_Flyers/HyWays_executive_summary_FINAL_22Feb2008.pdf [Accessed 3 March 2008]

Irwin, A., (2001), *Sociology and the Environment*, Cambridge: Polity.

Irwin, A., (2007), 'Public dialogue and the scientific citizen', in R. Flynn and P. Bellaby (eds), *Risk and the Public Acceptance of New Technologies*, Basingstoke: Palgrave-Macmillan.

Irwin, A. and Michael, M., (2003), *Science, Social Theory and Public Knowledge*, Maidenhead: Open University Press.

Irwin, A. and Wynne, B., (1996), 'Introduction' in A. Irwin and B. Wynne (eds), *Misunderstanding Science?* Cambridge: Cambridge University Press.

Jackson, T., (2004), *Motivating Sustainable Consumption: a review of evidence on consumer behaviour and behavioural change*. A report to the Sustainable Development Research Network and ESRC, University of Surrey, from: http://www.portal.surrey.ac.uk/pls/portal/docs/PAGE/ENG/STAFF/STAFFAC/JACKSON/PUBLICATIONS Accessed 17 Nov 2006

Kollmuss, A. and Agyeman, J., (2002), 'Mind the gap', *Environmental Education Research*, 8, 3: 239–260.

Macnaghten, P. and Urry, J., (1998), *Contested Natures*, London: Sage.

Macnaghten, P., (2003), 'Embodying the environment in everyday life practices', *The Sociological Review*, 51(1): 63–84.

McDowall, W. and Eames, M., (2006), 'Forecasts, scenarios, backcasts and roadmaps to the hydrogen economy', *Energy Policy*, 34: 1236–1250.

Mohr, A., (2007), 'Against the stream: moving public engagement on nanotechnologies upstream', in R. Flynn R. and P. Bellaby (eds), *Risk and the Public Acceptance of New Technologies*, Basingstoke: Palgrave-Macmillan.

Newby, H., (1991), 'One world, two cultures: sociology and the environment', *Network* (British Sociological Association), 50, May.

O'Garra, T., Pearson, P. and Mourato, S., (2007), 'Public acceptability of hydrogen fuel cell transport and associated refuelling infrastructures', in R. Flynn and P. Bellaby (eds), *Risk and the Public Acceptance of New Technologies*, Basingstoke: Palgrave-Macmillan.

Park, A., Curtice, J., Thomson, K., Jarvis, L. and Bromley, C., (eds), (2002), *British Social Attitudes: the 18th Report*, London: Sage.

Park, A., Curtice, J., Thomson, K., Phillips, M., Johnson, M. and Clery, E., (eds), (2008), *British Social Attitudes: the 24th Report*, London, Sage.

Poortinga, W., Steg, L. and Vlek, C., (2004), 'Values, environmental concern and environmental behaviour', *Environment and Behaviour*, 36, 1: 70–93.

Ricci, M., Flynn, R. and Bellaby, P., (2006), *Public Attitudes towards hydrogen energy: preliminary analysis of focus groups in London, Teesside and Wales*, Report for UK Sustainable Hydrogen Consortium, June 2006, ISCPR, University of Salford. Available from: http://www.psi.org.uk/ukshec

Ricci, M., Newsholme, G., Bellaby, P. and Flynn, R., (2007a), 'The transition to hydrogen-based energy: combining technology and risk assessments and lay perspectives', *International Journal of Energy Sector Management*, 1(1): 43–50.

Ricci, M., Bellaby, P. and Flynn, R., (2007b), 'Stakeholders' and publics' perceptions of hydrogen energy technologies', in R. Flynn and P. Bellaby (eds), *Risk and the Public Acceptance of New Technologies*, Basingstoke: Palgrave-Macmillan.

Ricci, M., Bellaby, P. and Flynn, R., (2008), 'What do we know about public perceptions and acceptance of hydrogen? A critical review and new case study evidence', *International Journal of Hydrogen Energy*, 33: 5868–5880.

Rifkin, J., (2002), *The Hydrogen Economy*, New York: Tarcher & Putnam.

Rowe, G. and Frewer, L., (2004), 'Evaluating public engagement exercises: a research agenda', *Science, Technology and Human Values*, 29 (4): 512–556.

Stern, N., (2007), *The Stern Review: The Economics of Climate Change*, London: Cabinet Office & HM Treasury.

Stern, P. C., (2000), 'Towards a coherent theory of environmentally significant behaviour', *Journal of Social Issues*, 56(3): 407–424.

Stirling, A., (2005), 'Opening-up or closing down? Analysis, participation and power in the social appraisal of technology' in M. Leach, I. Scoones and B. Wynne (eds), *Science and Citizens*, London: Zed Books.

Stradling, S., Anable, J., Anderson, T. and Cronberg, A., (2008), 'Car use and climate change: do we practise what we preach?', in A. Park *et al.*, (eds), (2008), *British Social Attitudes: the 24th Report*, London: Sage.

Sustainable Development Commission, (2006), *I will if you will: towards sustainable consumption*, Report by the Sustainable Development Round Table, 1 May 2006, from: http://www.sd-commssion.org.uk/publications.php?id=367 Accessed 24 Aug 2006.

UK Committee on Climate Change, (2008), 'Building a low carbon economy: the UK's contribution to tackling climate change', First Report, December 2008, London: The Stationary Office.

United Nations, (2006), *The Hydrogen Economy: a non-technical review*, United Nations Environment Programme, New York: UN.

Urry, J., (2008), 'Climate change, travel and complex futures', *British Journal of Sociology*, 59(2): 261–279.

Wilsdon, J. and Willis, R., (2004), *See-through Science: why public engagement needs to move upstream*, London: Demos.

Wynne, B., (2005), 'Risk as a globalizing "democratic" discourse? Framing subjects and citizens', in M. Leach, I. Scoones and B. Wynne (eds), *Science and Citizens*, London: Zed Books.

Yearley, S., (2005), *Cultures of Environmentalism*, London: Palgrave-Macmillan.

Technologies in place: symbolic interpretations of renewable energy

Carly McLachlan

> Wave Hub's government approval is good news for Cornwall and for the future of renewable energy generation in the UK. We look forward to using the same energy we've used to ride waves to light up our homes as well. (Surfers Against Sewage, 2007)

> It is bioenergy but it is not your all-singing all-dancing clean energy is it? (Eccleshall, resident interview 10: 8)

This chapter considers stakeholder (including the public) responses to two specific energy technologies in two particular places – the Wave Hub, Cornwall, UK and Eccleshall Biomass, Staffordshire, UK. The focus is on the role of different interpretations of place and technology in shaping the responses that stakeholders had to these developments. Investigation of a bioenergy and a wave energy development allows comparison of terrestrial and marine issues and widens the dominant focus upon wind in studies of the social acceptability of renewable energy. It is argued that stakeholder responses to renewable energy developments are, in part, related to interpretations of what the technology and the location or 'place' are seen to represent or symbolize. Symbolism refers to more abstract meanings that stakeholders associate with the physical developments themselves. In particular, the interest is in the multiple and potentially conflicting symbolic interpretations of both place and the technology, and how these can explain why the development does or does not 'fit' in a particular location for different stakeholders.

Previous work on renewable energy siting controversy has identified that opposition to particular renewable energy developments may be a substantial barrier to meeting renewable energy targets (Wüstenhagen et al., 2007). Although some authors have developed theoretical frameworks (eg Bell et al., 2005), much of the work on renewable energy siting controversy has tended to focus on description rather than explanation (Devine-Wright, 2005). Notions of NIMBYism (Not In My Back Yard) have been commonplace in both applied and academic contexts and are used as a way of discrediting objectors (Burningham, 2000). Calls for more information provision and more 'rationality' (eg Upreti, 2004) or describing objectors as NIMBYs (with the accusations of selfishness that the term implies), have failed to take on the task of developing an under-standing of the different reasons for opposition and support. Rather than focus-sing on the provision of scientifically informed 'answers' or on seeking to prove certain positions right and others wrong, the concern here is with identifying and *understanding* positions of opposition and support.

Firstly, the role of place and symbolic interpretations of technology in previ-ous renewable energy siting controversy work is discussed. Then some theoreti-cal background to the concepts of place and technology symbolism is presented, before the case studies are discussed.

Previous work on renewable energy siting controversy

Although identified as a potential source of opposition and support and there-fore a valuable line of academic enquiry, symbolic interpretations have largely been neglected in the analysis of renewable energy siting controversy (Devine-Wright, 2005). However, there are a few notable exceptions. For example wind turbines have been seen to represent: 'stewardship', 'ugly technology', 'respon-sible energy policy', 'destroying landscape', 'progress' and 'harking back to the past' (Thayer and Freeman, 1987; Thayer and Hansen, 1988; Lee *et al.*, 1989; Gipe, 1993). Such studies make clear that there can be a wide range of different symbolic meanings attributed to a development. However, the studies have tended to be quantitative in nature and have therefore lacked an exploratory approach, which could investigate the various different symbolic meanings *already* given to the development. Although Pasqualetti, (2000), identifies the importance of the 'congruency' between landscape and wind turbines, he does not explicitly discuss the contested nature of what the landscape and the tech-nology represent and the resulting, potentially diverse, reasons for assessments of congruence or incongruence. Rather his focus is upon aesthetic design rules that are argued to improve this 'fit'. Further study is required to identify the reasons behind such assessments of 'fit'.

Case studies of bioenergy developments have also identified interesting sym-bolic interpretations. The authors of one study state that the plant was viewed by 'the public' as a factory with smoking chimneys rather than a 'state of the art environmentally friendly facility to produce green electricity to benefit all' (Upreti and Van der Horst, 2004: 67). This potentially valuable line of enquiry receives no further attention. The reader is left to infer that the assessment of chimneys and their related 'industrialness' will lead to opposition but this would benefit from more explicit analysis. Is it 'industrialness' itself that is a negative concept or is there a more complex interaction of place symbolism and technol-ogy symbolism (ie industrialness doesn't fit in this location for some reason)? There is also no further analysis of those who view the plant as environmentally friendly or their reasoning behind this. Another study lists the reasons given for a development being 'unfair' as: 'it should be in the city', 'we don't need the power' and 'it shouldn't be in the countryside' (Sinclair and Lofstedt, 2001).

These reasons indicate interesting concepts of ownership and responsibility for the production of energy but are again not analysed in any more detail.

Place

Geographers have used the concept of 'place' to discuss the significance of locations beyond their physical characteristics. Place is defined as a location with 'meaning' and this meaning can be attributed on vastly different scales (from an armchair to the entire earth) (Tuan, 1977; Cresswell, 2004). Meaning is not inherent in the physical characteristics of a particular place but is given by humans and may be closely linked to notions of identity and sense of 'belonging' (Cresswell, 2004; Simmons and Walker, 2004). It is unsurprising, therefore, that strong reactions may be encountered when something (eg a renewable energy development) is seen to threaten what a place means. Wind farm controversy work has focused on landscape, with developments often being referred to as 'a blot' on a treasured landscape. However, landscape is an 'intensely visual' concept, of which the viewer is outside. In contrast, *places* are something to be inside of and connected with (Cresswell, 2004). From the case studies discussed here, and a close reading of other papers on renewable energy siting controversy, a more interactive relationship with the site/location is evident. It is more than the visual amenity that is 'valued' by respondents and it is these broader meanings that this chapter is concerned with exploring.

Places can mean different things to different people but official assessments may obscure this pluralism. By stressing certain aspects or histories of the location, respondents, both supporters and opponents of the developments, can create particular images of the place (Jess and Massey, 1995; Hubbard *et al.*, 2004). Drawing on historic images of a place can bolster the validity and credibility of claims to define the essence of that place. Activities that do not fit with this essence are seen as being 'out of place' and therefore unacceptable. Through the example of aboriginal people's relationships with areas of land that have strong meaning and a close link to their identity, Massey (1995) identifies the importance of notions of 'ownership' of places. This 'ownership' may not be a legal definition but rather a legacy or moral ownership. A moral sense of ownership, or indeed a moral sense that the place is 'un-ownable' (ie that it belongs to everyone) can be a strong factor in actors' sense of what the place 'is' and how it should be used or protected.

There is much discussion of the impact of the modern, globalized world on sense of place. For some, place is being lost due to increased personal mobility and the globalization of products and brands. However, Massey (1995) argues that, in this faster and less stable world, a sense of place is strongly desired. In addition, she calls for a more fluid and porous approach, which sees place as being defined both by what is within it and its connections to the wider world, rather than drawing impermeable boundaries around places. It is not the purpose of this chapter to declare what type of place respondents should be thinking of and identifying with. Rather, the concern is with how place is used by different actors in the case studies. Exclusionary notions of place are evident in the cases. However, the changing nature of UK energy policy, with more decentralized developments being proposed as well as a focus on renewable energy and energy security (DTI, 2007), mean that actors that previously had little interaction with energy, beyond its delivery through a socket on the wall, may now find that energy is changing what a valued place means and how it is connected to other places. This wider context is often discussed by respondents and it is important to consider how these changing pressures of energy production may alter interpretations of places.

Technology symbolism

Technology is a prominent theme in much environmental discourse, often being presented as the answer to all environmental ills, or indeed as the creator of them. For example it is now common to see nuclear energy presented as both the creator of negative environmental and human health legacies and as an important way of mitigating climate change (eg Greenpeace, 2008, BERR 2008). Shiva indicates the different symbolic meaning with which technological debates can be imbued, and the different levels at which this symbolism can be enacted through discussion of genetically modified organisms:

> . . . in the seed, cultural diversity converges with biological diversity. Ecological issues combine with social justice, peace and democracy. (Shiva, 1998: 126)

Discussions of controversy over technologies are often focused upon the impacts that the technology will have. Such a focus is evidence of the technological determinism that is dominant in much of the siting controversy discourse. Impact assessments imply that technologies are amenable to a single objective and independent assessment, rather than multiple interpretations. Irwin (2001: 136) argues that 'technologies are not simply 'given' but are varyingly constructed, experienced, worried over and enjoyed'.

Zonabend's (1993) work on nuclear plant workers found that they often used symbolic interpretations of the technology to 'fill the gaps' in their understanding of, and access to, the processes which they worked alongside. This accessibility and 'observability' relates to the distinction between 'devices' and 'things'. Under the 'device paradigm' it is argued that bodily engagement with technologies is increasingly seen as burdensome. Therefore, progress has been in the direction of the provision of goods and services which have minimal human interaction with the mechanism of provision. For example, a log stove is argued to be a *thing*, in that it requires bodily engagement to provide heat and it plays a wider role than simply the provision of heat. It can work to define roles in the family (collection of wood, stoking the fire, etc). It can also act as the centrepiece of the home and as the centre of social interactions. In contrast, a boiler which provides the same level of heat to the home is thought of as a *device*. Interaction with it is minimal as heat is provided with very little direct human effort (Borg-mann, 1984). There is much room for discussion in this distinction. It is clear that what may be a *device* to one person may be a *thing* to someone else, and that the social engagement embodied in a *thing* may be interpreted both posi-tively and negatively (Tatum, 1994). Rather than seeking to present either wave energy or bioenergy technologies as *devices* or *things*, concern here is with iden-tifying how these concepts may lead to different symbolic interpretations.

Some argue that constellations of policies and institutional arrangements have facilitated the dominance or development of certain technologies, at certain times, in certain places (MacKenzie and Wajcman, 1999). From an energy technology perspective, the climate change and energy security agendas are important factors in the justification and explanation of how these particular developments have 'come about'. It is unsurprising that respondents may decide upon the acceptability of this specific technology in this specific location based, at least partially, on assessments of its related social and institutional constellations. Therefore, as Owens (2002) has identified, local opposition to particular facilities is often tied up with concerns over much wider policies and issues.

Case studies

The Wave Hub project is funded by the South West Regional Development Agency (SWRDA), and is envisaged as a final pre-commercial facility (offering developers the opportunity to deploy and monitor arrays of their devices before developing single-device commercial farms). The hub is explained as an 'under-water socket'. Up to four arrays of Wave Energy Converters (WECs) can then 'plug in' to the socket on the sea bed, allowing the electricity that they produce to be brought on shore to a sub-station that is connected to the National Grid.

In Wave Hub, objections to the proposal came primarily from three groups. Firstly, some surfers claimed that the development would have a detrimental impact on the height and quality of waves in the area. Secondly, some maritime stakeholders expressed concern over the impact on the safety of navigation in the area. Finally, there were concerns over the potential impact on tourism. SWRDA issued numerous press releases about the benefits for the local area and the impact on surfing. Support came from local energy and environmental stakeholders, including Surfers Against Sewage (SAS), who organized support-ive PR activities including a 'Mexican Wave of Support'. The Wave Hub was granted planning permission in September 2007, and is expected to be opera-tional in 2011.

The Eccleshall Biomass development was first discussed with local residents in early summer 2003 *before* any formal submission was made to the local plan-ning authority, Stafford Borough Council. Originally the 2.6 MW plant was to be fuelled by Miscanthus (an energy crop), to be grown within a 25 mile radius

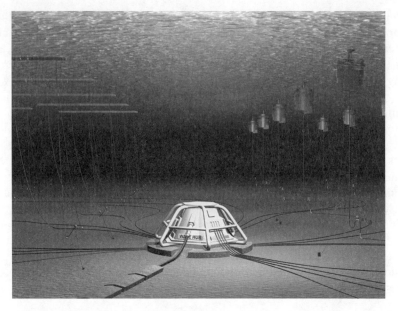

Figure 1: *Artist's impression of Wave Hub, Illustration by Industrial Art Studio, www.ind-art.co.uk.*

of the plant. The project was presented as one of rural diversification that would help local farmers whilst producing renewable electricity.

The application received planning permission in October 2003. In November 2005, changes were made to the proposed development and a new application was made. The new proposal identified that there was a shortfall of Miscanthus and therefore 'clean woodchip' would be used as an interim fuel (Miscanthus is only harvestable at least three years after initial planting). In seeking a Power Purchase Agreement, the developers were required to store more fuel on site to ensure reliability, and planned to construct buildings to cover this fuel.

The new proposal was submitted without any direct contact between the developer and the local residents. Therefore the first official notice that the local residents had of the new proposal was when they received a letter from the planning department to inform them that a plan had been submitted. At this point, some of the local residents started to raise concerns with the council and organized a public meeting, which the developers also attended. Residents' concerns mainly arose once the altered proposal had been submitted. These included the health impacts of woodchip fuel, the monitoring of fuels and the possibility of waste being used as a fuel in the future. The move to woodchip made some objectors question both the environmental and rural benefits of the project. The project did gain planning permission and was connected to the National Grid in August 2007.

Figure 2: *The Eccleshall Biomass Development, ©Eccleshall Biomass.*

In Eccleshall, concerns were raised primarily by local residents rather than different stakeholder groups as they were in the Wave Hub. However, in both cases, objections were raised about the process of consultation itself.

Method

The research for each case was conducted through collection of secondary data and in-depth interviews with relevant stakeholders. Interviews were sought with 'active' stakeholders (Walker, 1995) in the cases, ie those that were already in the debate before the research commenced, rather than seeking to collect responses from a representative local sample. Concern was with mapping the controversy over the developments rather than reflecting local 'public perceptions' in a statistically representative way. In order to access the reasons behind different support and opposition positions, the interview schedule was open-ended. Interviews started with a broad question, asking the respondents to tell the interviewer about the development and what, if any, the main issues were. This was designed to minimize the impact of prompting and to try to capture what the respondent would intuitively report as the key issues. The issues mentioned by the respondent were probed by asking for more detail and explanation before moving on to the preset topic areas identified from the secondary data. It should be noted that the respondents were not at any time asked specifically about what the development 'symbolized'. This in-depth qualitative approach allowed identification of the symbolic meaning attached to both the technology and place, and consideration of how such meanings were mobilized to bolster opposition and support.

'Place' in the case studies

As has been identified from discussion of the concept of place, there can be multiple and conflicting ways in which the location of a proposed renewable energy development is experienced and defined by different stakeholders. The historic meaning, and sense of belonging that a particular place can hold for people, makes it unsurprising that a proposed development can meet with strong reaction if it is felt to change or not to 'fit' with that place. Although landscape issues may form a significant part of place, it cannot be reduced solely to this. Place is interpreted in numerous ways in each of the case studies. Original spelling and grammar have been maintained in the quotes taken from written material.

Scale

Just as Tuan (1977) stressed that widely different scales of place can have significance, the relevant scale of place that the development is seen to influence varies widely within each of the cases (from the site boundary to the global). The development is seen to pose different opportunities and threats at these different scales. For the Wave Hub, the threats at the sea-bed level are the potential impacts on marine life in and around the site and the impact on localized waves and surfing beaches. The Cornish coast is threatened by the potential further expansion of the Wave Hub or developments like it (this relates to the technological symbolism of *precedent* which will be discussed later). Alternatively the development is seen to put Cornwall, the South West region and the UK 'on the map' in terms of renewable energy development. For Eccleshall, there is also discussion of what the development means for Staffordshire and UK energy and climate change strategy. In addition, the construction of who is 'local' at different scales also plays an important role, with the developers being portrayed as not *really* local as they do not live in the immediate vicinity. Both traditional and more porous conceptions of place are evident.

> The Wave Hub isn't about Cornwall and the South West, it is about the whole of the UK and maintaining the leading position the UK has already got. (Wave Hub, Interview, SWRDA, p. 18)

> ...path finding project of national significance (Eccleshall, Letter submitted to planning department from developer)

Economically vulnerable

In the Wave Hub case, Cornwall is generally described as economically vulnerable. This image of a deprived area is used both as a reason to object to the project and to support it. In terms of objections it is argued that the project will affect the surf and the image of surfing in the region and have a knock-on effect on tourism which is seen as a major and vital local industry. Alternatively, the economic vulnerability of the area is used as a way of justifying what is deemed to be a small, insignificant or acceptable impact on the surf, to attract a sustainable industry to the area. In Eccleshall, there is widespread support for rural diversification in principle, and the farming industry is often presented as being in need of protection and encouragement. The fragility of the rural economy is underlined by references to financial and job losses should the project not go ahead. However, once woodchip replaced the Miscanthus as the primary fuel, the value and the relevance of the project to farmers was questioned and therefore so was its acceptability.

> The surfing industry has become massively important to Cornwalls fragile economy. Most of our industries are in steep decline...' (Wave Hub, Email objection, p. 8a)

> Fuel supply will help to safeguard up to 60 local farm businesses with a new diversification opportunity for farmers to produce energy crops under long term fuel supply contracts. (Eccleshall, Developer's supporting statement to Planning Department)

Ownership

The notion of ownership is invoked in symbolic and moral ways rather than in a legal sense (Massey, 1995). In Cornwall, there are numerous references to 'our waves' and to their being 'stolen'. In addition, there is discussion around the rights of access to certain areas of the sea from fishing and shipping interests, with this discourse drawing on the interpretation of the sea as a resource.

> The hubs pinching something up to 35% of the waves energy. (Wave Hub, Email objection, p. 23a)

In Eccleshall, there is a sense of the 'countryside' being a public good, owned by everyone, that everyone has a right to enjoy, which is counter to the legal ownership of specific fields. There is an additional ownership issue over the potential impact that the development may have on local house prices.

In both cases the development is promoted in terms of the locals 'doing their bit' for climate change or energy security by supporting the development. This draws on a sense of place to mobilize support for the development, through showing what 'our place' stands for.

> The Eccleshall plant provides the opportunity for the people of Staffordshire to show their colours and make a real difference. (Eccleshall, National Farmers' Union, letter of support to planning department)

However, along with mobilization of sense of place in favour of the development, comes the related issue of energy distribution. Who will actually receive the electricity produced by the development and what will it cost? For some objectors, particularly in the Eccleshall Biomass case, as soon as the power goes in to the National Grid, anyone can use it and it therefore loses its 'localness'. The development is no longer about providing electricity for this place, as the electricity could have been produced anywhere.

> Two hundred homes and when the whole country is short of electricity, and the lights are out, and this that and the other – Eccleshall will be booming and have loads of electricity – load of shit! They'll sell it to the National Grid and it just goes in. It don't go to Eccleshall. (Eccleshall, resident interview 2, p. 57)

There are two counter arguments to this. One is simply that everyone's electricity has to be put in to the grid so although the relationship is mediated, they are still putting electricity 'in' here and taking electricity 'out' here. Alternatively a more technical point of view argues that due to the operation of the grid, electricity will automatically be distributed as locally as possible.

Claims that the energy is for local use may work to develop a sense of symbolic ownership but can backfire when objectors think this does not ring true with notions of the *National* Grid.

Place as nature or a natural resource

In the Wave Hub case, the place is discussed in the context of being a resource, to be used with maximum efficiency.

> The reality is that in future you are going to have to get as much as you can out of a sea area. If you have got one square mile you can't just spread out right across – because of the competing interests from stakeholders and because of cabling and because of organization and operational costs. (Wave Hub, Interview, SWRDA, p. 30)

In Eccleshall, 'the countryside' is also seen by some stakeholders as a resource to be used by farmers to make their living. For others, the countryside and the sea are seen as 'nature' – delicate to human intervention and in need of protection.

> The sea is a delicate world of its own, that has taken millions of years to get to the balance that it is in now, it should be respected and admired, not used to try to cover up what we've done on land. (Wave Hub, Email objection, p. 120a)

> I feel it would be much better if it was not virtually on the doorstep of a beautiful village and its surroundings. Too much of this countryside is being wasted on projects such as this. (Eccleshall, resident (85) objection pro forma)

The idyllic rural image presented by some in Eccleshall is attacked by describing this particular site as *already* being industrial. Although the site is 'Greenfield', the adjacent industrial estate is used to stress that the *relative* impact in this area is minimal or acceptable.

> Clearly if the plant has to be located outside an existing industrial estate or site, a location adjacent to an existing industrial estate is likely to have less of an impact than would an isolated Greenfield site within open countryside. (Eccleshall, Planning Officer's report)

Technology symbolism from the case studies

These technologies and developments are not seen simply as 'sustainable' or 'green' projects with only positive impacts, but are viewed in multiple ways by different stakeholders. Rather than considering the developments in isolation, they are compared with other renewable energy technologies and with energy demand reduction options. Their importance and significance are discussed in the context of other climate change and energy policies and judgements on the effectiveness of these.

It should be noted that the Wave Hub itself is not a wave energy technology, rather wave energy devices will connect to it. Stakeholders talked about the Wave Hub in an operational sense, ie with the devices attached rather than the hub or 'socket' on its own. Whilst some respondents used certain devices as examples to make their points, particular wave energy devices were not identified as having particular symbolic interpretations, rather it was wave energy in general that was discussed. Clearly this may come to change as different devices are proposed and installed and their impacts and effectiveness are discussed, monitored and compared.

Contested environmental status

Many stakeholders, with differing assessments of the desirability of the project, share a consensus on its environmental status. Some argue that its carbon benefits outweigh any other, more localized environmental impacts. The pitting of one set of environmental values (the protection of the local natural environment), against the more longterm target of environmental protection through avoiding climate change, leads to various 'green on green' battles, where different factions compete for the environmental high ground (Warren *et al.*, 2005). Many respondents preface their objection with an acceptance of the general desirability of the project. Potentially this could be seen as an example of respondents learning to 'sound like environmentalists' (Barr, 2004). Some stakeholders argue that to retain credibility it is necessary to accept at least the general desirability of the project, even if they still wish to raise concerns about this specific development. Respondents tended to not want to be seen as anti-environment and so often described their own pro-environmental behaviour when discussing their opposition to the development.

> I understand the need for green energy, but there are other places the waves hubs could be placed. (Wave Hub, Email objection, p. 90a)

Despite the perceived taboo of objecting to any sort of 'green' project, some people do openly question the rationale behind the development. In particular, there is an accusation that it is about being 'seen to be green' rather than the benefits of the project itself. The following quotes demonstrate this theme of 'Greenwash'.

> It seems that the proposed siting off Cornwall is motivated by the regional ego of a few people, rather than by science. (Wave Hub, Email objection, p. 117b)

> with this global warming there is a lot of political posturing and they don't really look in to the background of things. (Eccleshall, resident interview (3) p. 13)

This sense of 'Greenwash' is backed up by questions about the overall carbon impact of the project with claims that, over the lifecycle of the project, the amount of carbon dioxide saved will be negligible or indeed that emissions may even increase. The environmental status of the project is often implicitly questioned through the use of quotation marks when using the term green. This is particularly the case in Eccleshall when woodchip, introduced to make up the Miscanthus shortfall, was seen by some to undermine the green status of the development.

> What about the carbon emissions caused by these lorries and the tractors harvesting and delivering the miscanthus. (Eccleshall, letter from local resident (11) to planning department)

> Even a small reduction in wave energy would mean people will choose not to surf in Cornwall, instead travelling abroad to surf with the dual affect of losing an important money generator for the region and creating further carbon emissions through increased plane travel! (Wave Hub, Email objection, p.82a)

These different interpretations of the technology indicate that 'greenness' is rarely a universally accepted intrinsic property of a technology. Understanding how respondents are assessing claims to greenness and how tradeoffs with other social and green goals are made is important in understanding how the desirability of this and other projects are assessed. Respondents' desire to ensure that they are not seen as anti-environment, indicates the dominance of the environmental and green discourses, both within stakeholders' organizations and more generally in the media and public spheres (Segnit and Ereaut, 2007).

Significance and precedent

As mentioned above, the scale of the problem of climate change is often used to justify the acceptability of more localized environmental impacts.

> Whatever the detrimental effects are, they are a very small price to pay for longterm climate stability. (Wave Hub, Interview, Surf Magazine Editor, p. 7)

Whilst this respondent does not believe that Wave Hub alone will provide climate stability, the project is seen as a significant and necessary step to achieving such a goal. A strong theme of precedent emerges from many stakeholders. On one hand it is perceived as a boundary-pushing development, ie this development is key and others will flow from it, which supports claims of materiality and significance. Alternatively, those that see it as an intrusion on this valuable and sensitive natural environment worry that this is the first of many developments and are concerned about the cumulative impact.

> If the hub works, great! But will this mean hub after hub being installed along the best surfing coast line in the UK? One may cause little effect, but what about one hundred in a line. (Wave Hub, Email objection, p. 17a)

> The [Parish] council would not be in favour of the development if it were likely to be the precursor to any extension of Raleigh Hall outside of the existing boundaries and on to a green field site. (Eccleshall, Parish council response to proposal)

In Eccleshall, the notion of precedent applies not just to the extension of the industrial estate adjacent to the site, but to the types of fuels that will be used. There are concerns that a shift from Miscanthus to woodchip sets a precedent for using other fuels in the future.

> Concerns have been expressed in respect to the use of the plant and if there is a plan to ultimately include the processing of domestic waste. (Eccleshall, letter from resident(5) to planning department)

> Reading some articles and concerns of Tony Blair [to] reduce emissions targets and winning public views over nuclear power stations and introducing small nuclear plants, there is a lot of speculation as to what Eccleshall Biomass Plant is really going to become. (Eccleshall, Letter from resident (1) to planning department)

This concern, that the plant may become a nuclear facility, was picked up by the local newspaper. The resident's own letter to the planning department clearly demonstrates how technologies are experienced in context, drawing upon wider current political and social conditions in order to frame their concerns over this particular development. At first glance, the notion that a biomass combustion plant could be turned in to a nuclear plant could easily be cast as misunderstanding or ignorance. However, as the quote above explains the justification for this position, it becomes easy to understand why such a concern developed. Concerns over precedent support previous calls for local and regional limits on renewable energy to be set so as to give stakeholders a guide on how much renewable energy they may expect to see in their region (Woods, 2003; Upham and Shackley, 2006).

The scale of the emissions reductions required to combat climate change makes some respondents more sceptical about the significance, and therefore acceptability, of this particular project. Setting the development in the context of leading the UK's fight against climate change works to increase its significance, whereas the contribution of the developments in terms of national or regional energy demand is used to undermine the 'difference' that they will make.

> The wave hub is likely to deplete wave height and therefore local revenue [...] which relies heavily on the surf industry in exchange for only 3% of the power requirement of Cornwall. It is not an equal payoff. It is not enough to make an impact on global warming, or fossil fuel consumption...(Wave Hub, Email objection, p. 106b)

Commercial project or symbolic ownership

Opposition to renewable energy developments is often labelled as NIMBYism. This term holds accusations of selfishness and of individuals' unwillingness to make a personal sacrifice for the social good. However, many respondents feel they are being asked to make a personal sacrifice for the personal gain of others (ie developers and energy companies), rather than the social good of carbon dioxide reductions. When the trade-off is set up in this way, it is unsurprising that some respondents find it unacceptable.

> Go to Scotland please, we're not stupid, and this is ultimately a commercial venture its set-up costs are reduced by its proposed location, but its output reduced! (Wave Hub, Email objection, p. 34a)

This discourse relates to the sense that this development is not 'for the locals'. This feeling is often explained through the argument that they will receive no reduction in their energy bill. This stands counter to much of the promotional work around renewable energy developments, which draws upon images of common goals and of 'saving our planet'. This is clearly identified in the opening quote from Surfers Against Sewage who are looking forward to using the waves *they* have been using for surfing to light *their* homes. This position makes no reference to the fact that local people will still be required to pay for the electricity that they use, regardless of whether it comes from the Wave Hub. By omitting this from the image of *local* natural resources being used for *local* energy generation, they increase the projects' inclusivity and sense of symbolic local ownership. Whilst many renewable energy developers do offer some form of local community benefit or ownership, neither of the cases presented here had such a scheme.

Experiment or pioneering

The technology is seen by many stakeholders as being 'experimental'. However, this 'experimental' status is interpreted both positively and negatively by different stakeholders. On the one hand the project is seen as pushing at the boundaries of solutions for climate change and energy security. Being at the forefront of innovation demonstrates the technical competence and potential commercial strength of the industry in the regions and in the UK as a whole.

> This is a vital project for the local rural economy and is of national significance to the future of the biomass industry and agriculture in the UK. (Eccleshall, Letter of support from BiEcc growers group to the Development Control Committee)

Alternatively, the 'experimental' status is seen as evidence that the impacts are unknown or unknowable. This results in calls either for more research to be done on the impacts or for the project to be abandoned as the impacts are thought to be inherently 'unknowable'. The negative interpretation of the experimental status also links to concerns over irreversibility. There is a sense that, due either to the delicate balance of the place or the procedures of the planning process, once the development has been built there is no way of removing it or reversing any damage it has done. The question is therefore posed, given the importance and value of this 'place' why 'experiment' here?

> If you're going to conduct a chemistry experiment you don't do it in your best china. Likewise, if you're going to conduct a wave hub experiment you don't conduct it off your best coastline. (Wave Hub, Internet Discussion Forum)

It is all experimental so how can they say it is going to be no noise and no fumes and nothing like that? They don't know yet, not really. They have only experimented on a small scale. (Eccleshall, resident interview (4) p. 8)

Industrial or at one with Mother Nature?

For some supporters the Wave Hub fits seamlessly with images of nature and the need to value and protect it. Using nature to solve an environmental problem has a certain 'fit' and wave technology is often described in terms such as 'benign' (Pelamis Wave Power, 2007). Surfers Against Sewage, for example, see the development as 'fitting' with surfing, because the same waves are used to light 'our' homes and for surfing. There is no new intrusion in this analysis, just an extension of what is already, harmoniously, occurring. Here, engagement with the technology as a thing can be seen with renewable energy representing a positive relationship between humans and nature. In Eccleshall, the 'natural-ness' of the fuel is discussed and analogies are often drawn with open fires that people have in their homes, which makes the technology seem more accessible and *thing-like*.

> Won't cause any harm to anyone, cause you can't beat natural products can you? (Eccleshall, Interview 6, p. 14)

Alternatively the developments are presented as industrial installations and therefore potentially as intrusions in a natural environment. This is achieved for the Wave Hub by drawing on industrial images, such as pistons and pumps, or referring simply to the development as a power station. For Eccleshall, the development is referred to as a 'power station', a 'factory' and an 'incinerator' by respondents. The 'clean woodchip' that the developers say will fuel the plant is often referred to as 'waste wood' by local residents. These terms strip the developments of their green credentials, giving them a more traditional 'dirty' and industrial power station image.

> The proposed power station [...] will involve anchoring 20 sets of turbines, pistons and pumps 10 miles offshore in the path of the Atlantic swell...(The Times, 2006)

> We are in danger of our wonderful view being obscured by a huge chimney belching out god knows what. (Eccleshall, resident objection pro forma (90))

There is engagement here with the technologies as devices. They are described as being either just another industrial development with no real human or natural connection, or as being unknowable due to the inaccessible or unobservable nature of the process or impacts.

Conclusions: technologies in place

> Fancy spoiling a lovely rural location with a power station. (Eccleshall, comment on local objection petition)

The multiple interpretations of place and technology discussed above, come together to explain different assessments of 'fit' between the place and the technology. For example, whilst the status of being an 'experiment' can be interpreted positively or negatively, a negative interpretation combined with a sense of place as fragile nature that must be protected will cause a clash. A positive interpretation of the experimental status, combined with seeing the place as a resource that must be exploited with maximum efficiency fits well. The assessment of place as 'nature' can still fit with a positive assessment of the development if the technology is seen as being benign or 'at one with Mother Nature'. Figure 3 illustrates some of these potential symbolic logics of opposition and support.

Previous work on renewable energy siting controversy has not focussed upon the role of symbolic interpretations of technology and place. It is clear from the cases presented here that these are multiple and often conflicting. Consideration of both place and technology works to illuminate better both support and opposition positions and assessments of 'fit' (ie why this particular development does or does not fit in this particular location). Just as it is important to consider both opposition and support if a fuller understanding of renewable energy siting controversy is to be gained, it is of fundamental importance that both place *and* technology symbolism be considered. This chapter has argued that these interpretations come together to form very different logics behind both opposition and support positions. Rather than casting objections as evidence of selfish NIMBYism or support as evidence of promoting global over local environmen-

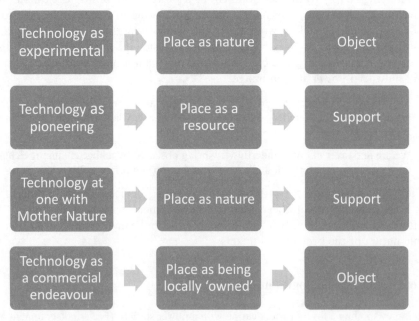

Figure 3: *Symbolic logics of opposition and support.*

tal issues, considering the reasons for, rather than only the levels of, opposition and support builds a better understanding of these positions. This understanding potentially opens up new and alternative mitigation, communication, compensation and consultation activities that respond to these issues and concerns, rather than repetition of activities that are operating potentially at cross purposes.

The interpretations of place found in the cases, indicate that engagement with location, although including visual impact, is much broader than the purely visual notion of landscape that has dominated work on wind energy. A sense of place can also be used to mobilize support for developments, as local residents and stakeholders are called on to support the development and show what 'our place' stands for. 'Impacts' have traditionally be considered at a very localized level but the relevant scale for symbolic impacts can be drawn very differently by different stakeholders. Some of these interpretations use the development as a way of linking this particular place with others, eg through the meeting of regional or national targets indicating a 'porous' conceptualization of place. However, more traditional exclusionary concepts of place are also evident as developers are presented by some as unwelcome 'outsiders'.

The technologies were interpreted in many ways including; 'experimental', 'pioneering', 'at one with nature', 'industrial', 'for profit' and having a sense of local 'ownership'. It is clear that any sense that marine energy will be an opposition-free alternative to wind energy, welcomed by all stakeholders, is misplaced. Wave energy and bioenergy have not, in these cases, been viewed universally positively, and in a similar way to wind energy, green-on-green controversy has occurred, with different actors mobilizing environmental arguments to bolster their conflicting positions. These different interpretations of the technology indicate that 'sustainability' is rarely a universally accepted intrinsic property of a technology. The technologies are experienced as both 'things' and 'devices' and are interpreted and assessed in the context of energy planning and climate change policies.

Promotional or communication materials may entrench positions, or even widen the gap between opposition and support, if they present the place or the technology in a singular image, without regard for how it is being alternatively interpreted. For example, providing more information on the pioneering status of the development, may reinforce concerns over the development being 'experimental' and therefore having 'unknown' impacts. A focus on more 'facts and figures' on carbon savings and energy production may represent misplaced effort if substantial concerns arise from other issues such as the industrial intrusion into a precious natural location. Whilst information provision must be included in any successful consultation strategy, approaches that rely solely upon it, and do not attempt to understand how the place and technology are seen by stakeholders, may fail to uncover why support and opposition positions exist.

Many of the issues raised in the cases and the symbolic interpretations of the place and the technology, have the potential to be important factors in any renewable energy development. The categories discussed in this chapter are not presented as a theory of what will be found in other cases but, rather, a useful collection of 'things to look for' and 'ways of looking' that may allow academics, planners and developers to better understand and anticipate the sorts of responses that local residents and stakeholders may have to proposed developments and the reasons for these.

Acknowledgements

The research discussed here is part of a project funded by the Tyndall Centre for Climate Change Research and the Supergen Bioenergy Consortium. I would like to thank all of the stakeholders who spared time to talk with me. I would also like to thank Paul Upham and Sally Randles for their guidance throughout the project and Sarah Mander and Claire Ebrey for their thoughtful comments on earlier versions of the chapter.

References

Barr, S., (2004), 'Are we all environmentalists now? Rhetoric and reality in environmental action', *Geoforum*, 35(2): 231–249.

Bell, D., Gray, T. and Haggett, C., (2005), 'The 'Social Gap' in Wind Farm Siting Decisions: Explanations and Policy Responses', *Environmental Politics*, 14(4): 460–477.

Berr, (2008), Meeting the energy challenge: a white paper on nuclear energy, London: Department for Business Enterprise and Regulatory Reform.

Borgmann, A., (1984), *Technology and the character of contemporary life*, Chicago: University of Chicago Press.

Burningham, K., (2000), 'Using the language of NIMBY: a topic for research not an activity for researchers', *Local Environment*, 5(1): 55–67.

Cresswell, T., (2004), *Place*, Oxford: Blackwell Publishing Ltd.

Devine-Wright, P., (2005), 'Beyond NIMBYism: towards an integrated framework for understanding public perceptions of wind energy', *Wind Energy*, 8(2): 125–139.

DTI, (2007), *Energy White Paper: meeting the energy challenge*: Department of Trade and Industry.

Gipe, P., (1993), 'The wind industry's experience with aesthetic criticism', *Leonardo*, 26(3): 243–248.

Greenpeace, (2008), *End the Nuclear Age*, http://www.greenpeace.org/international/campaigns/nuclear Accessed 26 Nov 2008.

Hubbard, P., Kitchin, R. and Valentine, G., (2004), *Key thinkers on space and place*, London: Sage.

Irwin, A., (2001), *Sociology and the Environment*, Cambridge: Polity.

Jess, P. and Massey, D., (1995), 'The contestation of place' in D. Massey and P. Jess (eds), *A place in the world?* New York: Oxford University Press Inc.

Lee, T., Wren, B. and Hickman, M., (1989), 'Public responses to the siting and operation of wind turbines', *Wind engineering*, 13(4): 188.

Mackenzie, D. and Wajcman, J., (1999), 'Introductory essay and general issues', in D. Mackenzie and J. Wajcman (eds), *The social shaping of technology*, 2nd edn, Buckingham: Open University Press.

Massey, D., (1995), 'The conceptualization of place', in D. Mackenzie and J. Wajcman (eds), *The social shaping of technology*, 2nd edn. Buckingham: Open University Press.

Owens, S., (2002), ' "A collision of adverse opinions?": major projects, planning inquiries and policy change', *Environment and Planning A*, 34(6): 949–957.

Pasqualetti, M. J., (2000), 'Morality, space and the power of wind-energy landscapes', *Geographical Review*, 90(3): 381–394.

Pelamis Wave Power, (2007), *Environmental Impact*, http://www.pelamiswave.com/content. php?id=154 Accessed 28 Mar 2009.

Segnit, N. and Ereaut, G., (2007), Warm Words II, IPPR and Energy Savings Trust.

Shiva, V., (1998), *Biopiracy: the plunder of nature and knowledge*, Dartington Totnes: Green Books.

Simmons, P. and Walker, G., (2004), 'Living with Technological Risk: Industrial Encroachment on Sense of Place' in A. Boholm and R. Lofstedt (eds), *Facility Siting. Risk, Power and Identity in Land Use Planning*, London: Earthscan.

Sinclair, P. and Lofstedt, R., (2001), 'The influence of trust in a biomass application: the case of Sutton UK', *Biomass and Bioenergy*, 21(3): 177–184.

Surfers against Sewage, (2007), *Surfers' NGO welcomes wave hub planning approval*, http://www.sas. org.uk/pr/2007/wave_hub_2.php Accessed 06 Dec 2007.

Tatum, J. S., (1994), 'Technology and values: Getting beyond the 'Device Paradigm' Impasse', *Science Technology Human Values*, 19(1): 70–87.

Thayer, R. L. and Freeman, C. M., (1987), 'Altamont: Public perceptions of a wind energy landscape', *Landscape and Urban Planning*, 14: 379–398.

Thayer, R. L. and Hansen, H., (1988), 'Wind on the Landscape', *Landscape Architecture*, March, 1988.

The Times, (2006), Get off our waves, surfers tell greens, *Booth, R*, London, 2nd July.

Tuan, Y. F., (1977), *Space and Place: The Perspective of Experience*, Minneapolis: Minnesota Press.

Upham, P. and Shackley, S., (2006), 'The case of a proposed 21.5 MWe biomass gasifier in Winkleigh, Devon: Implications for governance of renewable energy planning', *Energy Policy*, 34(15): 2161–2172.

Upreti, B. R., (2004), 'Conflict over biomass energy development in the United Kingdom: some observations and lessons from England and Wales', *Energy Policy*, 32(6): 785–800.

Upreti, B. R. and Van Der Horst, D., (2004), 'National renewable energy policy and local opposition in the UK: the failed development of a biomass electricity plant', *Biomass and Bioenergy*, 26(1): 61–69.

Walker, G., (1995), 'Renewable energy and the public', *Land Use Policy*, 12(1): 49–59.

Warren, C., Lumsden, C., O'Dowd, S. and Birnie, R., (2005), 'Green On Green': Public perceptions of wind power in Scotland and Ireland', *Journal of Environmental Planning and Management*, 48(6): 853–875.

Woods, M., (2003), 'Conflicting Environmental Visions of the Rural: Windfarm Development in Mid Wales', *Sociologia Ruralis*, 43(3): 271–288.

Wüstenhagen, R., Wolsink, M. and Bürer, M. J., (2007), 'Social acceptance of renewable energy innovation: An introduction to the concept', *Energy Policy*, 35(5): 2683–2691.

Zonabend, F., (1993), *The Nuclear Peninsula*, Cambridge: Cambridge University Press.

'Doing food differently': reconnecting biological and social relationships through care for food

Elizabeth Dowler, Moya Kneafsey, Rosie Cox and Lewis Holloway

'Food' is essentially a biological entity, consumed by living creatures: plants, fungi, fish, animals or their products, are processed by various means at domestic or factory sites to produce the cornucopia of dishes, cuisines and ways of eating which have long characterized food systems (Tansey and Worsley, 1995; Beardsworth and Keil, 1997). A marked feature of the modern global food system is its divorcing of foodstuffs from the biological: increasingly, food is an industrialized product of global capitalism. Thus the drive is to make it uniform (remove as much natural variation as possible – carrots are always orange, and largely taste the same), safe (containing as few pathogens or contaminants as possible, and as good for consumer health as possible with minimum effort on the consumers' part) and predictable in processing, appearance, cost, preparation and taste. These attributes apply to raw ingredients (such as vegetables, fruit, meat) as much as to processed foodstuffs (whether longstanding and familiar such as bread, or newer, ready prepared dishes) (see for example Tansey and Worsley, 1995; Lawrence, 2004; Steel, 2008). Furthermore, this separation contributes to the emotional, intellectual and cultural distancing which people experience in their understanding of and relationship to food, a circumstance lamented by primary producers and policy makers and subject to growing academic attention (eg Cook and Crang, 1996; Cook *et al.*, 1998; Pretty, 2002; Morgan *et al.*, 2006).

Until recently environmental and social sustainability were largely ignored in the interests of industrialization and commercialization of what had traditionally been an eclectic relational exchange (Beardsworth and Keil, 1997; Pretty, 2000). Over the last few decades, however, the realities of the food system's contribution to greenhouse gas emissions, depletion of water, oil and other key resources, as well as predictions about the implications for future food production from climate change, have achieved more mainstream recognition both in writing and research (eg Pretty *et al.*, 2005; Ericksen, 2008; Garnett, 2008; Leahy, 2008; Roberts, 2008), and in policy discourse (eg The Strategy Unit, 2008).[1] Furthermore, challenges over the social sustainability of an industrialized, neo-colonial global food system increasingly come, not only from academics and writers (eg Tansey and Worsley, 1995; Friedmann, 1998; Tudge, 2007; Patel, 2007; McMichael, 2009) but also in the growing practice of the food sovereignty movement,[2] a global, largely majority world, network of NGOs and civil society organizations working to implement the right to food, which includes the right to land and self determination over food.

Some of these aspects are age-old: food trading has a long history, and the search for new seeds or commodities with economic potential, or of ways to preserve or enhance food, has long driven colonial exploration and commercial expansion (Tansey and Worsley, 1995; McMichael, 2009). Furthermore, the swapping, mixing and developing of cuisines across continents and kinships is not new. What is different in the contemporary global food system is the harnessing of science and technology to establish tight, usually vertical control over seeds, planting, tending, harvesting and processing specifications, and increasing centralization of considerable commercial and intellectual power in transnational corporations (Lang and Heasman, 2004; Tansey and Rajotte, 2008; McMichael, 2009). New forms of ownership are emerging, also concentrated in fewer and fewer hands, with the advent of Intellectual Property Rights over products and processes of plant and animal genetic engineering.[3] There is also a growing tendency to medicalize food: despite familiar notions of a 'balanced diet' for health, in practice, a combination of reductionist focus on the benefits of specific nutrient(s) or 'non-nutritive substances' and technological innovation in both human molecular biology and food manipulation, are contributing to promotion not so much of a 'healthy dietary regimen' as of the potential health gain from the consumption of specific foods, which have been technically manipulated to contain certain key nutrients, ostensibly suitable for people with specific medical conditions (such as high blood pressure or osteoporosis) (Lawrence and Germov, 2004; Pollan, 2008). Furthermore, the interaction between nutrients in foods and the human individual's genome, which is partly the basis of the emerging science of nutrigenomics, is seen by some as a critical and major prospective contribution in future public health (Chadwick, 2004; Lampe, 2006).

Thus the distancing of people from the 'natural' in food is increasing fast. Of course, plant and animal breeding and food processing have long histories too: very little food eaten today is 'natural' but equally, much of it is increasingly divorced from what most people think of as natural processes of growing and transforming foodstuffs. These issues are discussed in a number of literatures (see Pretty, 2000; Tudge, 2007; Pollan, 2008, among many), but are also increasingly recognized by the general public, who to some extent seek to address them in their role as 'consumers', in the economic, social and nutritional senses of the word. Few in industrialized rich countries can operate completely outside mainstream food sourcing and retailing – and this increasingly applies to middle and upper income consumers in the global south (Reardon and Berdegue, 2002; Hawkes, 2005) – but many do seek different ways of relating to and using food. The motivations and practices of both producers and 'consumers' seeking to grow, rear, sell, buy and eat food outside the mainstream food system are varied (see, for instance, Morgan *et al.*, 2006 and Maye *et al.*, 2007b) but often include recognition of the demand on the natural environment from mainstream practices and different sets of explicit ethical values. This chapter draws on recent research which was framed to explore the possibilities of 'reconnecting' people, both to the biological in food production and consumption, and to renewed social and ethical relationships between food system actors (Kneafsey *et al.*, 2008).

Food system alternatives

As already implied, there is an academic and policy tradition of positioning contrasting versions of contemporary food systems, which draw on binary oppositions. Thus, the 'mainstream' or 'conventional' modern global system is one where power and management are concentrated in fewer and fewer multi- or transnational corporations, where economic efficiency and rationality are key to driving profits, so that increased market share and shareholder gains measure success. Turnover is in the £billions, and regulation is largely led by the private sector, with the state and superstate catching up (Marsden *et al.*, 2000; Millstone and van Zwanenberg, 2002). Food produced and sold has to be safe and consistent (in appearance, taste, handling) and is increasingly presented divorced from production realities (thus, for instance, vegetables are washed, fruit may be peeled, meat and fish are gutted or shorn of indicators of animal origin and wrapped in plastic). This process reaches its apotheosis in the commonly named 'ready meal' – the purchaser can notionally choose from any number of international or historical cuisines, but need only remove outer packaging and place in a conventional or microwave oven to consume; no further knowledge, skill or engagement is required.

The so-called 'alternative', by contrast, is characterized by assorted diverse, smaller scale enterprises and initiatives, led sometimes by producers, sometimes by consumers. They may be wholly in the private sector (ie commercial businesses such as farm shops, Farmers' Markets, Box Schemes);[4] initiated or supported by the public sector (eg community growing or school vegetable gardens); a mix of charitable and non-governmental organizations; or a public-private mix (such as food growing and distributional cooperatives and Community Supported Agriculture).[5] Such enterprises, whose turnover can be of hundreds or thousands of pounds, and whose producer or customer base can similarly vary by orders of magnitude, may have very different goals and philosophies from each other, as well as from the mainstream; they also encompass different histories and can often appear inefficient or irrational in economic or business terms, notwithstanding the commercial origins and structures of some. They have in common a 'notion of struggle to take control and develop visions of possible food systems which, for those involved, seem to improve on existing arrangements' (Holloway *et al.*, 2007a: 78), eg a rejection of this withdrawal from the relational (to people, plants, animals and soil), and of the single minded pursuit of profit.

Nevertheless, the theoretical and practical capture of such diversity is hard: even the label 'alternative' is contested (see for instance, Morgan *et al.*, 2006; Maye *et al.*, 2007a) and was by actors within our empirical research described below. Seyfang (2006) and Maxey (2007), among others, argue that the term 'sustainable' food systems would better represent the realities of diverse attempts to renegotiate relationships between food system actors and to challenge the extractive framework of more conventional food systems. However, 'sustainable', like 'food security', is a term increasingly used with multiple meanings and often captured by government and the industrialized food system. And although 'environmental' as well as 'social and economic' survival may be specified,[6] this is usually in the manner of an exhortive or utopian hope rather than a more radical understanding (though see Sumberg, 2009 for a recent more challenging approach to sustainable food). Furthermore, Jackson and his colleagues (2009) question the tendency to polarize moral and ethical values as solely located within the 'non-conventional' food system; morality and markets, they argue, are not necessarily oppositional terms. Another debate, particularly in the USA, questions the role of such 'alternative' systems within an essentially capitalist framework: can they represent truly resistant, oppositional economies, or do they remain yet another, more 'consumer and environmentally friendly' version of the neoliberal, not least in the uncritical adoption of 'ideas of localizm, consumer choice, and value capture – ideas [...] standard to neoliberalism' (Guthman, 2008: 1174) which, Guthman argues, can increasingly be the face of agro-food activism? In considering our own empirical data, we moved away from binary categorizations of schemes or enterprises as 'alternative' or 'conventional' to employ a series of interrelated analytical fields or areas of engagement as a heuristic device which avoids such oppositions (Holloway *et al.*, 2007b; Kneafsey *et al.*, 2008).

We can identify consequences, however, for both 'producers' and 'consumers', from the industrializing tendencies within the so-called 'conventional' system with its divorce from the 'biological'. From our own and others' research, producers speak of the loss of traditional knowledges and experiences of relating to land, seed, genetic lines, as well as actual skills; they become managers rather than growers or rearers, and some explicitly see this as detrimental to environmental care. It could even be argued that, in the UK at least, those who buck these trends and retain more direct connection (such as in upland sheep farming) seem to be undervalued and thus unable to sustain a livelihood, which contributes to the loss of young workers from farming. Producers also regret opportunities for expressing emotional and social ties, again, with land, produce, animals, and fellow food system workers, to say nothing of customers (see Pretty, 2002; Kneafsey *et al.*, 2008, especially chs. 1 and 4). Also, of course, producers have lost autonomy: they are small players in the major global systems, which are largely dominated by economic managers and corporate buyers (Tansey and Worsley, 1995; Lang and Heasman, 2004).

Consumers – the general public, seen only in their economic roles – while apparently embracing their deskilled, disconnected, purchasing roles, in practice often seem to welcome the chance to re-establish relationships with others in the food system through their use of farmers' markets and box schemes, or to demonstrate values other than concern for price alone, through increased purchase of food with value or 'ethical' credentials – fair trade, organic, free-range, outdoor reared, etc (IGD, 2006; IGD, 2008). And while diverse in their understandings, some are quite well informed about contemporary food production practices and the loss of connection with primary producers (Weatherell *et al.*, 2003). However, if they shop in the major supermarkets (which in the UK most do),[7] consumers have little scope for contact with how and where food is produced, relying on product narratives and labels of origin; they also have to trust that labels of production values (ie 'fair trade', 'free range', 'organic' etc) represent consistent indications. Despite the strong assertion by retailers of the sovereignty of consumer choice, consumers using such outlets have little real autonomy for decision making in practice: they can only choose between available commodities, over whose conditions of production, processing and distribution they have little control.

The biological dimensions of the food system and implications for the 'natural' and social worlds nevertheless remain salient. Recent concern internationally and nationally, in the UK and elsewhere, is now increasingly with environmental, and to a lesser extent, social sustainability as part of growing anxiety over national and international food security (eg DEFRA, 2002; IAASTD, 2008). Despite policy rhetoric on the need for consumers to change their eating and waste disposal practices, in practice much of the emphasis is on 'choice editing' and internal system improvement by retailers and major food companies (SDC, 2008). The responsibility to improve food system sustainability is thus seen by government, internationally and nationally, as belonging primarily to the corporate sector; technology is promoted as the answer to solving what are essentially social and biological problems (salination, water shortage, flooding, pests and disease, reduced yields as well as climatic instability and insecurity of fossil fuel supply). There have been trenchant critiques from academia and civil society (eg Tudge, 2007; IAASTD, 2008), that enabling appropriate social and ethical relationships is as critical as getting the technical aspects right (see FEC, 2008 for examples on water). But these voices are readily sidelined, so that the instrumentality of the food system is maintained in technical and corporate management of plants, animals, and the natural environment; the role of consumers has been to 'behave better', while maintained in a position of knowing or understanding little.

Researching 'reconnection'

The growing literature on 'alternative food networks' (in the US and the UK/ Europe) and on local food initiatives, is testament to the discontents we have outlined. Our empirical enquiry was extensively grounded in these literatures, with particular focus on examining motivations for people to join such schemes, or become customers or shareholders in enterprises, and the impact on their food and other behaviours, with the exploration of 'reconnection' as a fundamental theme (Kneafsey *et al.*, 2008). 'Reconnection' as an intellectual idea and practical experience implies 'disconnection' in the food system, some of which was outlined earlier. Such ideas, which we argue emerged in relationship with, rather than necessarily in opposition to, each other, became apparent in policy discourse particularly in the 1990s, partly in response to BSE and other crises of confidence.[8] In broad terms, 'reconnection' implies the bringing together of different elements of the food system – producers, consumers, markets, knowledges and nature. It is a rather portmanteau term (like 'local': see for example Heinrichs, 2003; Feagan, 2007), some of whose various meanings were explored in our research.[9]

Of course the very word 'reconnection' carries overtones of revival or re-establishment of a 'lost' or damaged connection, with echoes of nostalgia for a 'Golden Age' when things were better, consumers knew where their food came from, farmers earned a decent living, the environment was not degraded and human health was not threatened. We were aware that such discourses of 'reconnection' are readily appropriated in marketing by retailers whose procedures may bear little resemblance to practices of 'reconnection' being performed by other actors in the food system (see for eg Jackson *et al.*, 2007). Our interest was in the articulation of 'reconnection' by 'producers' and 'consumers' themselves. What emerged were complex thinking, understanding and ingrained behaviours, to which a host of related actors, material and social institutions – spouses, partners, children, friends, colleagues, soil, animals, plants, certification, institutions, technologies and artefacts – contributed in mediating 'reconnection' (Kneafsey *et al.*, 2008). Indeed, we came to see 'reconnection' as a process rather than an end-state: a sense of 'doing and becoming', so that 'alternative' food practices were embedded in people's lives, sometimes resonating with other ethical ideologies and practices.

The discourses of 'reconnection' which different food system actors employ (and which can serve different ethical, commercial or political ends) include 'reconnecting' producers with their market; consumer with product, process and place; and people with nature or the 'natural'. In particular, campaigning organizations and individuals wanting to emphasize the environmental, health, socio-cultural and economic benefits of re-engaging with nature argue strongly for 'reconnection' through relationships between farmers and consumers, often located within the context of greater 'sustainability' and sometimes extending to commodification of the farmed environment through rural tourism and leisure (CPRE, 2001; Countryside Agency, 2002). An alternative view within this framing comes strongly from Pretty (2002), who argues for food as a commons rather than a commodity, and for the fundamental importance of human connectedness with nature in interdependent systems. Only when this is recognized can a truly environmentally sustainable agriculture be practised, to provide sufficient food for all the world's population, without which we face disaster.

If these actions are co-ordinated, then individuals will enjoy higher benefits (or reduced harm), when compared with acting alone. But if this joint management breaks down, then some may benefit greatly in the short term by extracting all the benefit for themselves. In this case, the likely outcome is damage to the whole system. (Pretty, 2002: 157)

His examples of participatory development, social learning and co-operative projects are part of what he argues is an urgently needed 'revolution', not only in agriculture and food production-consumption but also in human-nature relationships and understanding.

Thus, drawing on diverse understandings of 'reconnection', over three years (2004–2007) we worked with six food enterprises or schemes which privilege direct contact of some kind between food producers and consumers, using them as case studies to illuminate a wider range of such activities. They were selected from a purpose-built database, in turn informed by this literature and stakeholder consultation (Venn *et al.*, 2006). Setting aside heterogeneities of 'local' or 'alternative', what all our examples have in common is a direct relationship between producers and consumers, and we drew on this to devise a typology of 'reconnection', into which our database entries could be fitted. As the Table shows, the typology differentiates schemes according to the relative 'connectedness' of food consumers to the act of food production. The six illustrative case study enterprises or schemes are listed in the final column (see Venn *et al.*, 2006 for more detail). They were situated in contrasting geographical locations, five in the UK and one in Italy and included more of the 'direct sell' type (eg where producers sell to consumers) because these are more widespread.

The schemes differ from one another in terms of operation, scale, aims and organization, and their members and locations vary in terms of social and economic conditions. Salop Drive market garden, in the heart of an inner city housing estate in the English West Midlands, is run and managed by local people, and delivers weekly bags of fruit and vegetables to about 70 nearby households. EarthShare Community Supported Agriculture is located in the district of Nairn, North East Scotland, and serves around 200 households. Waterland Organic vegetable box scheme is run by one farming family just outside Cambridge who, at the time of study, were also members of Eostre Organics, a producer cooperative in East Anglia; they deliver boxes to around 100 households. Farrington's farm shop, run by a family farm, sells a range of home-made, locally and internationally sourced products to over 8,000 customers in Somerset. Moorland Farm Direct raises grass-fed beef, also in Somerset, and sells direct through its onsite farm shop and stalls at farmers' markets. Finally, 'Adopt-a-Sheep', located in the mountainous Abruzzo region of Italy, aims at sustainability of traditional grazing and social structures; consumers 'adopt' individual sheep and receive their products, including woollen goods, through the post in return.

For each enterprise or scheme, we carried out at least two in-depth interviews with producer or manager over a period of about a year; two rounds of 'consumer' workshops, involving about 90 consumers across the UK based schemes;

Table 1: *Typology of Producer-Consumer Relationships*

Type of producer-consumer relationship	Examples	Illustrative Case Studies
Producers as consumers Food is grown or produced by those who consume it. Often promote healthy lifestyles. Extent of commercial orientation varies. Produce is usually sold on a local level but may be targeted at specific groups eg low incomes, ethnic minorities.	Community gardens, community co-ops and allotments	Salop Drive market garden, West Midlands, England
Producer-consumer partnerships The risks and rewards of farming are shared – to varying degrees – due to subscription or share arrangements.	Community Supported Agriculture Schemes (CSA)	EarthShare community supported agriculture, Moray, Scotland
Direct sell Farmers or producers cut out middlemen and sell direct to consumers. Can be direct face-to-face or over the Internet.	Farm shops, farmers' markets, box schemes, adoption schemes	Waterland organic vegetable box scheme, Cambridgeshire, England Farrington's Farm Shop, Somerset, England Moorland Farm (grassland beef; direct retail and farmers' market stall Bristol), Somerset, England Adopt-a-Sheep, (internet) Abruzzo National Park, Italy

(taken from Kneafsey *et al.*, 2008; permission to name the case studies obtained)

44 in-depth and 32 telephone follow-up consumer interviews; and in-depth exploration of detailed practices using diaries and photographs with six households of different socio-economic and demographic characteristics. Questionnaires and an on-line discussion were used to engage with 'Adopt-a-Sheep' consumers in different locations around the world. Thus we obtained cross-sectional and longitudinal data.

Such enterprises are sometimes seen as a middle-class niche, but those we studied cut across class and income boundaries; for instance, Salop Drive is in an economically depressed urban borough and many participants (who also grew the food) were in receipt of disability benefits. Secondly, of those who attended the consumer workshops from five of the schemes (who were self-selected) about 10 per cent were living on state benefits and over a third had household incomes below £20,000 p.a. (modest for the UK at the time of surveying). The richest participants mostly came from 'Adopt-a-sheep', which reflects its being a more luxury consumption (many receive the subscription as a gift). There was a wide range of occupations and household structures among consumer workshop participants: about 60 per cent were women, over half were over the age of 55, and a third were under 45 years of age.

'Reconnection' is biological and social

Our research yielded rich data (Kneafsey *et al.*, 2008; Holloway *et al.*, 2007a,b,c; Cox *et al.*, 2008). There was clear evidence of many aspects of 'reconnection': producers more connected to their markets, consumers to product, process and place, and people to 'nature'. 'Reconnection' was not just in relation to structures and distance but embraced the 'biological' in food – soils, animals, seasonality; the 'social', in terms of feelings, perceptions, and the work of building relationships between producers and consumers over time, which was seen as critical for generating and maintaining trust and regard; and the possibilities of 'morality' in drawing on explicit ethical values in specific aspects of living. Discourses and practices of 'reconnection' were revealed as defining features of the enterprises studied.

Biological reconnection

Consumers in particular expressed recognition of variety, seasonality and other realities of soil, guts, feathers, etc which they largely attributed to using or being in the particular scheme under discussion. Producers of course know these aspects very well; some, such as Manuela Cozzi in Italy or Paul Robinson in Cambridge,[10] saw part of their role as educating their customers in the realities of non-industrialized food production, such as its seasonality:

> The other things is that at the start of the summer – people see the sun early May, late April, and they think we've got salads down here, and we haven't, we've got nothing [this is the hungry gap]. (Paul Robinson, Waterland Box Scheme producer)

For many consumers, learning to manage seasonal supply with its dearth and gluts, preparing vegetables which arrive covered in earth, choosing cuts of meat which relate to a living animal, are revelations and journeys of discovery:

> I don't mind a bit of dirt on my carrots. I mean there's something a bit sort of unhealthy looking about these carrots that are washed completely clean, they're

sweating in polythene…I don't like buying pre-packaged vegetables at all…I would rather just buy them as they come out of the ground. (Farrington's Farm Shop customer)

People, all of the people, are sort of divorced from meat production because if you go to the supermarket you buy it and it's all wrapped in a bit of plastic you know and you don't know where it's come from or what it looked like, or the bit of animal it is. (Farrington's Farm Shop customer)

Indeed, the physical and sensual realities of foodstuffs increasingly became part of 'reconnection' journeys (Holloway *et al.*, 2007c).

Social reconnection

There was considerable evidence of the work needed to build relationships which also engender and support change. For example, Paul Robinson attributes some of his own motivation to continue working to his relationship with his customers:

I wanted to know that it was being sold locally and have that direct contact…When you are on your own a lot, and working with the boxes you don't actually get to see anyone that you don't already see everyday like family, so you end up grovelling around in the mud and you think 'well why am I doing this?' And it's not until you go off the farm and speak to people, and they say 'thanks' that you get real meaning, it gives you a sense of satisfaction.

The farmer at Moorland Farm, in discussing their direct marketing of beef, demonstrated his care for the authenticity, integrity and quality of the produce (which is bred and reared only on the farm), and his concern for honesty towards his customers, who can visit the farm and view the production processes.

The need to work at relationships was also emphasized by many consumers; getting to know the producer over time engenders trust in them and the product.

And you get an awful lot of trust in the setup because for instance, […] Trish's got this eye for detail, […] You feel there's a person for you, who wouldn't let anything else slide past her, so it's a very personal investment of trust […] and her staff, yes, it extends to her staff as well. (Farrington's Farm shop customer)

My impression is that it would be really difficult to fake it. […] it would be very hard for somebody to farm the land and tend their livestock if they were completely uncaring and devoid of any environmental principles or ethics and then come to a farmer's market and act like you were kind of, you know, a person that you wanted to do business with. (Moorland Farmer's Market customer)

Such trust contributes to the pleasure restored to shopping by the personal relationships which build up:

I think it's more of an enjoyable experience shopping in different places, meeting different people, talking to them about their different products and you know they're experts in their fields, they know their meat or their veg or whatever. (Moorland Farmers' Market customer)

Moral reconnection

These straightforward acknowledgements of the ways different structures enabled better ways of knowing and building trust in food and its provenance were consistently expounded and were clearly important. However, it also emerged, particularly among consumers, that people's motivations and desires, combined with different circumstances, prompted or promoted different forms of 'reconnection' in varied and complex ways which fit less easily into the standard characterizations. For instance, consumers usually found it easier initially to talk about their motives for becoming involved in a particular enterprise or scheme, than to generalize about wider principles; only on reflection were they able to point to patterns in decision-making and practices which offered them the opportunity to shop and eat in ways that increasingly chimed with their values and understandings, which themselves were reinforcing change as well as evolving over time. While some described having had strong views which led to certain behaviours, including obtaining and using food differently, for many, it was the increasing involvement with the scheme which had drawn them into thinking about, reacting to, engaging with, different ways of obtaining and using food; they described continual processes of discovery (which were not always immediately satisfactory, so that sometimes people had had to rethink how they shopped/cooked etc). Indeed, for many, the self actualization as 'ethical' consumers grew over time; for example, to use renewable energy sources, buy with less packaging – even though few were members of organizations or movements encouraging such practices.[11] While it would be false to assume all who used the schemes were actively trying to reduce their consumption footprint (and there were some who simply found life too demanding to try), it was clear that not only had people's practices involving food been transformed by participation, through growing, rearing or obtaining and preparing food in different ways, but that this had often led to changes in other consumption practices.

Thus, there was evidence of a 'graduation' effect: that by purchasing or growing food outside the 'mainstream', people found themselves rethinking and refining other consumption practices to match their ethical frameworks:

> Then you sort of think 'ok I've got these vegetables now and this is really working for me' and then you maybe […] think oh well maybe I should be thinking about […] if I'm putting that in my body what am I putting on my body? So then you think oh, well actually I'd quite like to live the simpler lifestyle…(Earthshare member)

> Because of the scheme we now try and buy all our meat locally, at the local butchers and choose products with less packaging, we've also found that we are recycling more. (Waterland Box Scheme member)

For others, changing food practices followed on from other ethical decisions and behaviours:

> [Buying more] local foods was part of an ethos and lifestyle that I was committed to and I got interested in this sort of thing around 1990, 1991, that sort of time. I think,

I remember being really positive when I heard that the Centre for Alternative Technology [in Machynlleth, Wales] were having a share offer, and I thought yes I've got to do this. And I joined Cambridge LETS[12] in 1993 and I've been a member of that since the start. (Waterland Box Scheme member)

Indeed, some had moved jobs or homes to live differently so as to express commitment to what they regarded as more socially and environmentally sustainable lifestyles:

We were talking about lifestyle change I made over the last three years and it's really kind of significant and positive lifestyle changes but you know, they've been quite difficult as well. One was taking a massive drop in salary to kind of try and get this sort of career change [...] and living, you know, in a more sustainable fashion but trying to sort of integrate things that I just wanted to do as part of my everyday living. [...I] have always sort of been on the side of questioning anyway. [...] non-violence, not tolerating racism and concerned about environment and things like that. [...] Social issues. Fairness. Justice, I suppose. Those aspects. [...] that's an important thing, to act. To do something about it. (Earthshare member)

Some adhered to these different ways of living with tenacity, although few were active campaigners trying to change others' views and behaviours outside their own immediate circles – they remained largely privately held passions.

Producers had clearer narratives of motivation and personal identities, as of wanting to practise certain ways of managing soil, seed, land, animals, processing, retail, and taking pleasure in doing so, although, again, there were complex histories and contemporary uncertainties; they, too, were in a state of constant 'becoming' rather than arrival in their 'reconnective' behaviours. All exemplified the work of building relationships, which were not just one-way communications of values and products, with their consumers. Some, such as Earthshare or Salop Drive, have explicit processes of consultation and participation:

...we want people to come on to the site to feed into producing the vegetable leaflet, and gain an understanding of what people need along with receiving a bag and this could be to do with storage of veg, preparation or identification of unusual veg etc. (Veronica Barry: Salop Drive producer)

Other schemes also made a point of being very open about how their farming and growing is practised, about other benefits from their way of working (such as wildlife monitoring), and on producers' problems with, for example, adverse weather or pests. Farrington's Farm Shop, for instance, while anxious not to 'turn people off by preaching', worked hard to establish a sense of community with familiar shop staff and regular customers, through newsletters and events, as well as a clearly written statement of its food policy.

Manuela Cozzi, the farmer behind 'Adopt-a-Sheep', is the most radical among the producers we met in her thinking and practice. She argues that she and others like her have a responsibility to 'reconnect' consumers, particularly those from urban areas who know little about food production, with the realities of farming, with the rural environment and thus with 'nature', as a way of addressing society's social and environmental problems. Her work with local schools, the adoption scheme and agritourism (also part of the farm business) are all grist to the mill of her mission to effect change in the wider society (over issues such as crime and the breakdown in families), through direct experience and the building of relationships:

> We try to teach children to care about the environment and to take care or responsibility for everything that they do. [...] to be an adult means to be able to care for things [...] only the rural community can teach people how to care for the environment. (Manuela Cozzi: 'Adopt-A-Sheep' producer)

Her strongly held view is that many adults have not fully 'grown up', because they do not know how to take care of, and responsibility for, others; thus she claims they cannot take care of society – or indeed, their physical environment. Contact with, and knowledge of, the countryside and food production she sees as being essential for moral maturity, which enables appropriate understanding of and behaviour in accordance with 'care'. This commitment to education, engagement and practice underpins all her work.

Interlocking 'cares'

This radical potential in thinking about 'reconnection' through taking care – of people, society, animals, the environment and 'nature' – was strengthened by looking through the lens of feminist thinking on an 'ethic of care', particularly, though not exclusively, the work of Tronto (1993), whose writing provided critical support to our analysis of motivations and actions. In simple terms, a broad 'ethic of care', which might be defined as a consideration of, and preparedness to take action over, the needs of others (not only human others), emerged as central to making sense of different identities, motivations and practices. Reconnecting people with nature is perhaps most obviously related to an 'ethic of care' because it is concerned with 'repairing and maintaining our world' (to paraphrase Tronto, 1993)[13] so that humans and non-humans can live in it as well as possible. Reconnecting people with product, process and place can also be located within an 'ethic of care': about the materiality of food, the people who produce it, and the natural environment. But we took the ideas further, identifying interlocking 'cares' which operated on different scales, from home through the local to wider communities, and were evident in concern for people, food, animals, soils and ecosystems. We identified three key themes in producer and consumer motivations: *first*, care for local economies, environments and future generations; *second*, care for health and wholeness; and *finally*, care about transparency and integrity in food systems, including matters of science and governance.

Care for local economies, environments and future generations

The care for local economies and the future was an obvious and familiar theme to many in workshops and interviews: it was where most people started their commentary. For instance, the dismay over loss of local shops because of the arrival of a major chain supermarket, with potential future loss of amenities, was usually mentioned very early in conversations:

> you know I think it is very sad how the little local shops are being squeezed out [...] you know, they opened a new [supermarket] in [nearest town] about, I don't know it must have been about three or four years ago, and within something like about two months the local fishmonger had closed. And he just put a big sign saying 'Closed because of [supermarket] (Earthshare, member)

This was not mere sentimentality: people felt strongly about how important a viable local economy was, in terms of jobs and food production ecology, and were often well informed about the economic and social processes at work to damage it. They expressed their willingness to support local communities and, where they existed, smaller producers in their localities, even if this was at a small extra cost to themselves:

> I think unfortunately these [supermarkets] will displace the local shops eventually, but we try and support numerous places including the local 10 o'clock shop as they are useful [...], to make them feel wanted. Plus, my milkman is struggling so I want to support him even though it's not the best milk. (Moorland Farm Shop customer)

Awareness of the realities of localized economies and livelihoods extended to those in different locations, ie it was not limited by proximity or geography; for instance, members involved in 'Adopt-a-Sheep', wherever they were themselves based, liked the fact they were supporting a system which showed respect for an ecosystem and traditional (transhumant) ways of farming even though it might be on a different continent. Such care was also evident in comments from many consumers about purchasing fairly traded goods, which in fact always came from overseas. While people were generally realistic about also having to use the major supermarkets for food shopping, they made it clear it was because they had little choice – and they mostly had less trust in the supermarkets (products and processes). Indeed, people sometimes sought a connection with producers and production precisely to resist what they perceived as consumer 'dumbing down' by retailers. Some were explicitly political in their resistance to the role of transnational corporations, of which the major supermarkets were seen as clear examples:

> I've been shopping there [Farmers' Market] for the last three years now, and it's just... I mean, for me, really why I shop there is just that I prefer to shop there than I do at a supermarket like [X], because I'm just quite anti-globalization and massive corporations. (Moorlands' Farmers Market stall customer)

In terms of the wider natural environment, there were also quite nuanced comments about the carbon footprinting of food. Few were simplistic in their understanding of 'food miles' (see Steedman and MacMillan, 2008 for a recent discussion), recognizing that, although their own purchase of local vegetables, say, might be less demanding than airfreighted goods, several of the schemes studied required members (eg of Earthshare) or customers (eg Farrington's Farm Shop) to drive on a regular basis for their shopping, and this was discussed realistically. Nevertheless, as mentioned above, some were fiercely idealistic in their concern for ecological sustainability and the part that the food system – and individuals' ways of living – played in contributing to damage to the planet and people, and in the potential for mitigation. Several, particularly in Earthshare, framed personal responsibility in terms of protecting or even enhancing the wellbeing of future generations, for which maintaining the integrity of the environment, particularly the soil, was essential: 'we feel this very deeply indeed, you cannot hand over to your incoming people, your incoming generations, soil that is so desperately polluted and inert' (Earthshare member).

Care for health and wholeness

These concerns were linked to strong desires to promote biological and social health and wholeness, both for oneself and for the wider environment. So, alongside respect for the soil was a call for integrity in treatment of other living creatures and for natural systems used to produce and promote growth and wellbeing. These goals were expressed by producers and consumers alike, all of whom clearly saw 'health' as more than an absence of disease or poisoning (even in relation to food): health is something holistic, which relates to a thriving and sustainable ecosystem. Many, despite often not being very wealthy, referred to their increasing pleasure in food, which they described in terms of wholeness and wellbeing. They said that they now liked where possible to take time for shopping, talking to producers, preparing and eating good food, and sharing with others. We gave some households cameras to document their food experiences, and several took photographs of people together, eating often quite simple dishes, but with much evident pleasure in them and in each other. Food was no mere fuel-stop, even for those with busy working and family lives, but something to celebrate and to share; it was a symbol of holistic health values.

There was evidence of conformity to contemporary guidelines for both healthy and sustainable eating (probably unwittingly, as few made reference to health or sustainable recommendations), in that people indicated they ate more locally sourced fruits and vegetables and better quality meat (the latter often less frequently) than before they had become involved in their scheme. In fact, such impact often went beyond using whatever they sourced from the scheme; for instance, those who had a regular fruit and vegetable box found they were changing the ways they purchased, prepared and ate other food commodities too, sometimes with knock-on effects on the food habits of friends and more distant family members. People had learnt new ways of using food, new skills in cooking and preparing it, and often family members who had not previously cooked got involved in cooking because they became more interested in food (Kneafsey *et al.*, 2008). Indeed, many consumers remarked that they ate far fewer supermarket 'ready meals' and less highly processed foods and snacks; many also commented on their increased knowledge about food, interest in it, and preparedness to try new things, as a result of their patterns of shopping and cooking:

> We eat veg probably every night now whereas a couple of times we might have had 'Oh, forget it, let's just have pizza' two or three, maybe twice a week, whereas now it's a case of 'No, we've got a casserole, we'll do this, we'll have this', so...(Waterland box-scheme member)

> Actually the variety, and [...] you got other stuff in there, it was nice to try things that I've never tried before. [...] And probably if I'd have gone to a supermarket I wouldn't ever have bought it. *[can you give me an example?]* The salad leaves, pak choi is it and things like this [...] I had lambs' cress which I would never have found before so that was a good thing that came out of it. (Salop Drive member)

Care about transparency in the food system

Many of those interviewed spoke of their mistrust of the mainstream food system in its lack of transparency over products, processes, and what is done to make food appealing to customers. This regularly emerged in discussions of motivations for choosing or producing food in different ways, sometimes in conjunction with an (unsolicited) reference to buying food labelled as 'organic'. Only some of the schemes produced or sold 'organic' food and there were mixed views on the significance of the production methods and the impact for consumers, and even on the integrity of the labelling. What was striking, however, was that consumers in particular tended to use the label as a shorthand for the types of food and production systems they desired. This usage was paralleled by a deep mistrust of the appropriateness, and potential 'cocktail effects', of the wide range of artificial chemicals known to be used in more mainstream food production. Again, this was not necessarily a naive desire for 'natural' food, but a deep sense that the technologizing of food production and processes had gone too far, and was insufficiently focussed on the wider costs and benefits to the environment (particularly the soil and water), animals and humans who absorb these powerful chemicals, whose long-term and collateral effects were insufficiently tested. And those who accepted the need for the latter nonetheless wanted more transparency and to be able to trust those in the food chain using them – particularly supermarkets:

> I just think that my feeling about the supermarkets is they skim in at the bottom level that they can to get away with something. So they'll come in at the lowest possible level to get something as...as certified organic. (Moorland Farm Shop customer)

Many particularly disliked the use of genetically modified organisms; although we did not specifically solicit views on GMOs, their usage within the food system was often spontaneously cited as an example of what were perceived as 'underhand' and deceptive behaviours by corporations using them 'by the back door'. This was not so much a suspicion or rejection of science and technology *per se*, nor a harking back to (imaginary) days of pure and unadulterated food, but a powerful caring about integrity in the food system: it was the lack of transparency which particularly incensed respondents. People were very wary of supermarket sourced processed products in general, which they saw as having been 'adulterated' by techniques to alter appearance or prolong shelf life artificially. Many were happy to purchase processed foods or even 'ready meals' from producers whose integrity they trusted and from whom they could obtain information about people, processes and places of manufacture if required. Again, it was what people saw as deception, particularly in the cause of promoting an industrialized, cheap product, which produced strong reactions. This was epitomized in the number who referred (again unsolicited) to the widespread availabilty of cheap chicken: food which may have been subject to means of maintaining 'freshness' to disguise potentially negative signs of travel, storage or processing.[14]

Conclusion

Choosing food is both a daily, often unconscious, act – a chore even – as well as a longer term, more deliberative process over where to shop and what to buy. Food choice contributes to expression of identity and culture, and, whether at individual, family, household or larger group level is influenced by biological, economic, social and cultural factors (Beardsworth and Keil, 1997; Murcott, 1998). Those who make such choice outside the home are usually seen primarily as economic agents, rather than in their social roles, even if they are capable of demonstrating what are termed 'ethical values' in their purchasing practices, as described earlier. Our research was based largely on people living and working in the UK, but the literature gives us no reason to suppose the findings cannot be generalized at some level to other industrialized, rich countries where the modern global food system has distanced people from the realities of food and its provenance.

What we found was that both producers and the majority of consumers we encountered demonstrate a care-oriented sense of self: they are aware of the needs of close and distant others, human and non-human, and 'are prepared to act on this awareness, in order to repair and sustain theirs and others' lifeworlds' (Kneafsey *et al.*, 2008: 162). They demonstrated care as action rather than mere expression of concern, through response to localities and the people, animals and natural environments in them, by trying to do something to contribute to their maintenance as locations of production and employment, thriving economies and communities. In so doing, growers, rearers, processors, customers, members, consumers – whatever the label – discovered and reinforced feelings of pleasure in and awareness of the sensuality of food (look, smell, texture, taste), and of the importance of knowing provenance in terms of place and people. Community and shared knowledge were built by becoming involved in growing food or otherwise helping out, hearing and seeing how things were done, discussing problems and talking to someone about their food. Being able to give and receive feedback, to say and hear 'thanks', contributed to relationships which reconnect people, place and food in more fundamental and lasting ways than merely the economic. Arguably they are acting as environmental citizens (despite the contested nature of such a description, see MacGregor *et al.*, 2005).

Our research was carried out at a time of optimism about the consumer society and the role of the modern global food system within it. Warnings about the sustainability of both were beginning, and have become considerably more strident since (eg Jackson, 2008; Ambler-Edwards *et al.*, 2009). Calls by government for a better understanding between producers and consumers continue, though consumers are usually constructed as ignorant or disaffected, knowing nothing of production and retail realities. Our research paints a different view of 'consumers' as nuanced economic and social agents, who may know some things and who have an aptitude for learning more, and who are well able to articulate and practice the complexities of sourcing and using food. Care-full relationships, between consumers, producers, and other actors in the food system, built over time through practice, are critical to processes of 'reconnection' which, arguably, are crucial for developing an ecologically sustainable system of food production.

Notes

1 See also publication summer 2009 by Defra (Department of Environment, Food & Rural Affairs) of policy documents (intended primarily for England) and online consultation on food security, which term has been adopted in response to anxieties about climate change effects, among others (MacMillan and Dowler, 2009 in press): http://www.defra.gov.uk/foodfarm/food/security/index.htm Accessed 16 Sep 2009.
2 'Food Sovereignty is the RIGHT of peoples, communities, and countries to define their own agricultural, labour, fishing, food and land policies which are ecologically, socially, economically and culturally appropriate to their unique circumstances....' http://www.foodsovereignty.org/new/whoweare.php Accessed 16 Sep 2009.
3 The introduction of the Trade Related Aspects of Intellectual Property Rights Agreement (TRIPS) as part of the World Trade Organization safeguards protection of economic interests in plant and animal genetic materials and processing (see Tansey and Rajotte, 2008).
4 These entities are variously defined in different national settings. Broadly, Farmers' Markets sell local produce (also variously defined), and in some instances, producers have to be present – they represent 'direct sell' (see eg Holloway and Kneafsey, 2000). Box schemes are direct sell from producer to consumer, usually of fresh produce and primarily vegetables and fruit, but also sometimes dried or other goods. Some operate in a small catchment area with delivery by producer; some are now larger businesses, which try to maintain relationships of trust and regard.
5 Community Supported Agriculture (CSA), at core, involves local people investing money and sometimes labour/time in a farm or crop in advance of harvest, in return for a share of produce. It guarantees income for the producer and shares the risk amongst subscribers (see eg Cox *et al.*, 2008).
6 For instance, the UK Government's overarching strategy for sustainable development sets out five policy framing principles of 'living within environmental limits; ensuring a strong, healthy

and just society; using sound science responsibly; promoting good governance and achieving a sustainable economy' (HMG, 2005).

7 Tesco, Asda-Walmart, Sainsbury and Morrisons command 70% market share in early 2009, the Co-op a further 6%: Nielson news release (28.04.09) http://blog.nielsen.com/nielsenwire/wp-content/uploads/2009/05/nielsen-retail-performance-summary-28-april.pdf Accessed 17 May 2009.

8 The 'BSE crisis' occurred in the mid 1990s when a potential link between Bovine Spongeform Encephalopathy in cattle ('mad cow disease') and human disease was announced in the UK Parliament; the British beef market collapsed, over 4 million cattle were slaughtered and public confidence in government and public health was massively reduced (see van Zwanenberg and Millstone, 2003.

9 Funded by the ESRC/AHRC *Cultures of Consumption* programme see: www.consume.bbk.ac.uk

10 Producers gave permission to use their names and saw quotations attributed to them; the enterprises are all identified.

11 At the time of the research there was little UK media coverage of the need for behavioural change to reduce environmental impact of climate change, and no campaigns in relation to food – which at the time of writing are now more common.

12 Local Exchange and Trading Schemes, see eg http://www.letslinkuk.net/ Accessed 16 Sep 2009.

13 Tronto defined caring as: 'a species activity that includes everything that we do to maintain, continue, and repair our 'world' so that we can live in it as well as possible. That world includes our bodies, our selves and our environment, all of which we seek to interweave in a complex, life-sustaining web' (cited in Tronto, 1993: 103).

14 There is an interesting issue here with a parallel *Cultures of Consumption* project by Jackson et al, '*Manufacturing meaning along the food commodity chain*', which sought producer, processor and consumer views, using chicken as one of its case examples. See: http://www.consume.bbk.ac.uk/research/jackson.html Accessed 16 Sep 2009.

References

Ambler-Edwards, S., Bailey, K., Kiff, A., Lang, T., Lee, R., Marsden, T., Simons, D. and Tibbs, H., (2009), *Food Futures: Rethinking UK Strategy*, London: Chatham House.

Beardsworth, A. and Keil, T., (1997), *Sociology on the Menu: an invitation to the study of food and society*, London: Routledge.

Chadwick, R., (2004), 'Nutrigenomics, individualism and public health', *Proceedings of the Nutrition Society*, 63: 161–166.

Cook, I. and Crang, P., (1996), 'The World on a Plate: Culinary Culture, Displacement and Geographical Knowledges', *Journal of Material Culture*, 1: 131–153.

Cook, I., Crang, P. and Thorpe, M., (1998), 'Biographies and geographies: consumer understandings of the origins of food', *British Food Journal*, 100: 162–167.

CPRE, (2001), *Sustainable Local Foods*, London: Council for the Protection of Rural England.

Countryside Agency, (2002), *Eat the View: Promoting Sustainable Local Products*, Wetherby: Countryside Agency Publications.

Cox, R., Holloway, L., Venn, L., Dowler, E., Ricketts Hein, J., Kneafsey, M. and Tuomainen, H., (2008), 'Common ground? Motivations for participation in community-supported agriculture scheme', *Local Environment*, 13(3): 203–218.

DEFRA, (2002), *Strategy for Sustainable Farming and Food: Facing the Future*, London: DEFRA (Department of Environment, Food and Rural Affairs).

Ericksen, P., (2008), 'Global Environmental Change and Food Security', *Global Change NewsLetter*, 71: 15–16.

FEC, (2008), 'Water' *Food Ethics* (Journal of the Food Ethics Council) 3 (1), available at: http://www.foodethicscouncil.org/node/342 Accessed 16 Sep 2009.

Feagan, R., (2007), 'The place of food: mapping out the "local" in local food systems', *Progress in Human Geography*, 31: 23–42.

Friedmann, H., (1998), 'A sustainable world food economy', ch 4 in: R. Keil, D. V. J., Bell, P. Penz and L. Fawcett, (eds), *Political ecology: global and local*, London: Routledge, 81–101.

Garnett, T., (2008), *Cooking up a Storm: food, greenhouse gas emissions and our changing climate*, University of Surrey: Food Climate Reseach Network. http://www.fcrn.org.uk/frcnPubs/index.php?id=6 Accessed 16 Sep 2009.

Guthman, J., (2008), 'Neoliberalism and the making of food politics in California', *Geoforum*, 39, (3): 1171–1183.

HMG, (2005), *Securing the Future: delivering UK sustainable development strategy*, Cm6467, London: The Stationery Office.

Hawkes, C., (2005), 'The role of foreign direct investment in the nutrition transition', *Public Health Nutrition*, 8: 357–365.

Heinrichs, C., (2003), 'The practice and politics of food system localization', *Journal of Rural Studies*, 20: 33–45.

Holloway, L. and Kneafsey, M., (2000), 'Reading the Space of the Farmers' Market: a Preliminary Investigation in the UK', *Sociologica Ruralis*, 40 (3): 285–299.

Holloway, L., Kneafsey, M., Cox, R., Venn, L., Dowler, E. and Tuomainen, H., (2007a), 'Beyond the 'Alternative'-'Conventional' Divide? Thinking Differently About Food Production-Consumption Relationships', ch 5 in: D. Maye, L. Holloway and M. Kneafsey (eds), *Alternative Food Geographies: Representation and Place*, London: Elsevier: 77–93.

Holloway, L., Kneafsey, M., Venn, L., Cox, R., Dowler, E. and Tuomainen, H., (2007b), 'Possible Food Economies: a Methodological framework for Exploring Food Production-Consumption Relationships', *Sociologia Ruralis*, 47: 1–19.

Holloway, L., Venn, L., Cox, R., Kneafsey, M., Dowler, E. and Tuomainen, H., (2007c), 'Dirty vegetables: connecting consumers to the growing of their food', ch 14 in: B. Campkin and R. Cox, (eds), *Dirt: New Geographies of Cleanliness and Contamination*, London I.B. Tauris: 178–188.

IAASTD, (2008), *Agriculture at a Crossroads: Global Summary for Decision Makers*, Washington: Island Press for the International Assessment of Agricultural Knowledge, Science and Technology for Development (IAASTD), see: http://www.islandpress.org/iaastd Accessed 17 May 2009.

IGD, (2006), *Shopper attitudes to ethical food*, Factsheet, Watford: Institute of Grocery Distribution.

IGD, (2008), *Shopper Trends in Product and Store Choice 2008 – 5 Years On*, Watford: Institute of Grocery Distribution; Summary available online at www.igd.com, ⟨accessed 17.05.09⟩.

Jackson, T., (2008), 'Where is the 'wellbeing dividend'? Nature, structure and consumption inequalities', *Local Environment*, 13 (8): 703–723.

Jackson, P., Russell, P. and Ward, N., (2007), 'The appropriation of 'alternative' discourses by 'mainstream' food retailers', in D. Maye, L. Holloway and M. Kneafsey (eds), *Alternative Food Geographies: Representation and Practice*, Oxford: Elsevier.

Jackson, P., Ward, N. and Russell, P., (2009), Moral economies of food and geographies of responsibility, *Transactions of the Institute of British Geographers*, 34: 12–24.

Kneafsey, M., Cox, R., Holloway, L., Dowler, E., Venn, L. and Tuomainen, H., (2008), *Reconnecting producers, consumers and food: exploring alternatives*, Oxford: Berg.

Lampe, J. W., (2006), 'For Debate: Investment in Nutrigenomics will Advance the Role of Nutrition in Public Health', *Cancer Epidemiology Biomarkers & Prevention*, 15: 2329–2330.

Lang, T. and Heasman, M., (2004), *Food Wars: the global battle for mouths, minds and markets*, London: Earthscan.

Lawrence, M. and Germov, J., (2004), 'Future Food: The Politics of Functional Foods and Health Claims' ch 6 in: J. Germov and L. Williams (eds), *A Sociology of Food and Nutrition: The Social Appetite*, Victoria, Australia: Oxford University Press. 2nd edn. pp 119–147.

Lawrence, F., (2004), *Not on the Label: what really goes into the food on your plate*, London: Penguin Group.

Leahy, T., (2008), 'Unsustainable Food Production: its Social Origins and Alternatives' ch 3 in: J. Germov, and L. Williams (eds), *A Sociology of Food and Nutrition: The Social Appetite*, 3rd edn., Victoria, Australia: Oxford University Press: 58–77.

McMichael, P., (2009), 'The World Food Crisis in Historical Perspective', *Monthly Review*, 61 (3), online at: http://www.monthlyreview.org/090713mcmichael.php Accessed 16 Sep 2009.

MacGregor, S., Pardoe, S., Dobson, A. and Bell, D., (2005), *Environmental Citizenship: the Good-enough Primer*, booklet and website : Public Space Ltd http://www.environmentalcitizenship.net/envcitprimer.html Accessed 16 Sep 2009.

MacMillan, T. and Dowler, E., (2009, under review), 'Secure and sustainable? Examining the rhetoric and potential realities of UK food and agriculture policy', *Journal of Agricultural and Environmental Ethics*.

Marsden, T., Flynn, A. and Harrison, M., (2000), *Consuming Interests: The Social Provision of Foods*, London: UCL Press.

Maxey, L., (2007), 'From 'Alternative' to 'Sustainable' Food', ch 3 in D. Maye, L. Holloway and M. Kneafsey (eds), *Alternative Food Geographies: Representation and Place*, London: Elsevier, 55–76.

Maye, D., Kneafsey, M. and Holloway, L., (2007a), 'Introducing Alternative Food Geographies', ch 1 in D. Maye, L. Holloway and M. Kneafsey (eds), *Alternative Food Geographies: Representation and Place*, London: Elsevier, 1–20.

Maye, D., Holloway, L. and Kneafsey, M., (eds), (2007b), *Alternative Food Geographies: Representation and Place*, London: Elsevier.

Millstone, E. and van Zwanenburg, P., (2002), The evolution of food safety policy-making instructions in the UK, EU and Codex Alimentarius, *Social Policy and Administration*, 36: 593–609.

Morgan, K., Marsden, T. and Murdoch, J., (2006), *Worlds of Food: Place, Power and Provenance in the Food Chain*, Oxford: University Press.

Murcott, A., (ed.), (1998), *The Nation's Diet: The Social Science of Food Choice*, Essex: Addison Wesley Longman Ltd.

Patel, R., (2007), *Stuffed and Starved: Markets, Power and the Hidden Battle for the World Food System*, London: Portobello Books.

Pollan, M., (2008), *In Defence of Food*, London: Allen Lane, Penguin Books.

Pretty, J., (2000), 'Towards sustainable food and farming systems in industrialized countries', *International Journal of Agricultural Resources, Governance and Ecology*, 1: 77–94.

Pretty, J., (2002), *Agri-Culture: Reconnecting People, Land and Nature*, London: Earthscan.

Pretty, J. N., Ball, A. S., Lang, T. and Morison, J. I. L., (2005) 'Farm costs and food miles: An assessment of the full cost of the UK weekly food basket', *Food Policy*, 30: 1–19.

Reardon, T. A. and Berdegue, J. A., (2002), 'The Rapid Rise of Supermarkets in Latin America: Challenges and Opportunities for Development, *Development Policy Review*, 20: 371–388.

Roberts, P., (2008), *The End of Food: the coming crisis in the world food industry*, London: Bloomsbury.

SDC, (2008), *Green, healthy and fair: a review of government's role in supporting sustainable supermarket food*, London: Sustainable Development Commission.

Seyfang, G., (2006), 'Ecological citizenship and sustainable consumption: examining local organic food networks', *Journal of Rural Studies*, 22: 383–395.

Steedman, P. and MacMillan, T., (2008), *Food Distribution: an ethical agenda*, Brighton: Food Ethics Council. (available online: http://www.foodethicscouncil.org/node/401) Accessed 17 May 2007.

Steel, C., (2008), *Hungry City: how food shapes our lives*. London: Chatto and Windus.

Sumberg, J., (2009), *Reframing the great food debate: the case for sustainable food*, London: New Economics Foundation.

Tansey, G. and Rajotte, T., (eds), (2008), *The Future Control of Food: A Guide to International Negotiations and Rules on Intellectual Property, Biodiversity and Food Security*, London: Earthscan.

Tansey, G. and Worsley, T., (1995), *The Food System: A Guide*, London: Earthscan.

The Strategy Unit, (2008), *Food Matters: Towards a Strategy for the 21ˢᵗ Century*, London: Cabinet Office.

Tronto, J. C., (1993), *Moral Boundaries: A Political Argument for an Ethic of Care*, London: Routledge.

Tudge, C., (2007), *Feeding People is Easy*, Pari: Pari Publishing.

van Zwanenberg, P. and Millstone, E., (2003), 'BSE: A Paradigm of Policy Failure', *Political Quarterly*, 74: 27–37.

Venn, L., Kneafsey, M., Holloway, L., Cox, R., Dowler, E. and Tuomainen, H., (2006), 'Researching European 'alternative' food networks: some methodological considerations', *Area*, 38: 248–258.

Weatherell, C., Tregear, A. and Allinson, J., (2003), 'In search of concerned consumer: UK public perceptions of food, farming and buying local', *Journal of Rural Studies*, 19: 233–244.

Unnatural times? The social imaginary and the future of nature

Kate Soper

I

These are highly charged times for thinking about the nature of 'nature' and its relations to the 'social'. On the one hand, we are poised on the brink of bio-technological interventions that are opening up a whole new domain of human interactions with 'nature', indeed have the potential to go well beyond interaction, into unprecedented forms of creativity. Such developments are hugely exciting to many because of what they might promise for the elimination of disease and the enhancement of human health or well-being. On the other hand, we are also suffering unprecedented forms of unease precisely in virtue of our new found powers to control and even create 'nature', and caught up in new anxieties verging on panic about the ways in which environmental 'nature' is, or seems to be, spinning out of control because of climate change and its unpredictable character and consequences. To add to the confusion, there is the seeming incapacity of affluent Westerners to act in any but the most contradictory ways in response: huge anxieties about the impact of genetic programming on future personal autonomy go together with continuing disregard for the ways in which global economic relations deny millions of less privileged individuals the minimum of self-realization. Faced with the indisputable need to cut carbon emissions to the minimum, people continue to drive and fly as never before, and are currently encouraged to do so in the UK by a government that has given the green light to major airport expansion even as it issues advice to its citizens on energy-saving lightbulbs.

There are complex, and in some ways quite contrary, discourses on nature underlying these responses to our times. Many of these are what I have elsewhere referred to as 'nature-endorsing': discourses that lament the loss or erosion of nature, emphasize human dependency on the planetary eco-system, and demand that we both acknowledge environmental limits and revise our consumption with a view to keeping within the confines they impose. Nature endorsers are sometimes committed to overtly normative and metaphysical conceptions of the nature of nature (viewing it, for example, as possessing 'intrinsic value' or as a source of redemption from social alienation, or as that we must now, in Heideggerian terms, 'let be'). But all that is essential to endorsement is recognition of 'nature' conceived as an independent domain that both enables and constrains human activities, and will not prove endlessly adaptable to the demands made on it by human beings.

At the same time, and running counter to any endorsement of nature as something distinguishable from, and other to, humanity, there is also much talk about its 'social' or 'cultural' construction' (eg Eder, 1996; McNaughten, and Urry, 1998; Wilson, 1990; Vogel, 1996, 2006). And this is talk that has prompted a number of 'post-humanist' demands to revise long held conceptual distinctions between human and other forms of being.

Sometimes those stressing the 'culture' of nature do so in their role as environmentalists who are keen to acknowledge the mediation of human work and culture in much of what is loosely referred to as 'natural'. Or else – less coherently – they do so because they want us to take action against what they claim is the disappearance from the planet of anything that is 'natural' in the sense of still unaffected (or, more pejoratively, 'uncontaminated' by human culture). The conservationist, Bill McKibben, for example, has argued that nature has come to an end in the sense that even the remotest and wildest parts of the environment now bear the mark of human occupation of the planet (McKibben, 1990).[1] I call this latter type of position less coherent because if nature has indeed come to an 'end', there is little point in the injunction to preserve it. As Stephen Vogel has argued, 'if nature has ended, then it isn't clear anymore what environmentalism is supposed to protect. Without nature, an environmental theory or practice oriented towards nature's protection has nothing left to do: the game is up, and we (and nature) have simply lost. If McKibben is right, defending nature makes no more sense than defending the Holy Roman Empire...' (Vogel, 2006).[2]

But many of those stressing the 'culturality' of nature do so not so much in virtue of our environmental impact, but in response to the situation that has been opened up by the huge advances that have been made of late in the field of genetics, and their actual or potential application in such areas as seed modification, stem cell research, cloning, and organ transplantation from other species. For these developments have all created uncertainty about where, if at all, the line can be drawn between the artificially contrived and the naturally given, and they are posing both cognitive and moral problems for existing definitions and criteria for being 'human'.

They have also coincided with the emergence of a range of theoretical calls associated with the politics of animal liberation and advocacy of cyborg posthumanism to replace rigid conceptual discriminations between humans and animals and between the organic and the inorganic, and to adopt instead an altogether more fluid ontology (Haraway, 1991, 1997; Gray, 1995; Peperell, 1995; Hardt and Negri, 2000: 215f.).[3] Support of a more general philosophical kind for this type of post-humanist ontological destabilization and revision has also come from the anti-foundationalist shift in philosophy, most influentially in the arguments of Foucault and Derrida: from Foucault in the form of a resistance to any final distinction between nature and culture; from Derrida both in his last writings on animals, and more generally in his suggestion that our intuitive demarcations between human and non-human 'others' are a form of unwarranted conceptual policing (Derrida, 1991, 1994, 2002). One might note here, too, the striking parallels between recent Continental philosophizing about vegetarianism or 'becoming animal' and arguments against human-animal dualism produced – albeit in a very different style – much earlier within Anglo-American environmental ethics (Atterton and Calarco, 2004).

II

One upshot of these various developments is a form of normative 'return to nature': the opening of a new chapter in philosophical questioning about the potential of 'nature' to figure as a countering constraint. Confronted with the prospects of planetary exhaustion or fears of the impact of technical advance on the ethics of human community we are looking again to 'nature' to see if it might provide some kind of policing role. Academics are now asking whether 'nature' can instruct us in any universally agreeable sense on what we should do, or not do, either to ourselves or in our management of the environment (Kaebnick, forthcoming; Vogel, 2006; Streiffer, 2003).

Thirty years ago, these questions would hardly have been addressed in the academy. Or if they had been, it would have been to challenge various spurious claims that were being made about the supposed 'perversity' of homosexuality, or about the 'naturally' ordained character of divisions and differences (relating to class, gender, ethnicity) that in reality owed more to social construction than to biological determination. It was, in short, to undermine reactionary attempts to invoke 'nature' as a means of policing behaviour (especially sexual behaviour), and the challenge, as Jonathan Dollimore and others have pointed out, was to the 'violence' being done in the name of 'nature' rather than to the offences being caused through its dismissal. Most of these objectors were left-leaning and saw their interventions as a progressive response to regrettable forms of social conservatism, or even bigotry (Dollimore, 1991: 114–115; Soper, 1995: 119–148, esp. 145, note 2). Hence the extent to which the appeal to 'nature' became a bone of contention in the social movement struggles of the period over class, gender and racial exploitations and their quests for emancipation.

In recent decades, however, the concern has been less to expose false forms of naturalisation of the social than to discover whether 'nature' might still provide an ontological basis or ultimate court of appeal for condemning a range of existing practices both in everyday production and consumption and in science and genetics. The protest, here, is that 'it's "not natural"'; but instead of coming from rightwing ideologues protesting against same-sex relations, women boxing, and other supposed 'perversities', it is a cry of those who are keen to protect society from what are seen as abusive and false forms of progress.

It is true that the most explicit concerns on these issues – both of experts and of the public at large – are voiced more usually in terms of success, utility and safety: in the case of the response in the UK to GM, for example, the main debates were about whether things would work out in the way claimed by the pro-GM scientists, whether GM production was expedient or necessary to achieve the ends proposed, and, perhaps, above all, whether it could be guaranteed to be safe in both human and ecological terms. And much conflicting scientific evidence was brought into play in the disputes around all these issues. There has also been justified concern about the immorality of the huge profits being made by the GM companies. But underlying or complexly caught up in these concerns – and arguably strongly influencing the reception and interpretation placed on the data offered, either for or against such developments as GM, by the scientists themselves – has been an intuitive sense of the counternaturality of the whole process: a questioning whether such developments are not a step too far in the manipulation of nature, an hubristic affront to the prevailing moral sense of what humans may properly do with their powers of intervention – and the notion of 'Frankenstein science' which is often invoked in this context is indicative of this revulsion.[4]

III

This reaction, however, immediately begs two questions. Firstly, on what grounds is the 'naturality' or otherwise of these new developments being determined, and how exactly, if at all, do they differ from earlier human constructions of or interactions with nature ? Secondly, why should the 'unnaturality' of certain practices be any more grounds for opposing them than it is in the case, say, of artistic production? After all, GM and similarly advanced bio-technological process is plainly unnatural according to one of the commonest definitions of the natural (and one, as noted above, invoked by many recent ecological writers) – where the kernel idea is that nature is that which is 'uncontaminated' by humans or in which humans have had no hand. But then so, too, are most of our other practices, including many that have been generally welcomed as uncontroversially beneficial. So even if there were agreement on the criteria that allowed certain applications of bio-technology to be specified as 'unnatural' (and, as indicated, this seems pretty unlikely) it is by no means clear that anything very much hangs thereby.

Theorists, then, have been justifiably wary of opting for any essentialist definition of 'nature' that could provide a criterion for distinguishing between our practices as 'natural' or 'unnatural' (whether, we might add, it be to applaud or reject them). Stephen Vogel, as indicated above (see note 2), has gone so far as to dismiss the idea that any helpful discriminations can be made through the concept. 'Not only,' he argues, '…might nature the thing have ended: the *concept* of 'nature' might be such an ambiguous and problematic one, so prone to misunderstanding and so riddled with pitfalls, that its usefulness for a coherent environmental philosophy might be small indeed.' (Vogel, 2006).

However, even though Vogel is right about the difficulties of invoking nature in any moral sense, he is too ready to elide the dismissal of nature in that sense with the rejection of *any* concept of nature at all. For there is *one* sense in which nature does always have its say in human activities, and this is the sense in which all our interventions, whether environmental or biological in respect of ourselves or other beings, are dependent on the workings of physical law and process, and have their outcomes determined by them. In making this point I am invoking what I and others influenced by Critical Realism have elsewhere argued is the difference between a 'realist' or theoretical concept of nature and other more phenomenological or metaphysical concepts (Benton, 1989, 1992; Soper, 1995, pp. 149–176, 1996). Nature in the 'realist' sense refers us to structures and processes that are independent of human activity (in the sense that they are not humanly created), and whose forces and causal powers are the condition of, and constraint upon, any human practice, however ambitious (be it, for example, genetic engineering, the creation of new energy sources, attempts to manipulate the weather or 'terraform' other planets, or any other Promethean scheme). This is the 'nature' to whose laws we are always subject, even as we harness them to human purposes, and whose processes we can neither escape nor destroy. This is the 'nature' that cannot be said to be 'ending' whatever we do to planet Earth, since it will persist in its workings even in the midst of nuclear holocaust or destruction by asteroid or solar combustion.

This realist concept of nature, I have argued in *What is Nature?*, is indispensable to the coherence both of ecological discourses about the 'changing face of nature' conceived as a surface environment, and to any discourse about the genetically engineered or cultural 'construction' of human beings or their bodies. Just as environmental transformations, whether humanly contrived or not, require us to distinguish between the naturally pre-given powers and processes at work in their creation and their more empirically observable (and humanly useful or damaging) environmental effects, so we must recognize the natural body as a condition of any cultural work upon it, whether voluntary or coerced, and however profound and intrusive in its alterations. I have made this point in the past essentially in reference to the so-called 'construction' of gender and sexuality, arguing that the very emphasis on the variable and culturally relative quality of human sexuality requires as its counterpart a recognition of the more constant and universal features of embodied existence if it is to be meaningful. But the same points apply in respect of any form of medical bio-engineering, given its reliance on the 'natural' laws and processes of human biology.

If, then, the theorists who tell us that 'there is no nature' are denying its reality and specific determinations in this understanding, they are committed to a form of idealism which is incoherent. Moreover, even though the appeal to nature in some looser and more normative sense is always vexed and troubled, it is worth noting how difficult it is to keep it out of the picture altogether. Thus we find that even those who are most critical of the attempts to provide a criterion of naturality often end up by gesturing towards the idea, if only implicitly. For example, the Nuffield Report seems happy conceptually to invoke *some* sort of criterion of what is more or less 'natural' even as it rejects the possibility of satisfactorily saying what it is. Thus it writes:

> 'Naturalness' and 'unnaturalness' are part of a spectrum. At one end of the scale, some modifications of the plants that are now being achieved by genetic modification might also have been achieved over time by conventional [ie more 'natural'] means of plant breeding. (The Nuffield Council, 1999: chapter 8. section 9).

Stephen Vogel, as we have seen, wants us to eschew all discourse on 'nature'. But he nonetheless defends his 'postnaturalism' by reference to the importance of avoiding environmental disaster and securing human flourishing. Thus he speaks of the 'correct' belief that the effects of human activity over the last two centuries have been 'baleful' and 'destructive' (Vogel, 2006: 5). Yet 'destruction' and 'disaster' only arise in respect to human values, needs and commitments to certain lifestyles, and once we have dispensed with any reference to nature, including – as Vogel insists – biological nature – then it is hard to argue that some forms of need/desire satisfaction should take preference over others. In the very vocabulary of 'looming environmental disaster' there is a reference to biological imperatives for survival and minimal flourishing that sits uneasily with Vogel's rejection of any appeal to nature.

Something similar applies, as I have argued at greater length elsewhere, in the case of Haraway's call to blur or collapse the organic-inorganic, human-animal distinctions, given that this is promoted in the name of improved animal well-being and human sexual emancipation. For a cyborg ontology hardly seems to provide the most promising basis for protesting against the bio-technological or agribusiness maltreatment of animals as if they were indeed Cartesian machines indifferent to fleshly suffering. Nor can it easily ground a proper respect for all those ways in which the pleasures and pains of human love and sexuality are quite distinctive from those of other creatures. In other words, unacknowledged though it may be, it is difficult not to discern an implicit gesture in Haraway's ethics towards the more romantic-redemptive understanding of nature that she has, at a more explicit level of argument, wanted us to eschew (Soper, 1999, 2003).

It remains true, however, that it is very difficult to appeal to 'nature' for endorsement of any particular way of living or being. In the case of the environment, realist nature will exercise an influence on what we do, or can even try to do, but it is we who have to decide what it is ethical to attempt within those limits. Likewise, as biological organisms, we have certain requirements or instinctual responses that we cannot resist (to breathe, take in food and drink, excrete, etc), but beyond those, the area of reduced or under determination is very vast. Even in the case of such a 'basic' need as that for food, the individual can decide to resist it – and does so in cases of anorexia or voluntary fasting. Or to invoke the example of sexuality once more: heterosexual relations, which have been presented in some gender theory, as an arbitrary and even coercive norm of human sexual conduct (Rich, 1983; Jeffreys, 1990; Butler, 1990, 1993) are a prescription of nature in the sense that they have been essential hitherto to the reproduction and thus history of the species. Yet it is in principle possible today to circumvent 'natural' reproduction of this kind, and were we to make an ethico-political decision to do so, 'realist' nature would not step in to prevent us, although it might make it pretty difficult to do (Soper, 1996: 32–33).

If, then, neither nature in my realist sense nor any other more universally applicable normative concept of 'nature' can readily supply us with an ethics, it might seem that we are brought back to more intuitive, and therefore fuzzier, ways of thinking about the forms of resistance to what is loosely deemed 'unnatural'. Might we, for example, do better to explore what, if anything, is distinctive to moral appeals to nature in specific contexts: to ask, not what feature of x makes x 'unnatural' but what is peculiar to the opprobrium attaching to the idea that it is, and how does it differ from other forms of moral disapproval? Why is it, for example, that we tend to condemn necrophilia and paedophilia as 'perverse' or 'unnatural' (as well as wrong), but not murder or rape (which we instead denounce simply as 'wrong' or 'evil')? Is this because we are implicitly discriminating here between acts that other animals cannot do and those they do not do? Other animals, of course, can, and do, kill each other very frequently, and regularly use force in sexual intercourse, but only humans can murder or rape, because these are acts that figure as morally culpable only in the context of the human community. Necrophilia, on the other hand, although certainly deemed immoral and criminalized by us, is also condemned as unnatural – in virtue, it might seem, of its proving the exception to rather than the norm for animal behaviour.

On the other hand, it can seem just as problematic to police human behaviour by reference to what is 'natural' for other animals, as to deal with animals as if they had moral understanding. According to Freud, moreover, the so-called perversions have an 'originary' status for human beings, being a given of human nature that has to be repressed as a condition of civilization. As he has written, 'society believes that no greater threat to its civilization could arise than if the sexual instincts were to be liberated and returned to their original aims. For this society does not wish to be reminded of this precarious portion of its foundations' (Freud, 1974–86: i: 48, vii: 86, viii: 268). Hence the reason, he suggests, why we feel such loathing towards manifest perversions:

> It is as though one could not forget that they are not only something disgusting but also something monstrous and dangerous – as though people felt them as seductive, and had at bottom to fight down a secret envy of those who were enjoying them (Freud, 1974–86: i: 363).

Indeed, this disgust with the perversions is presented by him as purely conventional, illogical and irrational (Freud, 1974–86: vii: 64, viii: 83–4). And yet, as

Jonathan Dollimore has pointed out, it would be naïve of Freud to expect us to rid ourselves of shame or disgust since these are – as he himself has argued (Freud, 1974–86: vii: 76 esp. n.1, vii: 75) – the fundamental principles of cultural order (Dollimore, 1991: 180).

The 'unnatural' or the 'perverse' in these contexts, one might therefore suggest, speaks to a species-specific and exclusive need for us to police divisions (between life and death, children and adults, nourishment and excretion, humans and animals) whose maintenance is seen as a condition of the possibility of any human community. In Kaja Silverman's words, perversion 'subverts many of the binary oppositions upon which the social order rests: it crosses the boundary separating food from excrement (coprophilia); human from animal (bestiality); life from death (necrophilia); adult from child (pederasty); and pleasure and pain (masochism)' (Silverman, 1988: 33).

So even if we cannot provide rigorous criteria for our intuitive discriminations, this is no reason to disregard them. Habermas has noted the 'symptomatic revulsion' we feel at the breaching of the species barrier that we had naively assumed to be inviolable – an 'ethical virgin soil', as he puts it, quoting Otfried Hoffe (2003: 39–4). He has also pointed out, against genetic programming, that:

> many of us seem to have the intuition that we should not weigh human life, not even in its earliest stages, either against the freedom (and competitiveness) of research, or against the concern with safe-guarding an industrial edge, or against the wish for a healthy child, or even against the prospect (assumed *arguendo*) of new treatments for severe genetic diseases (2003: 68).

And he has rightly, in this connection, spoken of a Rubicon that we should be very wary of crossing.

In this, I suggest, he echoes the warning of an earlier Critical Theorist, Theodor Adorno, who was always resistant *both* to false and fetishizing forms of naturalisation of history *and* to the 'enchantment of history', that is, to any view of history as if it were a form of 'mastery' of or 'escape' from nature. History, in fact, he suggested, creates nature in the negative sense (what he terms 'second nature') by delivering us up to new forms of fatedness, the apparent necessities of a given social order and economy, and viewed in this light, capitalist society is itself 'natural' or a-historical, since it is committed to the eternal reproduction of its relations of production and commodification. GM, nanotechnology and other forms of bio-technological appropriation of nature, however innovative, looked at in this optic would then be no more than business as usual and thus also 'natural' in a pejorative sense – since they are simply the latest vehicles for the reproduction of the market society and its profit-making and consumerist objectives.

On the other hand, in the more positive sense 'nature' (or 'first nature') for Adorno refers to all forms of concrete, individually existing beings that are mortal or transitory (that is, to both corporeal existence and to the products of labour), and in this understanding nature is the embodiment of history, and history the vehicle of nature. It might be said, then, that it is manifest both in the productions of bio-technology, but also in the resistance of all those who at any historical point in time, may pit themselves against the grain of dominant forces and tendencies. And one aspect of history that Adorno emphasizes in this dimension, partly under the influence of Walter Benjamin, is its 'one-timeness'. History is a transitory affair from which there is no going back, and in and through which the fate of first nature is always at any moment being decided. New technical developments, such as genetic engineering are always arresting because of the way in which we discern in them the irreversibility of our economic and political decisions and practices. To commit to them is to know that the 'innocence' of the pre-committed society will never return again and that, in that sense, the decision to enter into a new zone of instrumental rationality creates a certain fatedness, becoming part of 'second nature'. But we also know, at the same time, that there is nothing fated about the commitment itself (Adorno, 2006; 1973).

These Adornian arguments, however, cannot finally resolve the aporias of the natural/unnatural demarcation, since their ethico-political premises can always be contested. Susan Buck–Morss has written in her discussion of Ador-no's negative dialectics that 'where nature confronted men as a mythic power Adorno called for the control of that nature by reason; but where rational control of nature took the form of domination, Adorno exposed such instru-mental reason as a new mythology' (Buck-Morss, 1977: 58). This is an accurate summation; but it still leaves open the question of how we decide what consti-tutes a 'rational' control of nature and what exactly counts as its domination, and why. On the other hand, what we do know enough to know, and is captured in the Adornian argument, is that we cannot 'dominate' nature, either human or non-human, in any and every way and still expect to flourish. So even if we cannot point to any essential or universal aspects of ourselves that underlie our resistances, they are always to be attended to as signalling not so much the limits of what we *can* do to ourselves, and other creatures, and the rest of nature, but what we can do and *still expect to live well*, to be happy, and to experience the rewards of membership of an ethical community.

It would be a mistake, I have suggested, to overlook intuitive forms of revul-sion to cloning, to breaching the species barrier, and so forth. But I would here insist in conclusion that it would be even more mistaken to allow the awesome perspectives opened up by genetic engineering or other technical fixes to distract us from the currently more decisive role of social determinations on human (and other animal) modes of existence and forms of potential. Our developed powers over 'nature' in recent decades have brought about a situation in which we are today often more at the mercy of what culture and economic and social policy enforces than subject to biological dictate. Breast enhancement, face lifts, and other forms of cosmetic surgery, are far easier to accomplish than shifting ste-reotypes on beauty and sexual attraction. Much of the illness and misery afflict-ing the world's poorest could be easily eradicated were it not for the economic relations and political orders standing in the way. It is, in other words, often easier today to counter and alter what is genetically determined than to curb or transform the conventions of culture (Soper, 1995: 139–140). Habermas has argued that the challenge of new types of biological intervention relate to our Enlightenment sense of freedom and personal autonomy: we respond very differently, he claims, to the impact on individuals of the contingencies of socialization than we would to the irreversible determination of a pre-natal production of the genome. But we need also to accept that, reversible in principle though they may be, social determinations *in their actual effects* on the powers of self-realization and autonomy of massive numbers of persons can be just as decisive. Our alarms about the risks of genetic engineering should not be allowed to overwhelm more pressing concerns about the role of the global neo-liberal economic system in precipitating irreversible global warming and ecological barbarism on an unprecedented scale.

Changes in economic and social policy could therefore do much more to advance the autonomy *and* the pleasure and sensual and spiritual fulfilment of people worldwide than can be achieved by any genetic interventions and technical fix solutions. But the policies needed to redress the huge global disparities between rich and poor in their access to resources, and hence to the minimum material conditions essential to any further type of flourishing, are unlikely to make any headway unless and until the richer nations rethink their commitments to the growth economy and its currently dominant model of human progress and well-being.

This is why it is disappointing to find so little suggestion, in mainstream responses on global warming, that it might actually be more enjoyable to escape the confines of the growth-driven, shopping-mall culture than to continue to keep it on track. All the emphasis falls on the technical fixes that might allow us indefinitely to pursue consumerist lifestyles, and we hear very little of what might be gained by moving away from the obsession with such gratifications and pursuing a less work-driven and acquisitive way of life. My case for 'alternative hedonism' is all about countering this viewpoint through the development of a heightened sense of the pleasures, both sensual and spiritual, to be gained from restraining our more environmentally damaging forms of consumption. (Soper, 1993: 78–9).

Given the massive budgets devoted to advertisement of consumerist pleasures, it is hardly surprising that 'alternative hedonism' has made little impact to date. Yet despite the odds stacked against the promotion of counter-consumerist enjoyment, a dialectic may be now unfolding that will see it winning more adherents in the future. The indices of this are to be found not only in the alarms over climate change but also in growing concerns about the human consequences of the 'work and spend' economy and the new interest, both lay and academic, in what makes for the 'good life' and personal fulfilment. It is also a tension evident in the expansion of green and ethical consumption and in the centrality of the No Logo forms of opposition within the anti-globalization movement (Klein, 2000; Littler, 2005). All this, moreover, has found some backing in the findings from the 'Happy Planet' index of well-being recently published by the New Economic Foundation, and in the evidence of the so-called 'happiness economics' that contests the supposed correlation between increased wealth and increased well-being (Kasser, 2007; Layard, 2005; Purdy, 2005; Frey and Stutzer, 2000; Inglehart and Klingemann, 2000; Easterlin, 2001; Oswald, 1997; Durning, 1992: 23, 38–9, 41; Bauman, 1988: 96; Argyle, 1987: 161).

If, then, we are looking for the potential agents of a democratically achieved process of change in the West today, we need to take more account of the embryonic signs of consumer disenchantment with the so-called 'good life' and of the various ways in which consumption is now emerging as a site of political contention and campaigning. These embryonic signs, I have argued, are well captured in Raymond Williams' concept of a 'structure of feeling': what is at issue here are emergent or pre-emergent responses or qualitative changes of affect that, as he put it, 'do not have to await definition or rationalization before they exert palpable pressures and set effective limits on experience and on action' (Williams, 1977: 132, 128–136). The reference is in this sense to what may be experienced only in an as yet ambivalent and cloudy form, but may in future come to exert more definite and explicit forms of pressure.

Lest it appear, however, as if all the emphasis in this account is falling on the 'greening' of the individual consumer, it should be emphasized that the role of collective strategies for changing consumption will also be crucial. The two pressures for change are intimately related, at least in democratic societies, where more collective and institutionally based measures for environmental protection and conservation are always ultimately reliant on the support of the electorate. If I have here stressed the emergence of greater individual consumer equivocation, it is precisely because of its pivotal role in encouraging governments to promote more effective collective policies on the environment both at the national and international level. Collective and individual responses are not, in this sense, to be viewed as opposing or alternative forces for consumer change, but rather as interconnected and mutually reinforcing, since the 'greening' of individual consumers is a precondition of the kind of consensus around altered conceptions of prosperity that would permit the imposition of forms of collective control over the environment and public 'self-policing' of the more ecologically destructive types of consumption. Equally, and conversely, collective strategies which focus, for example, on the provision of public transport or the 'greening' of urban space, are likely themselves to issue in benefits (healthier environments, reduction in congestion, greater safety) that encourage more extensive individual consumer support.

Given this mutually reinforcing interaction between public response and policy intervention, it is important that government should act to confirm shifts in attitudes that will otherwise, without question, remain a marginal and ineffectual development. An 'avant-garde' consumer ethics deserves and requires a complementary response from those with the power to extend its reach. At the very least, policy makers have a duty to be more honest and straightforward in their engagement with the public on these issues. If there is a real commitment to environmental care, the alleviation of poverty, and sustainability, then every encouragement should be given to the affluent public to rethink the good life and to consume in less damaging ways, even if that comes at the cost of continued rates of economic growth. If there is no such commitment, then there should no longer be a pretence that there is, nor any lament at the implications in terms of climate change, global exploitation, and increased pollution and ill health.

Notes

1 Though today associated in particular with McKibben's ecological argument, this idea is not a new one. It has some register in Cicero's concept of 'second nature', and was already succinctly made by Marx and Engels in their claim in The *German Ideology* (1968: 59) that: 'The nature which preceded human history no longer exists anywhere (except perhaps on a few Australian coral-islands of recent origin).' But while for earlier thinkers, human interaction with 'nature' or the encroachment of second nature over an absolute and pristine otherness to human culture, was deemed on the whole a positive condition of the development and refinement of human needs and the flourishing of a distinctively human culture, it is today – at least among some of the deeper ecologists – the ground of altogether more negative assessments of our planetary impact.

2 It is because of these confusions and illogicalities in the deployment of the concept of 'nature' that Vogel himself has suggested we might do better to dispense with it altogether. This position is discussed further later in the chapter.

3 The 'Manifesto for Cyborgs' first appeared in the *Socialist Register* 80, 1985: 65–108. It has inspired numerous commentaries and articles. For an extensive selection, see Gray, 1995. For some more sceptical and polemical responses, see McCormick, 2000; Bordo, 1990; Soper, 1999.

4 The evidence cited by Kaebnick: 'Even among the wider public, surveys have reliably shown that a significant portion of the public finds them morally troubling (Hallman *et al.*, 2004; Marris, 2002). In a poll conducted by the Pew Initiative on Food Biotechnology, two-thirds of respondents said they were 'uncomfortable' about animal cloning even though less than half thought the products were unsafe (Pew Initiative on Food and Biotechnology, 2005). A market research firm hired by a company that clones livestock reported that over a third of those it polled said they would not buy such products even when first told that the FDA was likely to declare them safe (Sosin and Richards, 2005). Three-quarters of respondents to a poll paid for by the International Food Information Council said that they had an unfavourable impression of animal cloning (International Food Information Council, 2005)' in 'Putting Concerns about Nature in Context: The Case of Agricultural Biotechnology', forthcoming in *Perspectives in Biology and Medicine*.

References

Adorno, T., (1973), *Negative Dialectics*, Trans. E.B. Ashton, London: Routledge.
Adorno, T., (2006), *History and Freedom: Lectures 1964–5*, R. Tiedemann, (ed.) London: Wiley.
Argyle, M., (1987), *The Philosophy of Happiness*, New York: Methuen.
Atterton, P. and Calarco, M., (eds), (2004), *Animal Philosophy*, London and New York: Continuum.

Bauman, Z., (1988), *Freedom*, Milton Keynes: Open University Press.

Benton, T., (1989), 'Marxism and Natural Limits', *New Left Review* 178, November-December: 51–86, reprinted in P. Osborne (ed.), 1990, *Socialism and the Limits of Liberalism*, London: Verso: 241–269.

Benton, T., (1992), 'Ecology, Socialism and the Mastery of Nature: a reply to Reiner Grundrmann', *New Left Review* 194, July-August: 55–74.

Bordo, S., (1990), 'Feminism, Postmodernism, and Gender-Skepticism' in L. Nicholson (ed.), *Feminism/Postmodernism*, London & New York: Routledge.

Buck-Morss, S., (1977), *The Origin of Negative Dialectics*, London: Macmillan.

Butler, J., (1990), *Gender Trouble: feminism and the Subversion of Identity*, London: Routledge.

Butler, J., (1993), *Bodies that Matter*, London: Routledge.

Buck-Morss, S., (1977), *The Origin of Negative Dialectics*, London: Macmillan.

Derrida, J., (1991), ' "Eating Well," or the Calculation of the Subject: An Interview with Jacques Derrida' in E. Cadava *et al.*, (eds), *Who Comes After the Subject?* London: Routledge.

Derrida, J., (1994), 'The Deconstruction of Actuality' – an interview in *Radical Philosophy*, no. 68, Autumn.

Derrida, J., (2002), 'The Animal that Therefore I am (More to Follow)', trans, David Wills, *Critical Inquiry*, 28. (also included in Peter Atterton and Mathew Calarco (eds), *Animal Philosophy*, London: Continuum: 113–128)

Dollimore, J., (1991), *Sexual Dissidence Augustine to Wilde, Freud to Foucault*, Oxford: Clarendon.

Durning, A. T., (1992), *How Much is Enough?* London: Earthscan.

Easterlin, R.A., (2001), 'Income and Happiness: towards a unified theory', *Economic Journal*, 111: 465–494.

Eder, K., (1996), *The Social Construction of Nature*, London: Theory, Culture, Society.

Freud, S., (1974–86), *The Pelican Freud Library*, 15 vols., A. Rihcards (ed.), Hardmondsworth: Penguin.

Frey, B. S. and Stutzer, A., (2000), *Happiness and Economics: How the Economy and Institutions Affect Human Well Being*, New Jersey: Princeton University Press.

Goodland, R. and Daly, H., (1992), *Ten Reasons why Northern Growth is not the Answer to Southern Poverty*, Washington DC: Environmental Department: World Bank.

Gray, C. H., (ed.), (1995), *The Cyborg Handbook*, London: Routledge.

Habermas, J., (2002), *The Future of Human Nature*, Cambridge: Polity.

Hallman, W. K., Hebden, W. C., Cuite, C. L., Aquino, H. C., and Lang, J. T., (2004), 'Americans and GM food: Knowledge, opinion, and interest in 2004', (Publication no. RR-1104-007), New Brunswick, N.J.: Food Policy Institute, Cook College, Rutgers, The State University of New Jersey. At: http://www.foodpolicyinstitute.org/docs/reports/NationalStudy2004.pdf.

Haraway, D., (1991), *Simians, Cyborgs and Women: the reinvention of nature*, London: Free Association, Routledge.

Haraway, D., (1997). *ModestWitness@Second Millennium: FemaleMan© Meets OncoMouse™*, London & New York: Routledge.

Hardt, M. and Negri, A., (2000), *Empire*, Harvard, Connecticut: Harvard University Press.

Inglehart, R. and Klingemann, H-D., (2000), 'Genes, Culture, Democracy and Happiness' in E. Diener and E. Suh (eds), *Culture and Subjective Well-Being*, Cambridge Mass: MIT Press.

Jeffreys, S., (1990), *Anticlimax*, London: The Women's Press.

Kaebnick, G., (2007), 'Putting Concerns about Nature in Context: The Case of Agricultural Biotechnology', *Perspectives in Biology and Medicine*, 50(4): 572–584.

Kaebnick, G., 'Reasons of the Heart: Reason, Attitude, and "the Wisdom of Repugnance" ', Presentation to the Hastings Centre.

Kasser, T., (2007), 'Visions of Prosperity', Paper to the Sustainable Development Commission, 26th November, at: www.sd-commission.org.uk/publications.

Klein, N., (2000), *No Logo*, London & New York: Harper Collins.

Layard, R., (2005), *Happiness: Lessons from a New Science*, London: Allen Lane.

Littler, J., (2005), 'Beyond the Boycott: anti-consumerism, cultural change and the limits of reflexivity', *Cultural Studies*, Vol.19, no.2: 227–252.

Marris, C. *et al.*, (2002), 'Public perceptions of agricultural biotechnologies in Europe: Final report of the PABE research project', Commission of European Communities, Available at http://www.pabe.net.

Marx, K. and Engels, F., (1968), *The German Ideology*, Moscow: Progress Publishers.

McCormick, B., (2000), 'The Island of Dr. Haraway', *Environmental Ethics*, Vol. 22, Winter: 409–418.

McKibben, B., (1989), *The End of Nature*. New York: Random House.

McNaughten, P. and Urry, J., (1998), *Contested Natures*, Sage: London.

Nuffield Council Report, (1999), 'Genetically modified crops: The ethical and social issues.

O'Neill, J., (1994), 'Humanism and Nature', *Radical Philosophy* no. 66.

Oswald, A., (1997), 'Happiness and Economic Performance'. *Economic Journal*, 107: 1815–1831.

Peperell, R., (1995), *The Post-Human Condition*, Exeter: Intellect Books.

Purdy, D., (2005), 'Human happiness and the stationary state', *Soundings* 31, Autumn, pp. 133–146.

Rich, A., (1983), 'Compulsory Heterosexuality and Lesbian Existence' in E. and E. K. Abel (eds), *The Signs Reader*, Chicago: University of Chicago Press.

Silverman, K., (1988), 'Masochism and Male Subjectivity' in *Camera Obscura*, 17 May: 31–66.

Singer,P., (1989), 'All Animals are Equal' in T. Regan and P. Singer (eds), *Animal Rights and Human Obligations*, 2nd edn., New Jersey: Englewood Cliffs.

Sosin, J. and Richards, M. D., (2005), 'What will consumers do? Understanding consumer response when meat and milk from cloned animals reach supermarkets', Available at http://www.krcre-search.com/images/AnalysisWhatWillConsDo11-04-05.pdf.

Soper, K., (1993), 'To Each According to Their Need?' *New Left Review* 197, January-February: 112–128.

Soper, K., (1995), *What is Nature? Culture, Politics and the Non-Human*, Oxford: Blackwell.

Soper, K., (1996), 'Nature/ 'Nature'' in G. Robertson *et al.*, (eds), *FutureNatural*, London: Routledge: 22–34.

Soper, K., (1999), 'Of OncoMice and FemaleMen: Donna Haraway on Cyborg Ontology', *Women, a Cultural Review*, Vol. 10, no 2: 167–172.

Soper, K., (2003), 'Humans, Animals, Machines', *New Formations*, 49: 99–109.

Soper, K., (2006), 'Counter-Consumerism in a New Age of War', *Radical Philosophy*, no. 135, January-February: 2–8.

Streiffer, R., (2003), 'In defense of the moral relevance of species boundaries', *American Journal of Bioethics*. 3(3): 37–38.

UK Nuffield Council on Bioethics, (1999), *Genetically Modified Crops:the Ethical and Social Issues*.

Vogel, S., (1996), *Against Nature: the concept of Nature in Critical Theory*, Albany: Suny UP Press.

Vogel, S., (2006), 'Why 'Nature' Has No Place In Environmental Philosophy', Presentation to the Hastings Centre, Garrison NY, November 9.

Von Weizsacker, E. U., (1994), *Earth Politics*, Zed Books: London.

Williams, R., (1977), *Marxism and Literature*, Oxford: Oxford University Press.

Wilson, A., (1990), *The Culture of Nature: The Making of the North American Landscape from Disney to the Exxon Valdez*, Blackwell: Oxford.

Notes on contributors

Paul Bellaby is Research Professor of Sociology at the University of Salford. His research and publications have been in the sociology of health and the use of the internet in public health. He has also studied risks associated with hydrogen energy, and questions of trust in science and technology. He was guest editor of a special issue of *Energy Policy*, 2009, on trust among stakeholders in managing uncertainties surrounding sustainable energy. e-mail: p.bellaby@ salford.ac.uk

Ted Benton is Professor of Sociology at the University of Essex, UK. He is author of numerous publications in fields that include philosophy of social science, history and philosophy of the life sciences, and green and socialist thought. He was a founder member of the Red-Green Study Group and the subject of S. Moog & R. Stones (eds) *Nature, Social Relations and Human Needs: Essays in Honour of Ted Benton* (Palgrave, 2009). He is also a well known natural history writer and photographer. e-mail: tbenton@essex.ac.uk

Bob Carter is Associate Professor in the Sociology Department at the University of Warwick. He has published widely on the politics of racism and immigration and on social theory and sociolinguistics. He is the author of *Realism and Racism: Concepts of Race in Sociological Research* (Routledge, 2000) and the co-author (with Alison Sealey) of *Applied Linguistics as Social Science* (Continuum, 2004). He also co-edited (with Caroline New) *Making Realism Work* (Routledge, 2004). His current research explores the theory and politics of group formation and the impact of current knowledge of human genetic variation on social categorisations of race and ethnicity. e-mail: Robert.Carter@ warwick.ac.uk

Nickie Charles is Professor and Director of the Centre for the Study of Women and Gender in the Sociology Department at the University of Warwick. She has published widely on many aspects of gender including feminist social movements, the gendered division of paid and unpaid work and the refuge movement. She has recently completed an ESRC-funded research project investigating gender and political processes in the context of devolution and is developing new research on the relationship between humans and other animals. Her most recent book is *Families in Transition* (with Charlotte Aull Davies and Chris Harris, The Policy Press, 2008). Other books include *Gender in Modern Britain*,

(Oxford University Press, 2002), *Feminism, the State and Social Policy* (Macmillan, 2000), *Gender Divisions and Social Change* (Harvester Wheatsheaf, 1993) and (with Marion Kerr) *Women, Food and Families* (Manchester University Press, 1988). e-mail: Nickie.Charles@warwick.ac.uk

Rosie Cox is Senior Lecturer in Geography and Gender Studies at Birkbeck, University of London. She has a long-standing research interest in consumption within households, particularly the use of paid domestic labour, and has also more recently been researching food and DIY/ home maintenance. e-mail: r.cox@bbk.ac.uk

Daniel Nilsson DeHanas is a PhD candidate in Sociology at the University of North Carolina at Chapel Hill and a Visiting Research Fellow in Politics at SOAS, University of London. His current research concerns second-generation youth in London and the religious influences on their political and civic engagement. He is also interested in broader questions in the sociology of religion. e-mail: ddehanas@unc.edu

Peter Dickens is Visiting Professor of Sociology at the University of Brighton, U.K. and Visiting Senior Research Associate, Faculty of Politics, Psychology, Sociology and International Relations, University of Cambridge. His research interests are in the sociology of the environment and outer-space. See www.sociologyoftheuniverse.net. e-mail: p.dickens1@ntlworld.com

Elizabeth Dowler works on social and policy aspects of food and nutrition and their links to poverty, nationally and internationally; rights based approaches to poverty and food insecurity; evaluating local initiatives and national policy, and on 'reconnection' to sustainable food systems, especially consumers' perspectives. A registered Public Health Nutritionist, she is Professor of Food and Social Policy in the Department of Sociology at the University of Warwick. She is a member of Defra's Council of Food Policy Advisers, and is also a member/trustee of the Food Ethics Council – an independent research and advocacy group working to make the food system fairer and healthier (see www.foodethicscouncil.org). e-mail: Elizabeth.Dowler@warwick.ac.uk

Rob Flynn is Professor of Sociology at the University of Salford. He has researched and published extensively in urban sociology, health services research and medical sociology. Recently he has been investigating public perceptions of risk, and public engagement in hydrogen energy. He was co-editor of R.Flynn and P.Bellaby, *Risk and the Public Acceptance of New Technologies* (Palgrave-Macmillan, 2007). Previously he has been Chairperson successively of the Editorial Boards of *Sociology*, and *Sociology of Health and Illness*. He is also an Associate of the Tyndall Centre for Climate Change Research (Manchester University). e-mail: R.Flynn@salford.ac.uk

Lewis Holloway is Lecturer in Human Geography in the Department of Geography, University of Hull. His research concentrates on food, farming and the countryside. Recent projects have focused on alternative food networks, alternative rural lifestyles, the effects of genetic and robotic technologies on farming practices and identities, and the changing nature of human-nonhuman relations in agriculture. His most recent co-authored book is 'Reconnecting producers, consumers and food: exploring alternatives' (Berg, 2008). e-mail: L.Holloway@ hull.ac.uk

Moya Kneafsey is a Reader in Human Geography in the Department of Geography, Environment and Disaster Management at Coventry University. She is interested in 'alternative' and sustainable food systems, and has published research on local, regional and community food networks. She also maintains a research interest in tourism and development, particularly in rural contexts. e-mail: m.kneafsey@coventry.ac.uk

Sherilyn MacGregor is Lecturer of Environmental Politics in the School of Politics, International Relations and Philosophy at Keele University. Her research focuses on the politics/discourses of citizenship and sustainability from a critical feminist environmental perspective. She is author of *Beyond Mothering Earth: Ecological Citizenship and the Politics of Care* (University of British Columbia Press, 2006), reviews editor of *Environmental Politics* and currently working to co-edit (with Timothy J. Doyle) *Environmentalism: A Multicultural and World Perspective* (Praeger). e-mail: s.macgregor@pol.keele.ac.uk

Carly McLachlan is a research associate at the Tyndall Centre for Climate Change Research at the University of Manchester. Her research focuses on how people and organisations engage with energy and climate change issues. Particular areas of interest include: the contestation of knowledge claims, how consultation activities are designed and interpreted, and the symbolic meanings associated with energy projects. She has worked on a range of energy and climate change projects in multi-disciplinary teams including: an integrated climate change model, stakeholder assessments of carbon capture and storage and a policy assessment of UK tidal energy. e-mail: C.Mclachlan@manchester.ac.uk

Miriam Ricci is Research Fellow in the Centre for Transport and Society, University of the West of England, Bristol. Previously she was at the University of Salford as a Research Fellow for the EPSRC's *UK Sustainable Hydrogen Energy Consortium*, working with Bellaby and Flynn on risk assessment and public perceptions of risk. Having originally trained as a physicist, her doctoral and post-doctoral studies focused on socio-technical innovation, and she has a general interest in issues around public engagement. e-mail: miriam.ricci@uwe. ac.uk

Nikolas Rose is Martin White Professor of Sociology at the London School of Economics and Political Sciences, and Director of the LSE's BIOS Centre for the Study of Bioscience, Biomedicine, Biotechnology and Society. His most recent books are *The Politics of Life Itself* (Princeton, 2007) and *Governing the Present* (with Peter Miller, Polity, 2008). e-mail: N.Rose@lse.ac.uk

Chris Shaw is a PhD student in the Sociology Department at the University of Sussex. His thesis is a sociological account of how and why the climate change debate has become defined by the idea of a dangerous limit. e-mail: christopher_shaw@lineone.net

Kate Soper is a Professor Emeritus of Philosophy in the Institute for the Study of European Transformations at London Metropolitan University, and Visiting Professor at the University of Brighton. She has written extensively on social and cultural theory, feminist issues, the conceptualisation of nature and environmental issues. Her recent writings include: *What is Nature? Culture, Politics and the Non-Human* (Blackwell, 1995); To Relish the Sublime? Culture and Self-Realisation in Postmodern Times (Verso, 2002, with Martin Ryle). She has recently completed a research project funded by an AHRC/ESRC award in the 'Cultures of Consumption' Programme on 'Alternative Hedonism and the Theory and Politics of Consumption' (see www.consume.bbk.ac.uk under 'Research'), and is currently working on a number of publications in association with this. She is co-editor with Frank Trentmann of *Citizenship and Consumption* (Palgrave, 2008), and with Lyn Thomas and Martin Ryle of *Counter Consumerism and its Pleasures* (Palgrave, 2009). e-mail: k.soper@londonmet.ac.uk

John Urry is Distinguished Professor and Director of the Centre for Mobilities Research, Lancaster University. Recent/forthcoming books include *Mobilities* (Polity, 2007), *After the Car* (with Dennis Kingsley, Routledge, 2009), *Aeromobilities* (with Saulo Cwerner and Sven Kesselring (eds), Routledge, 2009), *Mobile Lives* (with Anthony Elliott, Routledge, 2010), *Mobile Methods* (with Monika Büscher and Katian Witchger (eds), Routledge, 2010), *Climate Change and Society* (Polity, 2011). e-mail: j.urry@lancaster.ac.uk

Index

abstraction 49–50, 57, 63
activism 150, 161; religion and 153;
    women's 16, 134–5, 151–2, 153
Adorno, T. 229–30
Alfven, H. 51
alienation 50–1, 62
alternative hedonism 18, 231
Alzheimer's 75, 76–7; MCI and 77–8
Anable, J. 163
Anaxagoras 56
animals, humans and 27, 38–9, 223–4,
    227
animism 8
anthropocentrism 6
anthropology 8, 26
Aristotle 56

Banerjee, D. 125, 126
Bangladeshis, in East End of London,
    environmentalism among 145, 152
Barr, S. 163
Bataille, G. 96
Bauman, Z. 90, 127
Bayly, C.A. 2
Beck, U. 9, 10, 90
behaviour: environmental values
    and 159, 161–5, 167–70, 174, 176,
    210–11
Bell, M.M. 125, 126
Bellaby, P. 16
Benton, T. 3–4, 10, 11, 13
Big Bang theory 51, 59, 60
bioenergy, attitudes to 182–3
biological determinism 6, 68–9
biological reductionism 7, 11
biology 4, sociology and 66–7
biosociality 70

biotechnology 13–14
black holes 59–60
Blake, J. 162
brain disorders 78–9, 80;
    Alzheimer's 76–7, 78
brain imaging 75, 77
brain state 76
brains, normality of 75–80
Bray, D. 104
Buck-Morss, S. 230
Burkett, P. 4
Burningham, K. 176
Burrill, S. 72
Bush, George W., on climate change
    112
business, distrust of 167, 172, 175, 176
Butt, S. 162
Byron, Lord 149

Callan, M. 70
Canguilhem, G. 66
capitalism 2–3, 11–12, 84–5; and climate
    change 85, 96; excess 91–6, 97;
    mobility and 91
car use, and climate change 162, 166
carbon emissions 89, 103, 108, 160, 166,
    192, 193
care 212, 216; for health and
    wholeness 214–15; for local
    economies 212–13; for transparency in
    food system 215–16
Caribbean tourism 94–5
Carson, R. 6
Christianity, and environmentalism
    142
Christie, I. 161–2
civil rights movement 5–6

climate change 16–17, 85–8, 104, 160;
'dangerous' 103–4, 105, 106, 108–18;
feminism and 127–8, 130–2, 133–4,
136–7; future scenarios 96–8; gender
and 125–6, 127, 129, 130, 132–6, 161;
impact on everyday life 130–2;
mobility and 88–91; precautionary
principle and 104, 108, 118, 119;
responses to 132–6, 159, 162, 163, 176;
science and 85–6, 109–10, 113, 115–16,
127–9; security and 127–9, 134; social
construction and 127–8, 137; sociology
and 16, 125, 127; 'value-added
gap' 162–5, 168–9, 175–6
climate sensitivity 109–10
consumers: biological reconnection
with food 208–9; care for the
environment 134, 210, 213–14; citizens
as 169–70; and food system 201, 202,
203, 215–16, 217; relationship with
producers 205–6, 207–8, 208–10,
211–12, 213
consumption (*see* also energy use) 90,
91–2, 93, 94; changing 231–2;
ethical 210–12; excessive 93–6;
wasteful 95–6; women's 134–5
cosmic elites 49, 62
cosmologies 51; dualistic 49–50, 51–3
cosmos 59–60, 63; alienation from 50–1,
62; dualistic 47, 58, 61; splitting 53–4,
56, 58
counter consumerism 231–2
Cox, R. 17
creationism 28
critical realism 63; and climate
change 105
culture, nature and 8, 9–10, 13, 223

dark matter 60
Darnton, A. 163
Darwin, Charles 11, 23, 24–5; on animals
and humans 38–9; *The Descent of
Man* 35–41, 42; encounter with
apes 25–6; and natural selection 36,
41–2; *The Origin of Species* 28, 29, 35;
and race 39–40
Davenport, C. 5
Davis, M. 93, 94, 95, 97
Dawkins, R. 23

De Chatel, F. 143–4
deCODEme 67, 72
DeHanas, D. 16
Dench, G. 144–5
Dennett, D. 23
Derrida, J. 224
The Descent of Man (Darwin) 35–41, 42
Descola, P. 8
devices/things 184–5, 197
Di Chiro, G. 131
Diamond, J. 97
Dickens, P. 8–9, 11, 13
Dietz, T. 127, 128–9
discipline 91–2
Dollimore, J. 224, 229
Dowler, L. 17
dualisms 5, 8, 48–9; and cosmology
49–50, 51–3; gender and 8
Dubai 94
Durkheim, E. 3, 54–5

Eccleshall Biomass development
185–7; responses to 185, 186, 190, 192,
193, 195; and a sense of place 188,
189–90
Eckersley, R. 105
ecofeminism 7–8, 126, 130–1, 136, 143
ecological crisis 15–17
ecological Marxism 11, 12
ecological modernization 9, 16, 105,
133
EcoMom Alliance 134–5
Ellul, J. 119
energy use (*see also* renewable energy):
environmental values and
behaviour 167–70, 174 willingness to
change behaviour 168–70, 176
Engels, F. 84
Enlightenment dualism 57
environmental attitudes 161; link with
behaviour 161–5
environmental justice 16, 44
environmental movement 6–7
environmental refugees 9
environmental risk, gender differences in
perception of 131–2
environmental security 127–9
environmental social science, gender
and 125–7

environmental values, effect on
behaviour 159, 167–70, 174,
210–11
environmentalism: Islamic 141, 143–8,
150–1, 153; sacralization of 141, 148–
50, 152–3
Epicurus 56
ethic of care 17, 18, 212–16
eugenics 2, 3, 4; challenges to 5–6
Eugenics Society 68
European Union 103, 104, 112; and
hydrogen technology 160; and
precautionary principle 107–8
evolution *see* human evolution
evolutionary change, Wallace and
26–7
excess energy 96

female nature 48
feminism 7–8, 125–7; and climate
change 127–8, 130–2, 133–4,
136–7
Flynn, R. 16–17
food 200; medicalization of 201;
natural 201; organic 204, 215
food miles 213–14
food schemes: case studies 206–12; and
an ethic of care 212–16
food sovereignty 217n
food systems 200; alternative 202–4;
global 200–1; reconnection to
nature 204–9; sustainable 203;
transparency in 215–16
Foucault, M. 223–4
Freud, S. 58, 228–9
Funtowicz, S. 108

Geddes, P. 4
gender (*see also* women) 8, 11; division
of labour 131, 135–6; and
environmental social science
125–7
gene sequencing 70, 71, 74
genetic citizenship 70
genetic engineering 223, 230–1
genetic inheritance 42–3
genetic testing 67–8, 72, 74
genetically modified organisms
(GMOs) 215, 225

genetics 13, 68; and biological
determinism 68–9; normality/
pathology 69–70, 73–4
genomic medicine 69–71, 72, 74
Giddens, A. 16, 90, 93–4, 130; *The
Politics of Climate Change* 125, 133,
134, 1137
Gilg, A. 163
global warming 85, 86–7, 96–7, 103;
responses to 231; two-degree
limit 103, 104, 106, 108–18
Golomb, J. 77
'good/bad' dichotomy 52–3, 54, 57, 58–
60, 61, 62, 63
government, distrust of 172, 175, 176
Grant, T. 59, 60
Great Chain of Being 56
Greeley, A. 142
green critical theory 105–6
green diplomacy 106
'Greenwash' 191–2
group selection 42
Grove-White, R. 164
Guthman, J. 203

Habermas, J. 229, 231
Hannigan, J. 15
Hansen, J. 89
Haraway, D. 13, 15, 227
Harvey, D. 93
Harvey, F. 113
Hawking, S. 59–60, 61
Heath, D. 70
Heelas, P. 143
hierarchical universe 55–6
hierarchies 2: of races 31–2; social 2, 3
history, Adorno and 229–30
Hobbes, T. 48
Hobson, K. 176–7
Holloway, L. 17, 202
Hood, L. 69
Hoppe, R. 119
Hopwood, A. 78
Horwitz, A.V. 78–9
human evolution 11, 30–2, 33; Darwin
and 35–41; Wallace and 33–5
Human Genome Project 68–9, 71
human nature 23, 25
human progress 26–7, 39

humanism 44
humans 6, 26, 32, 34–5; and animals 27,
    38–9, 223–4, 227; and language 37;
    mental capacity 33–4, 37, 39; moral
    sense 30, 33, 34, 37–8, 42; and natural
    selection 30–2, 33–4, 36, 41; Wallace
    and 30, 33
Huxley, T. 23
hydrogen energy 160–1; public attitudes
    to 166, 170–1, 173–5, 176; and
    transport infrastructures 173–5

Ignatow, G. 142
industry, distrust of 167, 172, 176
infant selfhood 52
information-deficit 164, 172
instrumental reason 105
Intergovernmental Panel on Climate
    Change (IPCC) 85–6, 129, 130
introjection/projection 52–3
Irwin, A. 164, 184
Islam, and environmentalism 143–4, 150;
    in UK 144–53
Islamic Foundation for Ecology and
    Environmental Sciences 145

Jackson, P. 203
Jamison, A. 5
Jarvis, L. 161–2

Keller, E.F. 70
Khalid, F.M. 143
King, David 128
Klein, M. 52–3, 63
Klein, N. 93
Kneafsey, M. 17
Kunstler, J.H. 87–8
Kyoto Protocol 103, 110

language 37
Latour, B. 105
Leahy, T. 97
Leggett, J. 88
Lever-Tracy, C. 85, 125, 127
Levi-Strauss, C. 48, 54
lifestyles 134, 162, 166, 176–7;
    changing 17, 163, 164, 168–9, 211, 231;
    choice of 94
local development 188–9, 190, 194, 197

local economies, care for 212–13
Lock, M. 77
Locke, J. 48
logic of domination 8
London Islamic Network for the
    Environment 145
London Muslim Centre 146, 151–2
Lovelock, J. 86, 89
Lukacs, G. 62
Lyell, C. 25, 26, 33
Lynas, M. 116

MacGregor, S. 16
Macnaghten, P. 176
manual/mental labour 50, 61, 62
market 50; neo-liberalism and 93
Marx, K. 3–4, 11–12, 84; and money 50
Masika, R. 132, 134
Mass Observation Survey 61, 65
Massey, D. 183
materialism 4
Maxey, L. 203
McKibben, B. 223
McLachlan, C. 17
media, coverage of climate change 113–
    14
Mellor, M. 7
mental/manual labour 50, 61, 62
Merchant, C. 7, 48
Mild Cognitive Impairment (MCI) 77
mobility 14, 94, 96; and climate
    change 89–91, 97, 174
Mol, A.P.J. 14
Monbiot, G. 86
money 50
Monk, D. 93, 94, 95, 97
moral sense 30, 33, 34, 37–8, 42
Muhammad (Prophet) ecological
    thought 143–4, 150
Mumford, L. 4
Muslim Community Radio,
    environmental broadcasting 141, 145,
    146–8
Muslim women, environmentalism
    of 141, 151–2, 153
Muslim Women's Collective 152

Nasr, S.H. 144
natural beauty 149–50

natural selection: Darwin and 36, 41–2; Wallace and 28–32, 33

naturalism 8, 41–3, 44

naturalization of the social 3

nature 2, 3, 7, 11, 223, 225–6; 'after nature' 12–14, 223; in crisis 9–10; cultural construction 223–4; moral 224–5, 228; norms of 224–5, 227–8; realist 226, 227; society and 1–5, 6–7, 13, 14–15; and unnatural 224, 225–30

neo-liberalism 92–3, 136

Newton, I. 58, 59

NGOs (nongovernmental organizations), and dangerous climate change 116–18

NIMBYism 181–2, 193–4

normal/pathological distinction 69, 73, 74–5, 80

normativity 66; of brain 75–80

norms: of nature 224–5, 227–8; social and vital 66–7, 80

Novas, C. 69, 70

nuclear energy 160

O'Brien, M. 119, 176

O'Connor, J. 12

oil 87; peak production 87–8

Oppenheimer, M. 108–9

The Origin of Species (Darwin) 28, 29, 35

Owens, S. 185

Pasqualetti, M. 182

Pearce, F. 86

peer-review network 116

perversions 228–9

Petsonk, A. 108–9

Pichot, A. 2

place 183–4, 197; as natural resource 190; 'ownership' of 183, 189–90; and renewable energy development 188–90

places of excess 93–5

Poortinga, W. 163

population 88

post-humanism 223

postnaturalism 223, 227

poverty, climate change and 130–1

power 92

precautionary principle 73, 107, 116; climate change and 104, 108, 118, 119

Pretty, J. 205–6

primitive societies: dichotomizing 54–5; splitting of cosmos 55–6

privatization 92

producers of food 203, 216; relationship with consumers 205–6, 207–8, 208–10, 211–12, 213

psyche 62; splitting 52–3

psychoanalysis 52

public consultation 164–5; and participation in decision-making 172–5

Qur'an, on nature 144

Rabeharisoa, V. 70

Rabinow, P. 70

race/s 2, 6, 25; Darwin and 39–40; Wallace and 25, 26, 31–2

racial differences 40, 41

racism 3

Ravetz, J. 107, 108, 116, 118

realism 15

reconnection 204–8; biological 208–9; and ethic of care 212–16; moral 210–12; social 209

religion (*see also* Islam) 141; and activism 153; and attitude to environment 16, 142–3, 153

renewable energy (*see also* hydrogen energy); attitudes to 165–6; experimental status of 194–5, 196; 'greenness' of 191–2; opposition to 181, 182–3, 185, 196–7; and place 183, 196, 197; siting of plants 181, 182–3, 188–90, 196; stakeholder responses to 181, 185, 186–7, 188–90; technologies of 184–5, 191–5, 196, 197

reproductive technology 9–10

Rial, J.R. 89

Ricci, M. 16

Rifkin, J. 87, 160

risk: gender differences in perception of 131–2; medical 73

risk society 9, 16
Rivers, P. 17
Roddick, Anita 151
Rohr, U. 129
Romanticism, and nature 3
Rosa, E. 127, 128–9
Rose, N. 13, 17
Rosenberg, C. 73–4
Rosenhan, D. 75

sacralization of environment 141, 148–
  50, 152–3
Sandilands, C. 136
science 2; and climate change 85–6, 109–
  10, 113, 115–16, 127–9; environmental
  movement 6; feminist critique 7;
  gender and 7–8; and nature 2–3; and
  risk society 9
scientization of the natural 2–3
self 52–3; and cosmos 54–8
Seyfang, G. 203
sexual selection 40–1, 42, 43
Shackley, S. 104
Shaw, A. 162
Shaw, C. 15
Sheller, M. 94, 95, 96
Shiva, V. 184
Silverman, K. 229
sites of renewable energy projects:
  economic vulnerability of 188–9; as
  natural resource 190, 196; ownership
  of 189, 190; scale of 188
social constructivism 15, 223; and
  climate change 104–5
social Darwinism 68
social domination 58, 63
social instincts 37–8, 42
social life: climate change and 89, 96;
  and human evolution 42–3
social norms, and vital norms 66–7, 80
social reproduction 131, 136
societies of control 92
societization of nature 10
society 9–10; nature and 1–5, 6–7, 13,
  14–15
sociology, natural and social in 3–5, 11–
  15

sociology of flows 14
Soper, K. 13, 17–18
Spaargaren, G. 14
spiritualism, Wallace and 34, 41
splitting 53–8
states, neo-liberalism and 92–3
Stehr, N. 85
Stern, N. 118
Stern, P.C. 163
Stern Review 87, 89, 96, 118, 159–60
Stirling, A. 164
Stradling, S. 162
Strathern, M. 9–10, 12–13
subjectivity 51–2
supermarkets, resistance to 213, 215,
  216
surveillance 92
Sustainable Development
  Commission 162, 164
Swyngedouw, E. 13

Tarnas, R. 56
technology 17; and symbolism in
  renewable energy development 184–5,
  191–5, 196, 197
Terry, G. 126, 132
Titmuss, R. 68
totemism 8
transport, hydrogen energy and 173–5
Tronto, J.C. 212
Tuan, Y.F. 188
Tucker, W.H. 5

UK Committee on Climate Change
  (2008) 160
uniformitarianism 26, 27
United Nations Framework Convention
  on Climate Change 110, 111, 115
universalism 62
unnatural 224, 225–30
Urry, J. 14, 15–16, 162, 176
use-inheritance 42

'value-action gap' 162–5, 168–9, 175–6
Value-Belief-Norm theory 163
Van der Sluijs, J. 109
Veblen, T. 95

Venter, C. 70, 74
Vogel, S. 223, 225–6, 227

Wakefield, J.C. 78–9
Wallace, A.R. 23, 24–6, 42, 43, 44; and
    evolutionary change 26–7; and human
    evolution 33–5; and natural
    selection 28–31, 33; and sexual
    selection 43–4; and spiritualism 34, 41;
    transformation of species 26, 27
Wave Hub project 185; responses to 192,
    194, 195; and sense of place 188–9,
    190
WBGU Reports 110, 112, 119–20
Weber, W.W. 81
Western knowledge, feminist critique 7–8
White, L. 141, 142, 153

Williams, R. 232
wind energy, attitudes to 165–6, 182, 183
women (*see also* Muslim women): effect
    of climate change on 128, 130–2; and
    nature 8; nature of 48; responses to
    climate change 134–5
Women's Environment and Development
    Organization (WEDO) 133–4
Women's Institute, and climate
    change 132, 135
Women's Manifesto on Climate
    Change 132, 135
Woodhead, L. 143
Woods, A. 59, 60
Wynne, B. 164

Zonabend, F. 184